Nikon D5500: From Snapshots to Great Shots

Rob Sylvan

Peachpit Press

Nikon D5500: From Snapshots to Great Shots
Rob Sylvan

Peachpit Press
www.peachpit.com

To report errors, please send a note to errata@peachpit.com

Peachpit Press is a division of Pearson Education

Acquisitions Editor: Susan Rimerman
Project Editor: Valerie Witte
Senior Production Editor: Lisa Brazieal
Copyeditor: Suki Gear
Composition: WolfsonDesign
Indexer: Karin Arrigoni
Cover Image: Rob Sylvan
Cover Design: Aren Straiger
Interior Design: Mimi Heft

ISBN-13: 978-0-134-18547-7
ISBN-10: 0-134-18547-1

9 8 7 6 5 4 3 2 1

Printed and bound in the United States of America

The camera used while writing this *From Snapshots to Great Shots* book was generously provided by B&H Photo.

PHOTO - VIDEO - PRO AUDIO

www.bhphotovideo.com

Dedication

For Uncle Tony—this one's for you!

Acknowledgments

My deepest thanks go to Jeff Revell, the author of a number of books in the *From Snapshots to Great Shots* series, and specifically the book on the D5000, which I had the honor and pleasure of updating for the D5100, D5200, D5300, and now the D5500. Jeff is a tremendous photographer and gifted teacher. Thank you for providing such a sound foundation upon which to build.

Any book that has reached the final stage of being published is actually the work of many hands (eyes, brains, and hearts, too) behind the scenes. I owe everyone at Peachpit a great deal of gratitude, but specifically Susan Rimerman, Valerie Witte, Suki Gear, Lisa Brazieal, WolfsonDesign, Karin Arrigoni, Sara Jane Todd, and Nancy Aldrich-Ruenzel, who were instrumental in getting this book finished, making it look so darn fantastic, and putting it out into the world. Thank you all.

A special thanks to David Brommer and B&H Photo Video for help in securing the D5500 I used to write this book.

I am grateful for all that I have learned from my friends at the National Association of Photoshop Professionals, from the fantastic instructors at Photoshop World, and of course from my friends and fellow photographers at www.stocksy.com and www.thedigitalphotoworkshops.com. You all have taught and inspired me over the years.

I also want to thank my wife, Paloma, for being the love of my life and my number one supporter during this project; my son, Quinn, for assisting me on many shoots and being the model in many more; and my family, friends, and neighbors—Adrienne, Emma, Julia, Paige, Shiela, Ron, Kris, Max, Otis, Hayden, Jaylin, Alden, Jayda, Maggie, Raymond, Kayla, Justin, Nekos, Ben, and Scott—for being a part of the book in large and small ways.

Also, a big shout-out to Crackskull's Coffee & Books and the New Hampshire Media Makers. Thanks, guys!

Contents

Introduction

The D5500 is an amazing piece of technology and a very capable tool for creating photographs that you will be proud to show others. The intention of this book is not to rehash the owner's manual that came with the camera or the downloadable Reference Manual PDF, but rather to be a resource for learning how to improve your photography while using your D5500. I am very excited and honored to assist you in that process, and to that end I have put together a short Q&A to help you get a better understanding of just what you can expect from this book.

Q: Is every camera feature going to be covered?

A: Nope, just the ones I feel you need to know about in order to start taking great photos. Believe it or not, you already own a great resource that covers every feature of your camera: the user's manual (there's also a free, comprehensive Reference Manual PDF that I recommend you download from Nikon). Writing a book that just repeats this information would have been a waste of my time and your money. What I did write about was how to harness certain camera features to benefit your photography. As you read, you will see callouts that point you to specific pages in the Reference Manual PDF that are related to the topic being discussed. For example, in Chapter 1, I mention touch-screen functionality, but more information on this feature is available in the manual.

Q: So if I already own the manual, why do I need this book?

A: The manual does a pretty good job of telling you how to use a feature or turn it on in the menus, but it doesn't necessarily tell you *why* and *when* you should use it. If you really want to improve your photography, you need to know the whys and whens to put all of those great camera features to use at the right time. In that respect, the manual just isn't going to cut it. However, the Reference Manual PDF (even more than the printed manual) is an excellent resource on the camera's features, and that's why I treat it like a companion to this book.

Q: What can I expect to learn from this book?

A: Hopefully, you will learn how to take great photographs. My goal, and the reason the book is laid out the way it is, is to guide you through the basics of photography as they relate to different situations and scenarios. By using the features of your D5500 and this book, you will learn about aperture, shutter speed, ISO, lens selection, depth of field, and many other photographic concepts. You will also find plenty of full-page photos that include captions, shooting data, and callouts so you can see how all of the photography fundamentals come together to make great images. All the while, you will be learning how your camera works and how to apply its functions and features to your photography. Also, while the main focus of this book is on shooting still photographs, I do devote a chapter to help you get started with the video functions of the camera.

Q: What are the assignments all about?

A: At the end of most of the chapters, you will find shooting assignments, where I give you some suggestions about how you can apply the lessons of the chapter to help reinforce everything you just learned. Let's face it—using the camera is much more fun than reading about it, so the assignments are a way of taking a little break after each chapter and having some fun.

Q: Should I read the book straight through, or can I skip around from chapter to chapter?

A: Here's the easy answer: yes and no. No, you shouldn't skip because the first four chapters give you the basic information you need to know about your camera. These are the building blocks for using the camera. After that, yes, move around the book as you see fit, because those chapters are written to stand on their own as guides to specific types of photography or shooting situations. So you can bounce from portraits to landscapes and then maybe to a little action photography. It's all about your needs and how you want to address them. Or, you can read the book straight through. The choice is up to you.

Q: Is there anything else I should know before getting started?

A: In order to keep the book short and focused, I had to be pretty selective about what I included in each chapter. However, there is a little more information that might come in handy after you've gone through all the chapters. So as an added value, I have written a bonus chapter: Chapter 12, "Creative Compositions." Chapter 12 will lead you through some photography tips and techniques to make your photographs even better. To access the bonus chapter, just log in or join peachpit.com (it's free), and then enter the book's ISBN on this page: www.peachpit.com/store/register.aspx. After you register the book, a link to the bonus chapter will be listed on your Account page under Registered Products. Note: If you purchased an electronic version of this book, you're set—Chapter 12 is already included in it.

Q: Is that it?

A: One last thought before you dive into the first chapter. My goal in writing this book has been to give you a resource you can turn to for creating great photographs with your Nikon D5500. Take some time to learn the basics and then put them to use. Photography, like most things, takes time to master and requires practice. I have been a photographer for many years, and I'm still learning.

Always remember, it's not the camera but the person using it who makes beautiful photographs. Have fun, make mistakes, and then learn from them. In no time, I'm sure you will transition from a person who takes snapshots to a photographer who makes great shots.

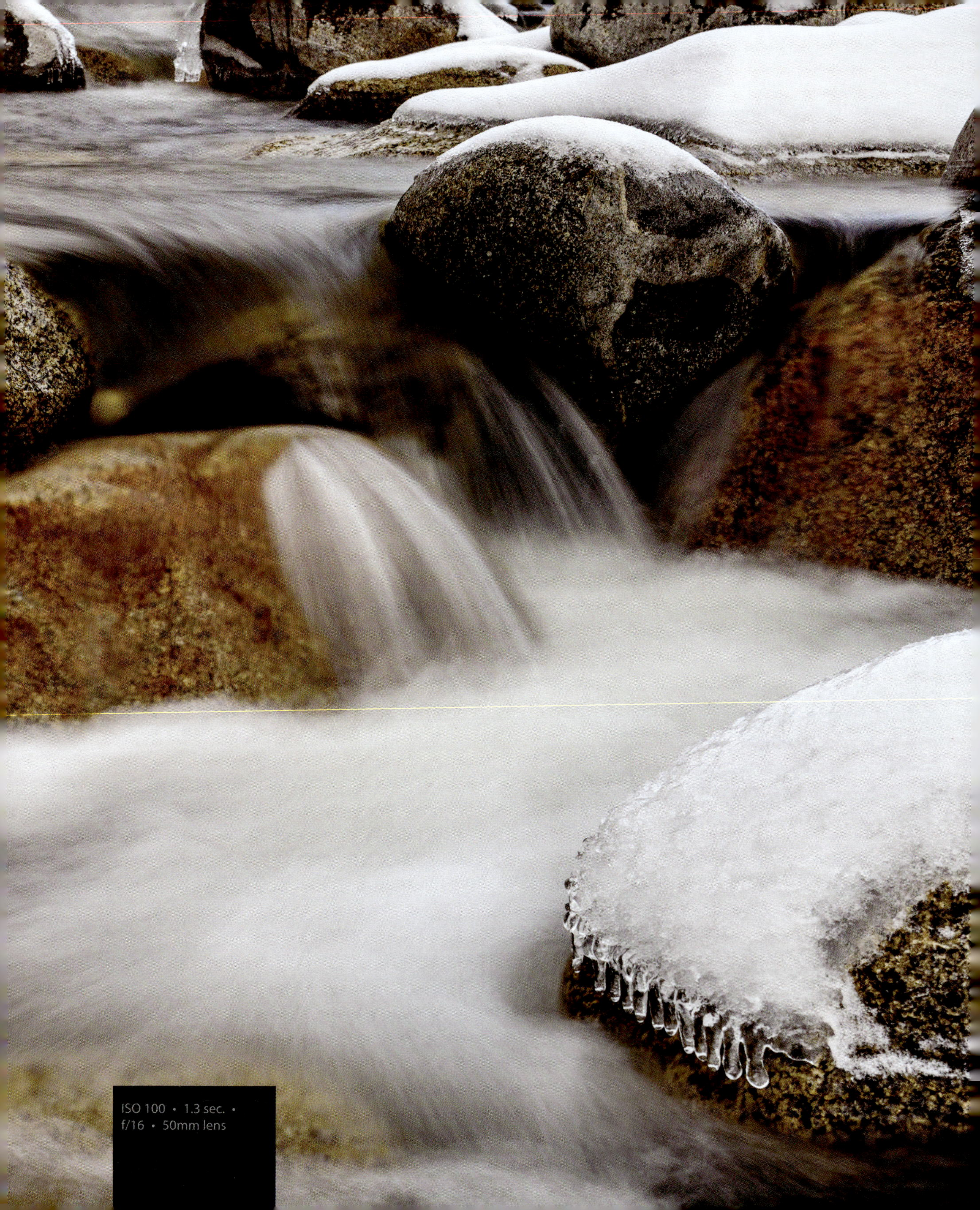

ISO 100 • 1.3 sec. • f/16 • 50mm lens

1

The D5500 Top Ten List

Ten Tips to Make Your Shooting More Productive Right Out of the Box

I'm going to go out on a limb here and guess that you've already taken your camera out of the box and played around with it. I mean, who can resist that delicious smell of new electronics and the thrill of playing with a new toy? I usually find it easier to sit down and read the manual after having taken the camera for at least one spin around the proverbial block. Of course, it is totally fine if you are reading this book before you've got the camera in hand, and I applaud your restraint.

So even if your camera is out of the box, here are some tips to help you get the most out of your D5500 experience. It's never too late to start over and take it from the top. As I mentioned in the introduction, the intention of this book is to extend the usefulness of your camera manual by expanding on subjects not covered in depth and by calling your attention to certain aspects that deserve closer inspection, all the while taking you places in your photographic journey that are far beyond the boundaries of the manual. To that end, there are some practical matters that will help you build the right foundation.

Poring Over the Camera

Camera Front

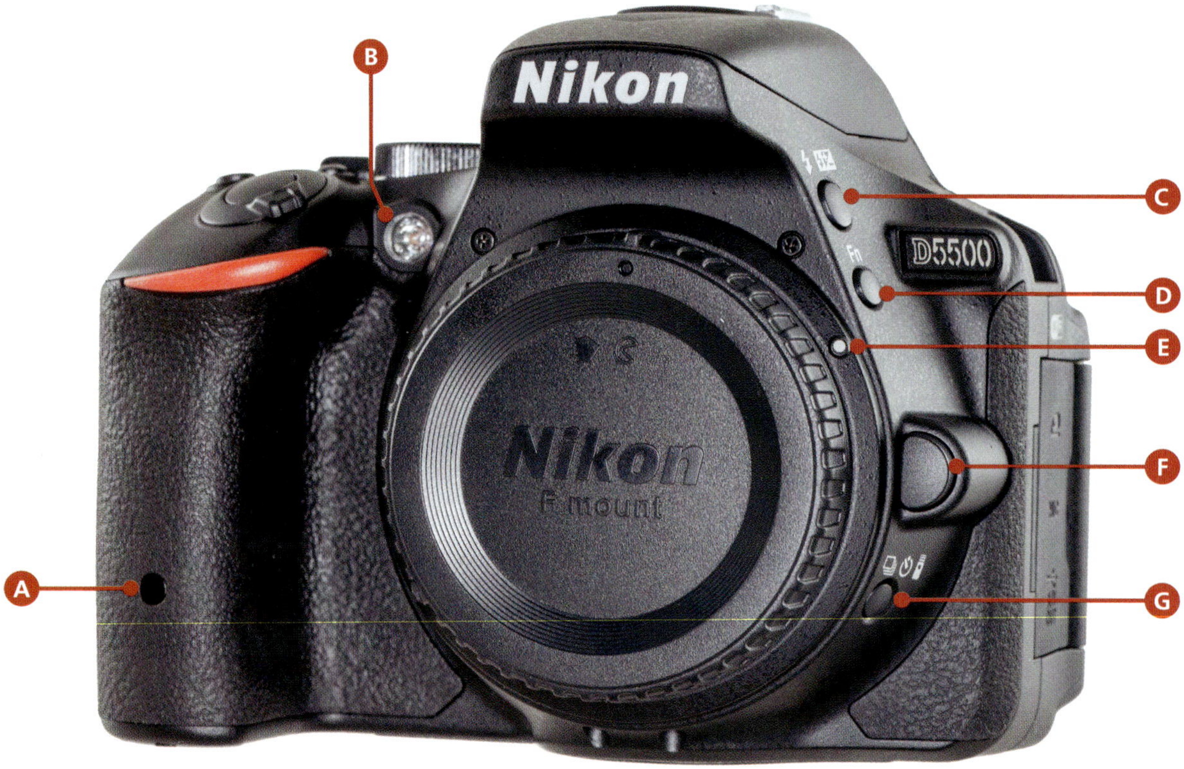

A	Infrared Receiver	E	Lens Mounting Mark
B	AF-Assist Illuminator	F	Lens Release Button
C	Flash Mode Button	G	Release Mode Button
D	Function Button		

Camera Back

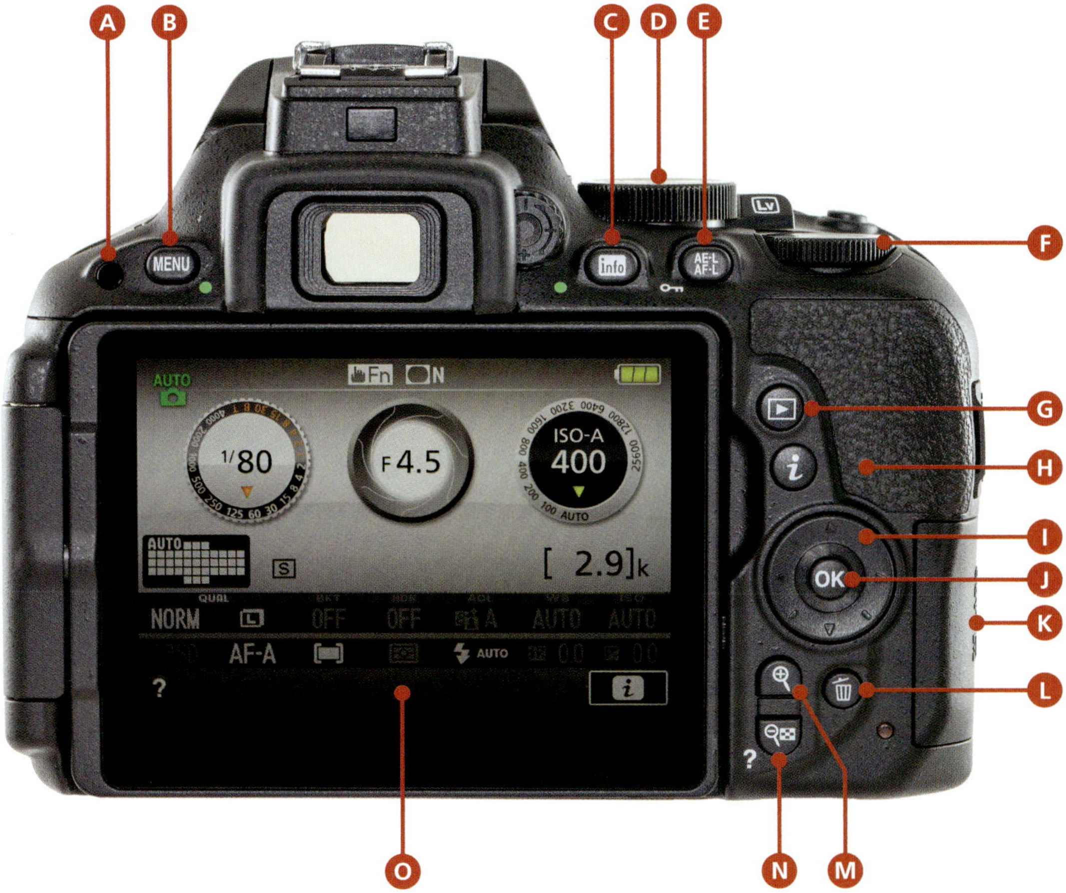

A Infrared Receiver	I Multi-Selector
B Menu Button	J OK Button
C Information Display Button	K Memory Card Door
D Mode Dial	L Delete Button
E Autoexposure/Autofocus Lock	M Playback Zoom In
F Command Dial	N Thumbnail/Playback Zoom Out
G Playback Button	O LCD/Information Screen
H Information Edit (i) Button	

Camera Top

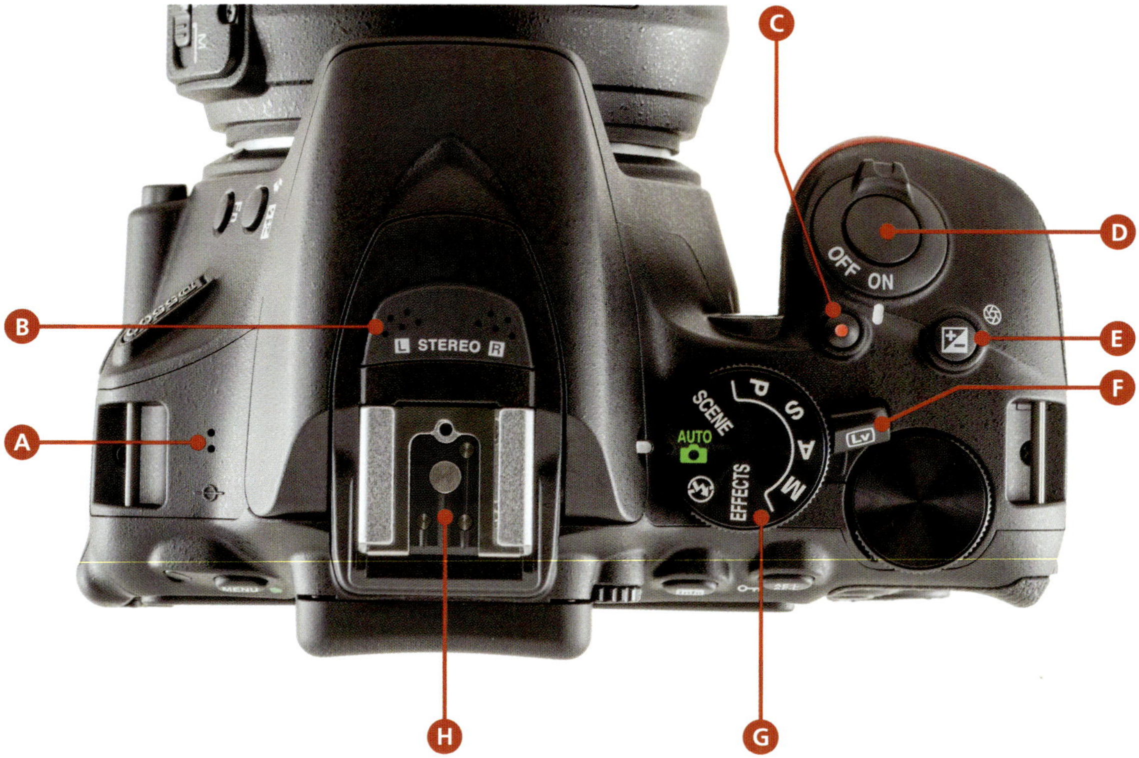

A Speaker
B Stereo Microphone
C Movie Record Button
D Shutter Release
E Exposure Compensation/Aperture Adjustment
F Live View Switch
G Mode Dial
H Flash Hot Shoe

1. Charge Your Battery

When you first open your camera and slide the battery into the battery slot, you will be pleased to find that there is probably juice in the battery and you can start shooting right away. What you should really be doing is getting out the battery charger and giving that power cell a full charge. Not only will this give you more time to shoot, it will start the battery off on the right foot. No matter what claims manufacturers make about battery life and charging memory, I always get better life and performance when I charge my batteries fully and then use them right down to the point where they have nothing left to give. To check your battery level, insert the battery into the camera, turn on the camera, and look for the battery indicator in the upper-right section of the information screen (**Figure 1.1**).

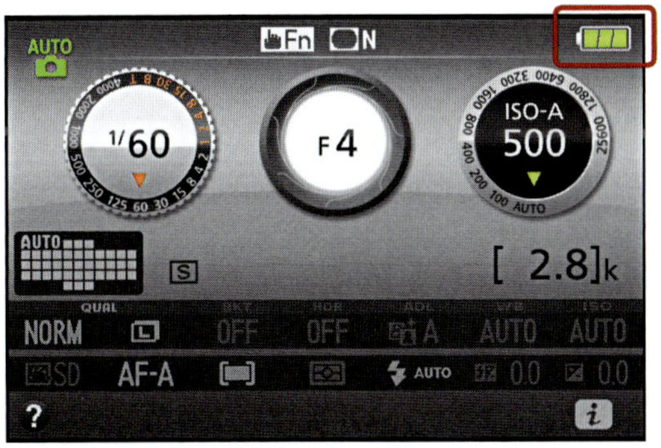

Figure 1.1 The LCD displays the amount of charge remaining on the battery.

Keeping a backup battery

If I were to suggest just one accessory that you should buy for your camera, it would be a second battery. Nothing is worse than being out in the field and having your camera die. Keeping a fully charged battery in your bag will give you confidence that you can keep on shooting without fail. Not only is this a great strategy to extend your shooting time, it also helps to lengthen the life of your batteries by alternating between them. No matter what the manufacturers say, batteries do have a life, and using them half as much will only lengthen their usefulness. Trust me, thanks to the increased quality of the LCD on the D5500, you will spend a lot of time gazing at your images (and eating up battery life).

Touch-screen goodness

One of the handiest new features of the D5500 is the touch-screen-enabled LCD monitor. The more I use the camera, the more I like using the touch-screen function to change settings while I am shooting, and even to focus the camera and trigger the shutter. That said, you can still change settings using the physical buttons on the camera (the Menu button, **i** button, Multi-selector, and OK button). There may be times when using the touch screen doesn't work, such as when you are wearing gloves or if you place a protective film over the screen that doesn't support touch-screen functionality, or maybe you just don't want to get fingerprints on your screen. You can even disable the touch controls completely if you choose.

I recommend getting used to using the touch controls, as they can be much faster for changing many settings, but I also want you to know how to change the settings using the physical buttons on the camera, as those always do the job (even when you're wearing gloves). To be consistent throughout the book and to keep the instructions clear, I will only refer to the physical buttons on the back of the camera when providing steps to change a setting.

There is a downloadable (PDF) Reference Manual for the D5500, which provides even more information on the camera than what's included in the printed User's Manual. Head to http://nikonimglib.com/manual and download the PDF from the Digital SLR Cameras menu. The Reference Manual has in-depth coverage on using the touch screen starting on page 17. Armed with that information, you can decide when you want to use the touch screen and when you want to use the physical buttons to get the job done.

2. Adjust Your Auto Off Timer Setting

One of the things that really bugged me when I first began shooting with the D5500 was the short duration of the Playback and Menu screens. When you are trying to learn about the camera and its features, it's frustrating when you have to keep pressing the Menu or Info button to bring the screen back to life. The short duration is also an issue when you're reviewing images on the screen after taking a picture.

The answer to this problem: Increase the timer setting to a longer duration. The D5500 has four different settings for the Auto Off function: Short, Normal, Long, and Custom. To make things easy, I set my camera to the Long setting when first learning how it works, which gives 10 minutes for playback/menus, 20 seconds for image review, 20 minutes for Live View, and 1 minute for standby. Once I've grown comfortable with the controls, I change the setting to Short to increase battery life. If you so choose, you can use the Custom setting to adjust each of these options individually.

Setting the Auto Off timers

1. Press the Menu button and navigate to Custom Setting Menu.
2. Select item c: Timers/AE Lock, and press the OK button (**A**).
3. Select item c2: Auto Off Timers, and press OK again (**B**).
4. Highlight your choice of timer settings, and press OK a final time to lock in your change (**C**).

A

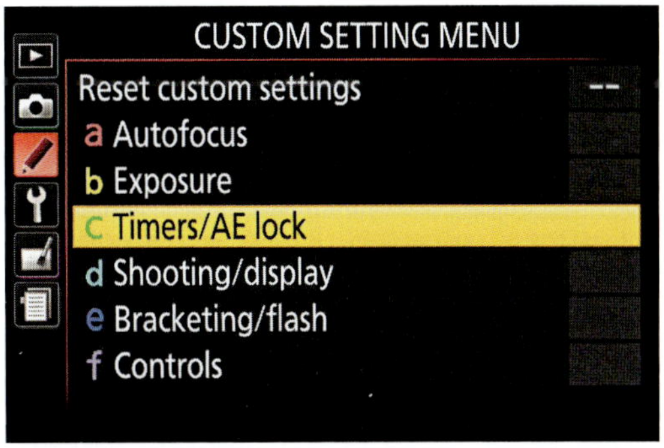

B

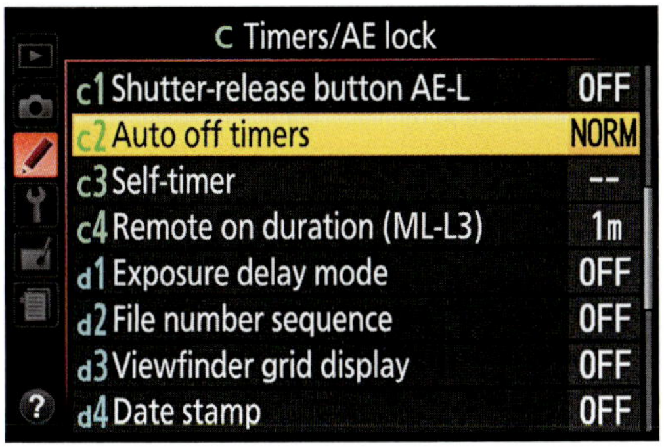

C

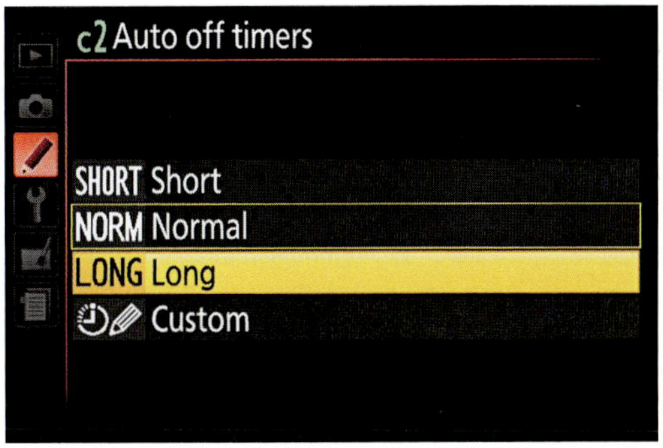

3. Set Your JPEG Image Quality

Your new D5500 has a number of image-quality settings to choose from, and you can adjust them according to your needs. Most people shoot with the JPEG option because it allows them to capture a large number of photos on their memory cards. The problem is that unless you understand what JPEG is, you might be degrading the quality of your images without realizing it.

The JPEG format has been around since about 1994. JPEG stands for Joint Photographic Experts Group, and the format was developed by this group as a method of shrinking digital images to a smaller size while retaining much of the original image information. (Technically, JPEG isn't even a file format—it's a mathematical equation for reducing image file sizes—but to keep things simple, we'll just refer to it as a file format.) The problem with JPEG is that in order to reduce file size, it has to throw away some information.

This is referred to as "lossy compression." This is important to understand, because while you can fit more images on your memory card by choosing a lower-quality JPEG setting, you will also be reducing the quality of your images. This effect becomes more apparent as you enlarge your pictures.

The JPEG file format also has one other characteristic: To apply the compression to the image before final storage on your memory card, the camera has to apply all of the image processing first. Image processing involves sharpening, color adjustment, contrast adjustment, noise reduction, and so on. Many photographers now prefer to use the RAW file format to get greater control over image processing. We will take a closer look at this in Chapter 2, but for now let's just make sure we are using the best-quality JPEG possible.

The D5500 has nine settings for the JPEG format. There are three settings each for the Large, Medium, and Small image-size settings. The three settings (Basic, Normal, and Fine) represent more or less image compression, based on your choice. The Large, Medium, and Small settings determine the actual physical size of your image in pixels. Let's work with the highest-quality setting possible. After all, our goal is to make big, beautiful photographs, so why start the process with a lower-quality image?

Setting the image quality

1. Press the **i** button on the back of the camera to activate the cursor in the information screen.
2. Use the Multi-selector to select the Image Quality setting, and press the OK button (**A**).
3. When the option screen appears, use the Multi-selector to choose the Fine setting, and press the OK button (**B**).

A

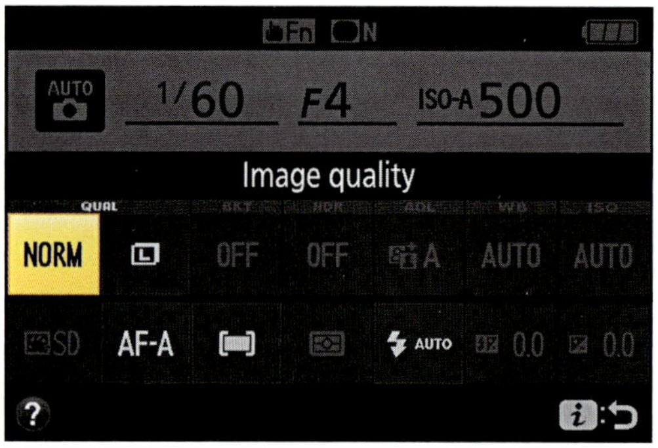

B

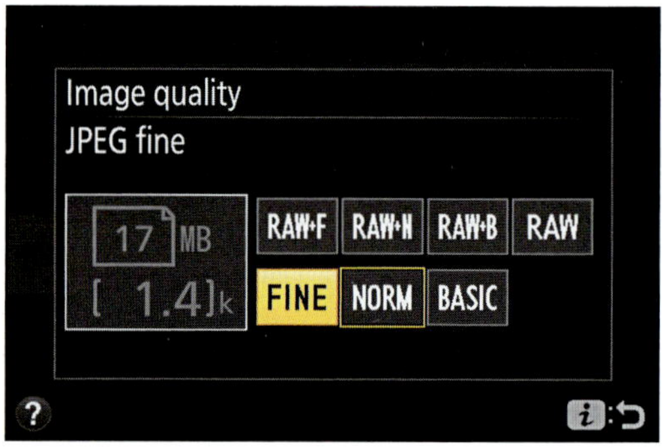

4. Now move the cursor to the right one step to choose the image size, and press OK to get to the options (**C**).
5. Select the L option to use the largest image size available, and press OK once more (**D**).
6. Press the **i** button again to return to shooting mode.

C

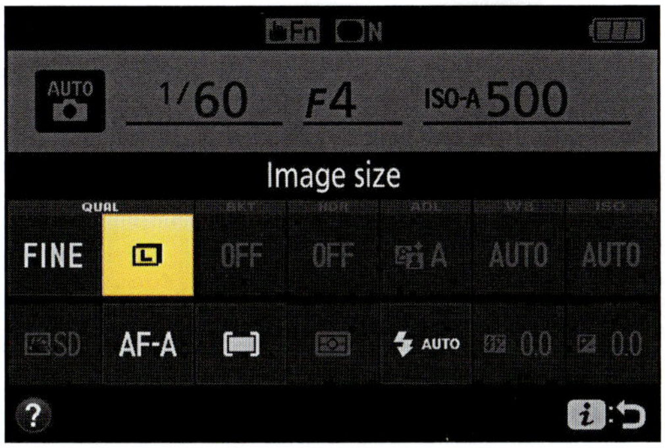

D

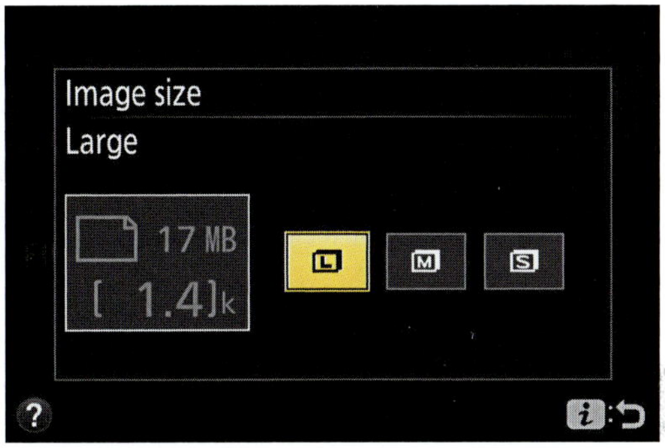

As you will see when scrolling through the quality settings, the higher the quality, the fewer pictures you will be able to fit on your card. If you have a 16 GB memory card, the quality setting we have selected will allow you to shoot about 1000 photographs before you fill up your card. Always try to choose quality over quantity. Your pictures will be the better for it.

Manual Callout

For a complete chart that shows the image-quality settings with the number of possible shots for each setting, turn to page 391 in the Reference Manual PDF, which you can download from the Nikon website.

4. Choose Your ISO Setting

The ISO setting on your camera allows you to choose the sensitivity level of the camera sensor to light. The ability to change this sensitivity is one of the biggest advantages to using a digital camera. In the days of film cameras, you had to choose the ISO by film type. This meant that if you wanted to shoot in lower light, you had to replace the film in the camera with one that had a higher ISO. So not only did you have to carry different types of film, but you also had to remove one roll from the camera to replace it with another, even if you hadn't used up the current roll. Now all you have to do is go to your information screen and select the appropriate ISO.

Having this flexibility is a powerful option, but just as with the Image Quality setting, the ISO setting has a direct bearing on the quality of the final image. The higher the ISO, the more digital noise the image will contain. Since our goal is to produce high-quality photographs, it is important that we master all of the camera controls and bend them to our will. When the Mode dial is set to Auto or Auto (Flash Off), the ISO will be set to Auto and cannot be changed manually. This means that the camera is determining how much light is available and will choose what it believes is the correct ISO setting. Since you want to use the lowest ISO possible, you will want to switch to a different mode and manually select the appropriate ISO. We'll cover all of the various modes in Chapters 3 and 4, but for now choosing P (for Program mode) is the safest choice.

Which ISO you choose depends on your level of available or ambient light. For sunny days or very bright scenes, use a low ISO such as 100. As the level of light is reduced, raise the ISO level. Cloudy days or indoor scenes might require you to use ISO 400. Low-light scenes, such as when you are shooting at night, will mean you need to bump up that ISO to 2000 or higher. Remember to shoot with the lowest setting possible for maximum quality.

Setting the ISO

1. Rotate the Mode dial to any setting other than Auto or Auto (Flash Off).
2. Press the **i** button on the back of the camera to activate the cursor in the information screen.
3. Use the Multi-selector to highlight the ISO Sensitivity option, and press the OK button (**A**).
4. In the option screen, select the appropriate ISO for the level of light you are shooting in, and press the OK button to lock in the change (**B**).

A

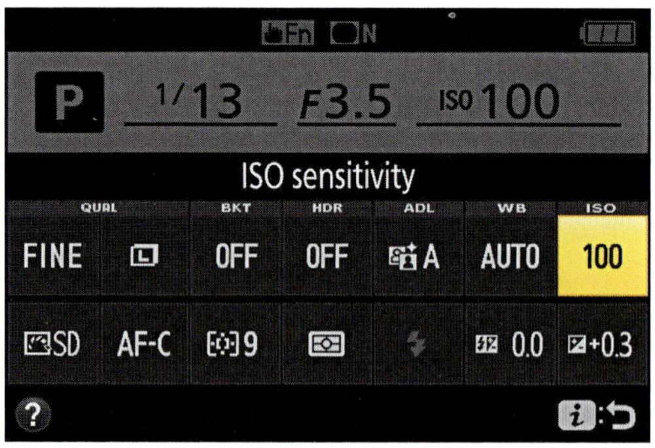

B

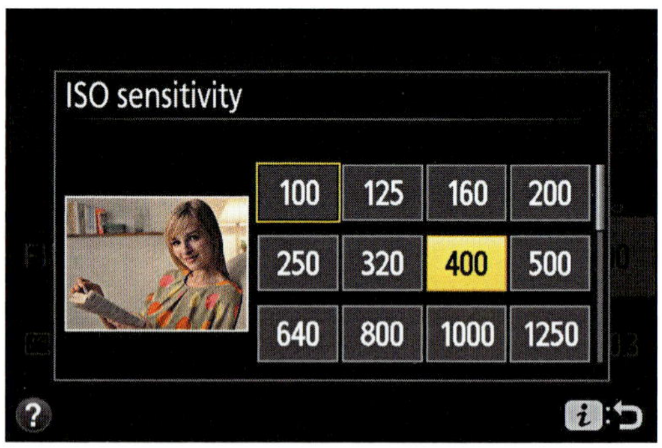

You should know that the Auto ISO option is enabled as a default only when you're using one of the automatic scene/effects modes. When you are using one of the professional modes (M, A, S, and P; covered in Chapter 4), the Auto ISO feature will be automatically turned off. If you wish to use Auto ISO in one of these modes, you must activate it and set the auto parameters in the Shooting menu. If you plan on shooting with the Auto mode, you cannot turn off the Auto ISO option at all.

Noise

Noise is the enemy of digital photography, but it has nothing to do with the loudness of your camera operation. It refers to the electronic artifacts that appear as speckles in your image. They generally appear in darker shadow areas and are a result of the camera trying to amplify the signal to produce visible information. The more the image needs to be amplified—raising the sensitivity through higher ISOs—the greater the amount of noise there will be.

Set your ISO on the fly

You can also change the ISO without taking your eye from the viewfinder. Although there is no dedicated ISO button on the D5500, you can still change this setting on the fly by setting the Function button to handle ISO sensitivity. Simply use Custom Setting Menu f1 to change the assignment of the Function button. Then, while you are looking through the viewfinder, just press and hold the Function button while turning the Command dial. You will see the ISO value change in your viewfinder display.

5. Set Your Focus Point and Mode

The Nikon focusing system is well known for its speed and accuracy. The automatic focus modes will give you a ton of flexibility in your shooting. There is, however, one small problem that is inherent with any focusing system. No matter how intelligent it is, the camera is looking at all of the subjects in the scene and determining which is closest to the camera. It then uses this information to determine where the proper focus point should be. It has no way of knowing what your main emphasis is, so it is using a best-guess system. To eliminate this factor, you should set the camera to single-point focusing to ensure that you are focusing on the most important feature in the scene.

The camera has 39 separate focus points to choose from. They are arranged in a diamond pattern, with 38 points around the outside of the diamond and one in the center. To start things off, you should select the focus point in the middle. Once you have become more

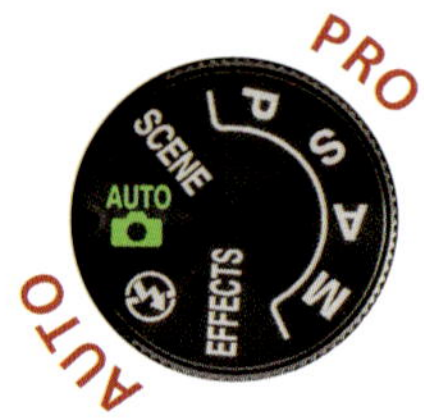

Figure 1.2 The camera's shooting modes are divided into the automatic scene/effects modes and the professional modes.

familiar with the focus system, you can experiment with the other points, as well as with the automatic point selection.

When possible, you should also change the focus mode to AF-S so you can focus on your subject and then recompose your shot while holding that point of focus. Your camera has two different "zones" of shooting modes to choose from. These are located on the Mode dial, which is separated into automatic scene/effects modes and what might be referred to as the professional modes. The automatic modes, which are identifiable by small icons, do not allow for much, if any, customization, which includes focus mode. The professional modes—defined by the letter symbols M, A, S, and P—allow for much more control by the photographer (**Figure 1.2**).

If the Mode dial is set to any of the automatic scene/effects modes, it is best to leave the focus mode set to AF-A, which means the camera will automatically select either single-servo autofocus or Continuous-Servo autofocus, based on whether the subject is stationary or moving. If the Mode dial is set to one of the professional modes, you will have the option to set the focus mode to AF-S (Single-Servo mode) if your subject is stationary.

Setting the focus point and focus mode

1. To choose a single point of focus, wake the camera (if necessary) by lightly pressing the shutter release button.
2. Press the **i** button on the back of the camera to activate the cursor in the information screen.
3. Use the Multi-selector to highlight the AF-Area Mode option, and press OK (**A**).
4. Select the top-left option, Single-Point AF, and press OK (**B**).

A

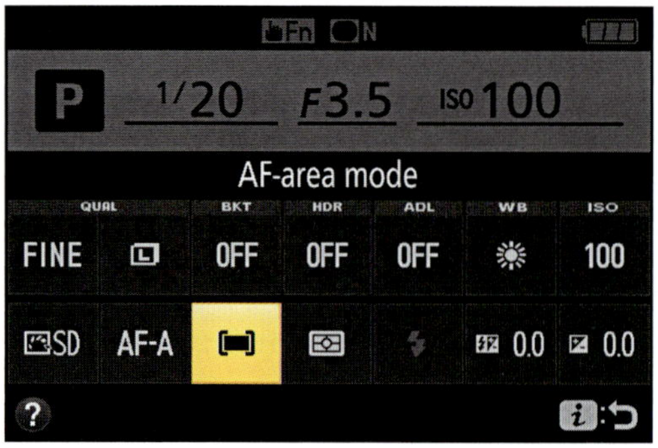

B

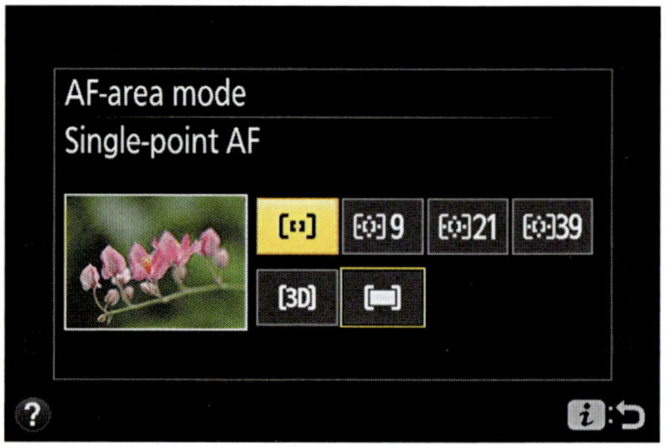

5. With the cursor still active, move left one item to the Focus Mode option, and press OK (**C**).
6. Select AF-A or AF-S, depending on the Mode dial setting, to configure the focus mode. Press the OK button to lock in your change (**D**).
7. Press the **i** button to return to the regular information screen.

C

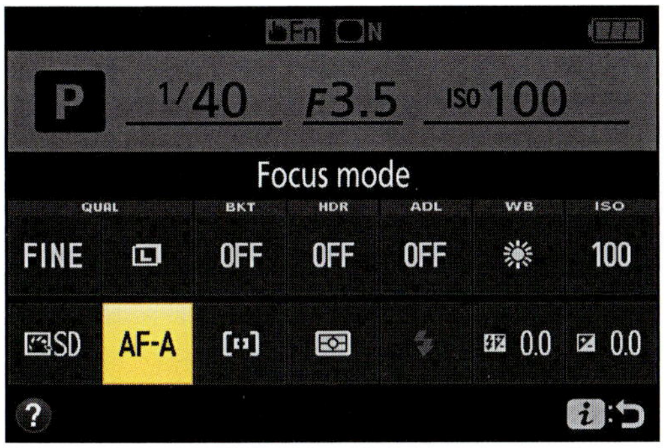

D

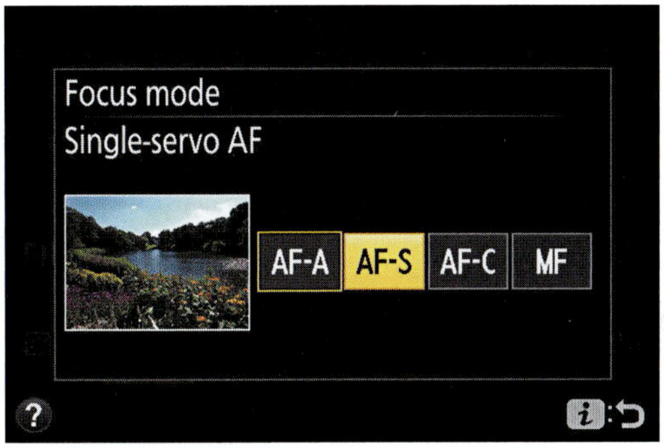

The camera is now ready for single-point focusing. You will hear a chirp when the camera has locked in and focused on the subject. To focus on your subject and then recompose your shot, just place the focus point in the viewfinder on your subject and depress the shutter release button halfway until the camera chirps. Without letting up on the shutter button, recompose your shot, and then press the shutter button all the way down to make your exposure.

6. Set the Correct White Balance

Color-balance correction is the process of rendering accurate colors in your final image. Most people don't even notice that light has different color characteristics because the human eye automatically adjusts to different color temperatures—so quickly, in fact, that everything looks correct in a matter of milliseconds.

When color film ruled the world, photographers would select which film to use according to what their light source was going to be. The most common film was balanced for daylight, but you could also buy film that was color balanced for tungsten light sources. Most other lighting situations had to be handled by using color filters over the lens. This process was necessary for the photographer's final image to show the correct color balance of a scene.

Your camera has the ability to perform this same process automatically, but you can also choose to override it and set the white balance manually. Guess which method we are going to use? You are catching on fast! Once again, your photography should be all about maintaining control over everything that influences your final image.

Luckily, you don't need to have a deep understanding of color temperatures to control your camera's white balance. The choices are given to you in simple terms. Your white-balance choices are:

- **Auto:** The default setting for your camera. It is also the setting used by all of the automatic scene/effects modes (see Chapter 3).
- **Incandescent:** Used for any occasion where you are using regular household-type bulbs for your light source. Incandescent (also called tungsten) is a very warm light source and will result in a yellow/orange cast if you don't correct for it.
- **Fluorescent:** Used to get rid of the green-blue cast that can result from using regular fluorescent lights as your dominant light source. Some fluorescent lights are actually balanced for daylight, which would allow you to use the Direct Sunlight white-balance setting.
- **Direct Sunlight:** Most often used for general daylight/sunlit shooting.
- **Flash:** Used whenever you're using the built-in flash or a flash on the hot shoe. You should select this white balance to adjust for the slightly cooler light that comes from using a flash. (The hot shoe is the small bracket located on the top of your camera, just above the eyepiece. This bracket is used for attaching a more powerful flash to the camera [see Chapters 8 and 11].)
- **Cloudy:** The choice for overcast or very cloudy days. This and the Shade setting will eliminate the blue color cast from your images.
- **Shade:** Used when working in shaded areas that are still using sunlight as the dominant light source.
- **Pre:** Indicates that you are using a customized white balance that is adjusted for a particular light source. This option can be adjusted using an existing photo you have taken or by taking a picture of something white or gray in the scene.

Setting the white balance

1. After turning on or waking the camera, select one of the professional shooting modes, such as P (you can't set the white balance when using any of the automatic modes).
2. Press the **i** button on the back of the camera to activate the cursor in the information screen.

3. Use the Multi-selector to highlight the White Balance mode, and press the OK button (**A**).
4. Using the Multi-selector, select the appropriate white balance, and then press the OK button (**B**).
5. Press the **i** button to return to the regular information screen.

A

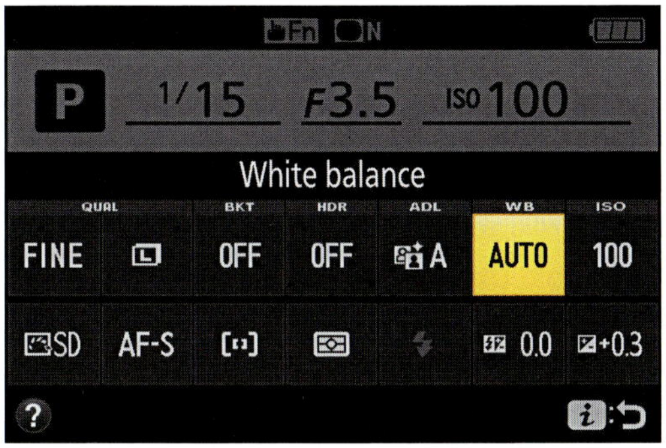

B

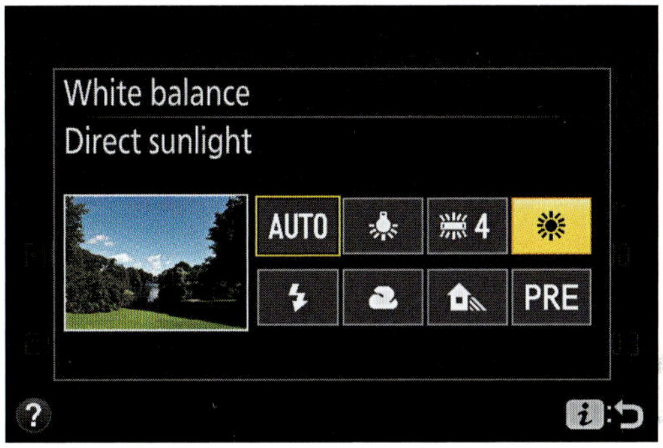

White balance and the temperature of color

When you select different white balances in your camera, you will notice that underneath several of the choices are numbers such as 5200K, 7000K, and 3200K. These numbers refer to the Kelvin temperature of the colors in the visible spectrum. The visible spectrum is the range of light that the human eye can see (think of a rainbow or the color bands that come out of a spectrum). The visible spectrum of light has been placed into a scale called the Kelvin temperature scale, which identifies the thermodynamic temperature of a given color of light. Put simply, reds and yellows are "warm" and greens and blues are "cool." Even more confusing can be the actual temperature ratings. Warm temperatures are typically lower on the Kelvin scale, ranging from 3000 degrees to 5000 degrees, while cool temperatures run from 5500 degrees to around 10,000 degrees. Take a look at this list for an example of Kelvin temperature properties.

Kelvin Temperature Properties			
Flames	1700K–1900K	Daylight	5000K
Incandescent bulb	2800K–3300K	Camera flash	5500K
White fluorescent	4000K	Overcast sky	6000K
Moonlight	4000K	Open shade	7000K

The most important thing to remember here is how the color temperature of light will affect the look of your images. If something is "warm," it will look reddish-yellow, and if something is "cool," it will have a bluish cast.

7. Set Your Color Space

The color space deals with how your images will ultimately be used. It is basically a set of instructions that tells your camera how to define the colors in your image and then output them to the device of your choice, be it your monitor or a printer. Your camera has a choice of two color spaces: sRGB and Adobe RGB.

The first choice, sRGB, was developed by Hewlett-Packard and Microsoft as a way of defining colors for the Internet. This space was created to deal with the way that computer monitors actually display images using red, green, and blue (RGB) colors. Because there are no black pixels in your monitor, the color space uses a combination of these three colors to display all of the colors in your image.

In 1998, Adobe Systems developed a new color space, Adobe RGB, which was intended to encompass a wider range of colors than was obtainable using traditional cyan, magenta, yellow, and black colors (called CMYK) but to do so using the primary red, green, and blue colors. It uses a more widely defined palette (or gamut) of colors than the sRGB space, and therefore can contain some colors farther toward the saturated end of the spectrum than sRGB.

The color space choice is applied only to the JPEG images produced by the camera. When you're shooting RAW, the color space is determined later, when you use software to process the photos. I typically use the Adobe RGB space when shooting JPEG because it has a wider gamut than sRGB, and it is always better to go from a wider color space to a narrower one when editing. That said, if you are shooting JPEG and sending photos straight to a printer or posting online without much (or any) editing, then sRGB is a good choice.

A little color theory

The visible spectrum of light is based on a principle called *additive color* and uses three primary colors: red, green, and blue. When you add these colors together in equal parts, you get white light. By combining different amounts of them, you can achieve all the different colors of the visible spectrum. This is a completely different process than printing, where cyan, magenta, and yellow colors are combined to create various other colors. This method is called *subtractive color* and has to do with the reflective properties of pigments or inks as they are combined.

Setting the color space

1. With the camera turned on, press the Menu button.
2. Using the Multi-selector, select Shooting Menu, and then highlight the Color Space option. Press the OK button (**A**).
3. Highlight your desired color space, and press the OK button once again (**B**).
4. Press the **i** button to return to the regular information screen.

A

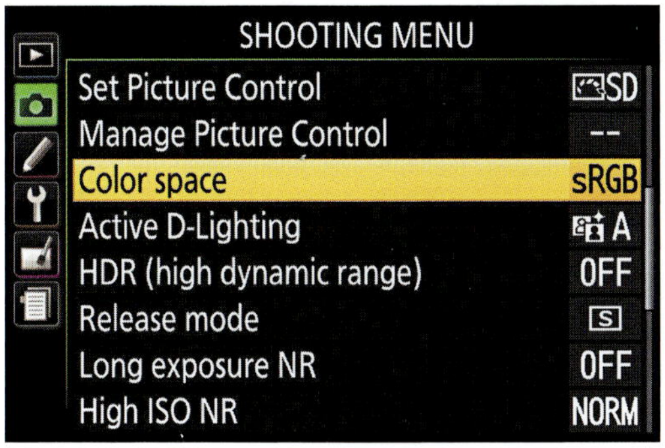

B

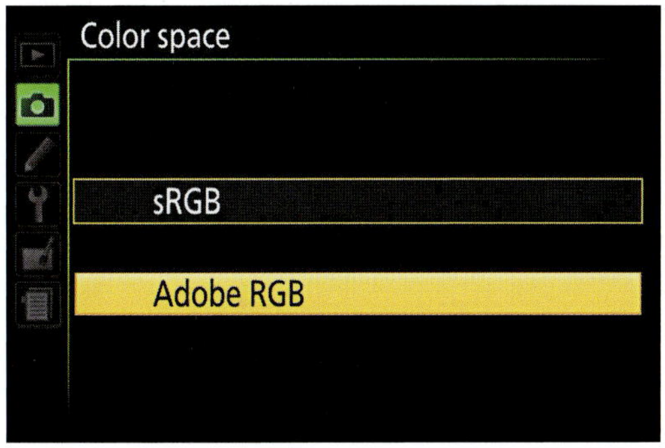

Note that if you choose Adobe RGB, the camera-generated filenames will start with an underscore.

8. Know How to Override Autofocus

As good as the Nikon autofocus system is, there may be times when it just isn't doing the job for you. This is often the case when you are using the camera on a tripod and can't prefocus and then recompose before shooting (as discussed earlier). To take care of this problem, you will need to manually focus the lens. I am only going to cover the lens that came with my D5500 (the 18–140mm VR), so if you have purchased a different lens, be sure to check the accompanying instruction manual for the lens.

On the 18–140mm lens, you simply need to slide the switch at the base of the lens (located on the lens barrel near the body of the camera) from the A setting to the M setting (**Figure 1.3**). You can now turn the focus ring on the lens to set your focus. Now that you're in manual focus mode, the camera will not give you an audible chirp when you have correctly focused.

We'll cover manual-focus situations in greater detail in future chapters.

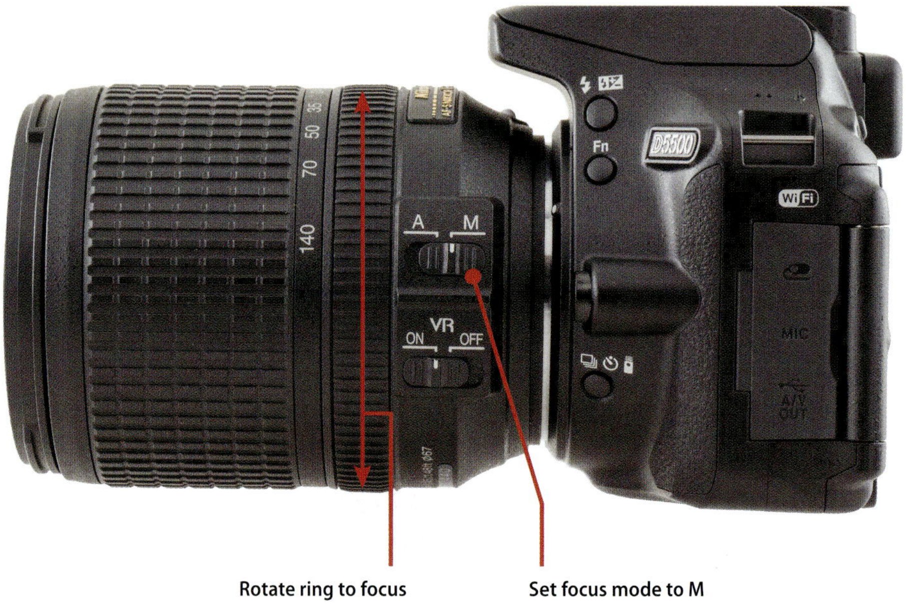

Figure 1.3
Slide the focus switch on the lens to the M position to manually focus.

9. Review Your Shots

One of the greatest features of a digital camera is its ability to give you instant feedback. By reviewing your images on the camera's LCD, you can instantly tell if you got your shot. This visual feedback allows you to make adjustments on the fly and make certain that all of those adjustments are correct before moving on.

When you first press the shutter release button, your camera quickly processes your shot and then displays the image on the LCD. In addition, you can press the Playback button at any time to review your shots on the card. The default playback view displays your image along with the folder name, image filename, frame number/total number of images on the card, date, time, image size, and image-quality setting.

There are other display options available that must be turned on using the camera menu. These options can be found in the Playback menu (**A**) under Playback Display Options (**B**). With this menu option, you can add display modes such as None (image only), Highlights (**C**), RGB histogram (**D**), Shooting data (**E**), and Overview (**F**).

A

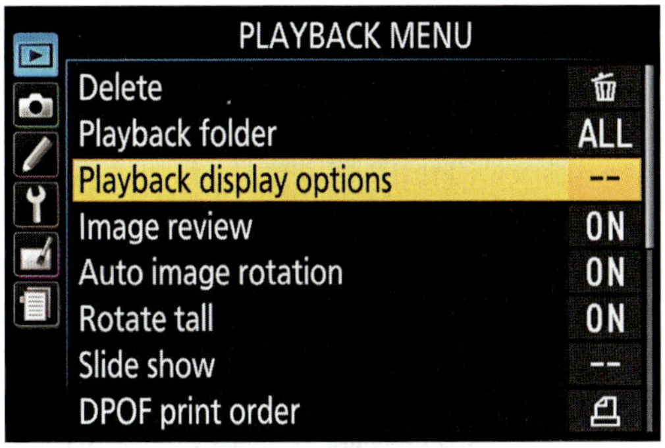

B

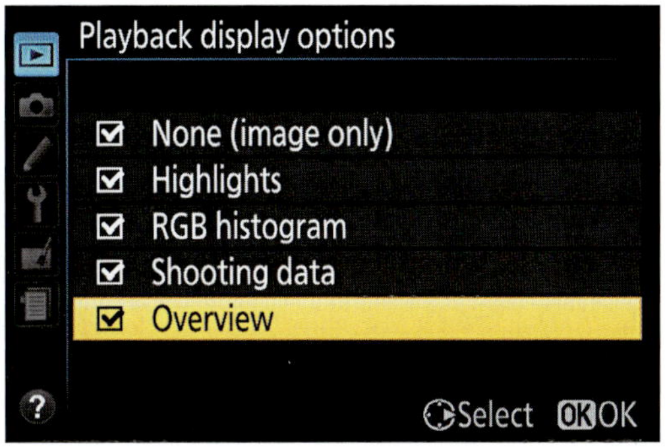

C

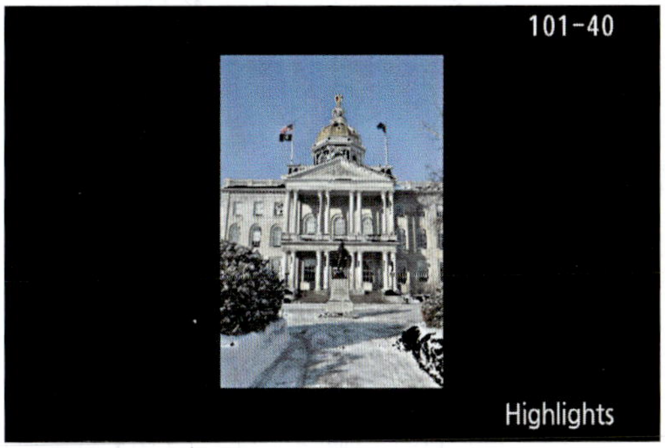

D

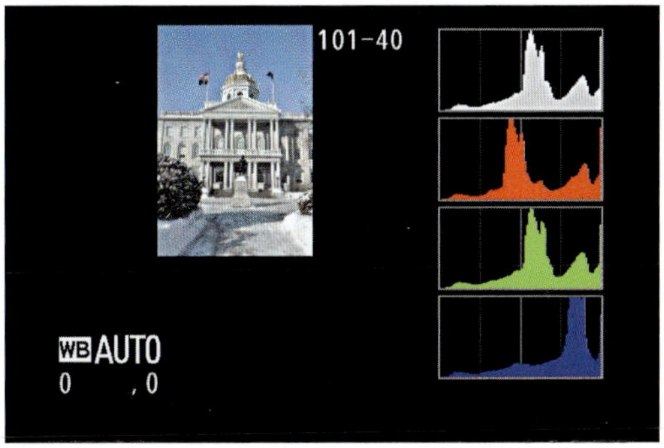

E

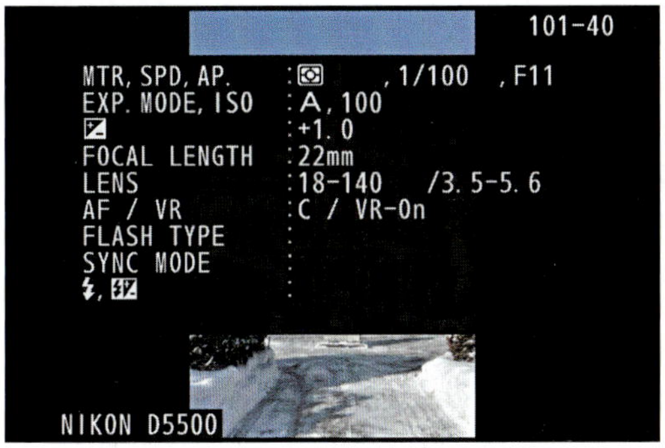

F

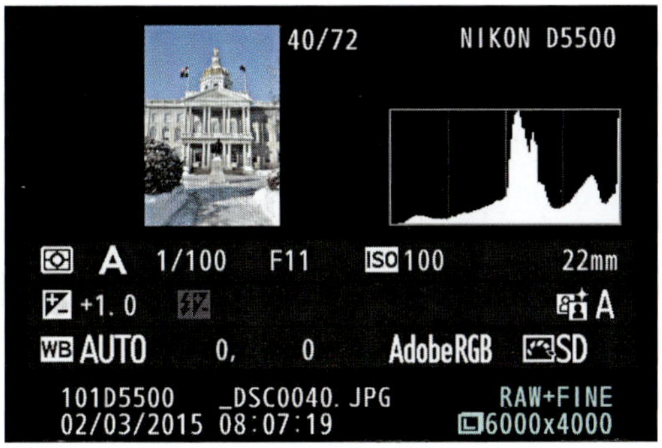

Press the Playback button to display the default view, and then press the Multi-selector up (or down) to cycle through each view. There is now a wealth of information—from shutter speed to the histogram (see the sidebar "The Value of the Histogram")—at your fingertips. Speaking of fingertips, the touch-screen functionality during playback is very intuitive, allowing you to swipe left and right to view other images, and use stretch and pinch gestures to zoom in and out of an image.

I find the Highlights display (sometimes referred to as the "blinkies") to be very helpful for quickly finding out if I have blown out the highlights in a photo, and I turn to the Overview display for everything else I need to know about a capture. I turn off all the other options to make it faster to cycle through the options I do use. There's more on the Highlights display view and how to use it to improve your image quality in the "How I Shoot" section in Chapter 4. For now, I suggest enabling all display options to get a feel for what each one offers. Then you can circle back and keep only the ones you find helpful.

Deleting images

Deleting or erasing images is a fairly simple process, covered on page 43 of the Reference Manual PDF. To quickly get you on your way, simply press the Playback button and use the Multi-selector to find the picture you want to delete. Then press the Delete button (with a trash can icon) located on the back of the camera. When you see the confirmation screen, simply press the Delete button once again to complete the process.

Caution: Once you have deleted an image, it is gone for good. Make sure you don't want it before you drop it in the trash.

10. Hold Your Camera for Proper Shooting

You might think this is a really dumb tip, but I hope you take a few seconds to read this and make sure you are giving yourself the best chance for great images. I can't begin to tell you how many times I've seen photographers holding their cameras in a fashion that is either unstable or just plain uncomfortable looking. Much of this probably comes from holding point-and-shoot cameras. There is a huge difference between point-and-shoots and dSLR cameras, and learning the correct way to hold a dSLR camera now will result in better images later. The purpose of correct shooting form is to provide the most stable platform possible for your camera (besides using a tripod, of course).

In general, dSLR cameras favor the right-handed and right-eyed individual. The basics of properly holding the camera begin with grasping the camera body with the right hand. You will quickly find that most of the important camera controls are within easy reach of your thumb and forefinger. The next step is to create a stable base for your camera to rest on. This is accomplished by placing the camera body on the up-facing palm of your left hand (**Figure 1.4**). Now you can curl your fingers around the lens barrel to quickly zoom or manually focus the lens.

When it comes to rotating the camera vertically to portrait orientation, most photographers favor rotating counterclockwise (**Figure 1.5**) because it keeps all the controls easily accessible to the right hand, allows the left eye to see, and keeps your nose off the LCD. That said, it can fling your right elbow into the crowd, and the pressure of your right arm can create a tendency to rotate the camera too far. Some people find it more comfortable to rotate the camera clockwise, which pulls your right hand under the camera and your right elbow tight against your chest. It decreases vision in your left eye and makes the controls a little more awkward to reach, but it can be more stable in a tight situation.

Now that you know where to put your hands, let's talk about what to do with the rest of your body parts. By using the underhand grip, your elbows will already be drawn closer to your body. You should concentrate on pulling them in even closer to your body to stabilize your shooting position. You should also try to maintain proper upright posture. Leaning forward at the waist will begin to fatigue your back, neck, and arms. You can ruin a day of shooting with a sore back, so make sure you stand erect with your elbows in. Finally, place your left foot in front of your right foot, and face your subject in a slightly wide stance. By combining all of these aspects into your photography, you will give yourself the best chance of eliminating self-imposed camera shake, resulting in much sharper photographs.

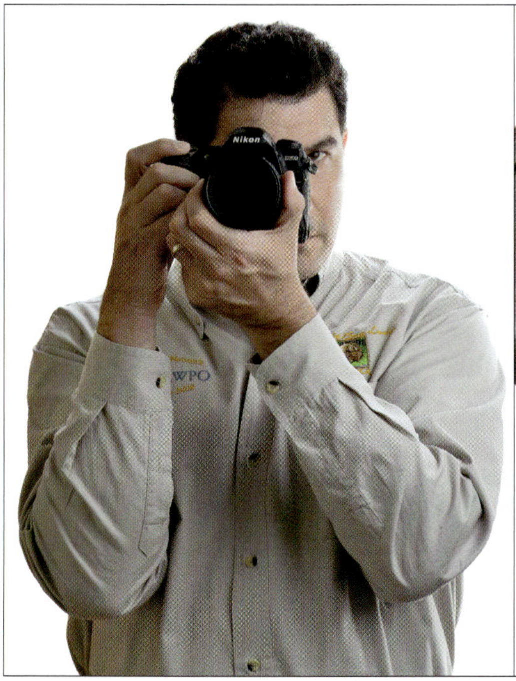

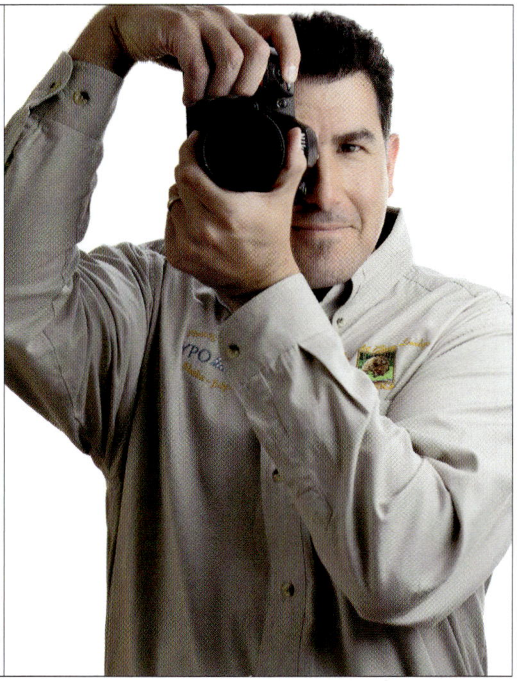

Figure 1.4 (left) This is the proper way to hold your camera horizontally to ensure sharp, blur-free images.

Figure 1.5 (right) The preferred way to hold your camera vertically. Practice rotating the camera each direction to find what is most comfortable and stable for you.

The value of the histogram

Simply put, histograms are two-dimensional representations of your images in graph form. There are two types of histogram that you should be concerned with: luminance and color. Luminance is referred to in your manual as "brightness," and this kind of histogram is most valuable when evaluating your exposures. In **Figure 1.6**, you see what looks like a mountain range. The graph represents the entire tonal range that your camera can capture, from the whitest whites to the blackest blacks. The left side represents black, all the way to the right side, which represents white. The heights of the peaks represent the number of pixels that contain those luminance levels (the tall peak near the middle means the image contains a large amount of medium-dark pixels). If I look at the histogram, I can see that the largest peak of the graph is near the middle and trails off as it reaches the edges. In most cases, you would look for this type of histogram, indicating that you captured the entire range of tones, from dark to light, in your image. Knowing that is fine, but here is where the information really gets useful.

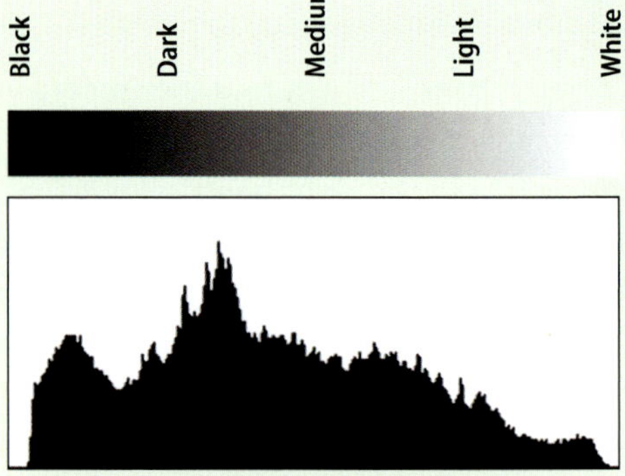

Figure 1.6 This is a typical histogram, where the dark-to-light tones run from left to right. The black-to-white gradient above the graph demonstrates where the tones lie on the graph and would not appear above your camera histogram display.

When you see a histogram that has a spike or peak riding up the far left or far right side of the graph, it means that you are clipping detail from your image. In essence, you are trying to record values that are either too dark or too light for your sensor to accurately record. This is usually an indication of over- or underexposure. It also means that you need to correct your exposure so the important details will not record as solid black or solid white pixels (which is what happens when clipping occurs). There are times, however, when some clipping is acceptable. If you are photographing a scene where the sun will be in the frame, you can expect to get some clipping because the sun is just too bright to hold any detail. Likewise, if you are shooting something that has true blacks in it—think coal in a mineshaft at midnight—there are most certainly going to be some true blacks with no detail in your shot.

The goal is not to clip any important visual information, and that is achieved by keeping an eye on your histogram. Take a look at **Figure 1.7**. The histogram displayed on the image shows a heavy skew toward the left, with almost no part of the mountain touching the right side. This is a good example of what an underexposed image's histogram looks like. Now look at the correctly exposed **Figure 1.8** and its histogram. Notice that even though there is a distinct peak on the graph, tones are distributed across the entire histogram.

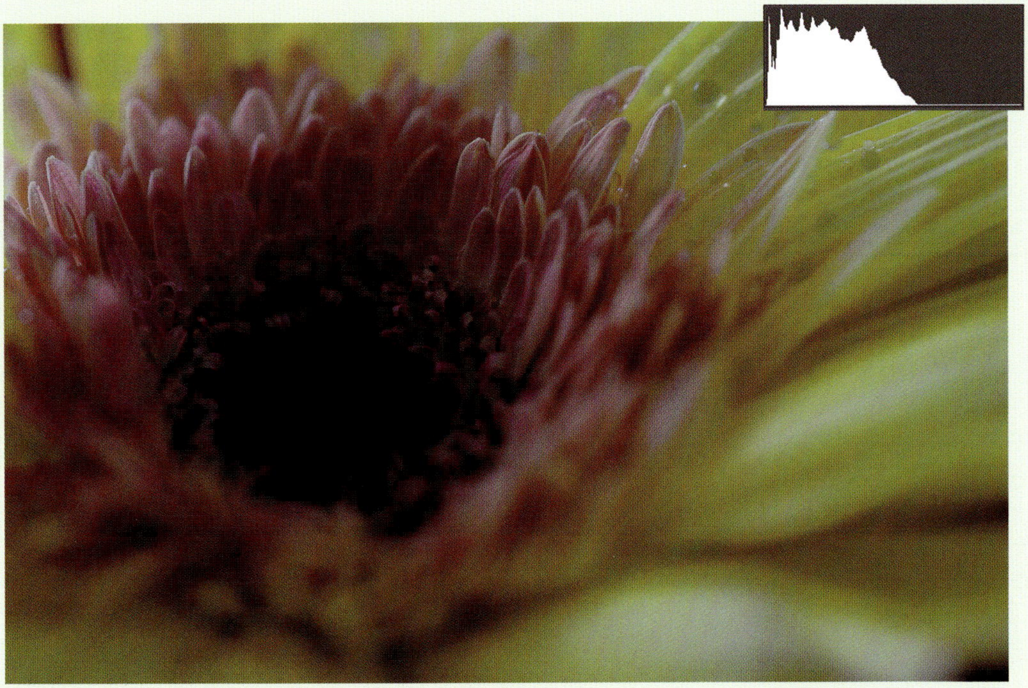

Figure 1.7
This image is about one stop under-exposed. Notice that the histogram is skewed to the left.

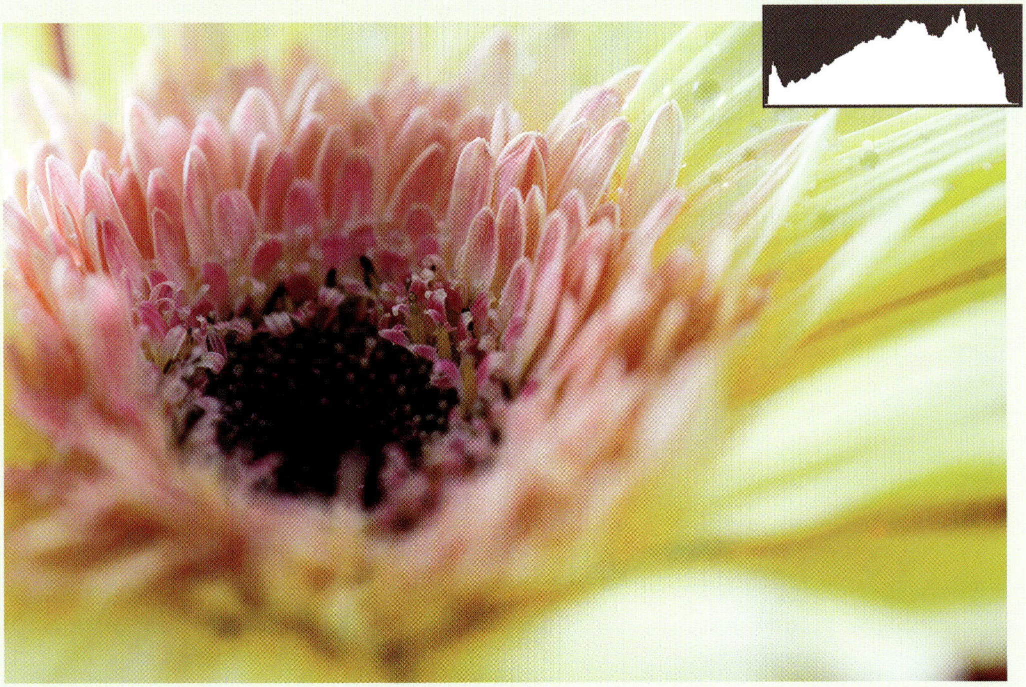

Figure 1.8
This histogram reflects a correctly exposed image.

Chapter 1 Assignments

Let's begin our shooting assignments by setting up and using all of the elements of the Top Ten list. Even though I have yet to cover the professional shooting modes, you should set your camera to the P (Program) mode. This will allow you to interact with the various settings and menus that have been covered thus far.

Touch-screen orientation

At the start of this chapter, I pointed you to the electronic Reference Manual you can download from Nikon. I'll be referencing pages in that PDF throughout the book, so make sure you download it and start with the section on touch-screen beginning on page 17.

Basic camera setup

Charge your battery to 100 percent to get it started on a life of dependable service. Next, using your newfound knowledge, address the following camera settings: Image Quality, Auto ISO, and Color Space.

Selecting the proper white balance

Take your camera outside into a daylight environment and photograph the same scene using different white-balance settings. Pay close attention to how each setting affects the overall color cast of your images. Next, move indoors and repeat the exercise while shooting in a tungsten-lighting environment. Finally, find a fluorescent light source and repeat one more time.

Focusing with Single-Point and AF-S

Change your camera setting so that you are focusing using the Single-Point focus mode. Try using all of the different focus points to see how they work in focusing your scene. Then set your focus mode to AF-S and practice focusing on a stationary subject and then recomposing before actually taking the picture. Try doing this with subjects at varying distances.

Evaluating your pictures with the LCD

Set up your image display properties and then review some of your previous assignment images using the different display modes. Review your shooting information for each image, and take a look at the histograms to see how the content of your photo affects the shape of the histograms.

Discovering the manual focus mode

Change your focus mode from autofocus to manual focus and practice a little manual-focus photography. Get familiar with where the focus ring is and how to use it to achieve sharp images.

Get a grip: proper camera holding

This final assignment is something you should practice every time you shoot: proper grip and stance for shooting with your camera. Use the described technique and then shoot a series of images. Try shooting a series using improper techniques to compare the stability of the grip and stance.

Share your results with the book's Flickr group!
Join the group here: flickr.com/groups/nikond5500_fromsnapshotstogreatshots

ISO 100 • 1/125 sec. • f/11 • 16mm lens

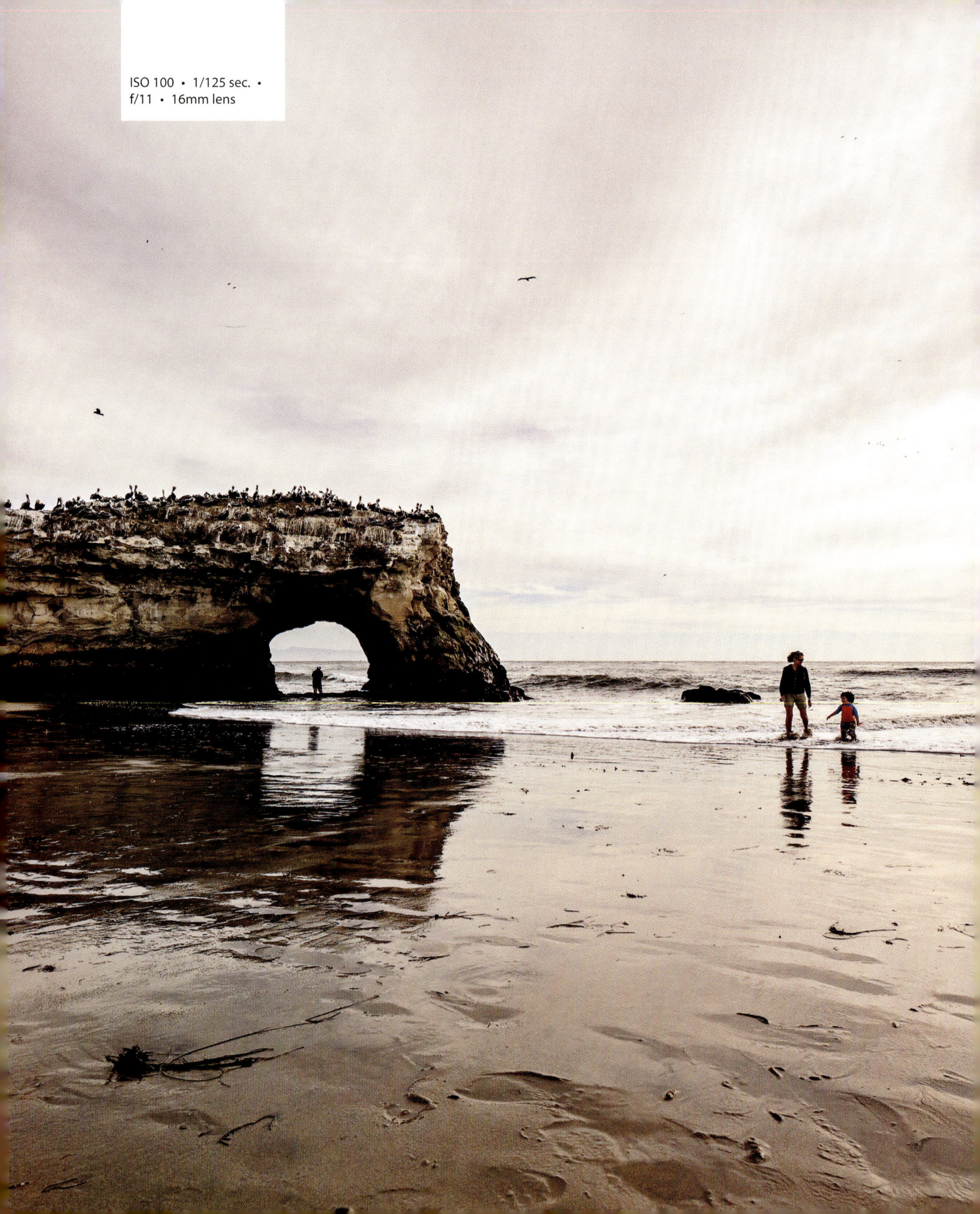

2

First Things First

A Few Things to Know and Do Before You Begin Taking Pictures

Now that we've covered the top ten tasks to get you up and shooting, we should probably take care of some other important details. You must become familiar with certain features of your camera before you can take full advantage of it. Additionally, we will take some steps to prepare the camera and memory card for use. So to get things moving, let's start off with something you will definitely need before you can take a single picture: a memory card.

Poring Over the Picture

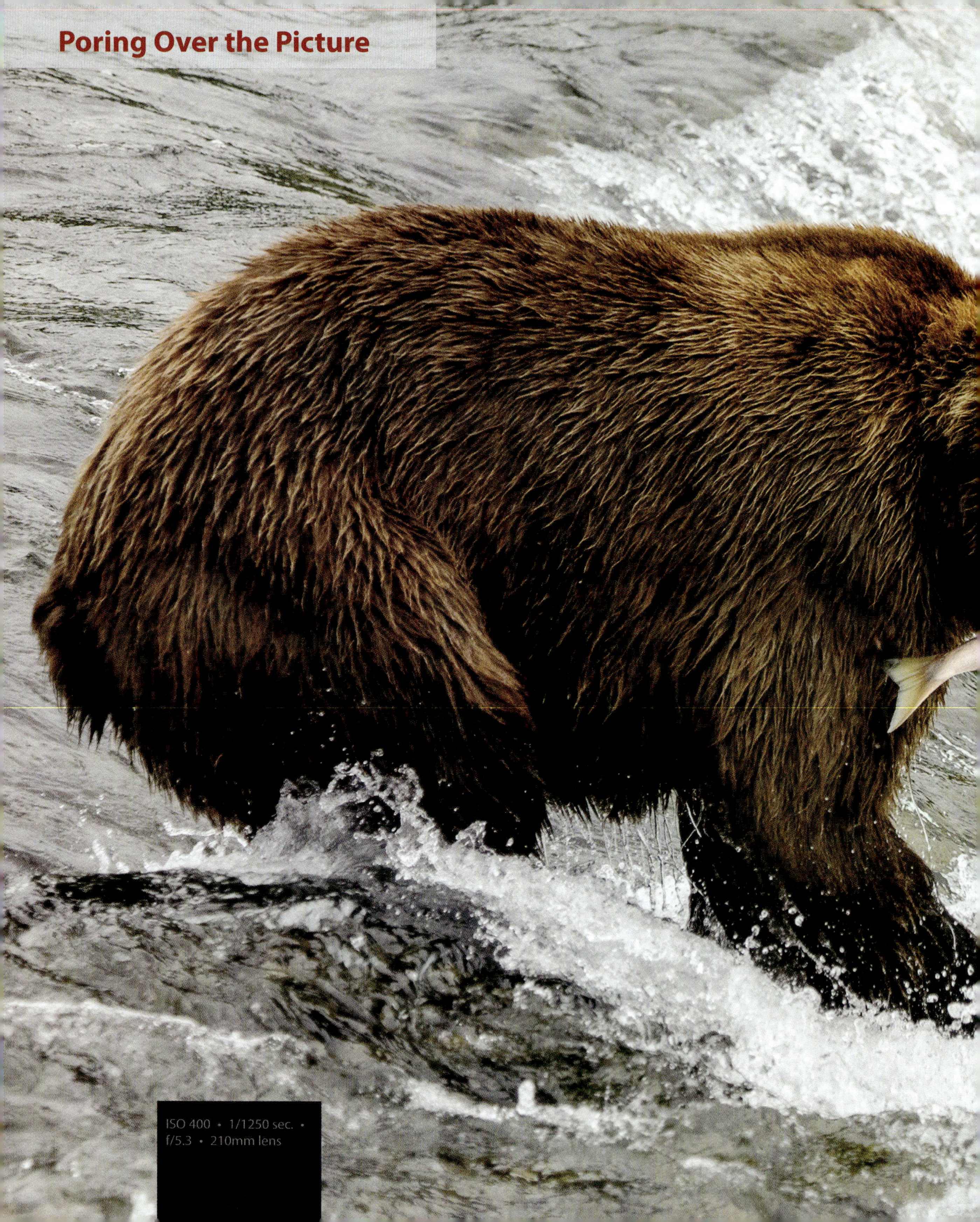

ISO 400 • 1/1250 sec. • f/5.3 • 210mm lens

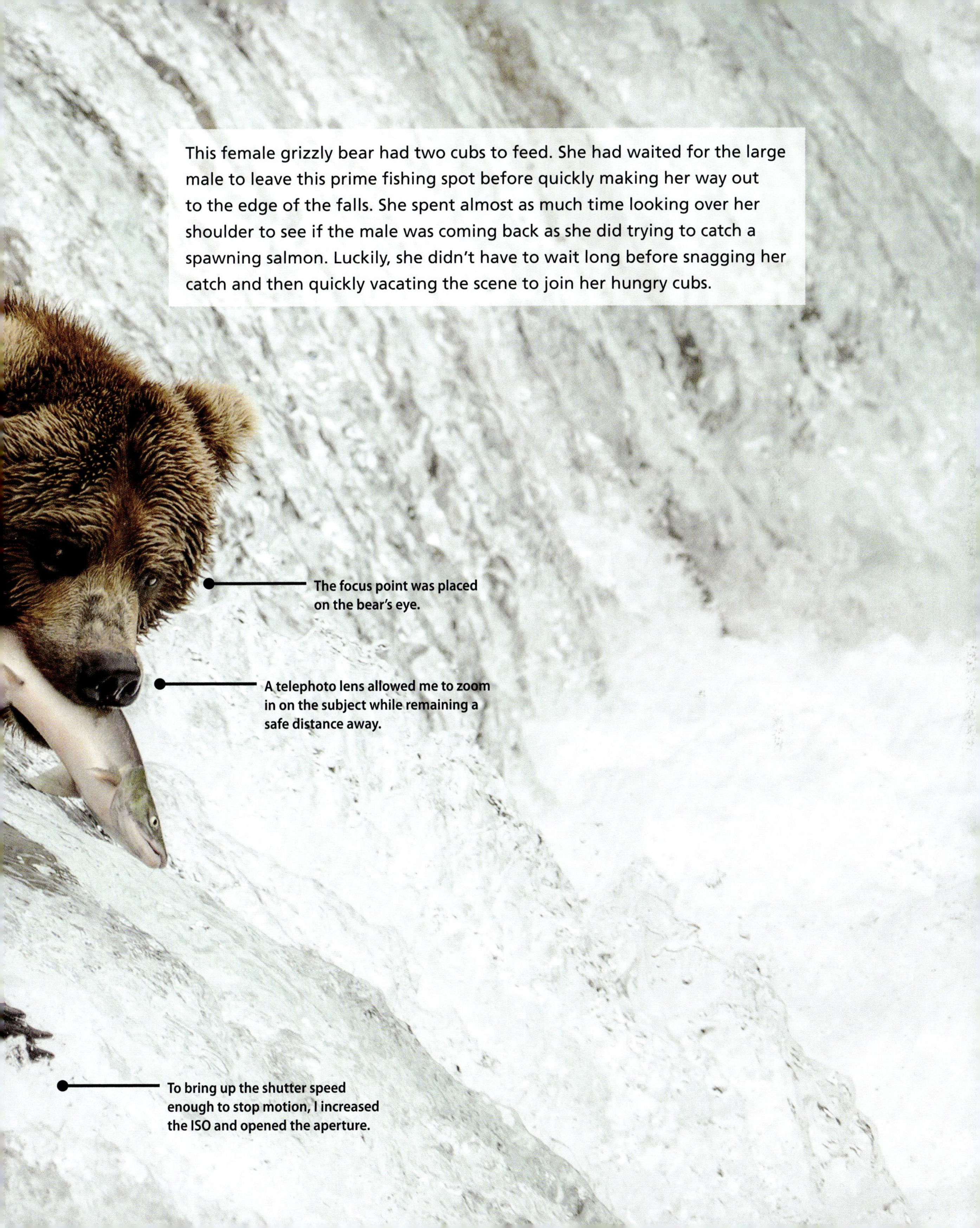

This female grizzly bear had two cubs to feed. She had waited for the large male to leave this prime fishing spot before quickly making her way out to the edge of the falls. She spent almost as much time looking over her shoulder to see if the male was coming back as she did trying to catch a spawning salmon. Luckily, she didn't have to wait long before snagging her catch and then quickly vacating the scene to join her hungry cubs.

Choosing the Right Memory Card

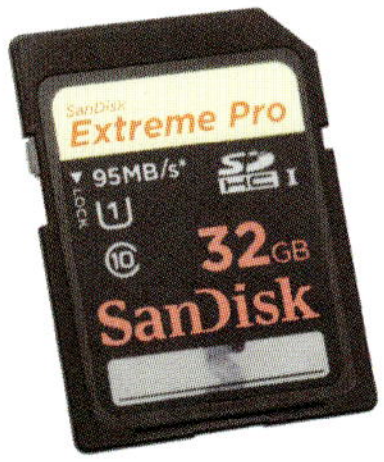

Figure 2.1
Make sure you select an SD card that has enough capacity to handle your photography needs.

Memory cards are the digital film that stores every shot you take until you move your images to a computer. The cards come in all shapes and sizes, and they are critical for temporarily storing your photos. It is important not to skimp when it comes to selecting your memory cards. The D5500 uses Secure Digital (SD) memory cards (**Figure 2.1**).

If you have been using a point-and-shoot camera, you may already own an SD media card. Which brand of card you use is up to you, but here is some advice about choosing your memory card:

- Size matters, at least in memory cards. At 24.2 megapixels, the D5500 will require a lot of storage space, especially if you shoot in the RAW or RAW+JPEG mode (more on this later in the chapter). You should definitely consider using a card with a storage capacity of at least 8 GB, but go with more if it is in your budget. If you plan on shooting high-definition video, be prepared for some large files. A 5-minute high-def video recording takes up approximately 700 MB of storage space. This means that you can fit about 30 minutes of video on a 4 GB card.
- Consider buying High Capacity (SDHC) cards. These cards are generally much faster, both when writing images to the card and when transferring them to your computer. If you are planning on using the Continuous mode (see Chapter 5) for capturing fast action, you can gain a boost in performance just by using an SDHC card with a class rating of at least 4 or 6. The higher the class rating, the faster the write speed. Class 6 or higher is recommended for video recording.
- Buy more than one card. If you have already purchased a memory card, consider getting another. Don't ruin a day of shooting by filling your card and then having to either erase shots or choose a lower-quality image format so you can keep on shooting. If photography matters to you, keeping a spare just makes good sense.

Manual Callout

For a list of Nikon-approved memory cards for the D5500, check out page 334 in the Reference Manual PDF you downloaded from the Nikon website.

Formatting Your Memory Card

Now that you have your card, let's talk about formatting for a minute. When you purchase any new SD card, you can pop it into your camera and start shooting right away—and probably everything will work as it should. However, what you should do first is format the card in the camera. This process allows the camera to set up the card to record images from your camera. Just as a computer hard drive must be formatted, formatting your card ensures that it is properly initialized. The card may work in the camera without first being formatted, but chances of failure down the road are much higher.

As a general practice, I always format new cards or cards that have been used in different cameras. I also reformat cards after I have downloaded my images and want to start a new shooting session. Note that you should always format your card in the camera, not in your computer. Using the computer could render the card useless. Also pay attention to the card manufacturer's recommendations with respect to moisture, humidity, and proper handling procedures. It sounds a little clichéd, but when it comes to protecting your images, every little bit helps.

Most people make the mistake of thinking that the process of formatting the memory card is equivalent to erasing it. Not so. The truth is that when you format the card, all you are doing is changing the file management information on the card. Think of it as removing the table of contents from a book and replacing it with a blank page. All of the contents are still there—for the moment at least—but you wouldn't know it by looking at the empty table of contents. The camera will see the card as completely empty, so you won't be losing any space, even if you have previously filled the card with images. Your camera will simply write the new image data over the previous data.

Formatting your memory card

1. Insert your memory card into the camera.
2. Press the Menu button and navigate to Setup Menu.
3. Use the Multi-selector on the back of the camera to highlight the Format Memory Card option, and press OK (**A**).

A

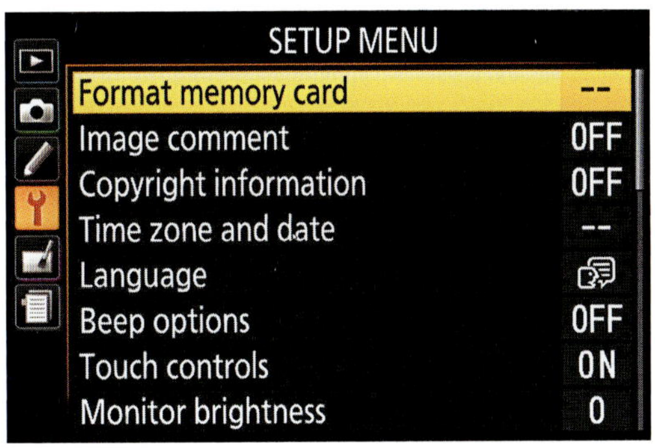

4. The next screen will show you a warning, letting you know that formatting the card will delete images (**B**). Select Yes, and press the OK button. The card is now formatted and ready for use.

B

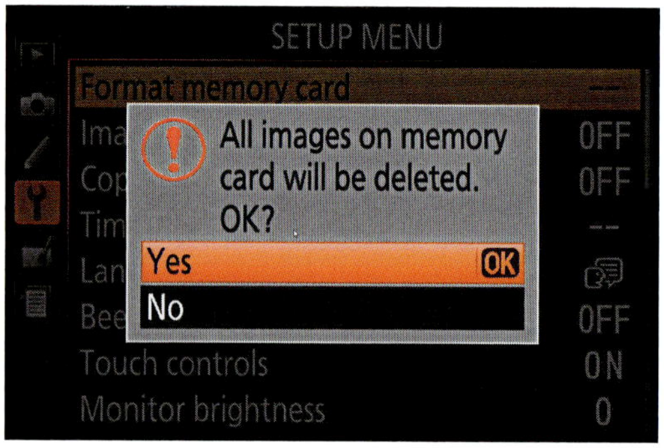

Updating the D5500's Firmware

The firmware of your camera is the set of computer operating instructions that controls how your camera functions. Updating this firmware is a great way to not only fix little bugs but also gain access to new functionality. I know that you want to get shooting, but having the proper firmware can affect the way the camera operates. You will need to check out the firmware information on the Nikon support page. Go to https://support.nikonusa.com and click the "Update your camera's firmware" link to see if a firmware update is available and how it will affect your camera. It is always a good idea to be working with the most up-to-date firmware version available.

Checking the camera's current firmware version number

1. Press the Menu button and navigate to Setup Menu.
2. Use the Multi-selector on the back of the camera to highlight the Firmware Version option, and press OK (**A**).

A

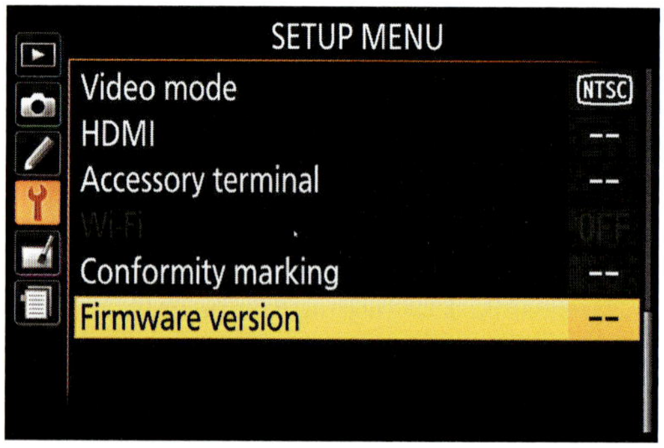

3. Take note of the current version numbers. There are two of them (**B**). Then check the Nikon website to see if you are using the current versions.

B

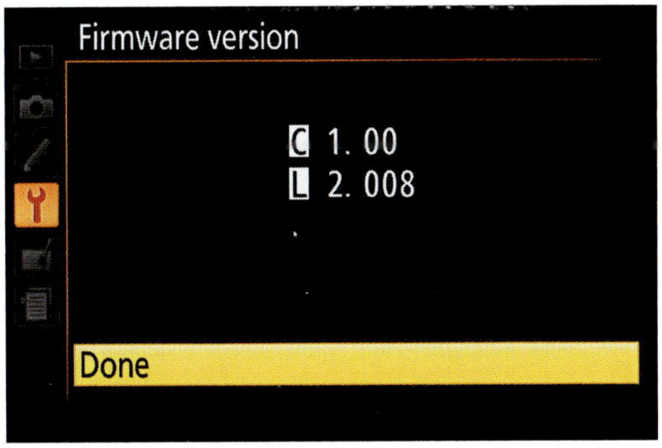

Updating the firmware from your SD Card

1. Download the firmware update file from the Nikon website. (Go to https://support.nikonusa.com, click "Update your camera's firmware," and locate the firmware update for your camera and computer operating system.)
2. Once you have downloaded the firmware to your computer and extracted it, you will need to transfer it to your SD card. The card must be formatted in your camera prior to loading the firmware to it.
3. Making sure you have a freshly charged camera battery, insert the card into the camera and turn it on.
4. Follow the instructions listed above for locating your firmware version. You will now be able to update your firmware using the files located on the SD card.

As this book is being written, firmware updates are not yet available for the D5500. After you check your camera firmware version and the Nikon site for updates, continue to check back periodically to see if there are updates available.

Cleaning the Sensor

Cleaning camera sensors used to be a nerve-racking process that required leaving the sensor exposed to scratching and even more dust. Now, cleaning the sensor is pretty much an automatic function. Every time you turn the camera on and off, you can instruct the sensor in the camera to vibrate to remove any dust particles that might have landed on it.

There are five choices for cleaning in the camera Setup menu: Clean at Startup, Clean at Shutdown, Clean at Startup and Shutdown, Cleaning Off, and Clean Now. I'm kind of obsessive when it comes to cleaning my sensor, so I like to have it set to clean when I turn the camera on and off.

The one cleaning function you will need to use via this menu is the Clean Now feature. This should be done every time you remove the lens from the camera body, because removing or changing a lens will leave the camera body open and susceptible to dust sneaking into the body. If you never change lenses, you shouldn't have too many dust problems. But the more often you change lenses, the more chances you are giving dust to enter the body. It's for this reason that I have added the Clean Now function to the custom My Menu list (see Chapter 9).

Every now and then, there will be a dust spot that is impervious to the shaking of the Auto Cleaning feature. This will require you to clean the sensor manually by raising the mirror and opening the camera shutter. When you activate this feature, it will move everything out of the way, giving you access to the sensor so you can use a blower or other cleaning device to remove the stubborn dust speck. The camera will need to be turned off after cleaning to allow the mirror to reset.

If you choose to manually clean your sensor, use a device that has been made to clean sensors (not a cotton swab from your medicine cabinet). There are dozens of commercially available devices such as brushes, swabs, and blowers that will clean the sensor without damaging it. To keep the sensor clean, always store the camera with a body cap or lens attached.

The camera sensor is an electrically charged device. This means that when the camera is turned on, there is a current running through the sensor. This electric current can create static electricity, which will attract small dust particles to the sensor area. For this reason, it is always a good idea to turn off the camera prior to removing a lens. You should also consider having the lens mount facing down when changing lenses so there is less opportunity for dust to fall into the inner workings of the camera.

Using the Clean Now feature

1. Press the Menu button and navigate to Setup Menu.
2. Use the Multi-selector on the back of the camera to highlight the Clean Image Sensor option, and press OK (**A**).
3. Highlight the Clean Now option, and press the OK button (**B**). The camera will clean the sensor for about 2 seconds and then return to the menu.

A

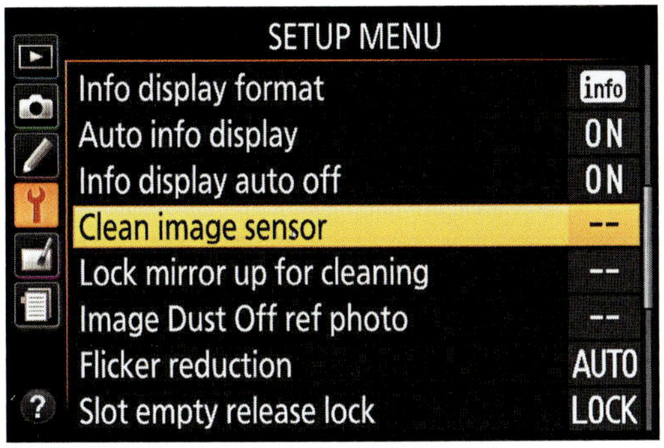

B

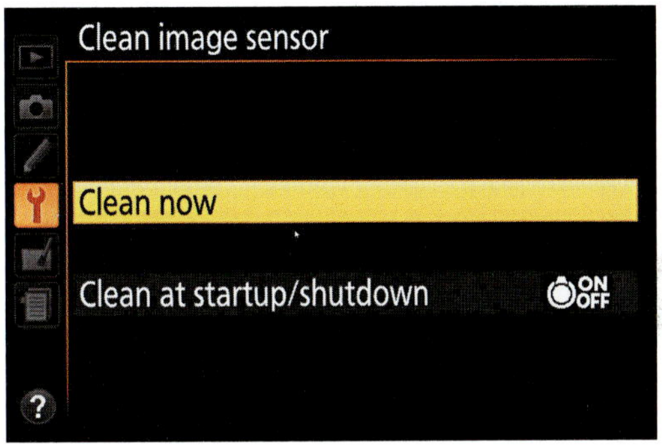

Using the Right Format: RAW vs. JPEG

When shooting with your D5500, you have a choice of image formats that your camera will use to store the pictures on the memory card. JPEG is probably the most familiar format to anyone who has been using a digital camera. I touched on this topic in Chapter 1, so you already have a little background on what JPEG and RAW files are.

There is nothing wrong with JPEG if you are taking casual shots. JPEG files are ready to use, right out of the camera. Why go through the process of adjusting RAW images of the kids opening presents when you are just going to email them to Grandma? For journalists and sports photographers who are shooting multiple frames per second and who need to transmit their images across the wire, again, JPEG is just fine. So what is wrong with JPEG? Absolutely nothing—unless you care about having complete creative control over all of your image data (as opposed to what a compression algorithm thinks is important).

As I mentioned in Chapter 1, JPEG is not actually an image format. It is a compression standard, and compression is where things go bad. When you have your camera set to JPEG—whether it is Fine, Normal, or Basic—you are telling the camera to process the image based on the in-camera settings and then throw away enough image data to make it shrink into a smaller space. In doing so, you give up subtle image details that you will never get back in post-processing. That is an awfully simplified statement but still fairly accurate.

So what does RAW have to offer?

First and foremost, RAW images are not compressed. (Some cameras, like the D5500, have what is called a compressed RAW format, but it is lossless compression, which means there is no loss of actual image data.) Note that RAW image files will require you to perform post-processing on your photographs. This is not only necessary, it is the reason that most photographers use it.

RAW images have a greater dynamic range than JPEG-processed images. This means that you can recover image detail in the highlights and shadows that just isn't available in JPEG-processed images.

There is more color information in a RAW image because it is a 12- or 14-bit image (depending on the camera), which means it contains more color information than a JPEG, which is always an 8-bit image. More color information means more to work with and smoother changes between tones—kind of like the difference between performing surgery with a scalpel as opposed to a butcher's knife. They'll both get the job done, but one will do less damage.

Regarding sharpening, a RAW image offers more control because you are the one who is applying the sharpening according to the effect you want to achieve. Once again, JPEG processing applies a standard amount of sharpening that you cannot change after the fact. Once it is done, it's done.

Image resolution

In discussions about digital cameras, "image resolution" is often used to describe pixel resolution, or the number of pixels used to make an image. This can be displayed as a dimension, such as 6000 x 4000 (the physical number of pixels in the width and height of the image sensor). Resolution can also be referred to in megapixels (MP), such as 24.2 MP. This number represents the total number of pixels on the sensor and is commonly used to describe the amount of image data that a digital camera can capture.

Finally, and most importantly, a RAW file is your negative. No matter what you do to it, you won't change it unless you save your file in a different format. This means that you can come back to that RAW file later and try different processing settings to achieve differing results and never harm the original image. By comparison, if you make a change to your JPEG and accidentally save the file, guess what? You have a new original file, and you will never get back to that first image. That alone should make you sit up and take notice.

Advice for new RAW shooters

Don't give up on shooting RAW just because it means more work. Hey, if RAW images take up more space on your cards, buy bigger cards or more small ones. Will downloading RAW images take more time? Yes, but good things come to those who wait. Don't worry about needing to purchase expensive software to work with your RAW files; Nikon gives away this software for free. Nikon's ViewNX 2 software can be downloaded from the Nikon website (go to https://support.nikonusa.com and click "Update your Nikon software") and gives you the ability to work directly on the RAW files and then output the enhanced results. That said, you will have more control with dedicated RAW processing software, such as Nikon's Capture NX-D (also a free download from Nikon) or Adobe's Photoshop and Photoshop Lightroom.

When you're starting out and learning from this book, my recommendation is to shoot in JPEG mode or RAW+JPEG mode (more on that in a moment). This will allow you to quickly review your JPEG images and study the effects of the lessons. Once you have become comfortable with all of the camera features, switch to shooting in RAW mode so you can start gaining more creative control over your image processing. After all, you took the photograph—shouldn't you be the one to decide how it looks in the end?

Shooting dual formats

Your camera has the added benefit of being able to write two files for each picture you take, one in RAW and one in JPEG. If you have a RAW+JPEG setting selected, your camera will save your images in both formats on your card.

I think shooting RAW+JPEG is actually a good way to transition to shooting RAW. You get the ease and safety of the familiar JPEG and the ability to compare the JPEG against your RAW processing experience. Obviously saving in both formats will take up more of the space on your memory card and hard drive, but think of it as a stepping-stone on the path to shooting only RAW in the future. It took me a little while to make the transition, and looking back, I took some shots in JPEG mode that I now wish were taken in RAW mode so I could improve upon them. Live and learn.

Shooting in RAW+JPEG

1. Press the **i** button to activate the cursor in the information screen.
2. Use the Multi-selector to highlight the Image Quality setting, and press OK (**A**).
3. Highlight the RAW+JPEG option of your choice. The options include RAW+B (Basic), RAW+N (Normal), and RAW+F (Fine) (**B**).
4. Press the OK button to lock in your changes.

A

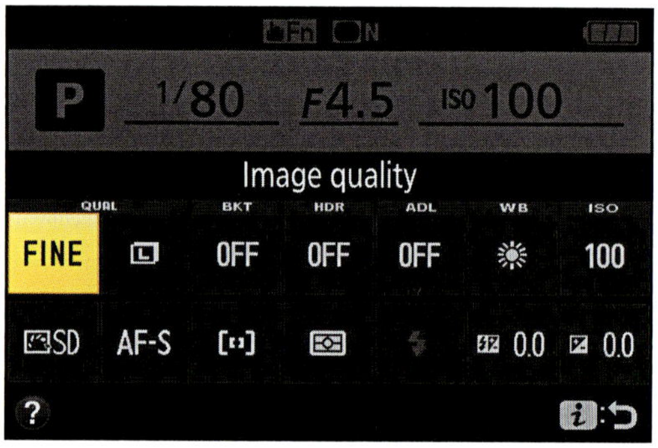

B

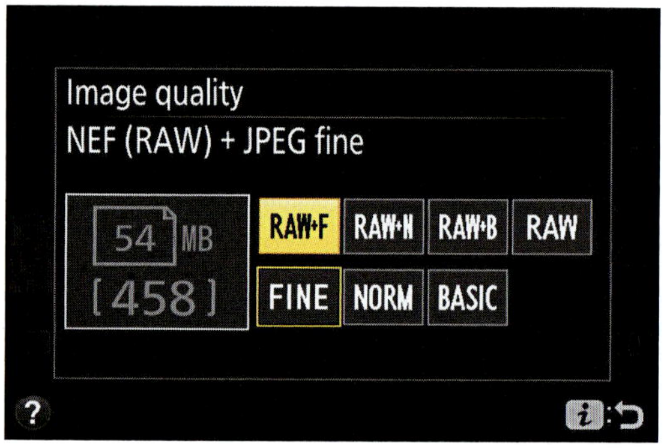

In the selection screen, you can see how much storage space each option will require on your SD card. The RAW+F option, which is the one I use, will take up approximately 54 megabytes of space for each photograph you take.

Lenses and Focal Lengths

If you ask professional photographers what they believe to be their most critical piece of photographic equipment, they will undoubtedly tell you it is their lens. The technology and engineering that goes into your camera is a marvel, but it isn't worth a darn if it can't get the light from the outside onto the sensor. The D5500, as a digital single lens reflex (dSLR) camera, uses the lens for a multitude of tasks, from focusing on a subject to metering a scene to delivering and focusing light onto the camera sensor. The lens is also responsible for the amount of the scene that will be captured (the frame). With all of this riding on the lens, we need to take a more in-depth look at the camera's eye on the world.

Lenses are composed of optical glass that is both concave and convex in shape. The alignment of the glass elements is designed to focus the light coming in from the front of the lens onto the camera sensor. The amount of light that enters the camera is also controlled by the lens, the size of the glass elements, and the aperture mechanism within the lens housing. The quality of the glass used in the lens will have a direct effect on how well the lens can resolve details and on the contrast of the image (the ability to deliver great highlights and shadows). Most lenses now routinely include things like an autofocus motor and, in some cases, a vibration-reduction mechanism.

One other aspect of the camera lens is often the first consideration of the photographer: lens length. Lenses are typically divided into three or four groups depending on the field of view they deliver.

Wide-angle lenses cover a field of view from around 110 degrees to about 60 degrees (**Figure 2.2**). Lenses that are extremely wide angle have a tendency to produce some distortion in your image, which will be apparent toward the outer edges of the frame. Generally anything 35mm or smaller could be considered wide angle.

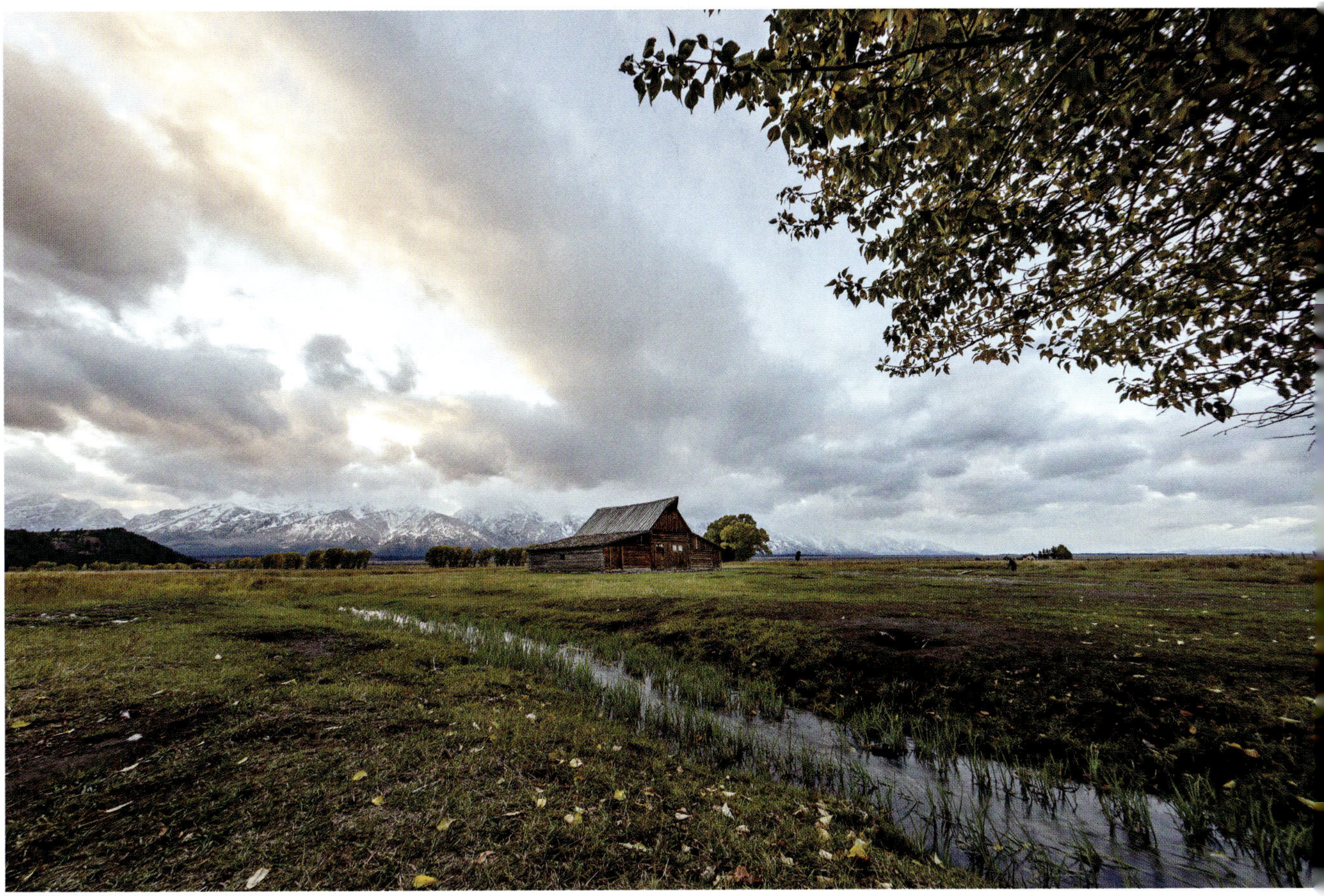

Figure 2.2 **The 16mm lens setting provides a wide view of the scene but little detail of distant objects.**

ISO 100 • 1/40 sec. • f/8 • 16mm lens

Wide-angle lenses can display a large depth of field, which allows you to keep the foreground and background in sharp focus. This makes them very useful for landscape photography. They also work well in tight spaces, such as indoors where there isn't much elbow room available (**Figure 2.3**). They can be handy for large group shots but, because of the amount of distortion, not so great for close-up portrait work.

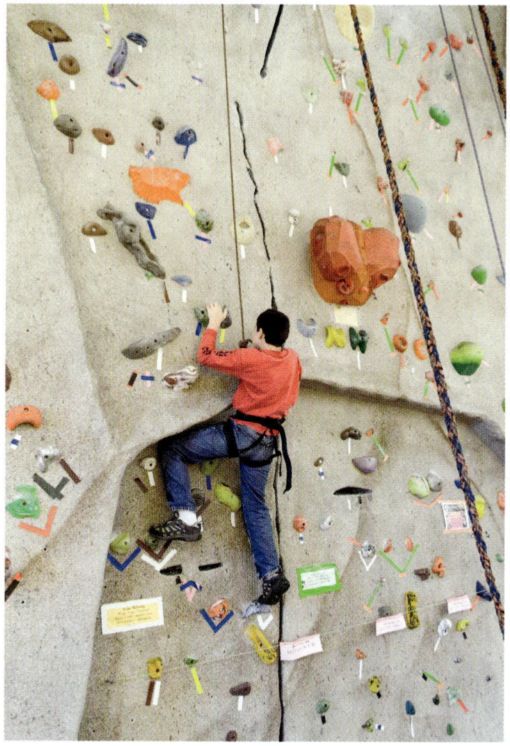

Figure 2.3 When you are shooting in tight spaces, such as indoors, a nice wide-angle lens helps capture more of the scene.

ISO 1000 • 1/60 sec. • f/3.5 • 24mm lens

A *normal* lens has a field of view that is about 45 degrees and delivers approximately the same view as the human eye. The perspective is natural, and there is little distortion in objects. The normal lens for full-frame and 35mm cameras is the 50mm lens (**Figure 2.4**), but for the D5500 it is more in the neighborhood of a 35mm lens because of its sensor's 1.5x crop factor. This photo of me tending my beehives was taken using the camera's interval timer (see Chapter 9).

Normal focal length lenses are useful for photographing people and architecture and for most other general photographic needs. They create very little distortion and offer a moderate range of depth of field.

Most longer focal length lenses are referred to as *telephoto* lenses. They range in length from 135mm up to 800mm or longer and have a field of view that is about 35 degrees or smaller. These lenses have the ability to greatly magnify the scene, allowing you to capture details of distant objects, but the angle of view is greatly reduced (**Figure 2.5**).

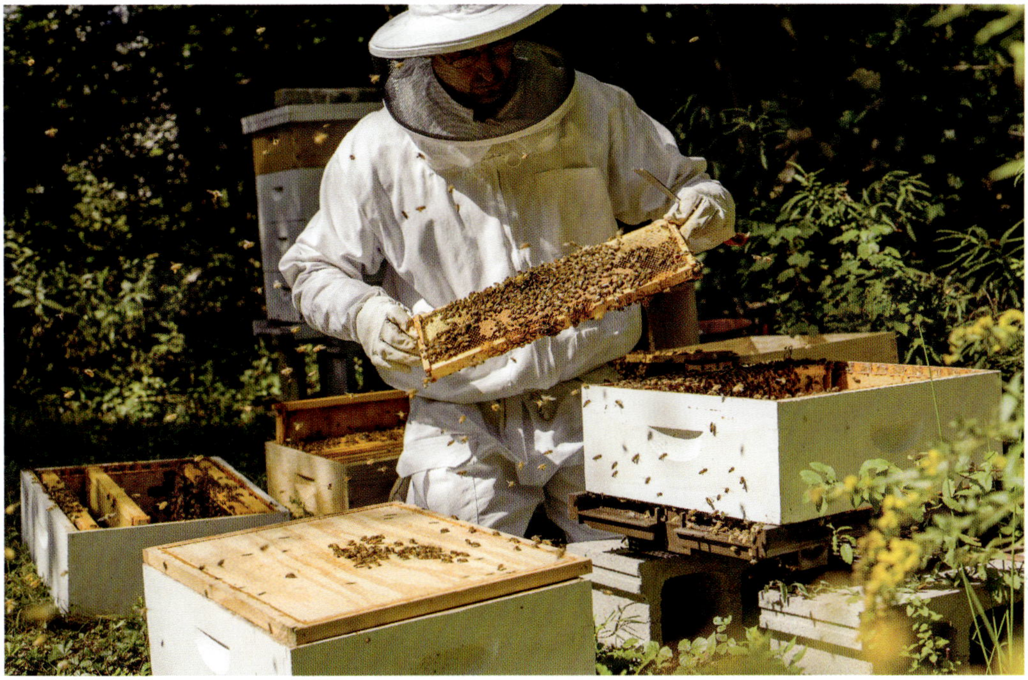

Figure 2.4
Long considered the "normal" lens for 35mm photography, the 50mm focal length can be considered somewhat of a telephoto lens on the D5500 because it has the same angle of view and magnification as a 75mm lens on a 35mm camera body.

ISO 200 • 1/800 sec. • f/5.6 • 50mm lens

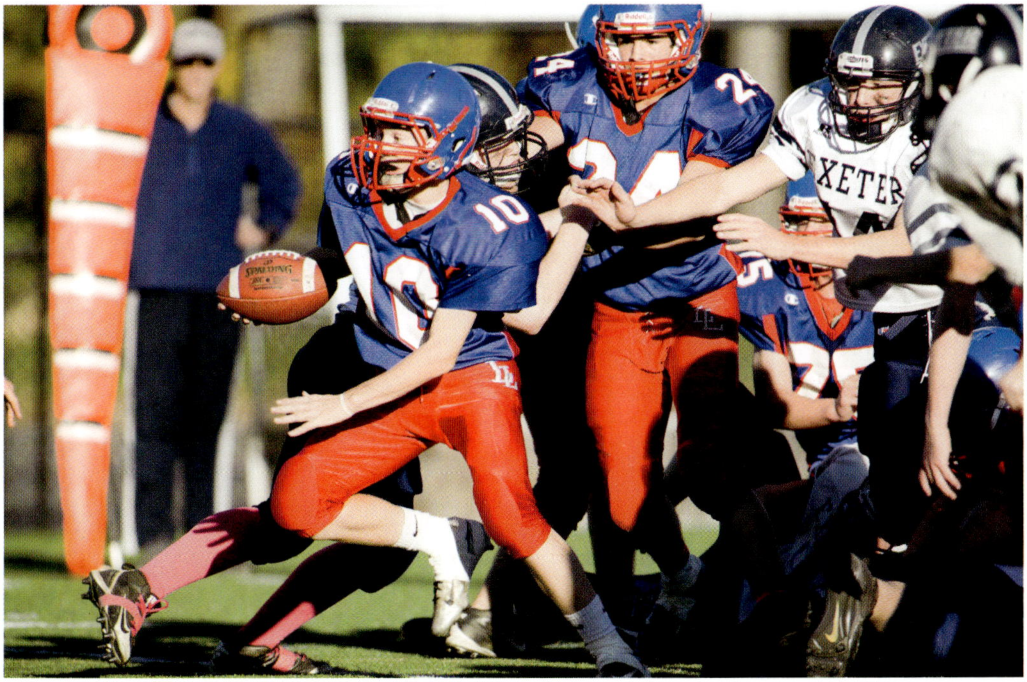

Figure 2.5
A 600mm lens can get you right into the action.

ISO 500 • 1/1000 sec. • f/5.6 • 600mm lens

Telephoto lenses are most useful for sports photography or any application where you need to get close to your subject. Note that they can have a compressing effect—making objects look closer together than they actually are (**Figure 2.6**)—and a very narrow depth of field when shot at their widest apertures.

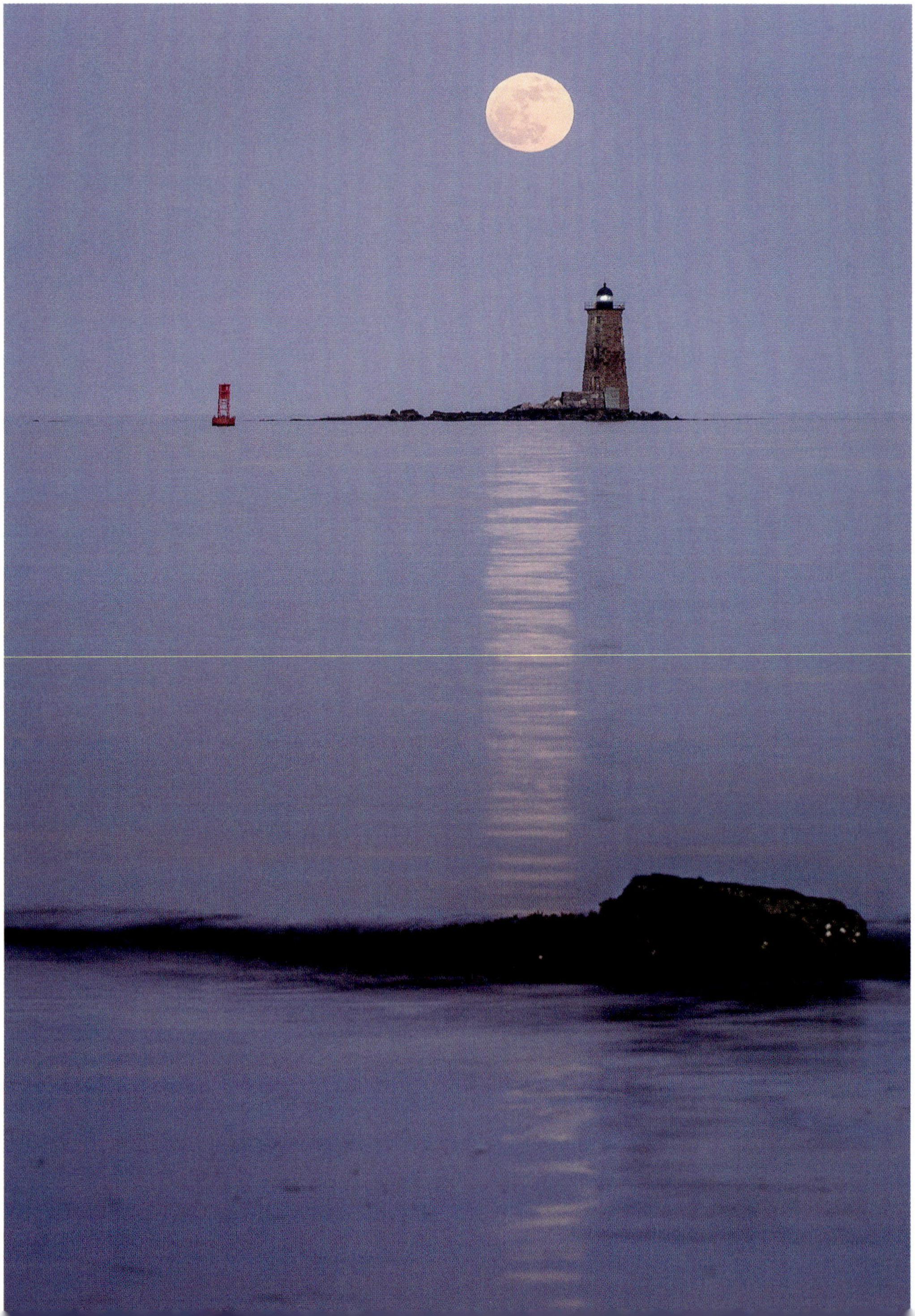

Figure 2.6
The long telephoto lens makes the rock in the foreground appear much closer to the lighthouse than it is in reality.

ISO 200 • 1/4 sec. • f/8 • 200mm lens

A *zoom* lens is a great alternative to carrying a bunch of single focal length lenses (also referred to as "prime" lenses). They can cover a wide range of focal lengths because of the configuration of their optics. However, because it takes more optical elements to capture a scene at different focal lengths, the light must pass through more glass on its way to the image sensor. The more glass, the lower the quality of the image sharpness. The other sacrifice that is made is in aperture. Zoom lenses typically have smaller maximum apertures than prime lenses, which means they cannot achieve a narrow depth of field or work in lower light levels without the assistance of image stabilization, a tripod, or higher ISO settings. (We'll discuss all this in more detail in later chapters.)

The D5500 can be purchased with the body only, but many folks will purchase it with a kit lens. The most common kit lens is the 18–140mm VR f/3.5–5.6. With my D5500, I have been working with the 18–140mm as well as the 70–200mm VR AF-S lens.

Throughout the book, I will occasionally reference lenses that are wider or more telephoto than these because I use a multitude of lenses. This doesn't mean you have to run out and purchase more lenses. It just means that if you do this long enough, you are sure to accumulate additional lenses that will expand your ability to be creative with your photography.

What Is Exposure?

In order for you to get the most out of this book, I need to briefly discuss the principles of exposure. Without this basic knowledge, it will be difficult for you to improve your photography. Granted, I could write an entire book on exposure and the photographic process—and many people have—but for our purposes, I will just cover some of the basics. This will give you the essential tools to make educated decisions in determining how best to photograph a subject.

Exposure is the process whereby the light bouncing off a subject reflects through an opening in the camera lens onto the camera sensor for a defined period of time. The combination of the lens opening, shutter speed, and sensor sensitivity is used to achieve a proper exposure value (EV) for the scene. The EV is the sum of the components necessary to properly expose a scene. A relationship exists between these factors, sometimes referred to as the "exposure triangle."

At each point of the triangle lies one of the factors of exposure:

- **ISO:** Determines the sensitivity of the camera sensor. ISO stands for the International Organization for Standardization, but the acronym is used as a term to describe the sensitivity of the camera sensor to light. The higher the sensitivity, the less light is required for a good exposure. These values are a carryover from the days of traditional color and black-and-white films.
- **Aperture:** Also referred to as the f-stop, this determines how much light passes through the lens at once.
- **Shutter Speed:** Controls the length of time that light is allowed to hit the sensor.

Here's how it works: The camera sensor has a level of sensitivity that is determined by the ISO setting. To get a proper exposure—not too much, not too little—the lens needs to adjust the aperture diaphragm (the size of the lens opening) to control the volume of light entering the camera. Then the shutter is opened for a relatively short period of time to allow the light to hit the sensor long enough for it to record on the sensor.

ISO numbers for the D5500 start at 100 and then double in sensitivity as you double the number. So 200 is twice as sensitive as 100. The camera can be set to use 1/2- or 1/3-stop increments, but for ISO just remember that the base numbers double: 100, 200, 400, 800, and so on. You also have a wide variety of shutter speeds available. The speeds on the D5500 range from as long as 30 seconds to as short as 1/4000 of a second. When using the camera, you will not see the 1 over the number in the viewfinder, so you will need to remember that anything shorter than a second will be a fraction. Typically, you will be working with a shutter speed from around 1/30 of a second to about 1/2000 of a second, but these numbers will change depending on your circumstances and the effect you are trying to achieve. The lens apertures will vary slightly depending on which lens you are using. This is because different lenses have different maximum apertures. The typical apertures at your disposal are f/4, f/5.6, f/8, f/11, f/16, and f/22.

When it comes to exposure, a change to any one of these factors requires changing one or more of the other two. This is referred to as reciprocal change. If you let more light in the lens by choosing a larger aperture, you will need to shorten the amount of time the shutter is open. If the shutter is allowed to stay open for a longer period of time, the aperture needs to be smaller to restrict the amount of light coming in.

How is exposure calculated?

We now know about the exposure triangle—ISO, shutter speed, and aperture—so it's time to put all three together to see how they relate to one another and how you can change them as needed.

Stop

You will hear the term "stop" thrown around all the time in photography. It relates to the f-stop, which is a term used to describe the aperture of your lens. When you need to give some additional exposure, you might say you are going to "add a stop." This doesn't just equate to the aperture; it could also be used to describe the shutter speed or even the ISO. So when your image is too light or dark, or you have too much movement in your subject, you will probably be changing things by a "stop" or two.

When you point your camera at a scene, the light reflecting off your subject enters the lens and is allowed to pass through to the sensor for a period of time as dictated by the shutter speed. The amount and duration of the light needed for a proper exposure depends on how much light is being reflected and how sensitive the sensor is. To figure this out, your camera uses a built-in light meter that looks through the lens and measures the amount of light. That level is then calculated against the sensitivity of the ISO setting and an exposure value is rendered. Here is the tricky part: There is no single way to achieve a perfect exposure, because the f-stop and shutter speed can be combined in different ways to allow the same amount of exposure. See, I told you it was tricky.

Here is a list of reciprocal settings that would all produce the same exposure result. Let's use the "sunny 16" rule, which states that when using f/16 on a sunny day, you can use a shutter speed that is roughly equal to the ISO setting to achieve a proper exposure. For simplification purposes, we will use an ISO of 100.

Reciprocal Exposures: ISO 100							
F-STOP	2.8	4	5.6	8	11	16	22
SHUTTER SPEED	1/4000	1/2000	1/1000	1/500	1/250	1/125	1/60

If you were to use any one of these combinations, they would each have the same result in terms of the exposure (how much light hits the camera's sensor). Also take note that every time we cut the f-stop in half, we reciprocated by doubling our shutter speed. For those of you wondering why f/5.6 is half of f/8, it's because those numbers are actually fractions based on the opening of the lens in relation to its focal length. This means that a lot of math goes into figuring out what the total area of a lens opening is, so you just have to take it on faith that f/5.6 is half of f/8 but twice as much as f/4. A good way to remember which opening is larger is to think of your camera lens as a pipe that controls the flow of water. If you had a pipe that was 1/2 inch in diameter (f/2) and one that was 1/8 inch (f/8), which would allow more water to flow through? It would be the 1/2-inch pipe. The same idea works here with camera f-stops; f/2 is a larger opening than f/4 or f/8 or f/16.

Now that we know this, we can start using this information to make intelligent choices in terms of shutter speed and f-stop. Let's bring the third element into this by changing our ISO by one stop, from 100 to 200.

Reciprocal Exposures: ISO 200							
F-STOP	2.8	4	5.6	8	11	16	22
SHUTTER SPEED	—	1/4000	1/2000	1/1000	1/500	1/250	1/125

Notice that, since we doubled the sensitivity of the sensor, we now require half as much exposure as before. We have also reduced our maximum aperture from f/2.8 to f/4 because the camera can't use a shutter speed that is faster than 1/4000 of a second.

So why not just use the exposure setting of f/16 at 1/250 of a second? Why bother with all of these reciprocal values when this one setting will give us a properly exposed image? The answer is that the f-stop and shutter speed also control two other important aspects of our image: motion and depth of field.

Motion and Depth of Field

Distinct characteristics are related to changes in aperture and shutter speed. Shutter speed controls the length of time the light has to strike the sensor; consequently, it also controls the blurriness (or lack of blurriness) of the image. The less time light has to hit the sensor, the less time your subjects have to move around and become blurry. This can let you control things like freezing the motion of a fast-moving subject (**Figure 2.7**) or intentionally blurring subjects to give the feel of energy and motion (**Figure 2.8**).

The aperture controls the amount of light that comes through the lens, but it also determines what areas of the image will be in focus. This is referred to as depth of field, and it is an extremely valuable creative tool. The smaller the opening (the larger the number, such as f/22), the greater the sharpness of objects from near to far (**Figure 2.9**). A large opening (or small number, like f/2.8) means more blurring of objects that are not at the same distance as the subject you are focusing on (**Figure 2.10**).

As we further explore the features of the camera, we will learn not only how to use the elements of exposure to capture properly exposed photographs, but also how to make adjustments to emphasize our subject. It is the manipulation of these elements—motion and focus—that will take your images to the next level.

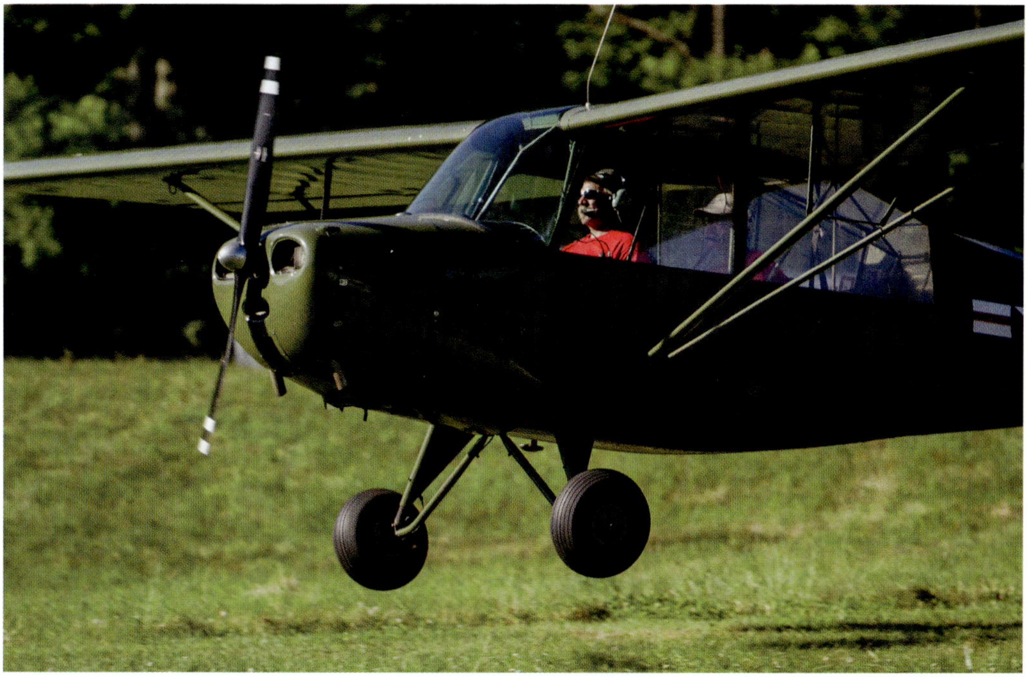

Figure 2.7
A fast shutter speed was used to freeze the action.

ISO 100 • 1/1250 sec. • f/2.8 • 200mm lens

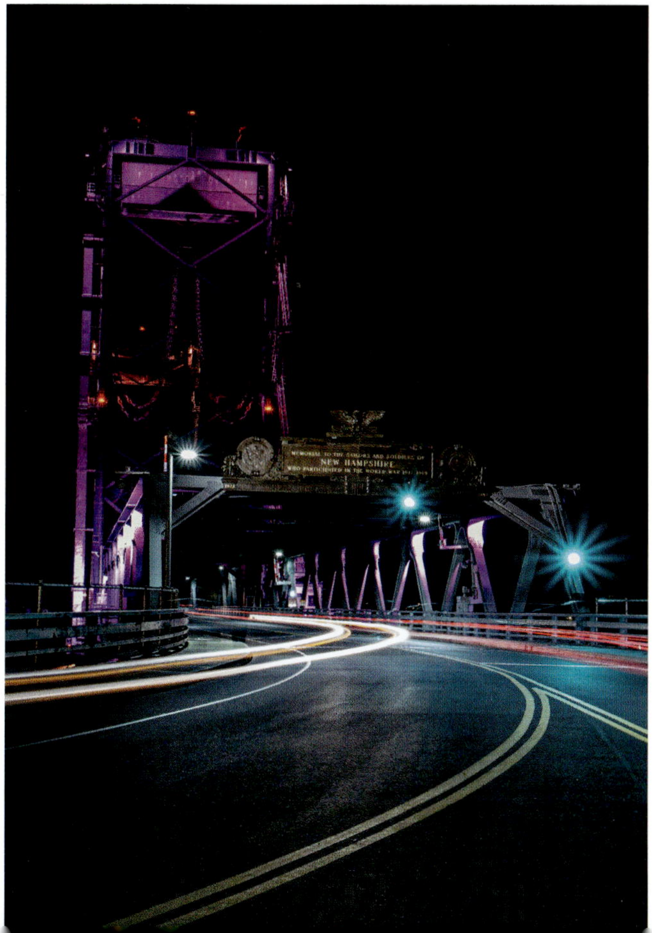

Figure 2.8
The slower shutter speed conveys a sense of motion.

ISO 250 • 30 sec. • f/16 • 42mm lens

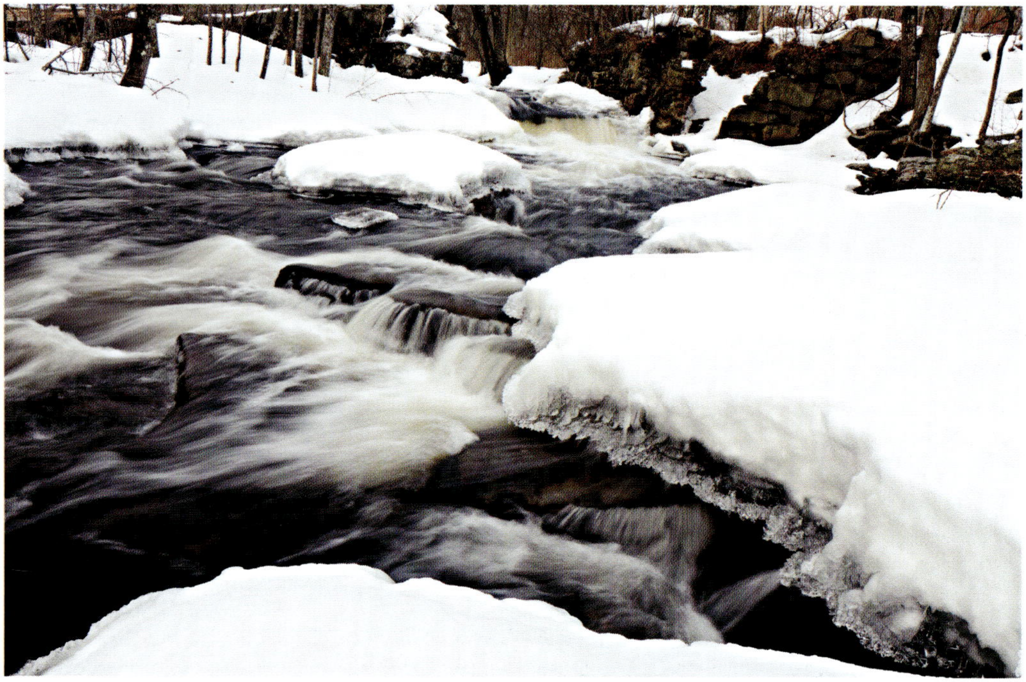

Figure 2.9
By using a small aperture, I've extended the area of sharp focus from a point that is near the camera all the way out to distant objects.

ISO 100 • 1/4 sec. • f/11 • 18mm lens

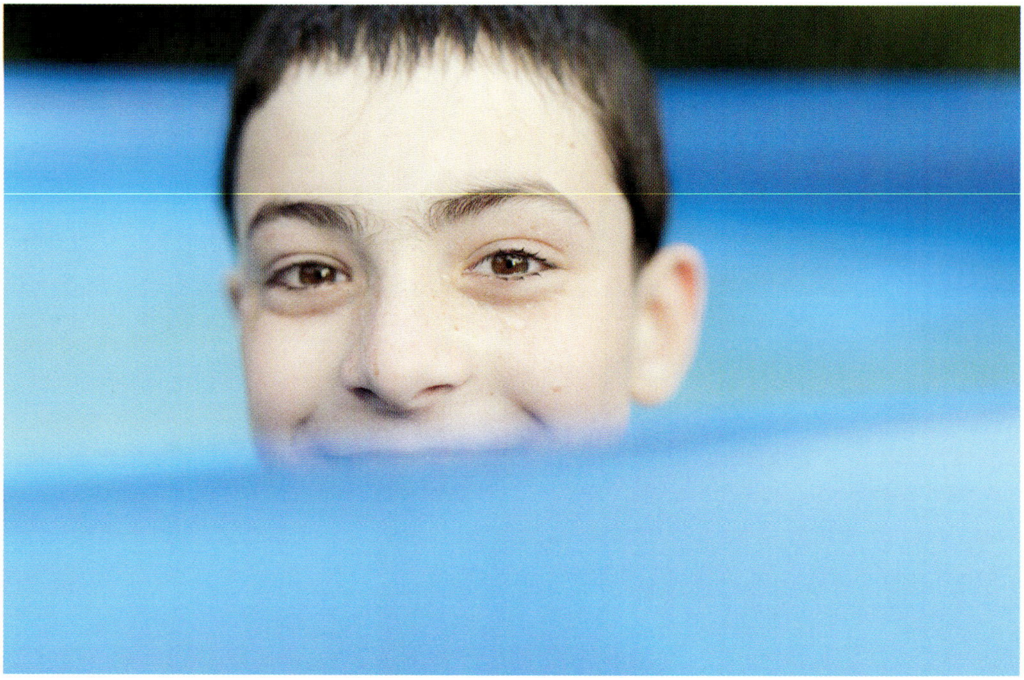

Figure 2.10
Isolating a subject is accomplished by using a large aperture, which produces a narrow area of sharp focus while blurring the foreground and background.

ISO 200 • 1/500 sec. • f/2 • 50mm lens

Chapter 2 Assignments

These assignments focus on helping you get to know your equipment better and ensuring that everything is in tip-top shape before you head out to shoot.

Formatting your card

Even if you have already begun using your camera, make sure you are familiar with formatting the Secure Digital (SD) card. If you haven't done so already, follow the directions given earlier in the chapter and format as prescribed (make sure you save any images to your computer first). Then perform the format function every time you have downloaded or saved your images or use a new card.

Checking your firmware version

Using the most up-to-date version of the camera firmware will ensure that your camera is functioning properly. Use the Setup menu to find your current firmware version, and then update as necessary following the steps listed in this chapter.

Cleaning your sensor

You probably noticed the sensor-cleaning message the first time you turned on your camera. Make sure you are familiar with the Clean Now command so you can perform this function every time you change a lens.

Exploring your image formats

I want you to become familiar with all of the camera features before using the RAW format, but take a little time to explore the Image Quality menu so you can see what options are available to you.

Exploring your lens

If you are using a zoom lens, spend a little time shooting with all of the different focal lengths, from the widest to the longest. See just how much of an angle you can cover with your widest lens setting. How much magnification will you be able to get from the telephoto setting? Try shooting the same subject with a variety of focal lengths to note the differences in how the subject looks, and also the relationship between the subject and the other elements in the photo.

Share your results with the book's Flickr group!
Join the group here: flickr.com/groups/nikond5500_fromsnapshotstogreatshots

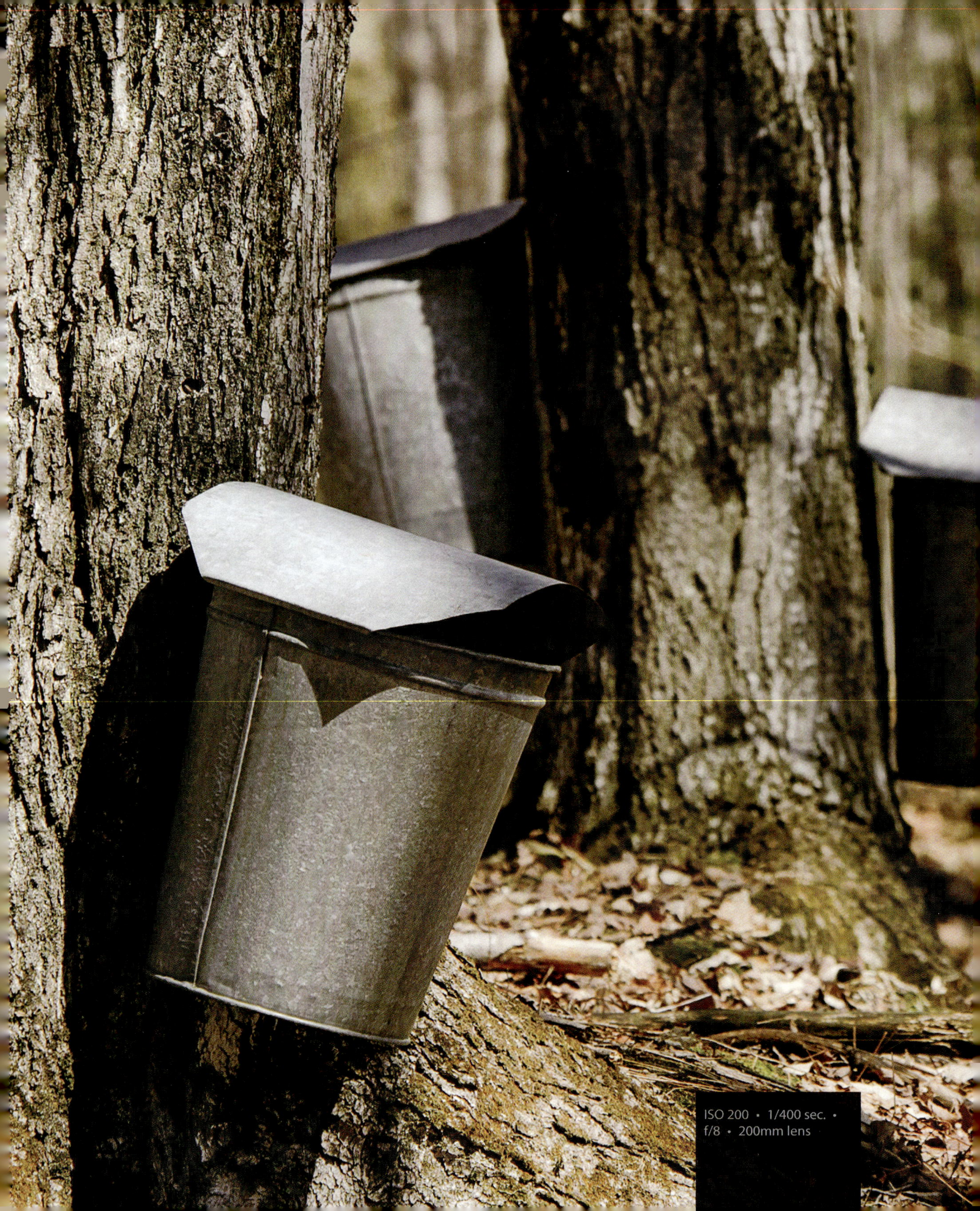
ISO 200 • 1/400 sec. • f/8 • 200mm lens

3

The Auto Modes

Get Shooting with the Automatic Camera Modes

The Nikon D5500 is an amazing camera with some incredible features. In fact, with all of the technology built into it, the D5500 can be pretty intimidating for someone new to dSLR photography. For that reason, the folks at Nikon have made it a little easier for you to get great-looking photographs without having to do a lot of thinking. Enter the scene modes. The camera modes on the automatic side of the Mode dial are simple, icon-labeled modes that are set up to use specific features of the camera for various shooting situations. In addition, there is a collection of in-camera special effects. Let's take a look at the different modes, and how and when to use them.

Poring Over the Picture

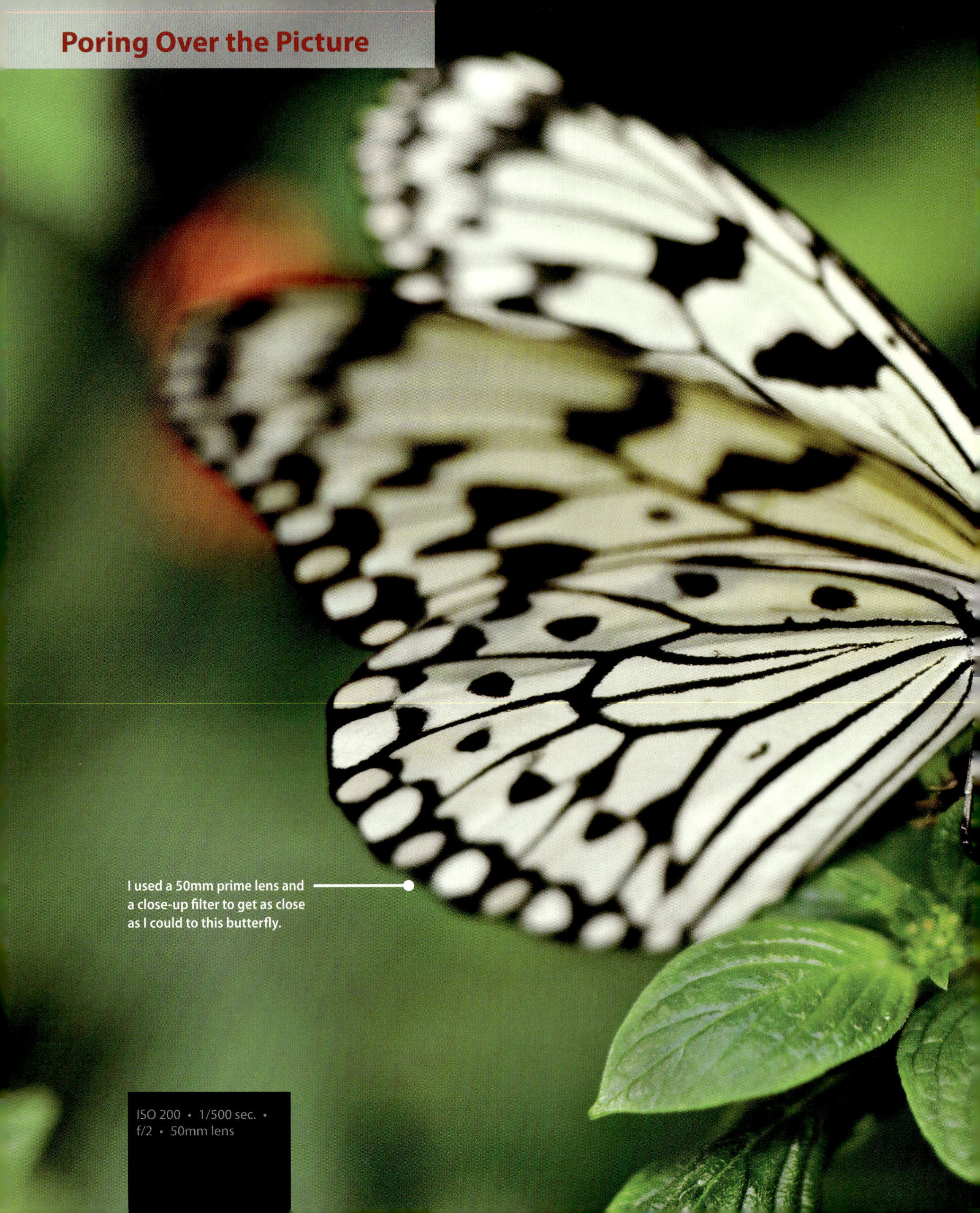

I used a 50mm prime lens and a close-up filter to get as close as I could to this butterfly.

ISO 200 • 1/500 sec. • f/2 • 50mm lens

Visiting a butterfly exhibit is a great way to spend quality time with these beautiful insects. You'll be able to photograph a variety of butterflies, many quite exotic and very large. The exhibits tend to be small, so you can stake out a spot and just wait for the butterflies to come to you. Plus, as the exhibits tend to be indoors, you don't have to contend with the pesky biting insects you encounter in fields and gardens. Butterfly exhibits are also great places to experiment with Close-up mode, getting as close as you can and filling the frame with colors and patterns.

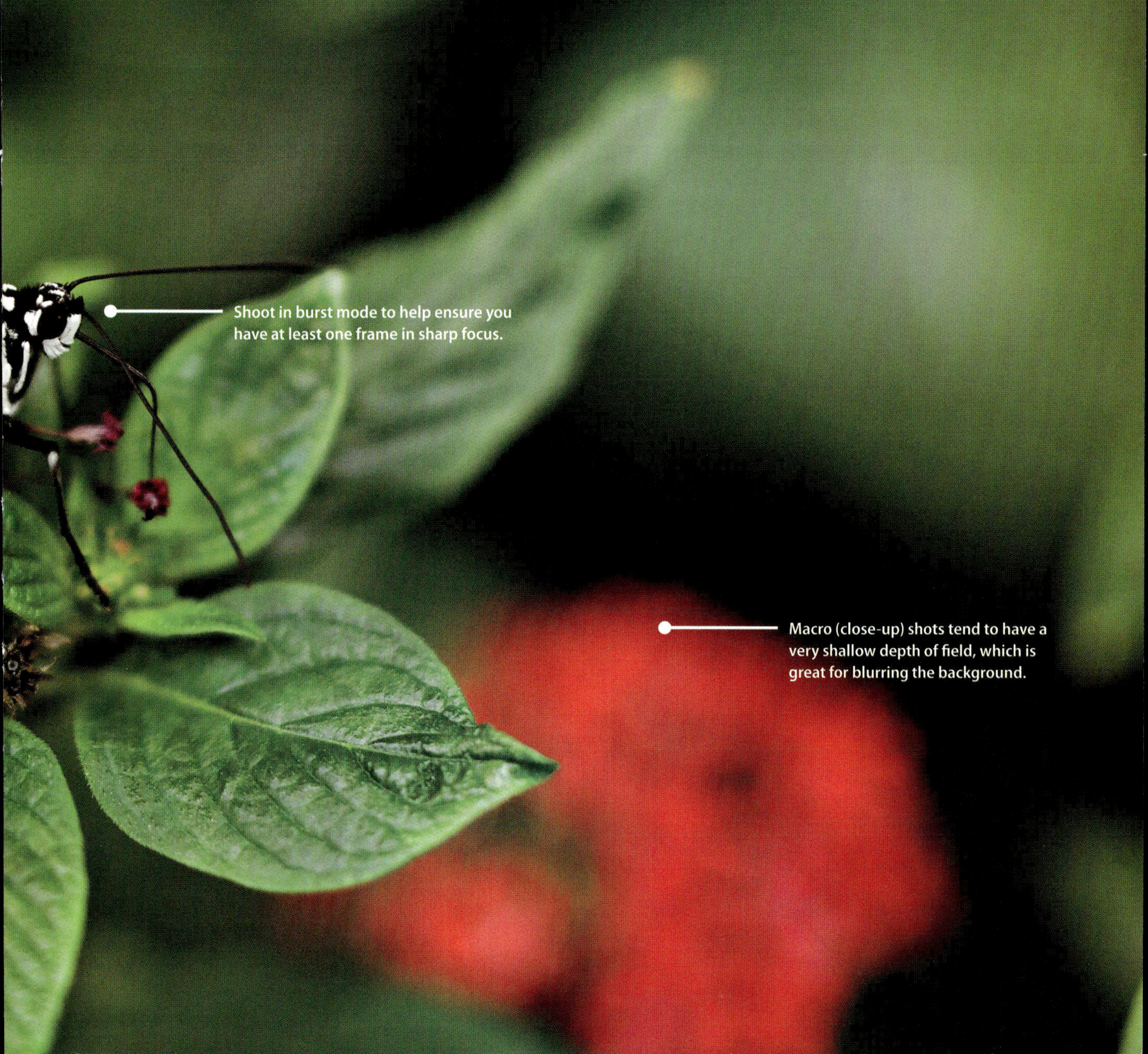

Auto Mode

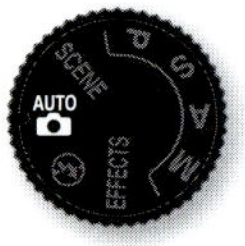

Auto mode is all about thought-free photography (**Figure 3.1**). There is little to nothing for you to do in this mode except point and shoot. Your biggest concern when using Auto mode is focusing. The camera will use the automatic focusing modes to achieve the best possible focus for your picture. Naturally, the camera is going to assume that the object closest to it is the one you want in sharpest focus. Simply press the shutter button down halfway while looking through the viewfinder, and you should see one of the focus points light up over the subject. Of course, you know that putting your subject in the middle of the picture is not the best way to compose your shot. So wait for the chirp to confirm that the focus has been set, and then, while still holding down the button, recompose your shot. Press the shutter button the rest of the way to take the photo. It's that easy (**Figure 3.2**). The camera will take care of all your exposure decisions, including when to use flash.

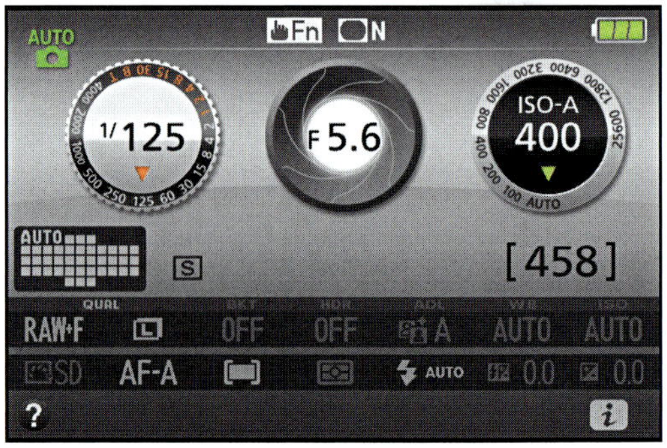

Figure 3.1 The Auto mode info screen.

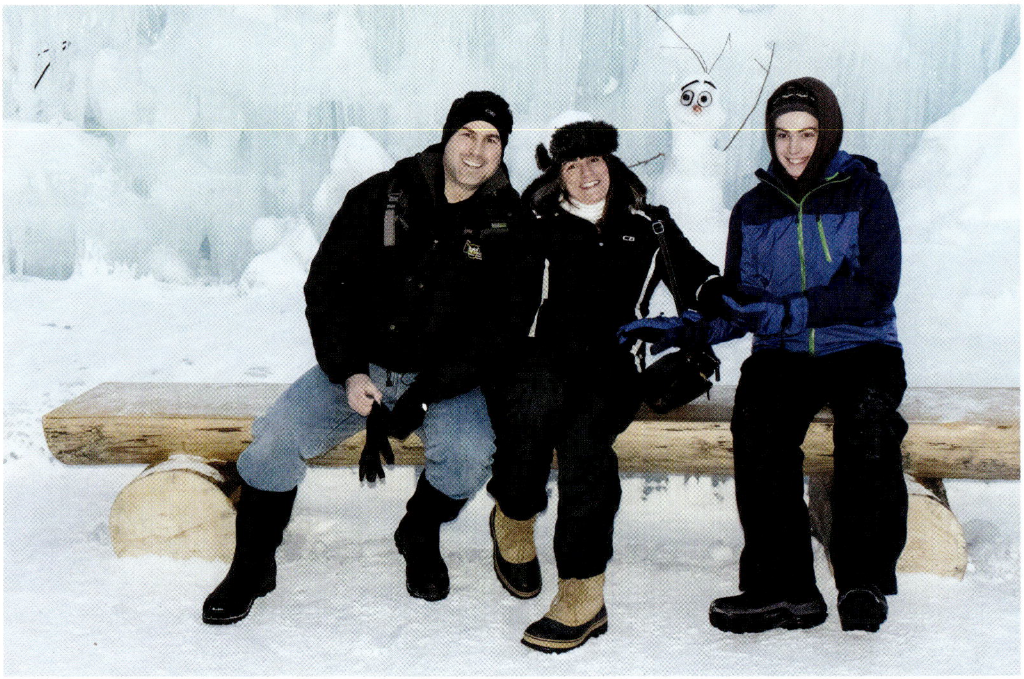

Figure 3.2
Auto mode works great when you don't want to think too much and just feel like snapping some shots.

ISO 18000 • 1/60 sec. • f/8 • 35mm lens

Let's face it: This is the lazy man's mode. But sometimes it's nice to be lazy and click away without giving thought to anything but preserving a memory. As you become more comfortable with your camera, though, you will want to start using its advanced features to improve your shots.

Auto (Flash Off) Mode

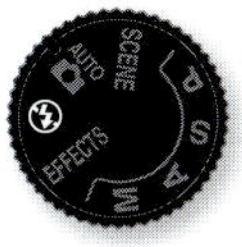

Sometimes you will be in a situation where the light levels are low but you don't want to use the flash. Maybe you are shooting in a place that restricts flash photography, such as a museum, or it could be a location where you want to capture the feel of the available light, such as an indoor scene lit by interesting lighting. This is where Auto (Flash Off) mode comes into play (**Figure 3.3**).

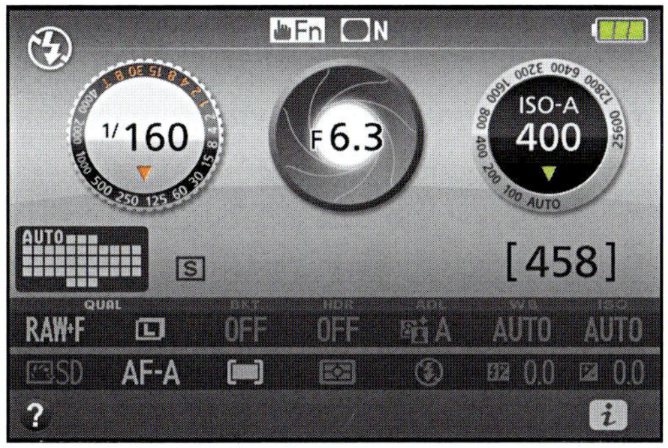

Figure 3.3 The Auto (Flash Off) mode info screen.

By keeping the flash from firing, you will be able to use just the available ambient light while the camera modifies the ISO setting to assist you in getting good exposures (**Figure 3.4**). If the camera detects that the shutter speed is going to be slow enough to introduce camera shake, it will give a warning on the rear information screen that reads "Subject is too dark." It will also flash the info in the viewfinder so you know to check the camera settings. Despite what the camera may say, you'll want to either use a tripod or brace yourself really well if the shutter speed is 1/60 of a second or slower to avoid blurred images from camera movement.

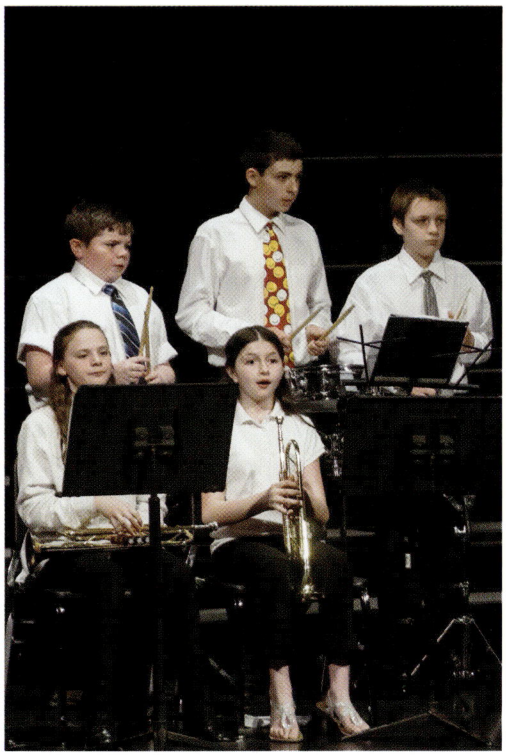

Figure 3.4 Auto (Flash Off) mode made sure the pop-up flash stayed disabled in the low-light environment.

ISO 3200 • 1/200 sec. • f/5.6 • 165mm lens

Fortunately, most of the new Vibration Reduction (VR) lenses being sold today allow you to handhold the camera at much slower shutter speeds and still get great results. The two downfalls to this mode are the Auto ISO setting, which will quickly take your ISO setting up high, and the fact that there is still the possibility of getting blur from subject movement if the shutter speed is slow.

Scene Modes

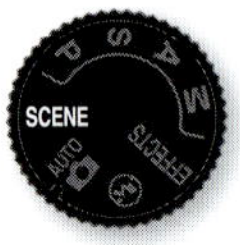

Most digital SLR cameras will have only seven or eight automatic modes at their disposal, but the D5500 takes things to a whole new level with 16 additional scene modes to choose from (plus the ten effects modes covered later in this chapter). Nikon has anticipated many of the typical shooting scenarios you will encounter and has created scene modes that are optimized for those situations. Let's take a quick look at these modes, but first, here's how to find them.

Using the scene modes

1. Set the Mode dial to the Scene setting.
2. Rotate the Command dial until the appropriate scene appears on the information screen.

Portrait

One problem with Auto mode is that it has no idea what type of subject you are photographing and therefore uses the same settings for each situation. Shooting portraits is a perfect example. When you take a photograph of someone, you usually want the emphasis of the picture to be on the person, not necessarily the stuff going on in the background.

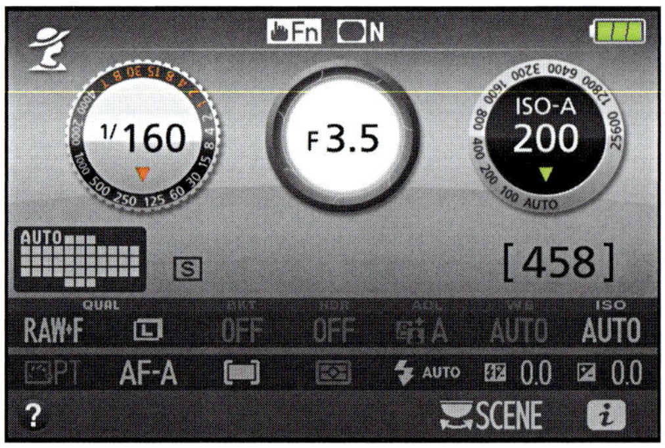

Figure 3.5 **The Portrait mode info screen.**

This is what Portrait mode is all about (**Figure 3.5**). When you set your camera to this mode, you are telling the camera to select a larger aperture so that the depth of field is much narrower and will blur objects in the background more. This blurry background places the attention on your subject (**Figure 3.6**). The other feature of this mode is the automatic selection of the D5500's built-in Portrait picture control (we'll go into more detail about picture controls in later chapters). This feature is optimized for skin tones and is a little softer to improve the look of skin.

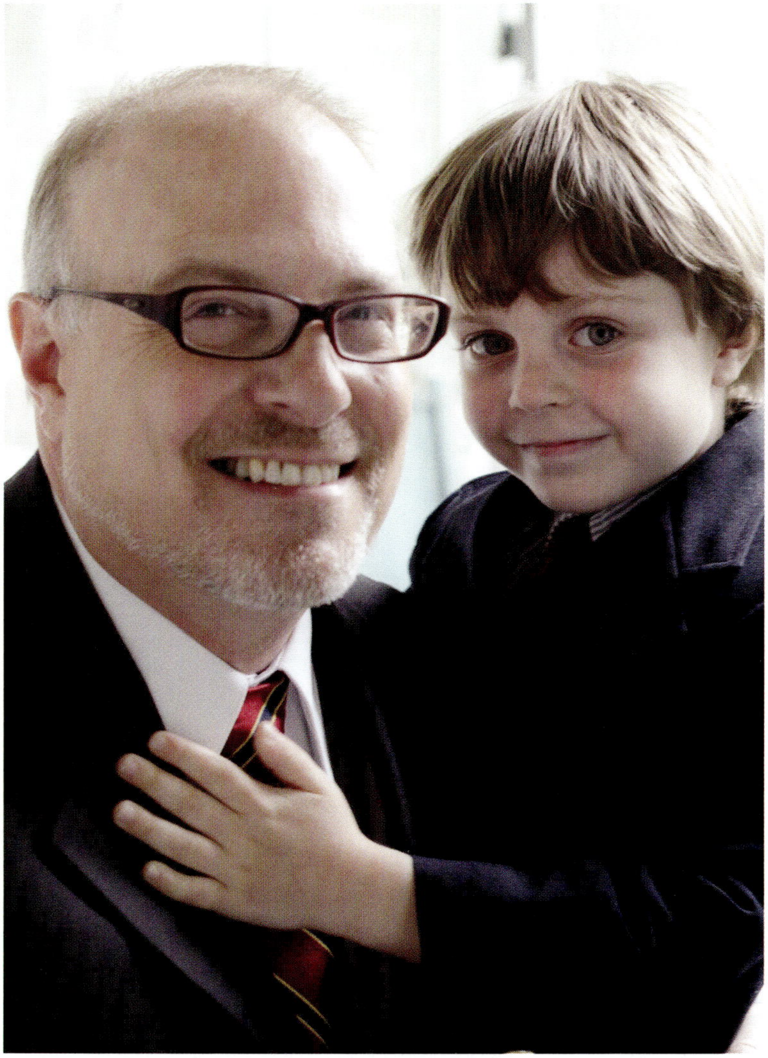

Figure 3.6
Portrait mode is useful for getting the right settings under the current lighting conditions for photos of people.

ISO 400 • 1/90 sec. • f/4.8 • 50mm lens

Using the best lens for great portraits

When using Portrait mode, use a lens that is 50mm or longer. The longer lens will give you a natural view of the subject as well as aid in keeping the depth of field narrow.

Landscape

As you might have guessed, Landscape mode has been optimized for shooting landscape images (**Figure 3.7**). Particular emphasis is placed on the picture control, with the camera trying to boost the greens and blues in the image (**Figure 3.8**). This makes sense, since the typical landscape is outdoors, where grass, trees, and skies should look more colorful. This picture control also boosts the sharpness that is applied during processing. In addition, the camera uses the lowest ISO settings possible in order to keep digital noise to a minimum. The downfall to this mode is that, once again, there is little control over the camera settings. The focus mode can be changed—but only from AF-A to Manual. Other changeable functions include image quality, ISO, and AF-Area. Note that the flash cannot be used while in Landscape mode.

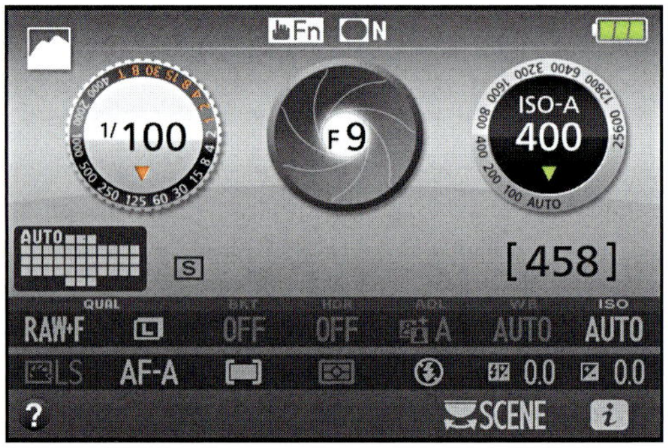

Figure 3.7 The Landscape mode info screen.

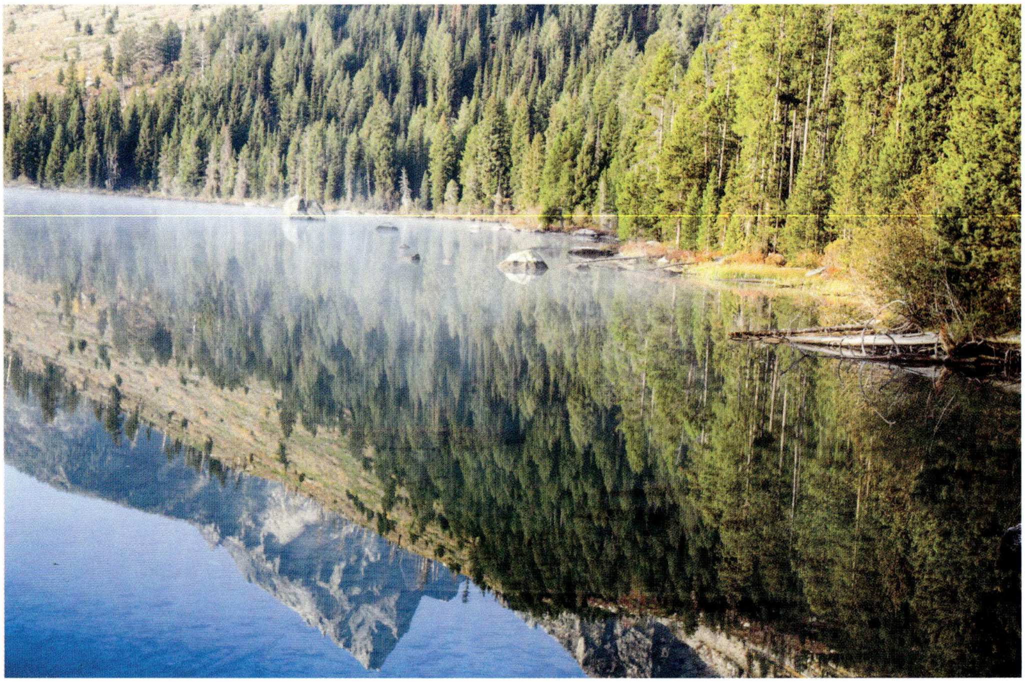

Figure 3.8 **Outdoor scenes with ample greens and blues are good candidates for Landscape mode.**

ISO 280 • 1/60 sec. • f/10 • 60mm lens

Child

The Child mode (**Figure 3.9**) is like a blend of the Sports and Portrait modes. Understanding that children are seldom still, the camera will try to use a slightly faster shutter speed to freeze any movement. The picture control feature has been optimized to render bright, vivid colors that one normally associates with pictures of children (**Figure 3.10**).

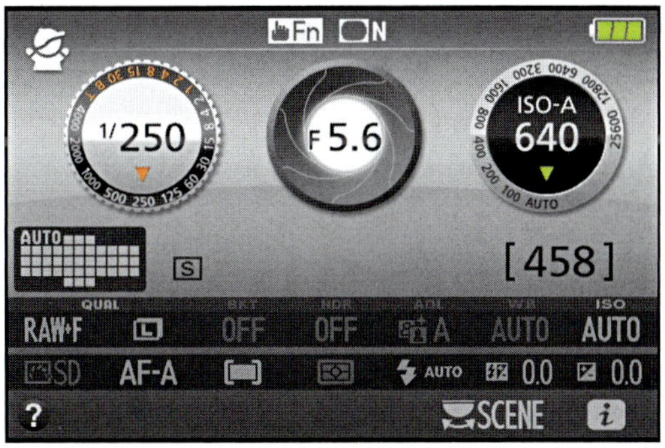

Figure 3.9 The Child mode info screen.

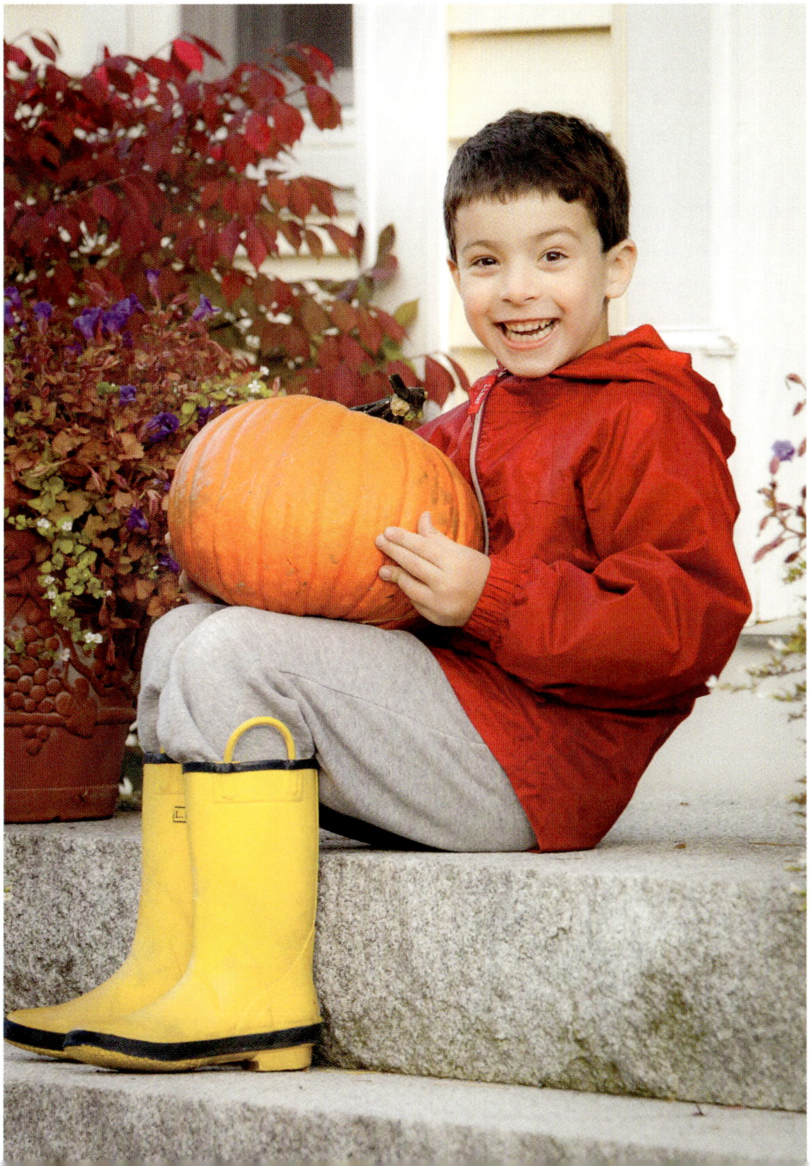

Figure 3.10
The Child mode tries to use a fast shutter speed as well as make colors more bright and vivid.

ISO 400 • 1/160 sec. • f/5.3 • 200mm lens

Sports

While this is called Sports mode, you can use it for any moving subject that you are photographing (**Figure 3.11**). The mode is built on the principles of sports photography: continuous focusing, large apertures, and fast shutter speeds (**Figure 3.12**). To handle these requirements, the camera sets the focus mode to Dynamic, the aperture to a very large opening, and the ISO to Auto. Overall, these are sound settings that will capture most moving subjects well. We will take an in-depth look at all of these features, like Continuous shooting mode, in Chapter 5.

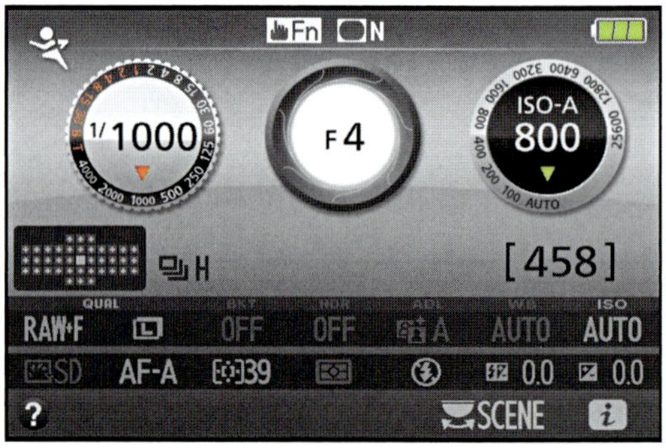

Figure 3.11 The Sports mode info screen.

You can, however, run the risk of too much digital noise in your picture if the camera decides that you need a very high ISO because the available light is low. This is why you have the ability to change some options within the Sports mode, such as ISO and the release mode (Single or Continuous). Also, when using Sports mode, you can change the focus mode from AF-A to Manual. This is especially handy if you know when and where the action will take place and want to prefocus the camera on a spot and wait for the right moment to take the photo.

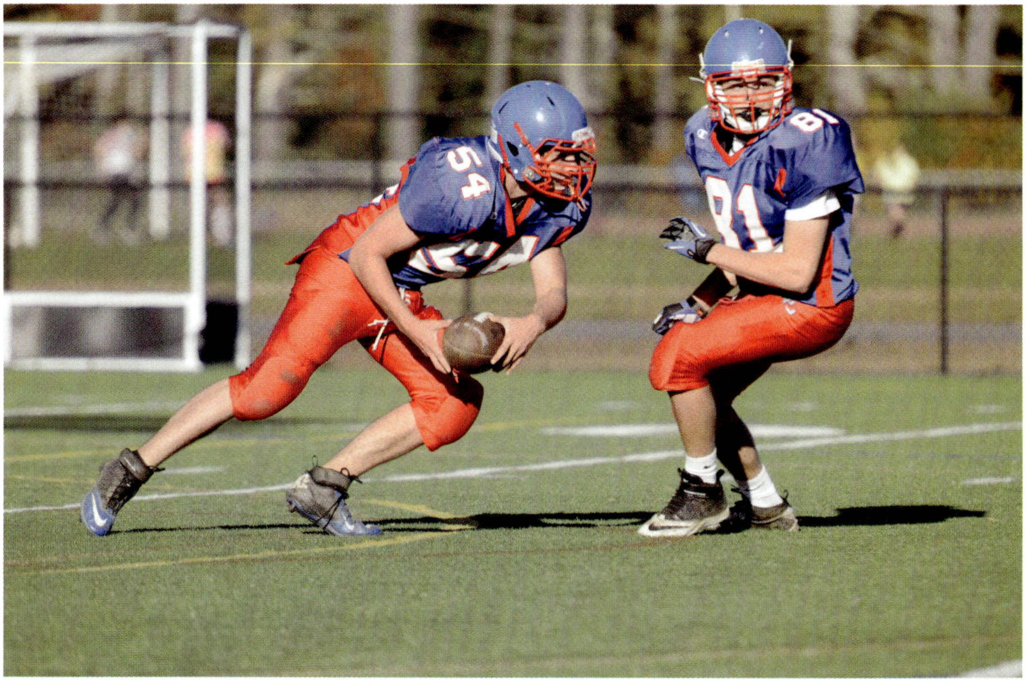

Figure 3.12
This is the type of shot that was made for Sports mode, where action-freezing shutter speeds and continuous focusing capture the moment.

ISO 320 • 1/1000 sec. • f/5.6 • 400mm lens

Close-up

Although most zoom lenses don't support true "macro" settings, that doesn't mean you can't shoot some great close-up photos. The key here is to use your camera-to-subject distance to fill the frame and still achieve sharp focus. This means you move yourself as close as possible to your subject while still being able to get a good, sharp focus.

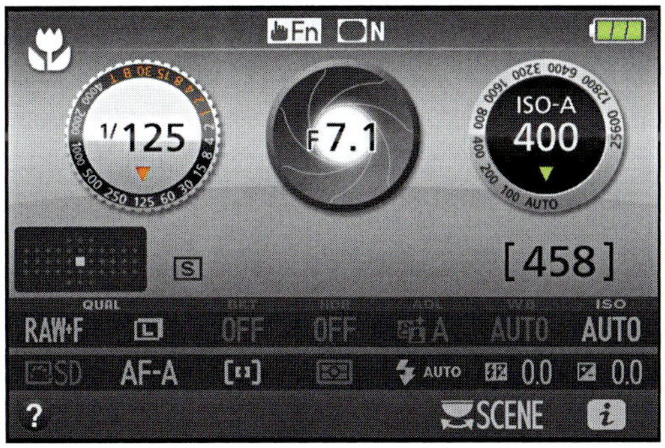

Figure 3.13 The Close-up mode info screen.

Oftentimes, your lens will be marked with the minimum focusing distance. On my 18–140mm zoom, it is about 1-and-1/2 feet with the lens set to 140mm. To help get the best focus in the picture, Close-up mode (**Figure 3.13**) will use the smallest aperture it can while keeping the shutter speed fast enough to get a sharp shot (**Figure 3.14**). It does this by raising the ISO or turning on the built-in flash—or a combination of the two. Fortunately, these are two of the settings that you can change in this mode. The flash will be set to Auto by default, but you can also change it to Auto Red-Eye or Off, depending on your needs. The ISO can be changed from the Auto setting to one of your own choosing. This probably only needs to be done in low-light settings when the Auto ISO starts to move up to maintain exposure values. Other settings that can be changed are the image quality, release mode, focus mode (AF-A or Manual), and AF-Area.

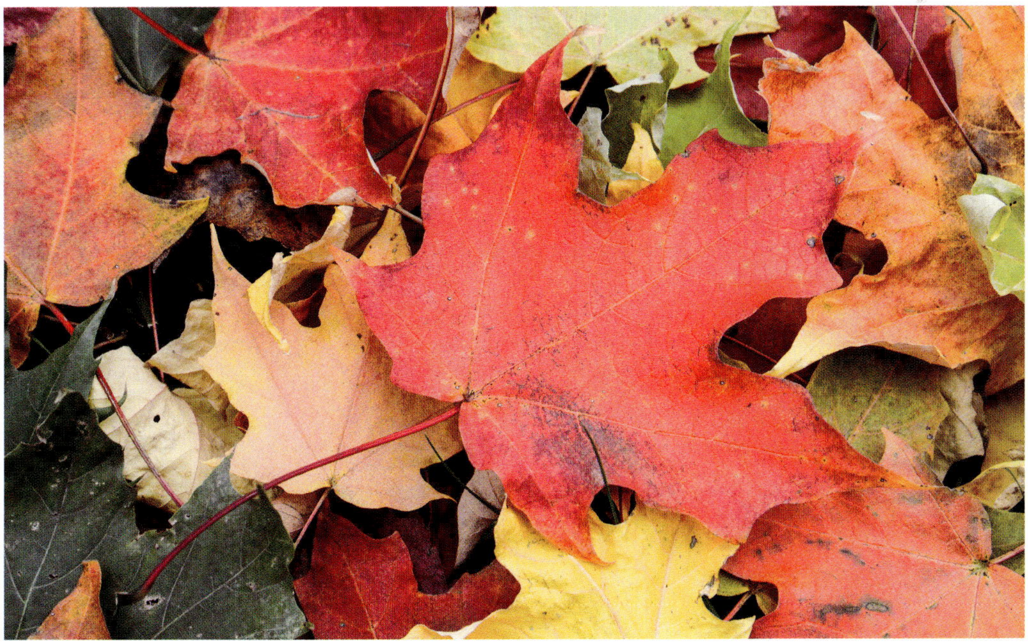

Figure 3.14 Close-up mode provided the proper exposure to capture the smallest of details.

ISO 100 • 1/60 sec. • f/8 • 50mm lens

Food

Food photography is very popular, and Nikon has provided you with a scene mode that is perfect for this type of photography (**Figure 3.15**). When you select this mode, the camera will use large apertures for fairly narrow depth of field, slightly overexposed settings to keep things bright, and a picture control that makes colors more vivid.

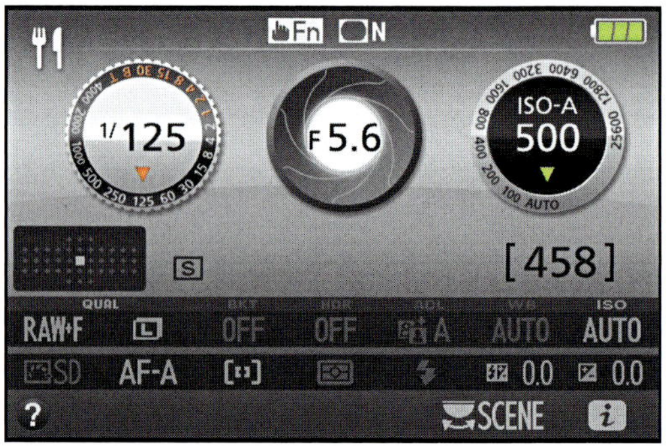

Figure 3.15 **The Food scene mode.**

Night Portrait

You're out on the town at night and you want to take a nice picture of someone, but you want to show some of the interesting scenery in the background as well. The solution is to use Night Portrait mode (**Figure 3.16**). When you set the dial to this mode, you are telling the camera that you want to use a slower-than-normal shutter speed so the background is getting more time (and, thus, more light) to achieve a proper exposure.

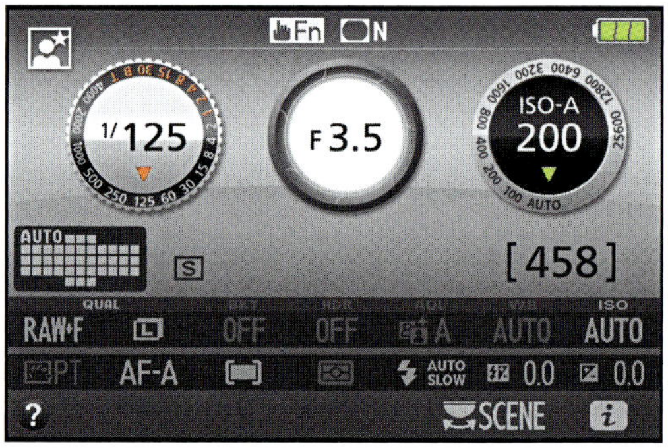

Figure 3.16 **The Night Portrait scene mode.**

The typical shutter speed for using flash is about 1/60 of a second or faster (but not faster than 1/200 of a second). By leaving the shutter open for a longer duration, the camera allows more of the background to be exposed so you get a much more balanced scene. Night Portrait is also a great mode for taking portraits during sunset. The camera uses an automatic ISO setting by default. You will want to keep an eye on it to make sure the setting isn't so high that the noise levels ruin your photo.

Night Landscape

A tripod or stable shooting surface is definitely recommended for the Night Landscape mode (**Figure 3.17**). By using low ISOs, longer shutter speeds, and noise reduction, you can capture great cityscapes with more accurate colors. The flash and focus-assist functions are turned off for this mode, so focusing might be a little difficult. If so, try moving your focus point to a different location or switch to manual focus.

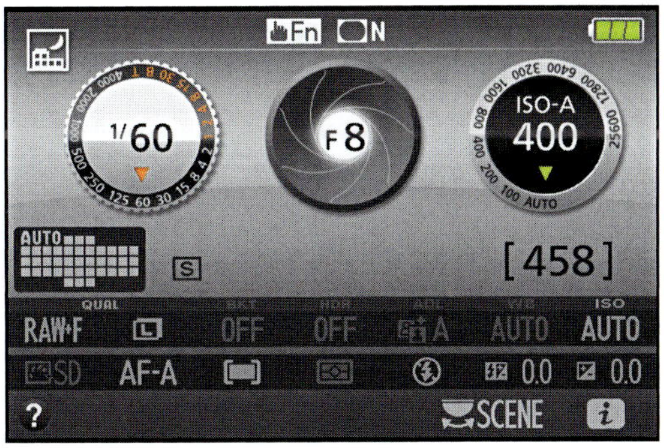

Figure 3.17 The Night Landscape scene mode.

Party/Indoor

This mode is very much like the Night Portrait mode except it is optimized for indoor use (**Figure 3.18**). The flash is automatically set to Auto+Red-Eye Reduction and will use the red-eye reduction lamp to help eliminate the red-eye problem that often occurs when using the flash indoors.

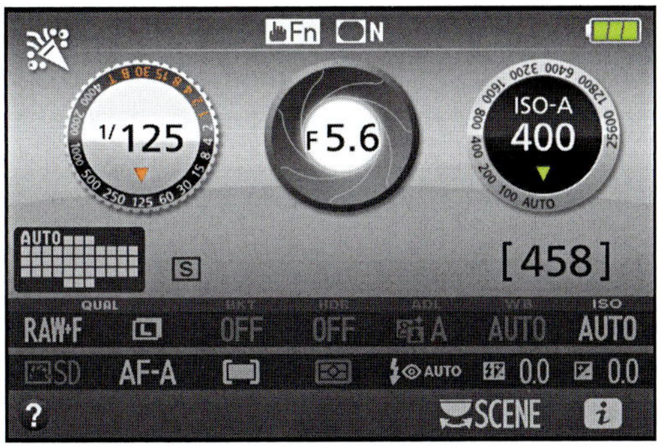

Figure 3.18 The Party/Indoor scene mode.

Beach/Snow

Shooting in a bright environment like the beach or a ski resort can have a bad effect on your images. The problem is that beaches and snow often reflect a lot of light and can fool the camera's light meter into underexposing. This means that the snow would come out looking darker than it should. To solve this problem, you can use the Beach/Snow scene mode (**Figure 3.19**), which will overexpose slightly, giving you much more accurate tones.

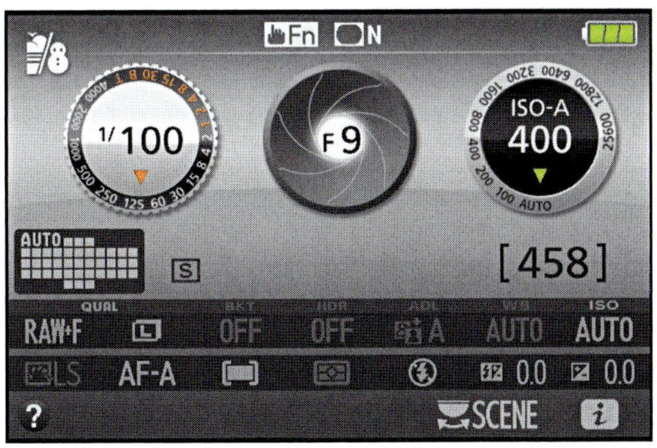

Figure 3.19 The Beach/Snow scene mode.

Sunset

This mode is set to optimize the colors that are present in a sunset (**Figure 3.20**). It will use slightly longer exposures, so a tripod or steady shooting surface is advised. You also won't be able to use the flash in this mode, since it would interfere with the settings necessary for capturing the sunset.

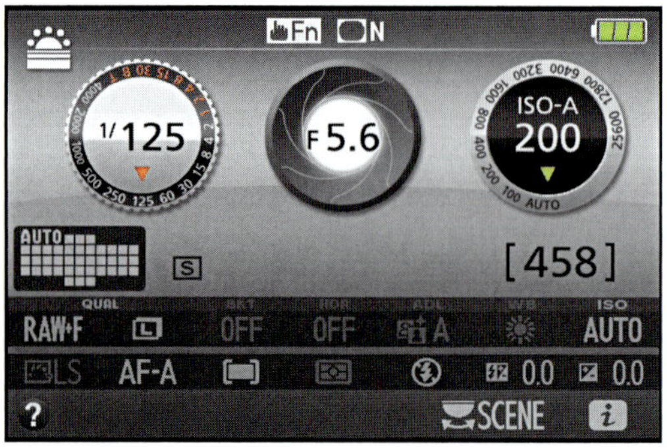

Figure 3.20 The Sunset scene mode.

Dusk/Dawn

Some great photo opportunities arise both before the sun rises and after it sets. The only problem is that typical camera settings don't truly capture the vibrancy of the colors. The Dusk/Dawn camera setting is optimized for low-light photography and helps boost colors and eliminate noise from longer exposures (**Figure 3.21**).

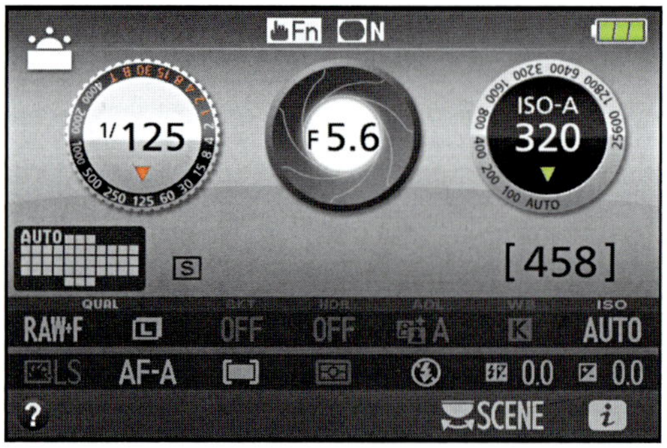

Figure 3.21 The Dusk/Dawn scene mode.

Pet Portrait

This mode is similar to the Portrait mode in that it uses larger apertures and faster shutter speeds (**Figure 3.22**). The difference is that the Portrait mode is optimized for human skin, with adjustments to the hues and color values. Pets normally don't have any skin showing, so the sharpness and hues are adjusted accordingly.

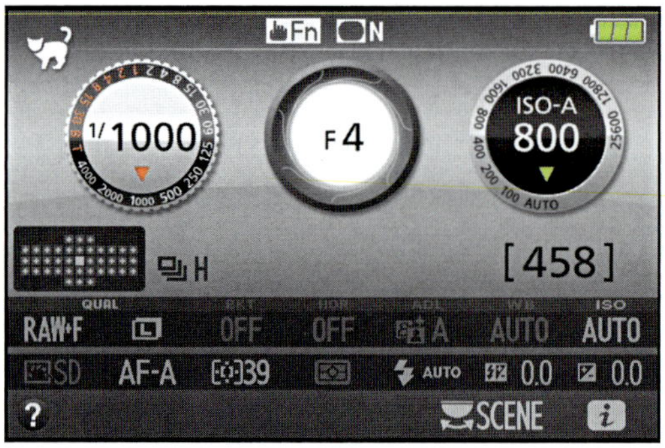

Figure 3.22 The Pet Portrait scene mode.

Candlelight

Sometimes it's pretty easy to know when to use a particular mode. The Candlelight mode is similar to the Auto (Flash Off) mode, but it is tweaked to work with the color of candlelight and will give you pleasing results (**Figure 3.23**). If you are photographing people in candlelight, try using a tripod and have them hold fairly still to reduce image blur.

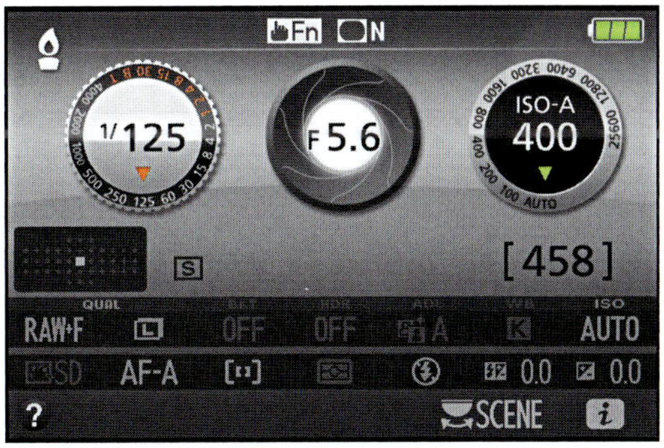

Figure 3.23 The Candlelight scene mode.

Blossom

This mode is very similar to the Landscape setting but with a few slight adjustments. The color settings for Blossom have been optimized for use outdoors where there are many flowers in full bloom (**Figure 3.24**).

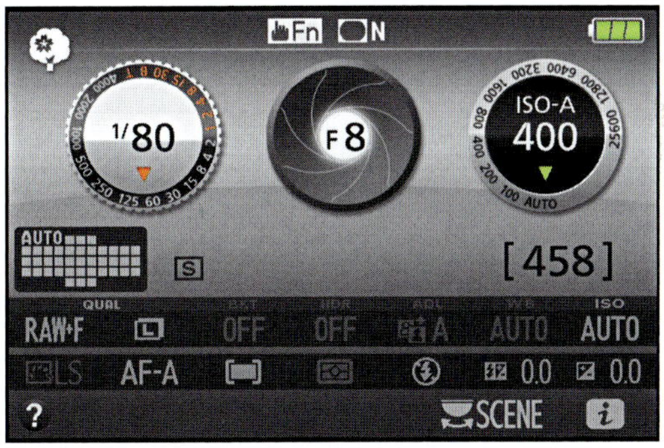

Figure 3.24 The Blossom scene mode.

Autumn Colors

If you live in an area that has great fall color, as I do, you will want to give this mode a try (**Figure 3.25**). The big advantage to this scene mode is that it is optimized for the red and yellow hues that are present in autumn, and it really makes them pop. It also turns off the flash, since the light from a flash can wash out the color in the leaves. Try using this mode when the leaves have turned and the skies are overcast. You will get some amazing color in your images.

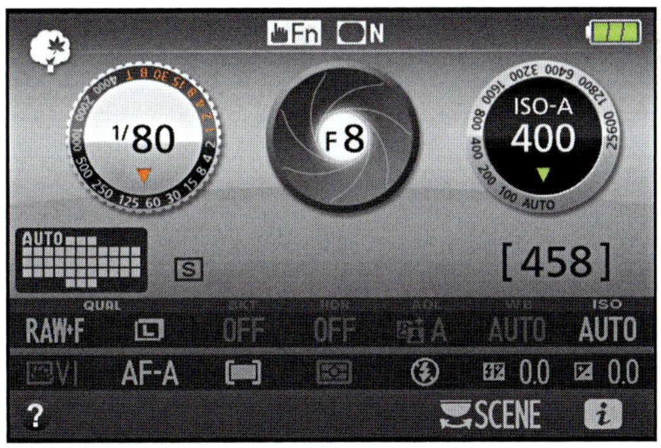

Figure 3.25 The Autumn Colors scene mode.

Effects Modes

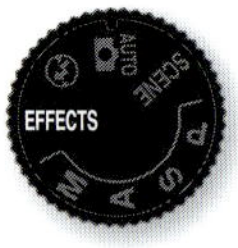

Beyond the scene-specific settings, the D5500 includes a collection of in-camera special effects that are fun to use. Remember, a digital camera is not only a light-capturing device but also a small computer. After an image is captured and saved to memory, these special effects modes give you the power to process your photos before they ever leave the camera. In fact, most of these effects can even be applied to video. Note that because the Night Vision, Miniature Effect, Toy Camera, Pop, Super Vivid, Photo Illustration, and Selective Color effects require additional in-camera processing, it is not possible to shoot in RAW mode with them. In addition, due to the extra work the camera has to do to process these effects, be prepared to wait between exposures, and expect the charge on the battery to be consumed faster.

I was a bit skeptical about these effects when I first heard about them. After all, one of the most important selling features of the D5500 is its stunning image quality, so it felt a bit risky to capture a good photo in, say, Photo Illustration mode but not have any way to work with the unprocessed original photo. But after giving each effect a thorough test drive, I found some of them quite enjoyable to use. And once I started getting used to the effects, I began to look for specific instances that might be suited to a given effect.

Using the effects modes

1. Set the Mode dial to the Effects setting.
2. Rotate the Command dial until the desired effect appears on the information screen.

Silhouette

The Silhouette mode (**Figure 3.26**) does things like adjust the exposure for the brightest area of the scene as well as turn off the Active D-Lighting feature (see Chapter 9 for more on Active D-Lighting). This is necessary, since Active D-Lighting tries to boost exposure in shadow areas, which is the opposite of the effect you want when trying to get a nice silhouette. Look for situations with strong backlighting behind your subject.

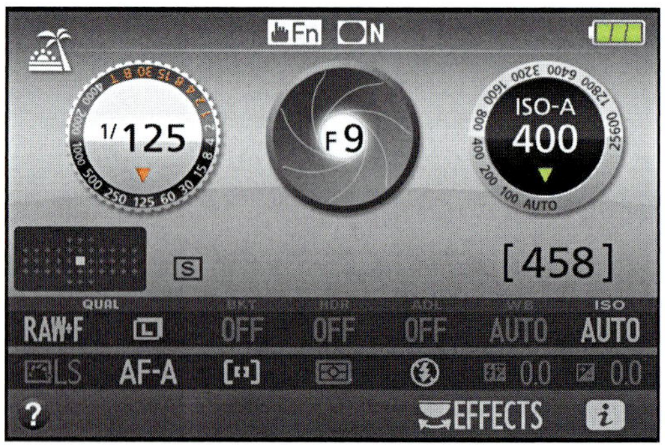

Figure 3.26 The Silhouette effects mode.

High Key

High-key photos are meant to have an overall bright, almost overexposed, look (**Figure 3.27**). Using the High Key setting forces the camera to overexpose a little and really lighten up those bright objects in your image. Subjects on bright backgrounds work well with this effect. Note that the internal flash turns off in this mode to make full use of available light.

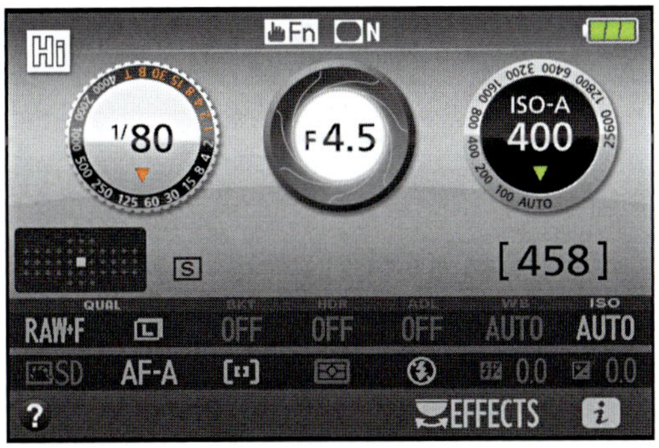

Figure 3.27 The High Key effects mode.

Low Key

Low-key photos are meant to have an overall dark look. Much like the beach/snow scenario in reverse, your camera's light meter will usually try to add some exposure when shooting a low-key scene to make everything brighter. If you want to keep things on the dark side, use the Low Key mode (**Figure 3.28**), which will keep the flash turned off and underexpose things just a little bit. Edgy and moody scenes lend themselves to this effect. Since the internal flash turns off and the scene may be dark, you'll want to have a solid base (or even a tripod) to avoid blur in your shots.

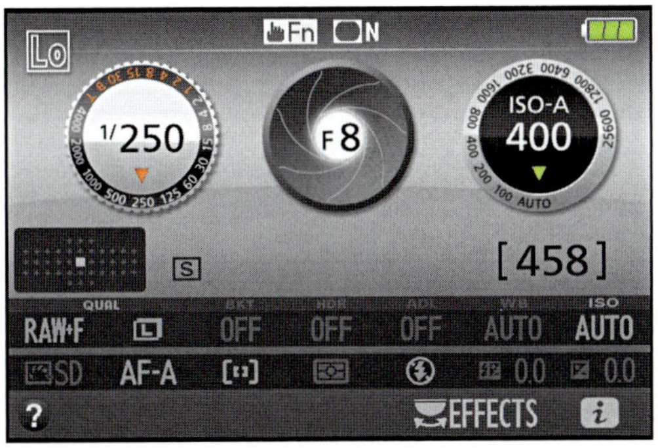

Figure 3.28 The Low Key effects mode.

Night Vision

For situations when it is so dark you're usually thinking it is time to put away the camera, the Night Vision effect (**Figure 3.29**) can be fun to experiment with. This was my favorite effect to use. The internal flash and AF-Assist Illuminator turn off, and autofocus is possible only when in Live View (it is on the slow side). You'll need a little light to see what you are doing. The camera will automatically adjust the ISO to the equivalent of 102400 ISO if needed, but the resulting JPEG images will be very noisy and only in grayscale. Think bad security-camera footage. Since you're most likely to use this in extremely low-light situations, I recommend a tripod or some other firm base.

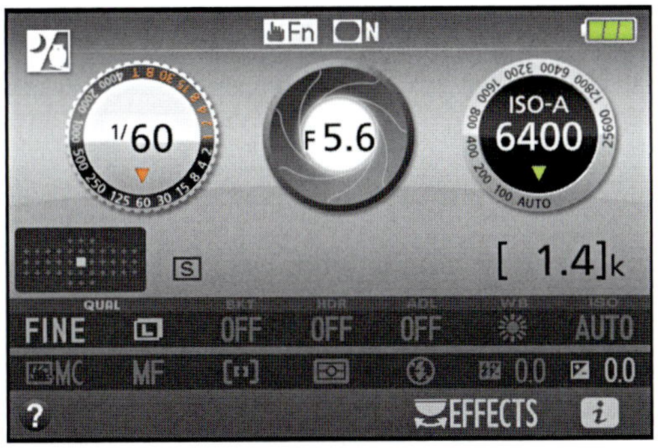

Figure 3.29 The Night Vision effects mode.

Super Vivid

Super Vivid (**Figure 3.30**) really pumps up the saturation of all colors and increases overall contrast for a truly vibrant result. Turn on Live View to see a real-time updated preview of the effect in action.

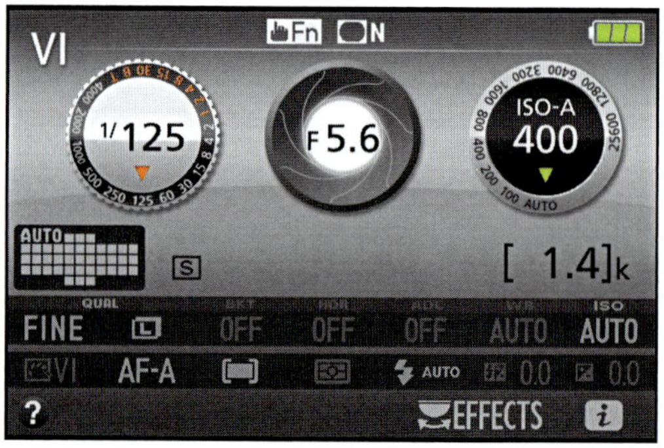

Figure 3.30 The Super Vivid effects mode.

Pop

Pop (**Figure 3.31**) is similar to Super Vivid except without the boost in contrast. This effect is for when you just want to boost the saturation of the colors in the image.

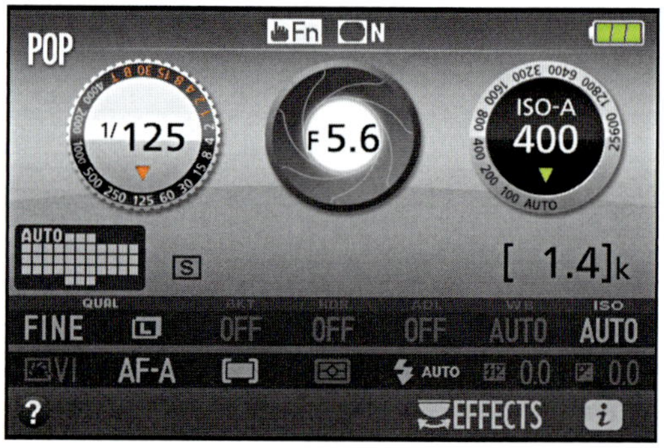

Figure 3.31 The Pop effects mode.

Photo Illustration

Photo Illustration (**Figure 3.32**) detects all the outlines in the scene and boosts the color to simulate an illustration-like effect. Bright and colorful scenes with recognizable shapes will benefit most from this effect. You can make light adjustments while in Live View.

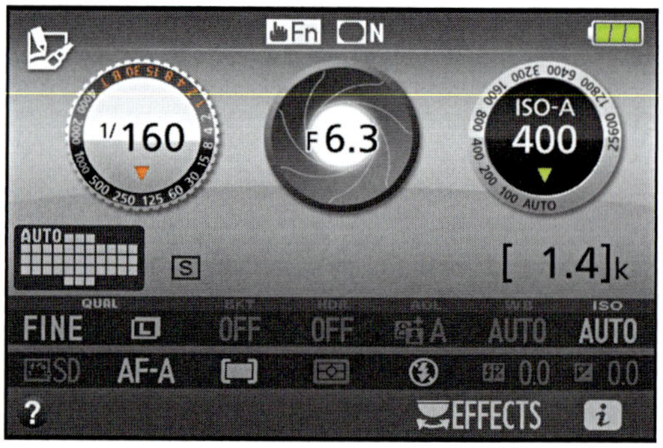

Figure 3.32 The Photo Illustration effects mode.

Toy Camera

I suspect this new effect was inspired by all the photo-filtering apps that are so popular for smartphones. The Toy Camera effect (**Figure 3.33**) adds a vignette (darkened edges) and tweaks the color of your photos to mimic the look of a cheap toy camera. I admit the purpose of this effect has me scratching my head a bit, but hey, I've certainly used those effects on my phone before. You can adjust the intensity of the effect in Live View.

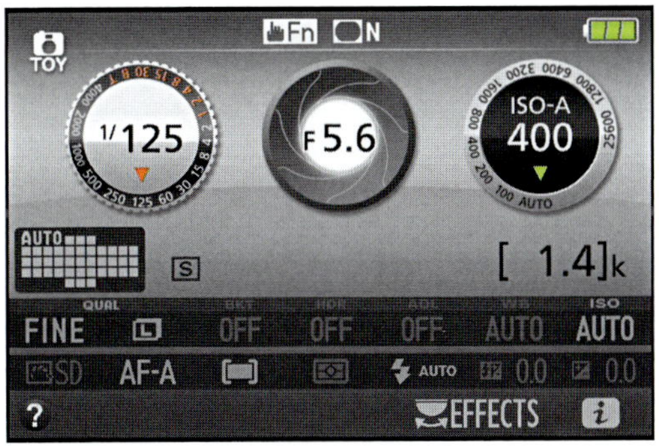

Figure 3.33 The Toy Camera mode.

Miniature Effect

A very popular effect seen in photography lately is achieved by using a tilt-shift lens to produce a narrow area of focus, which in certain scenes (typically photographed from a high vantage point) can make the subjects appear miniaturized. Something about the effect is indeed very eye-catching. The D5500 simulates this with the Miniature Effect mode (**Figure 3.34**) without a special lens by allowing only a narrow band of the image (which you can widen slightly while in Live View) to be in focus and then gradually blurring the rest of the scene.

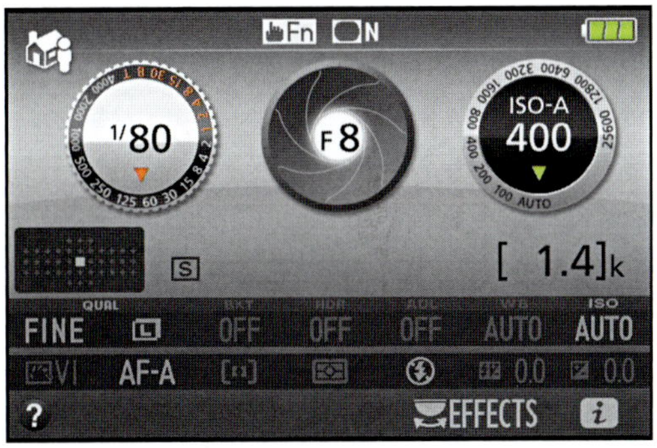

Figure 3.34 The Miniature Effect mode.

Selective Color

The Selective Color effect (**Figure 3.35**) can make a vibrantly colored object really stand out of the scene by desaturating all the colors in the scene except for the color or colors (up to three) you choose to keep. Color selection and a live preview are available when in Live View. It can be a little tricky selecting a color at first (use the image zoom button to zoom in on your color for easier selection), but it won't take long to get the hang of it. I'm a fan of doing this type of effect via software on my computer (to ensure I have a full-color original), but in a pinch or for use in a video, the effect works pretty well.

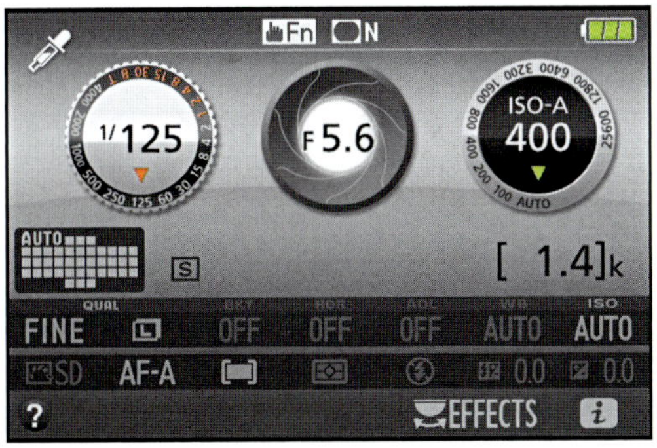

Figure 3.35 The Selective Color effects mode.

Manual Callout

You can learn more about the specific controls for each of these effects starting on page 61 of the Reference Manual PDF.

Why You May Never Want to Use the Auto Scene Modes Again

With so many easy-to-use camera modes, why would anyone ever want to use anything else? Well, the first thing that comes to my mind is control. It is the number-one reason for using a dSLR. The ability to control every aspect of your photography will open up creative avenues that just aren't available with the automatic scene modes. Let's face it: There is a reason that the Mode dial is split into two different categories. Let's look at what we are giving up when we work in the scene modes.

- **White balance.** There is no choice available for white balance. You are simply stuck with the Auto setting. This isn't always a bad thing, but your camera sometimes doesn't get it right. And in the scene modes, there is no way to change it.
- **Picture control.** All of the automatic modes have specifically tuned picture controls. Some of them use the control presets, such as Landscape or Vivid, but you have no way to change the characteristics of the controls while in the Auto modes.
- **Metering.** All of the automatic scene modes use the Matrix metering mode to establish the proper exposure. This is generally not a bad thing, but in scenarios that would benefit from a Center or Spot metering solution (which we'll cover in later chapters), you're out of luck.
- **Autofocus.** While each of the modes may use a specific focus area mode, such as Single or Dynamic, the actual focus mode for all of the scene modes is limited to either AF-A or Manual when shooting using the viewfinder. The problem is that you can't just use AF-S (Single) or AF-C (Continuous) as the default setting (unless you switch to Live View; see the sidebar "Live View").

Autofocus modes on the Nikon D5500

Four autofocus modes are available on the D5500. You can easily select the mode that will be most beneficial for the type of photography you are doing. The standard mode is called AF-S; it allows you to focus on one spot and hold the focus until you take the picture or release the shutter button. The AF-C mode will constantly refocus the camera on your subject the entire time you are depressing the shutter release button. This is great for sports and action photography. The AF-A mode is a combination of both of the previous modes, using AF-S mode unless the camera senses that the subject is moving, when it will switch to AF-C mode. When in Live View, you will also have the fourth choice of AF-F, which is when the camera automatically attempts to keep a moving subject in focus without pressing the shutter, such as during video recording.

- **Active D-Lighting.** This is another feature that can't be altered in the Auto modes. There are default settings for this feature that change from scene to scene, but you have no way to override the effect.
- **Exposure bracketing.** One way to make sure you have at least one good exposure is to use the bracketing feature of the camera, which takes images at varying exposures so you can get just the right look for your image. Unfortunately, this feature is also unavailable when using the scene modes.

Another thing you will find when using any of the automatic modes is that you have fewer choices to adjust in the camera menus. Each scene mode presents its own set of restrictions for the available menu items. These aren't the only restrictions to using the automatic scene modes, but they should concern you enough to make you want to explore the other side of the Mode dial, which I like to call the professional modes.

Live View

Live View is the feature on your D5500 that allows you to see a real-time view of what the camera is looking at via the rear LCD. Using Live View can be helpful when you want to see or shoot from an angle that doesn't allow you to place your eye to the viewfinder. It is also an excellent way of previewing any changes to white balance or the picture control because their effects will be visible on the screen. There's more on Live View in Chapters 6 and 7, but I want to mention that Live View does allow the AF-S autofocus mode while in the Auto scene modes.

Chapter 3 Assignments

These assignments will have you shooting in the various automatic scene and effects modes so you can experience the advantages and disadvantages of using them in your daily photography.

Shooting in Auto mode

It's time to give up complete control and just concentrate on what you see in the viewfinder. Set your camera to Auto and practice shooting in a variety of conditions, both indoors and outdoors. Take notice of the camera settings when you are reviewing your pictures. Try using the single-point autofocus (AF-S) area mode to pick a spot to focus on, and then recompose before taking the picture.

Checking out Portrait mode

Grab your favorite photogenic person and start shooting in Portrait mode. Try switching between Auto and Portrait mode while photographing the same person in the same setting. You should see a difference in the sharpness of the background as well as the skin tones. If you are using a zoom lens, set it to about 55mm if available.

Capturing the scenery with Landscape and Close-up modes

Take your camera outside for some landscape and macro work. First, find a nice scene, and then, with your widest available lens, take some pictures using Landscape mode. Switch back to Auto so you can compare the settings used for each image as well as the changes to colors and sharpness. Now, while you are still outside, find something in the foreground—a leaf or a flower—and switch the camera to Close-up mode. See how close you can get, and take note of the f-stop that the mode uses. Then switch to Auto and shoot the same subject.

Stopping the action with Sports mode

This assignment will require a subject in motion. That could be the traffic in front of your home or your child at play. The only real requirement is that the subject be moving. There isn't a lot to worry about here. Just point and shoot. Try shooting a few frames one at a time, and then hold down the shutter button and shoot a burst of about five or six frames. It will help if your subject is in good available light to start with so the camera won't be forced to use high ISOs.

Having fun with the effects modes

Carve out some time to give each of the effects a good test run, and have fun with it. It is all too easy to get hung up on getting the perfect shot, but with the effects modes you have permission to play. See how the world looks with just a single color; try envisioning things in miniature; check out your pets in Photo Illustration mode. Just get creative and explore the results. You never know when one of these effects might come in handy down the road.

Share your results with the book's Flickr group!
Join the group here: flickr.com/groups/nikond5500_fromsnapshotstogreatshots

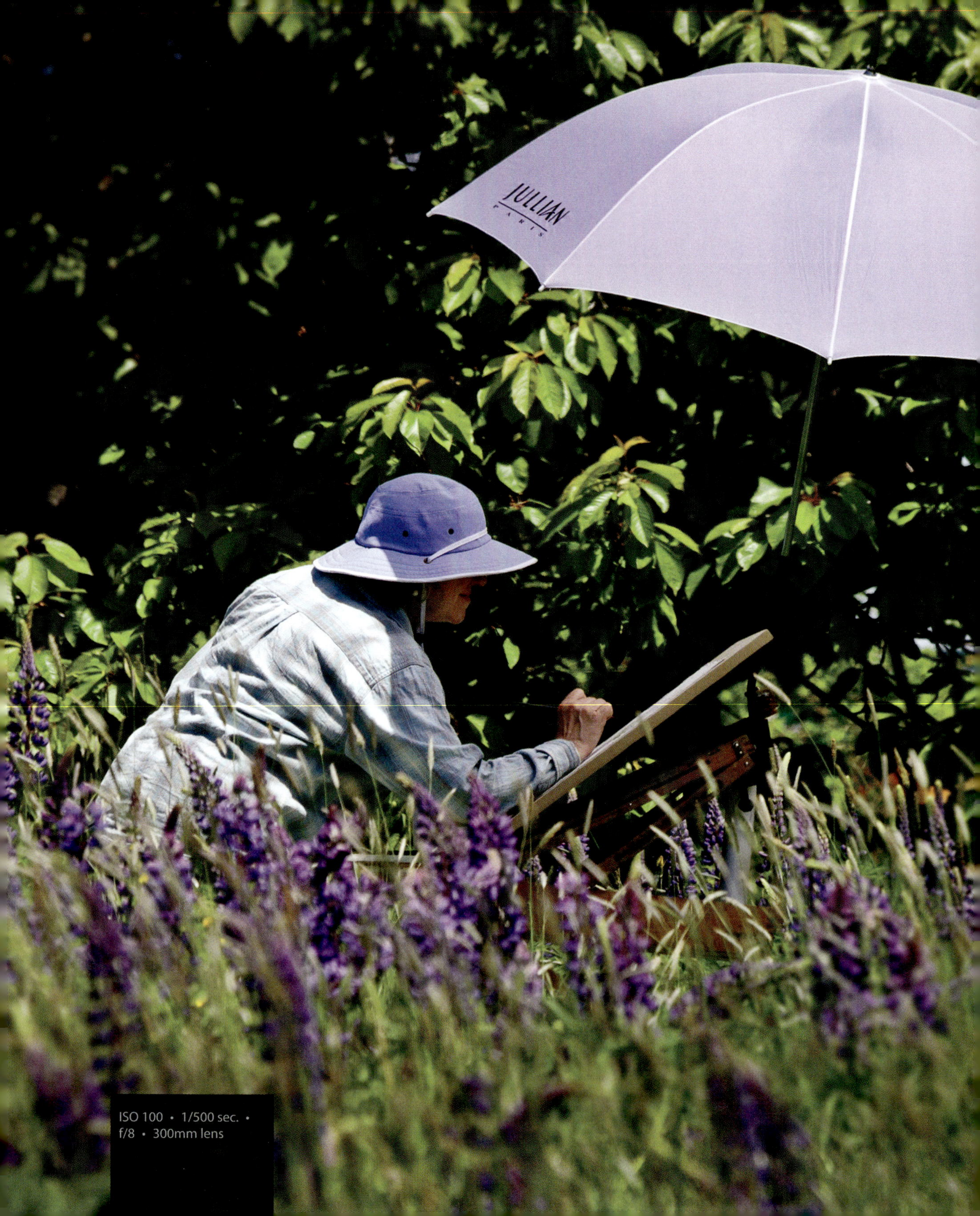

ISO 100 • 1/500 sec. • f/8 • 300mm lens

4

The Professional Modes

Taking Your Photography to the Next Level

If you talk to professional photographers, you will find that the majority of them use a few selective modes that offer the greatest amount of control. These modes are known as the backbone of photography. They allow you to influence two of the most important factors in taking great photographs: *aperture* and *shutter speed.*

To access these modes, you simply turn the Mode dial to one of the letter-designated modes and begin shooting. But wouldn't it be nice to know exactly what those modes control and how to make them do your bidding? If you want to take that next step in controlling your photography, it is essential that you understand not only how to control these modes but why you are controlling them. So let's move that Mode dial to the first of our professional modes: Program mode.

Poring Over the Picture

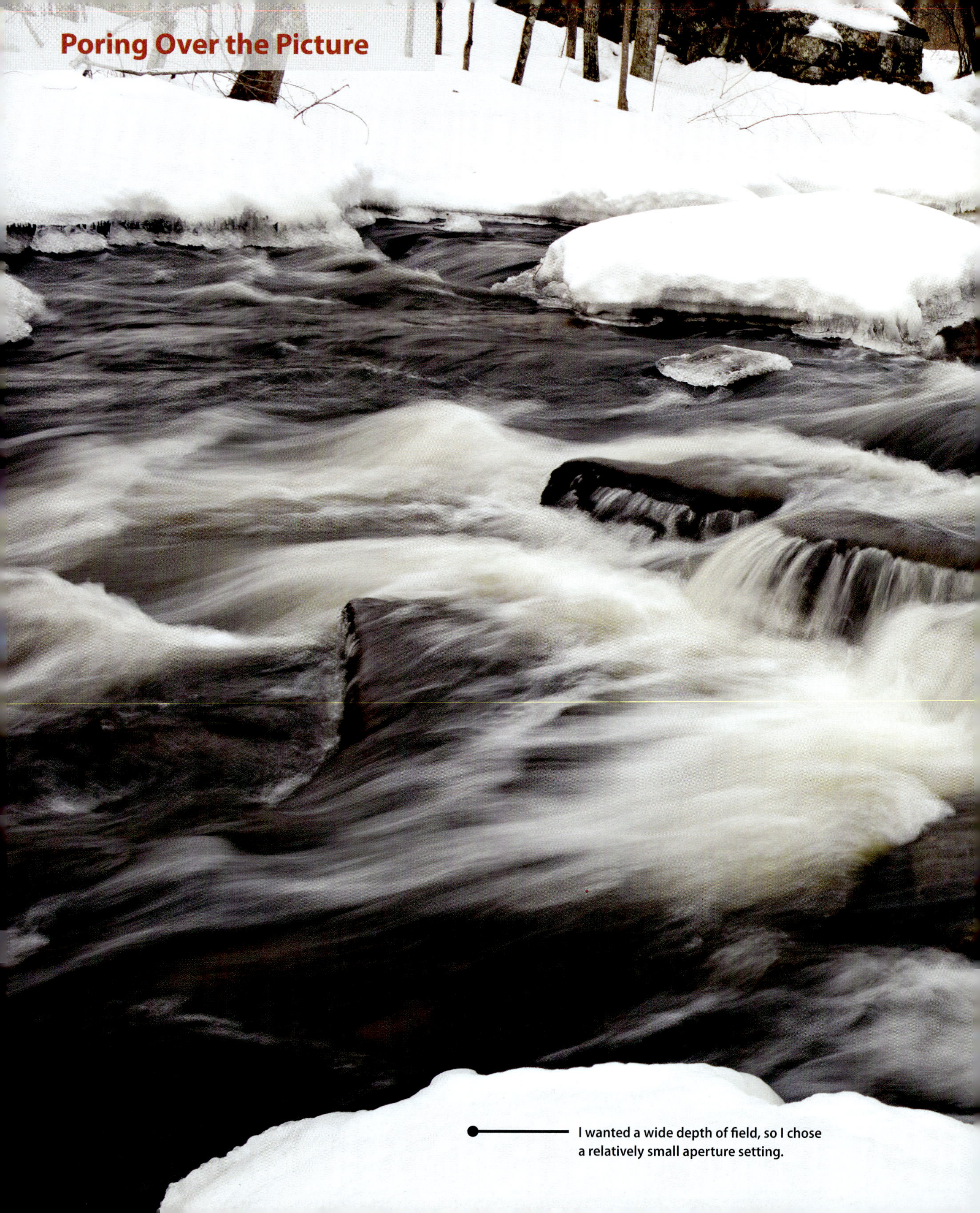

I wanted a wide depth of field, so I chose a relatively small aperture setting.

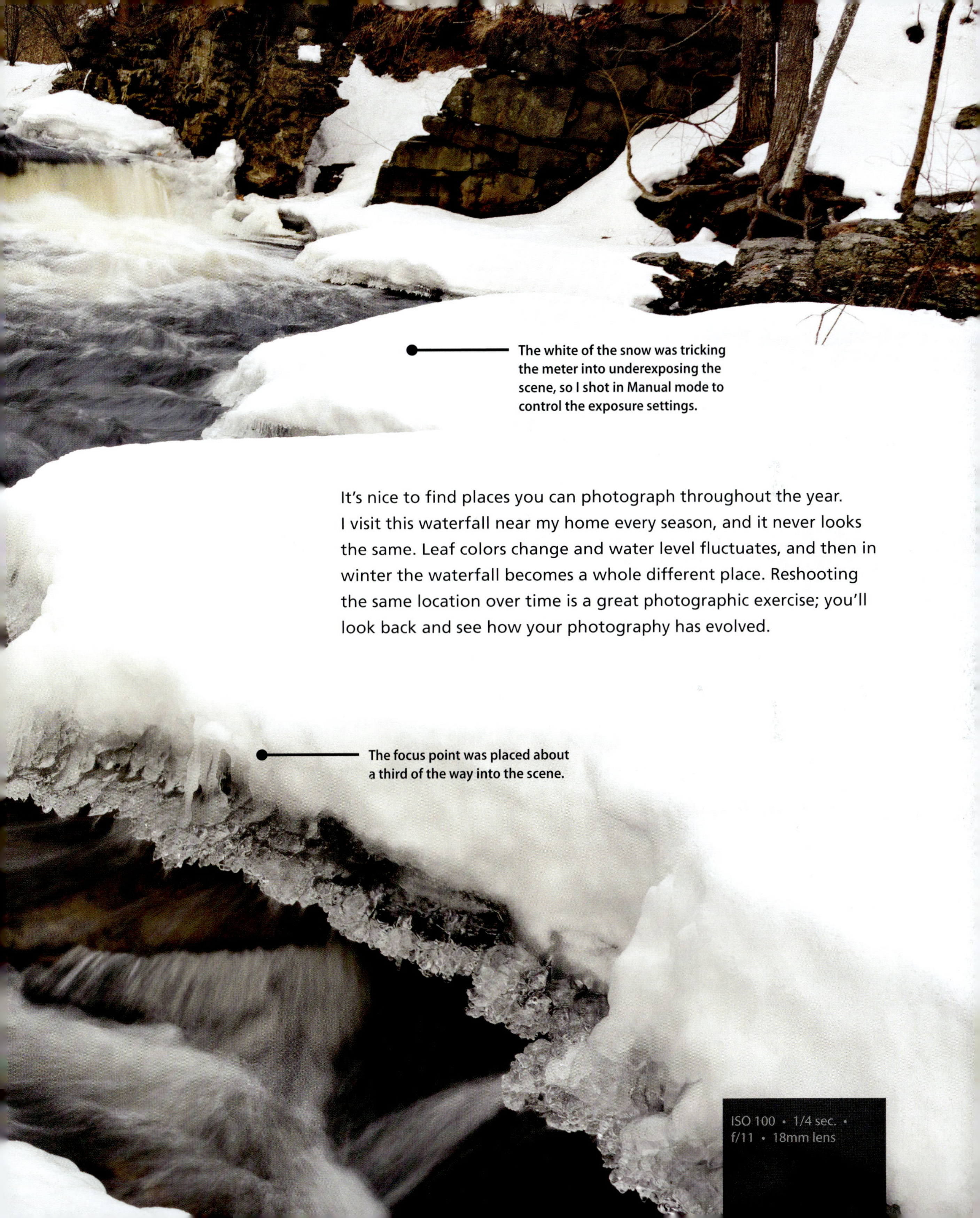

It's nice to find places you can photograph throughout the year. I visit this waterfall near my home every season, and it never looks the same. Leaf colors change and water level fluctuates, and then in winter the waterfall becomes a whole different place. Reshooting the same location over time is a great photographic exercise; you'll look back and see how your photography has evolved.

ISO 100 • 1/4 sec. • f/11 • 18mm lens

P: Program Mode

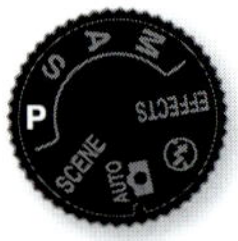

There is a reason Program mode is only one click away from the automatic modes: With respect to aperture and shutter speed, the camera is doing most of the thinking for you in this mode. So, if that is the case, why even bother with Program mode?

First, let me say that I rarely use Program mode because it just doesn't give as much control over the image-making process as the other professional modes. However, on occasion it comes in handy; for instance, when I am shooting in widely changing lighting conditions and don't have the time to think through all of my options, or when I'm not very concerned with having ultimate control of the scene. Think of a picnic outdoors in a partial shade/sun environment. I want great-looking pictures, but I'm not looking for anything to hang in a museum. If that's the scenario, why choose Program over one of the scene modes? Because it gives me choices and control that none of the scene modes can deliver.

Manual Callout

To see a comparison of all the different modes, check out the table on page 348 of the Reference Manual PDF.

When to use Program (P) mode instead of the automatic scene modes

- When shooting in a casual environment where quick adjustments are needed
- When you want more control over the ISO
- When you want to make corrections to the white balance
- When you want to change shutter speeds or the aperture to achieve a specific result

Let's go back to our picnic scenario. As I said, the light is moving from deep shadow to bright sunlight, which means the camera is trying to balance our three photo factors (ISO, aperture, and shutter speed) to make a good exposure. From Chapter 1, we know that Auto ISO is just not a consideration, so we have already turned that feature off (you did turn it off, didn't you?). Well, in Program mode, you can choose which ISO you would like the camera to base its exposure on. The lower the ISO number, the better the quality of photographs but the less light sensitive the camera becomes. It's a balancing act, with the main goal always being to keep the ISO as low as possible—too low an ISO and we will get camera shake in our images from a long shutter speed; too high an ISO and we will have an unacceptable amount of digital noise.

Starting points for ISO selection

We discuss ISO quite often in this and other chapters, but it might be helpful to know where your starting points should be for ISO settings. (Again, you should always try to use the lowest possible ISO setting.)

- 100: Bright, sunny day
- 200: Hazy or outdoor shade on a sunny day
- 400: Indoor lighting at night or cloudy conditions outside
- 800: Late-night, low-light conditions, or sporting arenas at night

These are just suggestions, and your ISO selection will depend on a number of factors that will be discussed later in the book. You might have to push your ISO even higher as needed, but at least now you know where to start.

For our purposes, let's select ISO 400 so we provide enough sensitivity for those shadows while allowing the camera to use shutter speeds fast enough to stop motion.

With the ISO selected, we can now make use of the other controls built into Program mode. By rotating the Command dial, we have the ability to shift the program settings. Remember, your camera is using the internal meter to pick what it believes are suitable exposure values, but sometimes it doesn't know what it's looking at and how you want those values applied (**Figures 4.1** and **4.2**). With the program shift, you can influence what the shot will look like. Do you need faster shutter speeds in order to stop the action? Just turn the Command dial to the right. Do you want a smaller aperture so you get a narrow depth of field? Then turn the dial to the left until you get the desired aperture. The camera shifts the shutter speed and aperture accordingly in order to get a proper exposure, and you will get the benefit of your choice as a result. Just keep in mind that the camera is always trying to maintain the right exposure at every setting, and so the available light and the maximum and minimum aperture values of the attached lens will limit the range of shutter speeds at a given ISO value.

You will also notice that a small star will appear above the letter P in the viewfinder and the rear display if you rotate the Command dial. This star is an indication that you modified the exposure from the one the camera chose. To go back to the default Program exposure, simply turn the dial until the star goes away, or switch to a different mode and then back to Program mode again.

Figure 4.1
This is my first shot using Program mode. I rotated the Command dial to the right to increase shutter speed and use a wider aperture for shallow depth of field.

ISO 100 • 1/1600 sec. • f/2 • 50mm lens

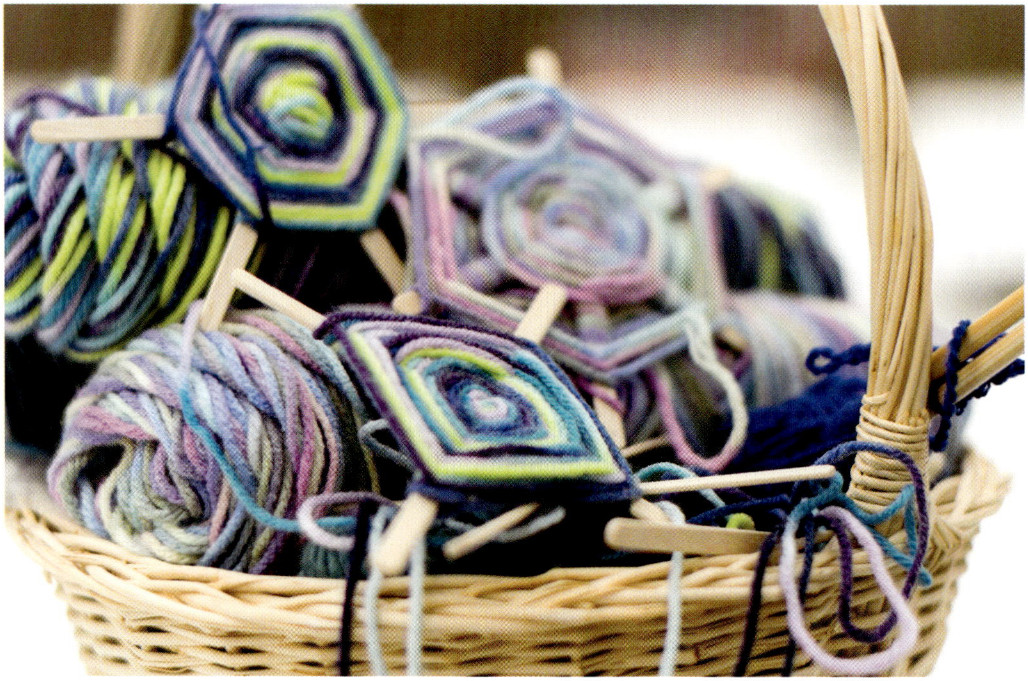

Figure 4.2
To increase the depth of field, I rotated the Command dial to the left to slow down shutter speed and decrease the size of the aperture.

ISO 100 • 1/80 sec. • f/9 • 50mm lens

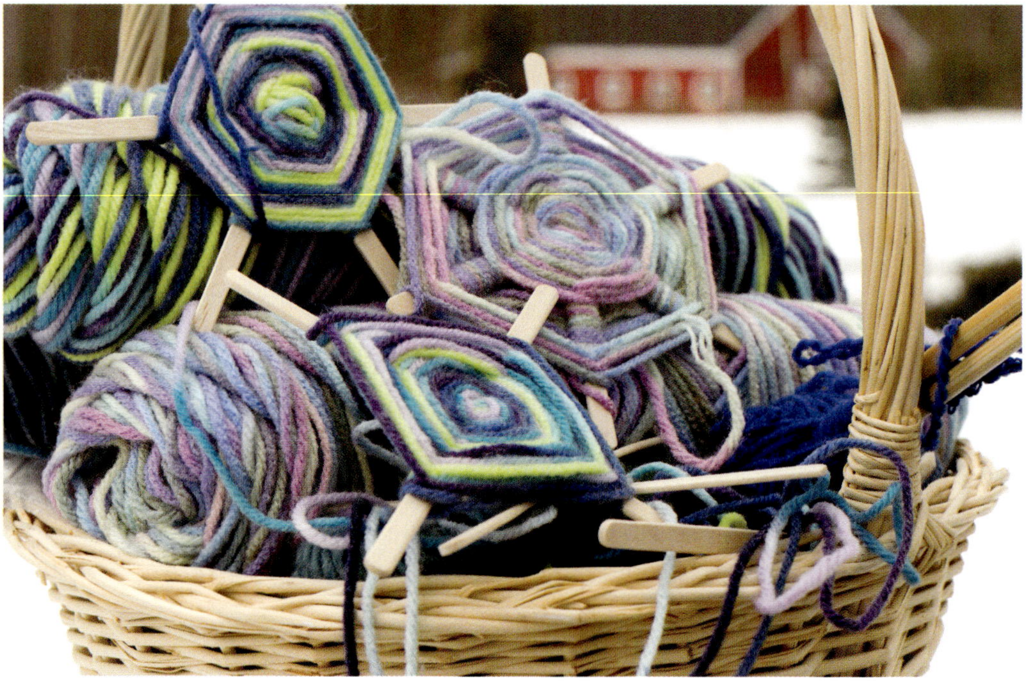

Let's set up the camera for Program mode and see how we can make all of this come together.

Setting up and shooting in Program mode

1. Turn on your camera, and then turn the Command dial to align the P with the indicator line.
2. Select your ISO by pressing the **i** button on the back of the camera.
3. Press up or down on the Multi-selector to highlight the ISO option, and then select OK.
4. Use the Multi-selector to select the desired ISO setting, and then press OK to lock in the change.
5. Point the camera at your subject, and then activate the camera meter by depressing the shutter button halfway.
6. View the exposure information in the bottom of the viewfinder or on the display panel on the back of the camera.
7. While the meter is activated, use your thumb to roll the Command dial left and right to see the changed exposure values.
8. Select the exposure that is right for you and start clicking. (Don't worry if you aren't sure what the right exposure is. We will start working on making the right choices for those great shots beginning with the next chapter.)

S: Shutter Priority Mode

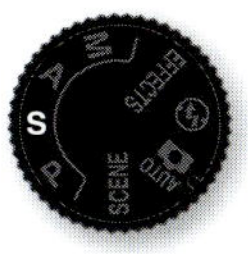

S mode is what we photographers commonly refer to as Shutter Priority mode. Just as the name implies, it is the mode that prioritizes or places major emphasis on the shutter speed above all other camera settings.

As with Program mode, Shutter Priority mode gives us more freedom to control certain aspects of our photography. The selected shutter speed determines how long you expose your camera's sensor to light. The longer it remains open, the more time your sensor has to gather light. The shutter speed also, to a large degree, determines how sharp your photographs are. This is different from the image being sharply in focus. Two of the major influences on the sharpness of an image are camera shake and the subject's movement. Because a slower shutter speed means that light from your subject is hitting the sensor for a longer period of time, any movement by you or your subject will show up in your photos as blur.

When to use Shutter Priority (S) mode

- When working with fast-moving subjects and you want to freeze the action (**Figure 4.3**); much more on this in Chapter 5
- When you want to emphasize movement in your subject with motion blur (**Figure 4.4**)
- When you want to use a long exposure to gather light over a long period of time (**Figure 4.5**); more on this in Chapter 8
- When you want to create silky-looking water in a waterfall (**Figure 4.6**)

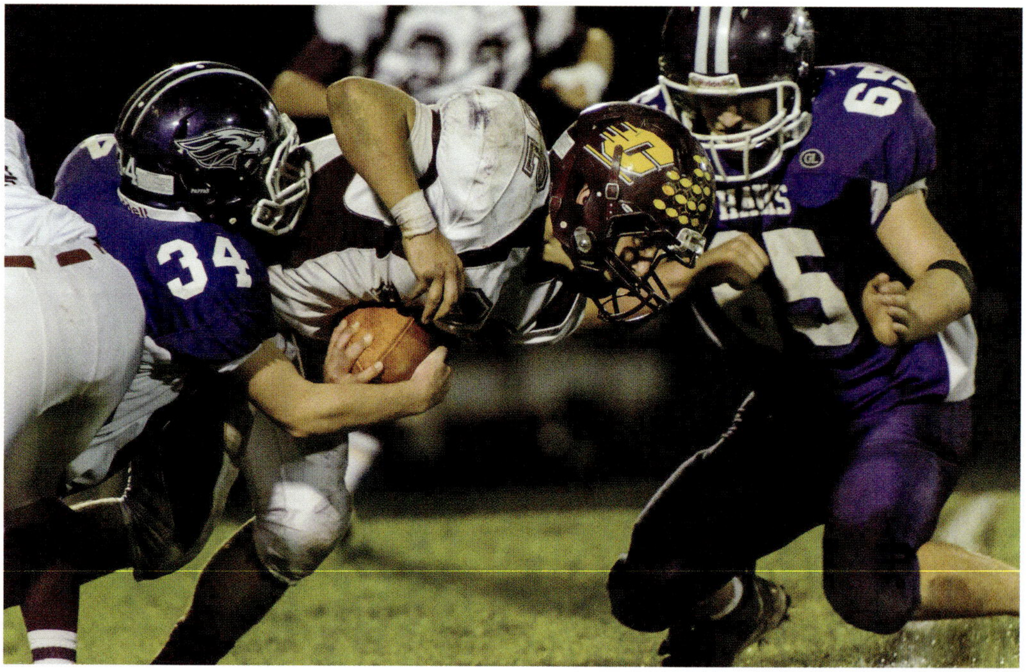

Figure 4.3 Even the fastest of subjects can be frozen with the right shutter speed.

ISO 25600 • 1/1000 sec. • f/5.6 • 400mm lens

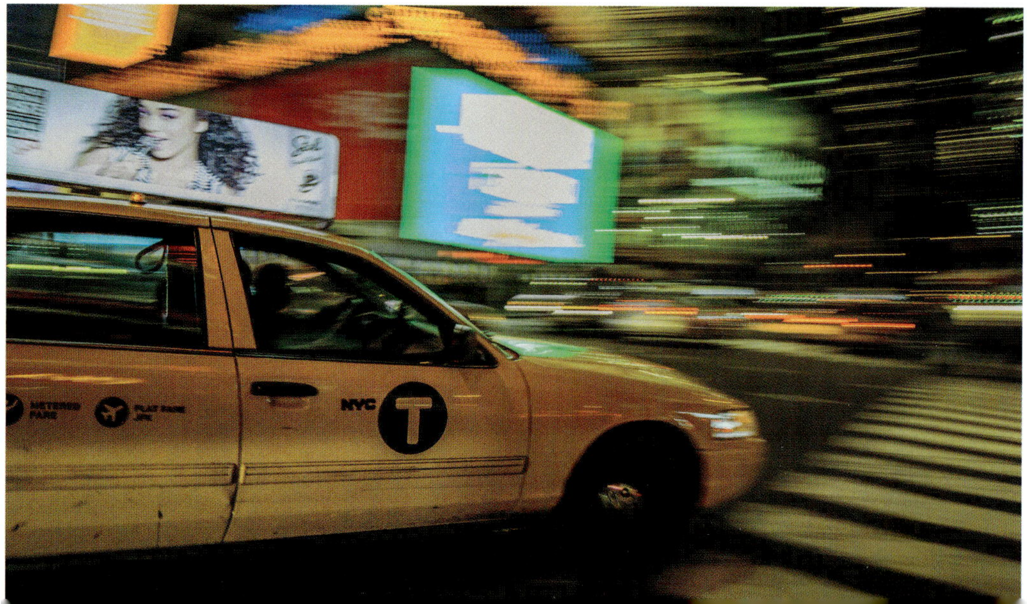

Figure 4.4 Slowing down the shutter speed and following the motion conveys a sense of movement in the shot.

ISO 800 • 1/10 sec. • f/8 • 24mm lens

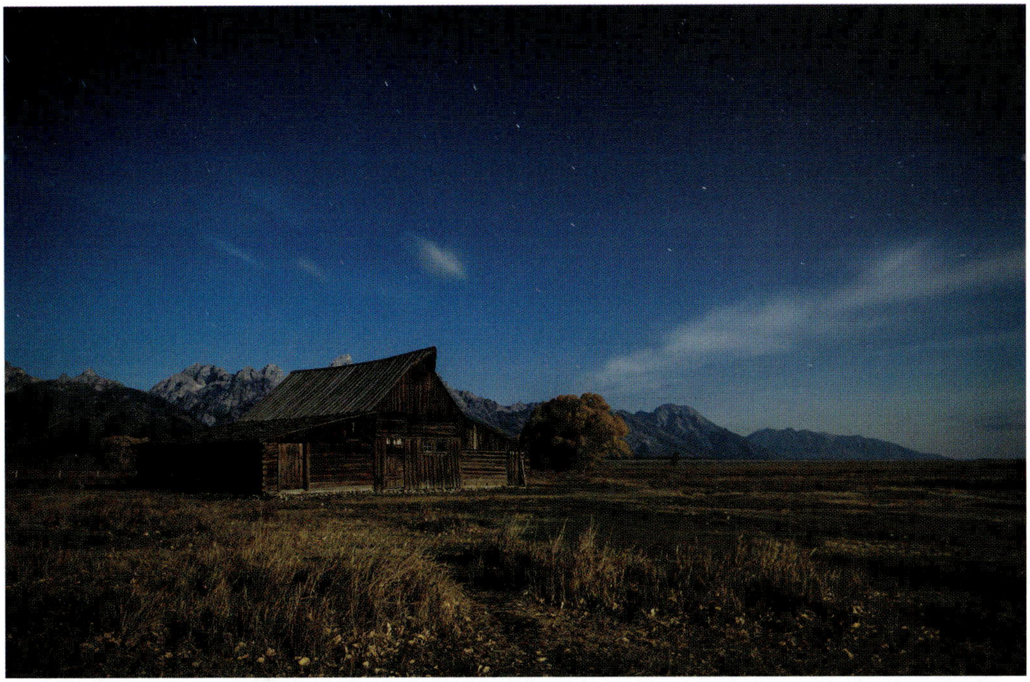

Figure 4.5

Long exposure coupled with a steady tripod can bring out the Big Dipper.

ISO 400 • 120 sec. • f/3.5 • 24mm lens

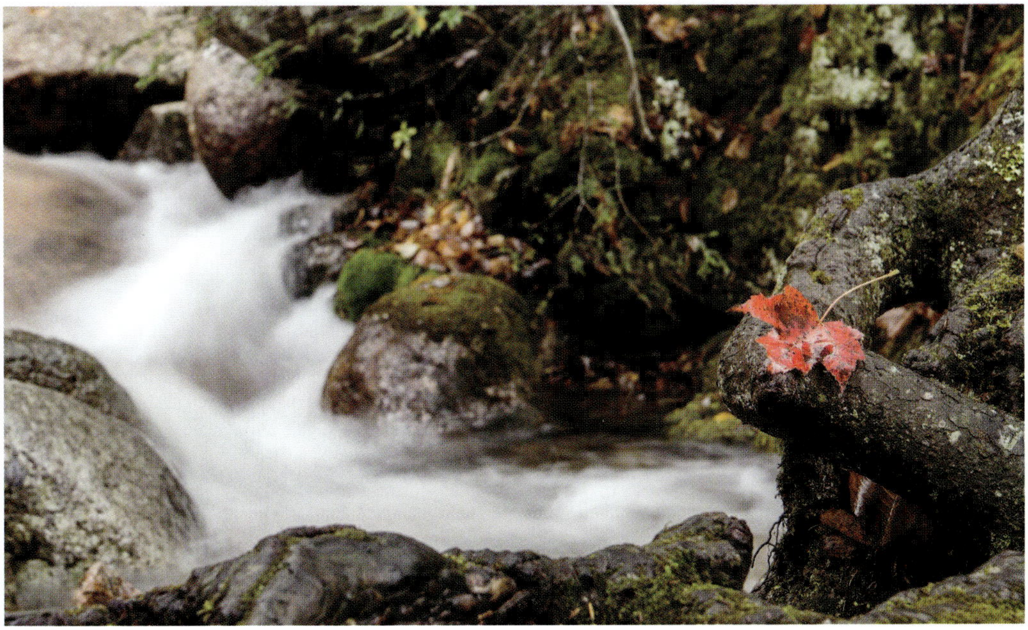

Figure 4.6

Increasing the length of the exposure time gives the flowing water a silky look.

ISO 100 • 1/2 sec. • f/13 • 70mm lens

As you can see, the subject of your photo usually determines whether or not you will use Shutter Priority mode. It is important that you be able to visualize the result of using a particular shutter speed. The great thing about shooting with digital cameras is you get instant feedback by viewing your shot on the LCD screen. But what if your subject won't give you a do-over? Such is often the case when shooting sporting events. You can't go ask the quarterback to throw that touchdown pass again because your last shot was blurry from a slow shutter speed. It's important to know what those speeds represent in terms of their capability to stop the action and deliver a blur-free shot.

Shutter speeds

A *slow* shutter speed refers to leaving the shutter open for a long period of time—like 1/30 of a second or longer. A *fast* shutter speed means that the shutter is open for a very short period of time—like 1/250 of a second or shorter.

First, let's examine just how much control you have over the shutter speed. The D5500 has a shutter speed range from 1/4000 of a second to 30 seconds. With that much latitude, you should have enough control to capture almost any subject. The other thing to think about is that Shutter Priority mode is considered a "semiautomatic" mode. This means you are taking control over one aspect of the total exposure while the camera handles the other. In this instance, you are controlling the shutter speed and the camera is controlling the aperture. This is important because there will be times when you want to use a particular shutter speed but your lens won't be able to accommodate your request.

For example, you might encounter this problem when shooting in low-light situations: If you are shooting a fast-moving subject that will blur at a shutter speed slower than 1/125 of a second, but your lens' largest aperture is f/3.5, you might find that your aperture display in the viewfinder and the rear LCD panel will blink. This is your warning that there won't be enough light available for the shot—due to the limitations of the lens—so your picture will be underexposed.

Another case where you might run into this issue is when you are shooting moving water. To get that look of silky, flowing water, you usually need to use a shutter speed of at least 1/15 of a second. If your waterfall is in full sunlight, you may see the aperture readout blink because the lens you are using only stops down to f/22 at its smallest opening. In this instance, your camera is warning that you will be overexposing your image. There are workarounds for these problems, which we will discuss in Chapter 7, but it is important to know that Shutter Priority mode has certain limitations.

Setting up and shooting in Shutter Priority mode

1. Turn on your camera, and then turn the Mode dial to align the S with the indicator line.
2. Select your ISO by pressing the **i** button on the back of the camera.
3. Press up or down on the Multi-selector to highlight the ISO option, and then press OK.
4. Use the Multi-selector to select the desired ISO setting, and then press OK to lock in the change.
5. Point the camera at your subject, and then activate the camera meter by depressing the shutter button halfway.
6. View the exposure information in the bottom area of the viewfinder or on the rear LCD panel.
7. While the meter is activated, use your thumb to roll the Command dial left and right to see the changed exposure values. Roll the dial to the right for faster shutter speeds and to the left for slower speeds.

A: Aperture Priority Mode

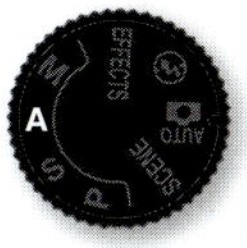

You wouldn't know it from its name, but Aperture Priority mode is one of the most useful and popular of all the professional modes. This mode is one of my personal favorites, and I believe it will quickly become one of yours as well. Aperture Priority mode is also deemed a semiautomatic mode because it allows you to control one factor of exposure while the camera adjusts for the other.

Why, you may ask, is this one of my favorite modes? It's because the aperture of your lens dictates depth of field. Depth of field, along with composition, is a major factor in how you direct attention to what is important in your image. It is the controlling factor of how much area in your image is sharp. If you want to isolate a subject from the background, such as when shooting a portrait, you can use a large aperture to keep the focus on your subject and make both the foreground and background blurry. If you want to keep the entire scene sharply focused, as with a landscape scene, using a small aperture will render the greatest amount of depth of field possible.

When to use Aperture Priority (A) mode

- When shooting portraits or wildlife (**Figure 4.7**)
- When shooting most landscape photography (**Figure 4.8**)
- When shooting macro, or close-up, photography (**Figure 4.9**)

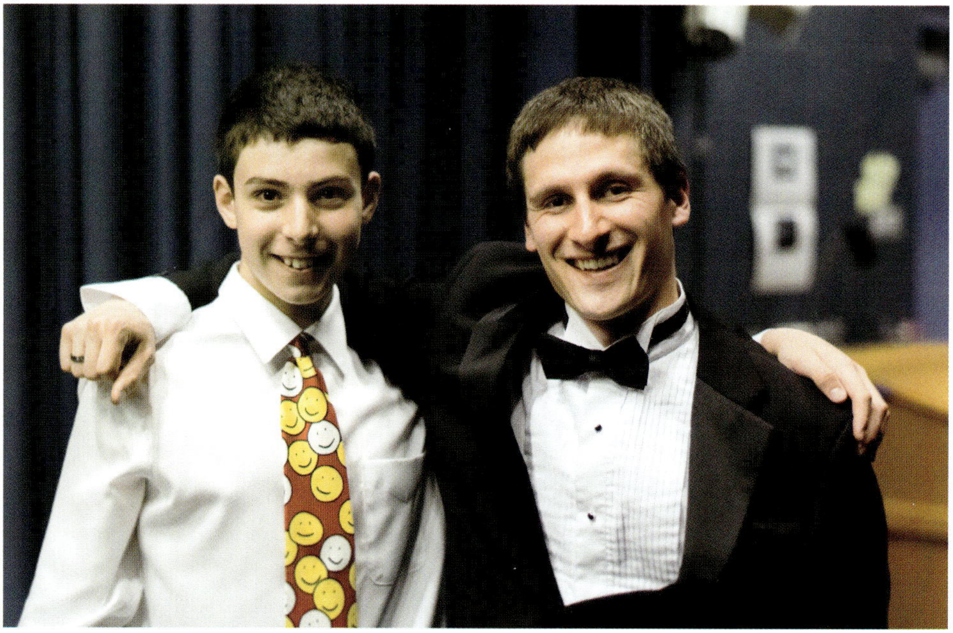

Figure 4.7
A large aperture created a very blurry background, so all the emphasis was left on the subjects.
ISO 3200 • 1/125 sec. • f/1.4 • 50mm lens

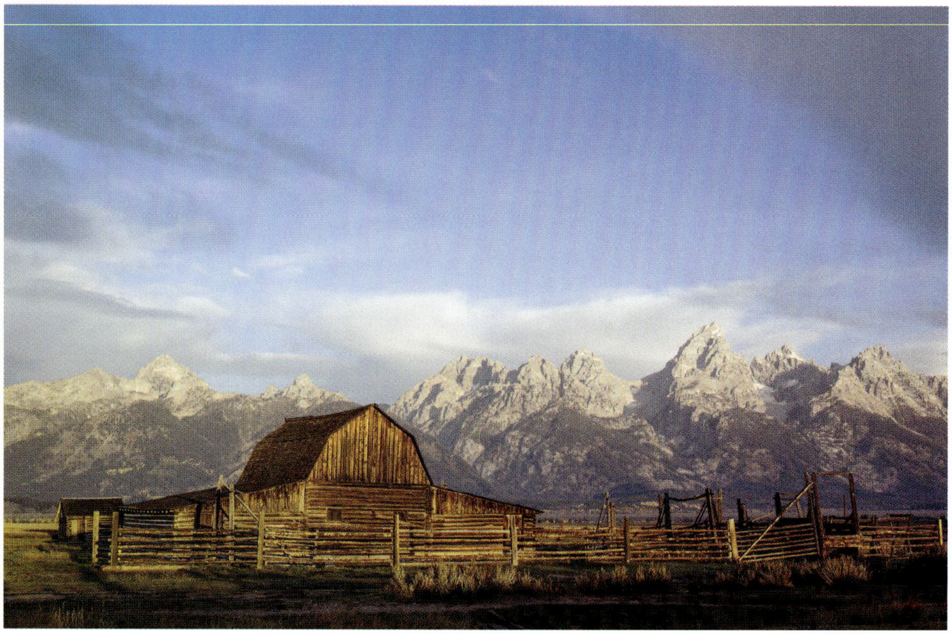

Figure 4.8
A smaller aperture setting brings sharpness to near and far objects.
ISO 100 • 1/15 sec. • f/11 • 45mm lens

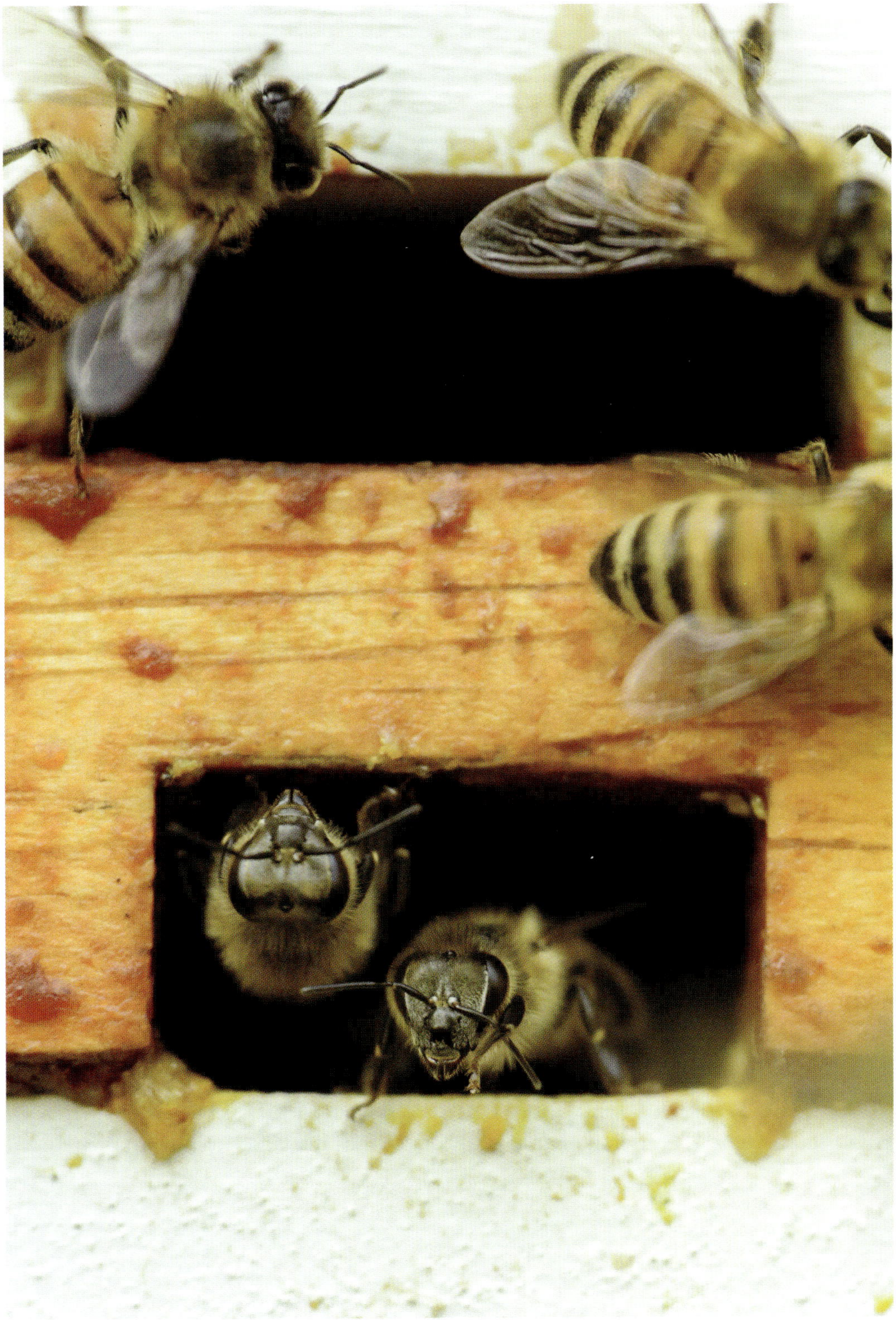

Figure 4.9

Small apertures give more sharpness in macro images.

ISO 4000 • 1/320 sec. • f/8 • 400mm lens

F-stops and aperture

As discussed earlier, the numeric value of your lens aperture is described as an *f-stop*. The f-stop is one of those old photography terms, which technically relates to the focal length of the lens (for example, 200mm) divided by the effective aperture diameter. These measurements are defined as "stops" and work incrementally with your shutter speed to determine proper exposure. Older camera lenses used one-stop increments to assist in exposure adjustments, such as 1.4, 2, 2.8, 4, 5.6, 8, 11, 16, and 22. Each stop represents about half the amount of light entering the lens iris as the larger stop before it. Today, most lenses don't have f-stop markings, since all adjustments to this setting are performed via the camera's electronics. The stops are also now typically divided into 1/3-stop increments to allow much finer adjustments to exposures as well as to match the incremental values of your camera's ISO settings, which are adjusted in 1/3-stop increments.

So we have established that Aperture Priority (A) mode is highly useful in controlling the depth of field in your image. But it's also pivotal in determining the limits of available light you can shoot in. Different lenses have different maximum apertures. The larger the maximum aperture, the less light you need in order to achieve an acceptably sharp image. You will recall that when using Shutter Priority mode, handholding your camera introduces movement or hand shake, which causes blurriness in the final picture. If your lens has a larger aperture, you can let in more light all at once, which means you can use faster shutter speeds. This is why lenses with large maximum apertures, such as f/1.4, are called "fast" lenses.

On the other hand, bright scenes require the use of a small aperture (such as f/16 or f/22), especially if you want to use a slower shutter speed. That small opening reduces the amount of incoming light, and this reduction of light requires that the shutter stay open longer.

Setting up and shooting in Aperture Priority mode

1. Turn on your camera, and then turn the Mode dial to align the A with the indicator line.
2. Select your ISO by pressing the **i** button on the back of the camera.
3. Press up or down on the Multi-selector to highlight the ISO option, and then select OK.
4. Use the Multi-selector to select the desired ISO setting, and then press OK to lock in the change.
5. Point the camera at your subject, and then activate the camera meter by depressing the shutter button halfway.
6. View the exposure information in the bottom area of the viewfinder or on the rear display panel.

7. While the meter is activated, use your thumb to roll the Command dial left and right to see the changed exposure values. Roll the dial to the right for a smaller aperture (higher f-stop number) and to the left for a larger aperture (smaller f-stop number).

Zoom lenses and maximum apertures

Some zoom lenses (like the 18–140mm lens) have a variable maximum aperture. This means that the largest opening will change depending on the zoom setting. In the example of the 18–140mm zoom, the lens has a maximum aperture of f/3.5 at 18mm and only f/5.6 when the lens is zoomed out to 140mm.

M: Manual Mode

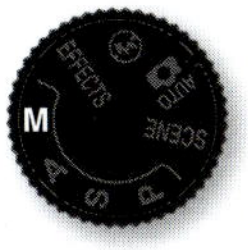

Once upon a time, long before digital cameras and program modes, there was manual mode. In those days it wasn't called "manual mode" because there were no other modes. It was just photography. In fact, many photographers cut their teeth on completely manual cameras. Let's face it—if you want to learn the effects of aperture and shutter speed on your photography, there is no better way to learn than by setting these adjustments yourself. However, today, with the advancement of camera technology, many new photographers never give this mode a second thought. That's truly a shame, as not only is it an excellent way to learn your photography basics, but it's also an essential tool to have in your photographic bag of tricks.

When your camera is set to Manual (M) mode, the camera meter will give you a reading of the scene you are photographing. It's your job to set both the f-stop (aperture) and the shutter speed to achieve a correct exposure. If you need a faster shutter speed, you will have to make the reciprocal change to your f-stop. Using any other mode, such as Shutter Priority or Aperture Priority, would mean that you just have to worry about one of these changes, but Manual mode means you have to do it all yourself. This can be a little challenging at first, but after a while you will have a complete understanding of how each change affects your exposure, which will, in turn, improve the way you use the other modes.

When to use Manual (M) mode

- When learning how each exposure element interacts with the others (**Figure 4.10**)
- When your environment is fooling your light meter and you need to maintain a certain exposure setting (**Figure 4.11**)
- When shooting silhouetted subjects, which requires overriding the camera's meter readings (**Figure 4.12**)

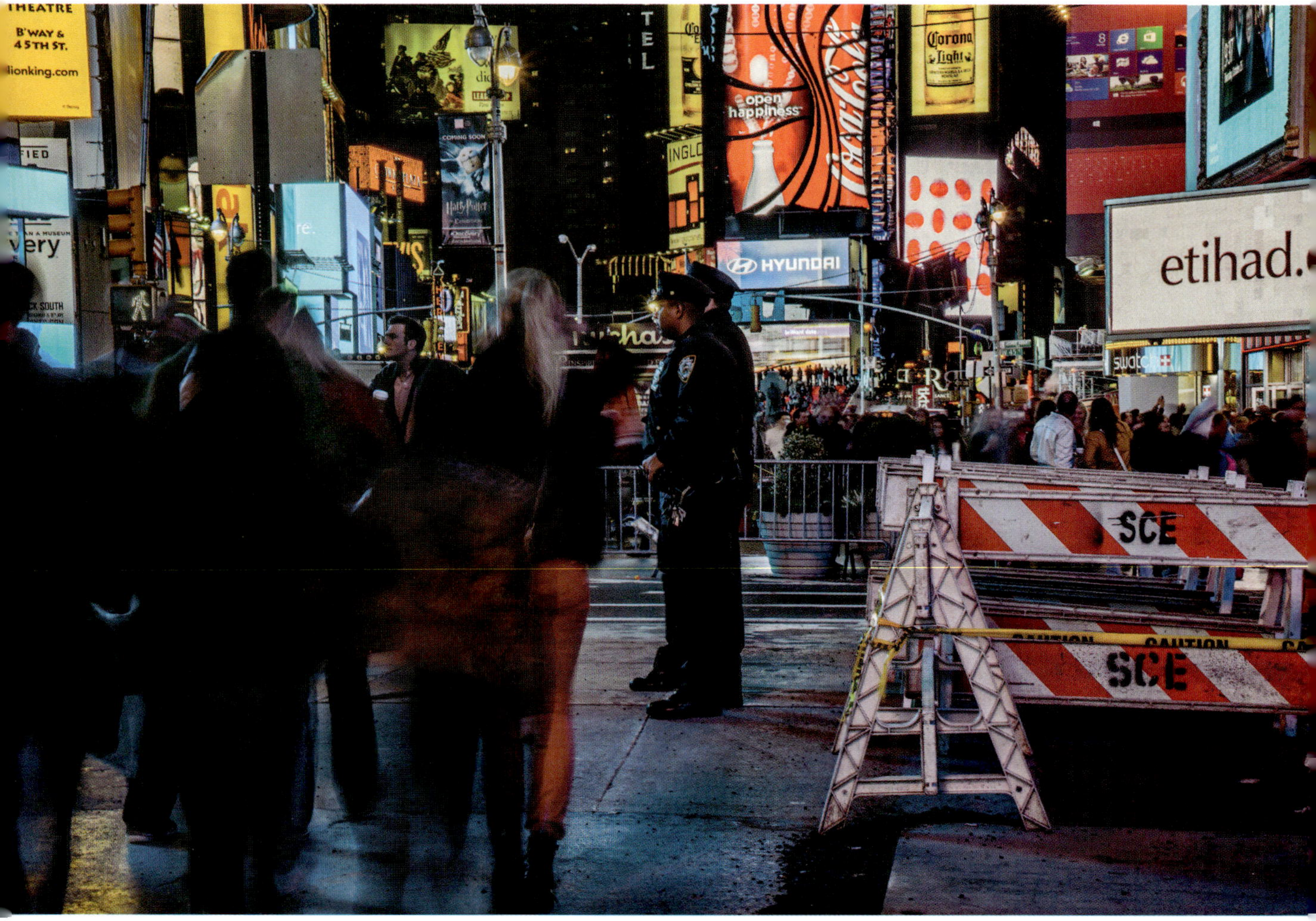

Figure 4.10 I wanted to expose for the bright signs to keep them from blowing out, but I also wanted to use a shutter speed that was slow enough to convey motion.

ISO 100 • 0.6 sec. • f/22 • 80mm lens

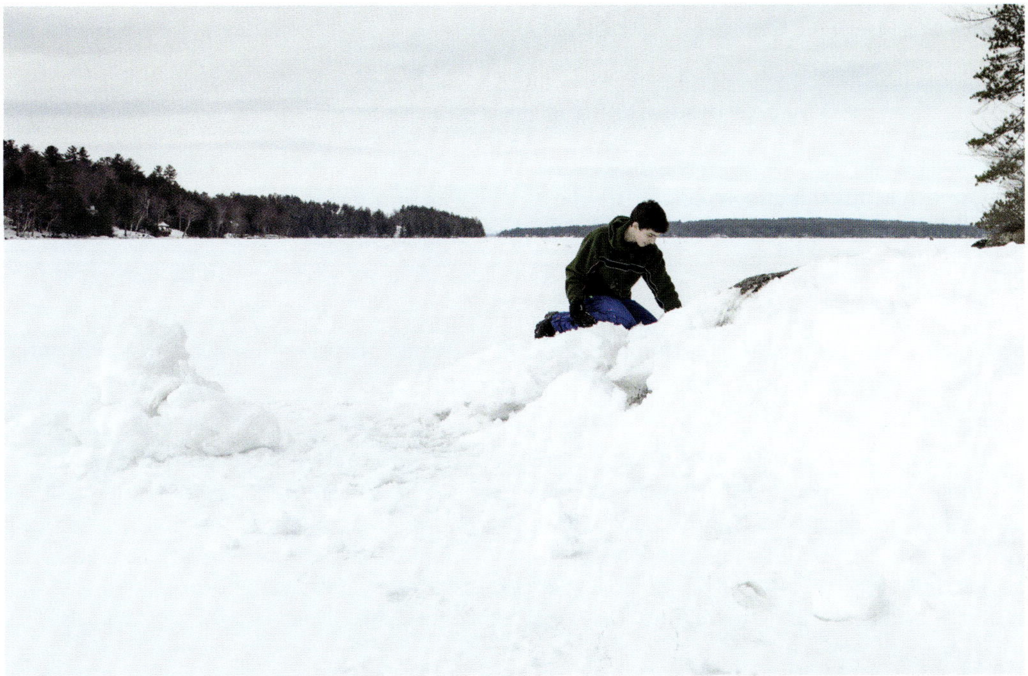

Figure 4.11
Sand and snow are always a challenge for light meters. Using Manual mode allowed me to prevent the scene from being underexposed.

ISO 100 • 1/400 sec. • f/6.3 • 22mm lens

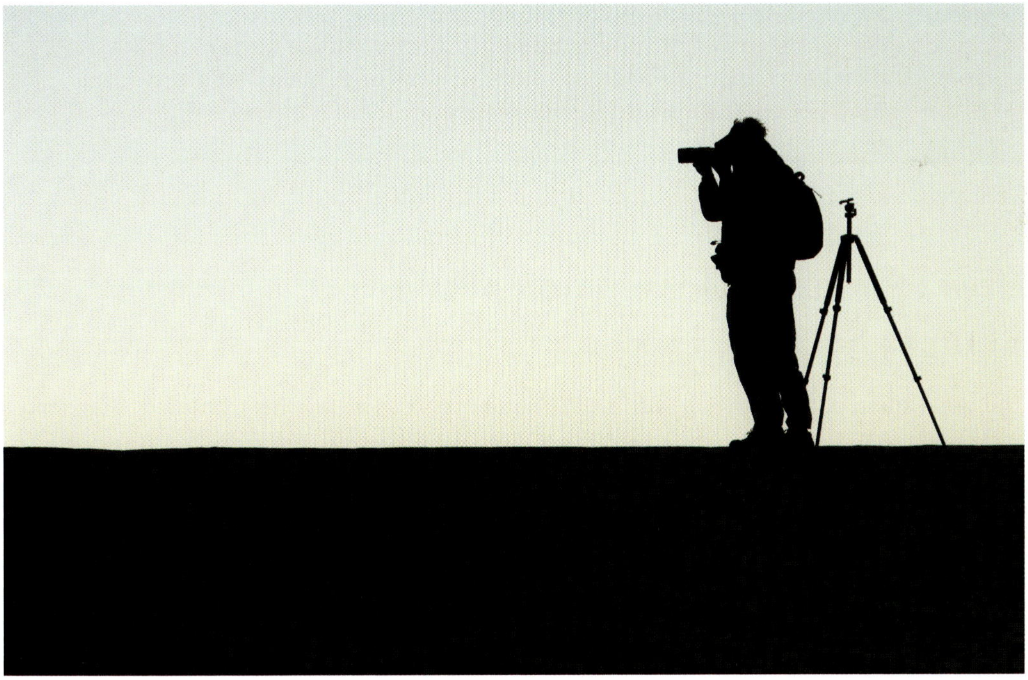

Figure 4.12
I used the spot meter on the bright background and adjusted exposure manually to put the subject into silhouette.

ISO 200 • 1/80 sec. • f/8 • 200mm lens

Setting up and shooting in Manual mode

1. Turn on your camera, and then turn the Mode dial to align the M with the indicator line.
2. Select your ISO by pressing the **i** button on the back of the camera.
3. Press up or down on the Multi-selector to highlight the ISO option, and then select OK.
4. Use the Multi-selector to select the desired ISO setting, and then press OK to lock in the change.
5. Point the camera at your subject, and then activate the camera meter by depressing the shutter button halfway.
6. View the exposure information in the bottom area of the viewfinder or on the display panel on the rear of the camera.
7. While the meter is activated, use your thumb to roll the Command dial left and right to change your shutter speed value until the exposure mark is lined up with the zero mark. The exposure information is displayed by a scale with marks that run from –2 to +2 stops. A proper exposure will line up with the arrow mark in the middle. As the indicator moves to the left, it is a sign that you will be underexposing (there is too little light on the sensor to provide adequate exposure). Move the indicator to the right and you will be providing more exposure than the camera meter calls for; this is overexposure.
8. To set your exposure using the aperture, depress the shutter release button until the meter is activated. Then, while holding down the Exposure Compensation/Aperture button (located behind and to the right of the shutter release button), rotate the Command dial to change the aperture. Rotate right for a smaller aperture (large f-stop number) and left for a larger aperture (small f-stop number).

How I Shoot: A Closer Look at the Camera Settings I Use

The great thing about working with a dSLR camera is I can always feel confident that some things will remain unchanged from camera to camera. For me, these are the Aperture Priority (A) and Shutter Priority (S) shooting modes. Regardless of the subject I am shooting—from landscape to portrait to macro—I am almost always going to be concerned with my depth of field. Whether it's isolating my subject with a large aperture or trying to maximize the overall sharpness of a sweeping landscape (**Figure 4.13**), I always keep an eye on my aperture setting. If I do have a need to control the action, I use Shutter Priority, my fallback mode: To create a silky waterfall effect, I can depend on Shutter Priority mode to provide that long shutter speed that will deliver. If I am shooting a soccer game, I definitely need the fast shutter speeds that will freeze the fast-moving action.

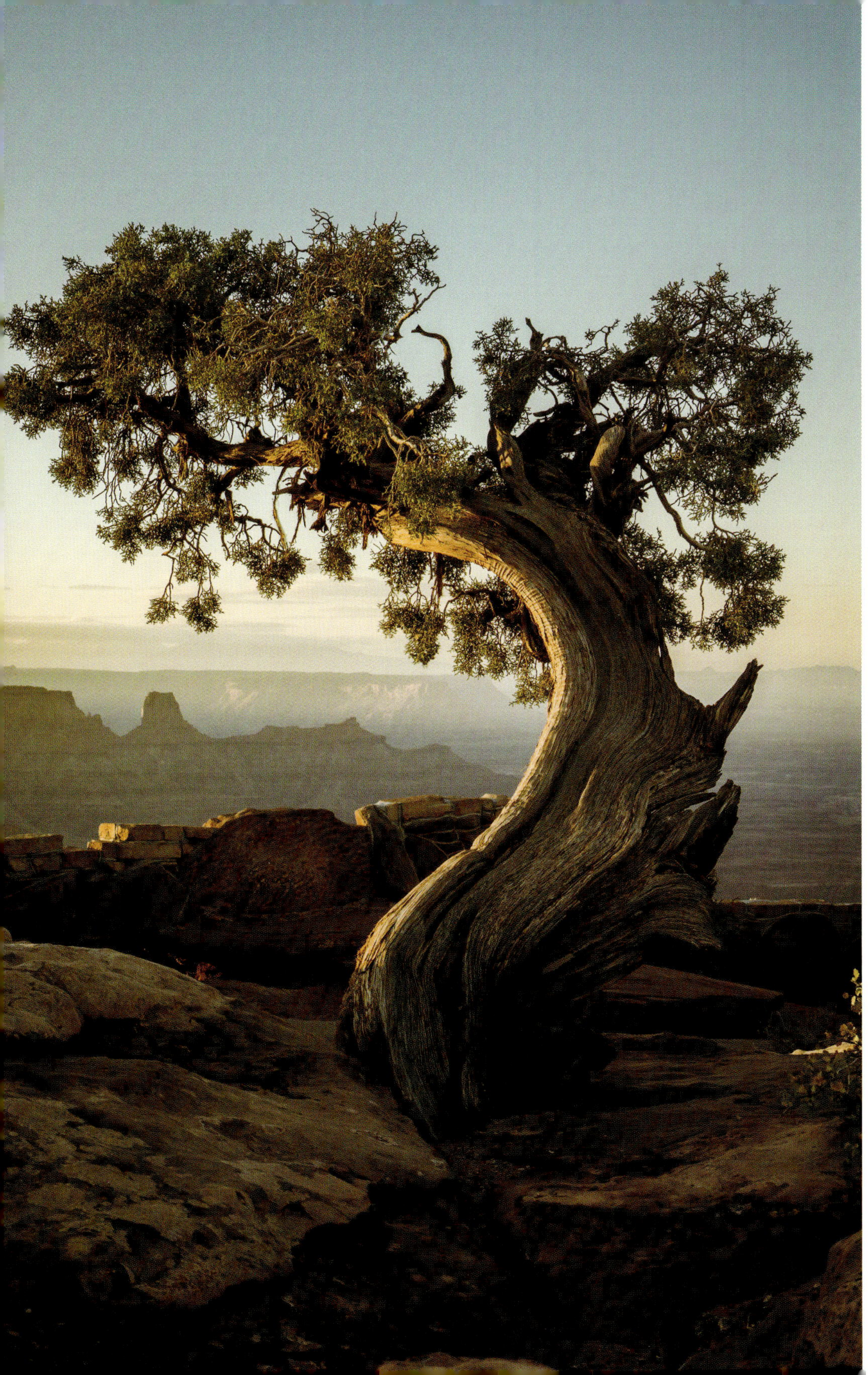

Figure 4.13
A small aperture increases the depth of field, which means more of the landscape is in focus.

ISO 100 • 1/3 sec. • f/13 • 52mm lens

While the other camera modes have their place, I think you will find that, like me and most other working pros, you will use the Aperture Priority and Shutter Priority modes for 90 percent of your shooting.

Another major concern I have when I am setting up my camera is just how low I can keep my ISO. This is always a priority for me, because a low ISO will deliver the cleanest image. I raise the ISO only as a last resort, because each increase in sensitivity is an opportunity for more digital noise to enter my image. To that end, I always have the High ISO Noise Reduction feature turned on (see Chapter 7).

To make quick changes while I shoot, I often use the Exposure Compensation feature (also covered in Chapter 7) so I can make small overexposure and underexposure changes. This is different than changing the aperture or shutter speed; it is more like fooling the camera meter into thinking the scene is brighter or darker than it actually is. To get to this function quickly, I press the Exposure Compensation/Aperture button and dial in the desired amount of compensation. Truth be told, I usually have this set to –1/3 so there is just a tiny bit of underexposure in my image. This usually leads to better color saturation. (Note: The Exposure Compensation feature does not work in the Manual shooting mode.)

One of the reasons I change my exposure is to make corrections when I see the "blinkies" in my rear LCD. Blinkies are the warning signal that part of my image has been overexposed to the point that I no longer have any detail in the highlights. When the Highlight Alert feature is turned on, the display will flash wherever the potential exists for overexposure. The black-and-white flashing will appear only in areas of your picture that are in danger of overexposure.

Setting up the Highlight Alert feature

1. Press the Menu button, and then use the Multi-selector to navigate to Playback Menu (**A**).
2. Move the Multi-selector to Playback Display Options and press OK (**B**).
3. Move the Multi-selector down to select the Highlights option, and then press OK to place a check mark next to the word Highlights (**C**).
4. Now move back up to select Done, and press OK again to lock in your change.

A

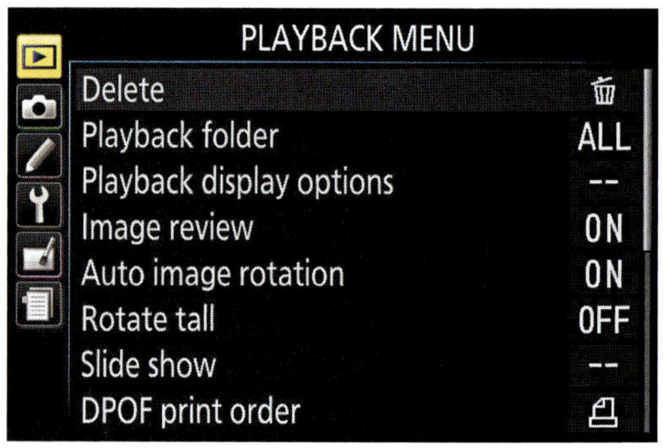

B

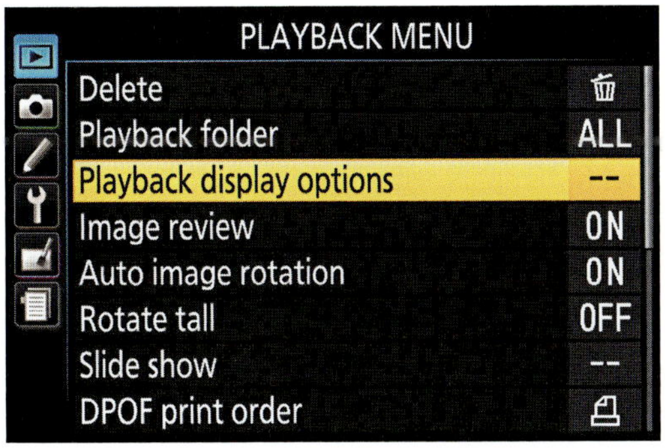

C

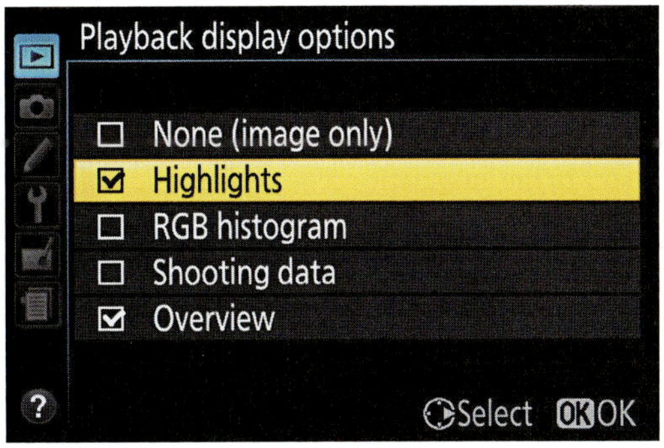

Once the highlight warning is turned on, I use it to check my images on the back of the LCD after taking a shot. If I see an area that is blinking, I will usually set the Exposure Compensation feature to an underexposed setting like –1/3 or –2/3 stops and take another photo, checking the result on the screen. I repeat this process until the warning is gone.

Sometimes, such as when you're shooting into the sun, the warning will blink no matter how much you adjust the exposure because there is just no detail in the highlight. Use your best judgment to determine if the warning is alerting you to an area where you want to retain highlight detail.

As you work your way through the coming chapters, you will see other tips and tricks I use in my daily photography, but the most important tip I can give is to understand the features of your camera so you can leverage the technology in a knowledgeable way. This will result in better photographs.

This will be more of a mental challenge than anything else, but you should put a lot of work into these lesson assignments because the information covered in this chapter will define how you work with your camera from this point on. Granted, once in a while you'll just want to grab some quick pictures and will resort to the automatic scene modes, but to get serious with your photography, you should learn the professional modes inside and out.

Starting off with Program mode

Set your camera on Program mode and start shooting. Become familiar with the adjustments you can make to your exposure by turning the Command dial. Shoot in bright sun, deep shade, indoors, anywhere you have different types and intensities of light. While you are shooting, make sure you keep an eye on your ISO, and raise or lower it according to your environment.

Learning to control time with the Shutter Priority mode

Find some moving subjects and set your camera to S mode. Have someone ride a bike back and forth, or even just photograph cars as they go by. Start with a slow shutter speed of around 1/30 of a second, and then start shooting with faster and faster shutter speeds. Keep shooting until you can freeze the action. Now find something that isn't moving, like a flower, and start with your shutter speed at something fast like 1/500 of a second and work your way down. Don't brace the camera on a steady surface. Just try to shoot as slowly as possible, down to about 1/4 of a second. The point is to see how well you can handhold your camera before you start introducing hand shake into the image, making it appear soft and somewhat unfocused.

Controlling depth of field with the Aperture Priority mode

The name of the game with Aperture Priority mode is depth of field. Set up three items—chess pieces or something similar—at different distances from you. Focus on the middle item, and set your camera to the largest aperture your lens allows (remember, large aperture means a small number, like f/3.5). Now, while still focusing on the middle subject, start shooting with ever-smaller apertures until you are at the smallest f-stop for your lens. If you have a zoom lens, try doing this exercise with the lens at the widest and then the most telephoto setting. Now move up to subjects that are farther away, like telephone poles, and shoot them in the same way. The idea is to get a feel for how each aperture setting affects your depth of field.

Giving and taking with Manual mode

Manual mode is not going to require a lot of work, but you should pay close attention to your results. Go outside on a sunny day and, using the camera in Manual mode, set your ISO to 100, your shutter speed to 1/125 of a second, and your aperture to f/16. Now press your shutter release button to get a meter reading. You should be pretty close to that zero mark. If not, make small adjustments to one of your settings until it hits that mark. This is when the fun begins. Start moving your shutter speed slower, to 1/60, and then set your aperture to f/22. Now go the other way. Set your aperture on f/8 and your shutter speed to 1/500.

Review your images. If all went well, all the exposures should look the same. This is because you balanced the light with reciprocal changes to the aperture and shutter speed. Go back to our original setting of 1/125 at f/16 and try moving the shutter speed without changing the aperture. Just make 1/3-stop changes (1/125 to 1/100 to 1/80 to 1/60), and then review your images to see what a 1/3-stop of overexposure looks like. Then do the same thing going in the opposite way. It's hard to know if you want to overexpose or underexpose a scene until you have actually done it and seen the results.

With each of the assignments, make sure you keep track of your modes and exposures so you can compare them with the images. If you are using software to review your images, you should also be able to check the camera settings that are embedded within the images' metadata.

Share your results with the book's Flickr group!
Join the group here: flickr.com/groups/nikond5500_fromsnapshotstogreatshots

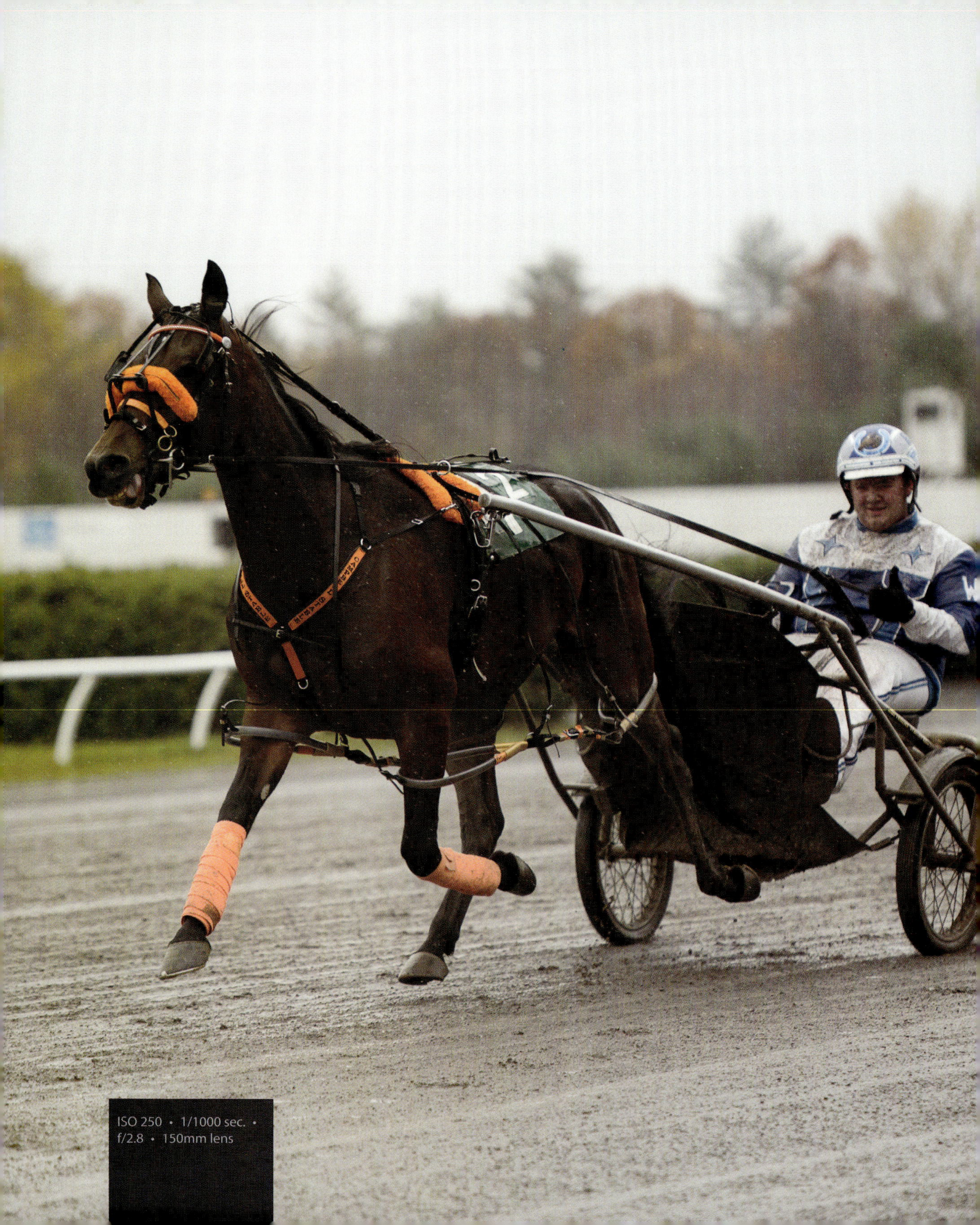

ISO 250 • 1/1000 sec. • f/2.8 • 150mm lens

5

Moving Targets

Tricks for Shooting Subjects in Motion

Now that you have learned about the professional modes, it's time to put your newfound knowledge to good use. Whether you are shooting the action at a professional sporting event, an osprey swooping for a fish, or a child on a merry-go-round, you'll learn techniques that will help you bring out the best in your photography when your subject is in motion.

The number one thing to know when trying to capture a moving target is that speed is king! I'm not talking about how fast your subject is moving but rather how fast your shutter is opening and closing. Shutter speed is the key to freezing the moment in time—but also to conveying movement. It's all in how you turn the dial. We'll also explore other elements vital for taking your shot to the next level: composition, lens selection, and a few more items. So strap on your seat belt and hit the gas, because here we go!

Poring Over the Picture

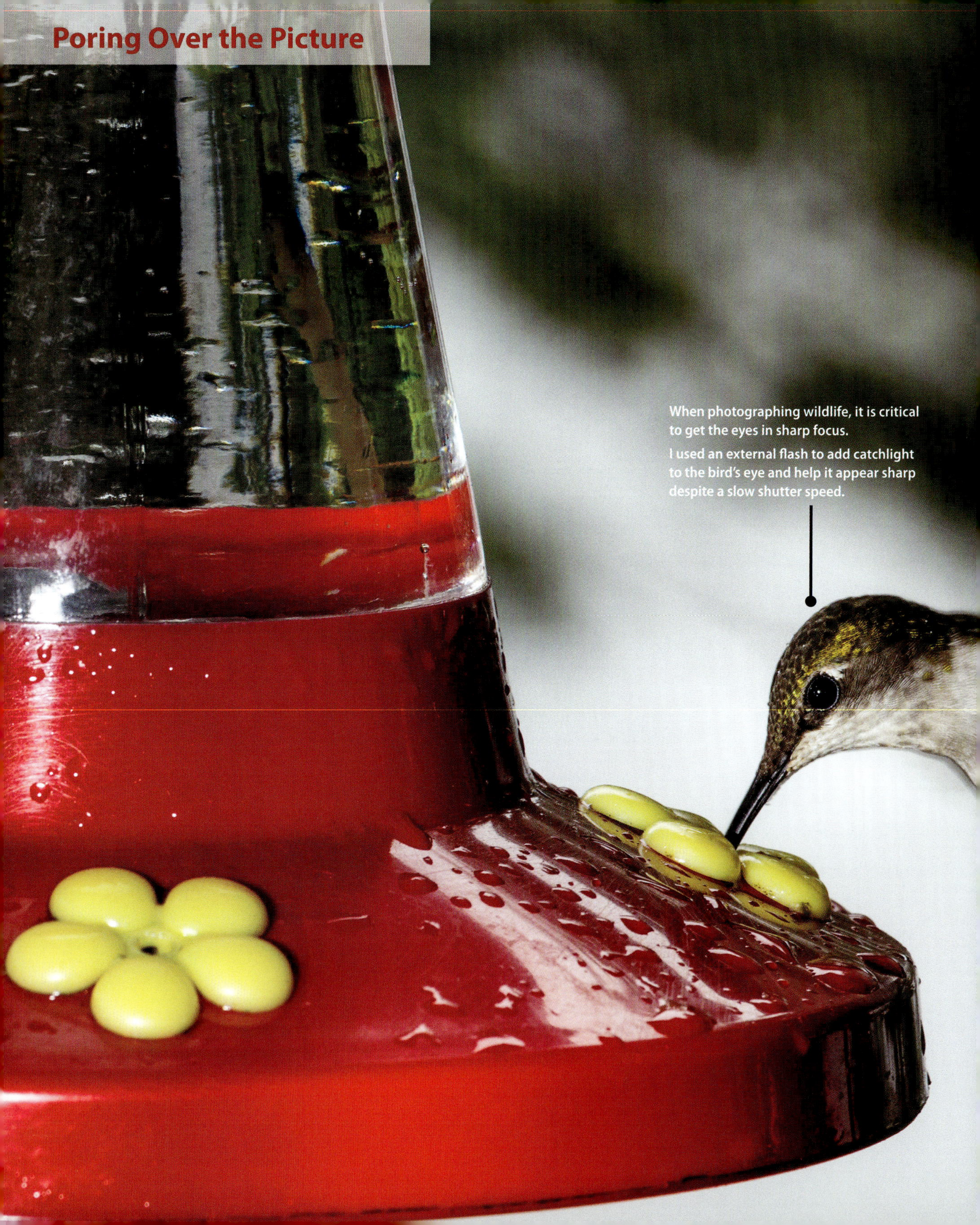

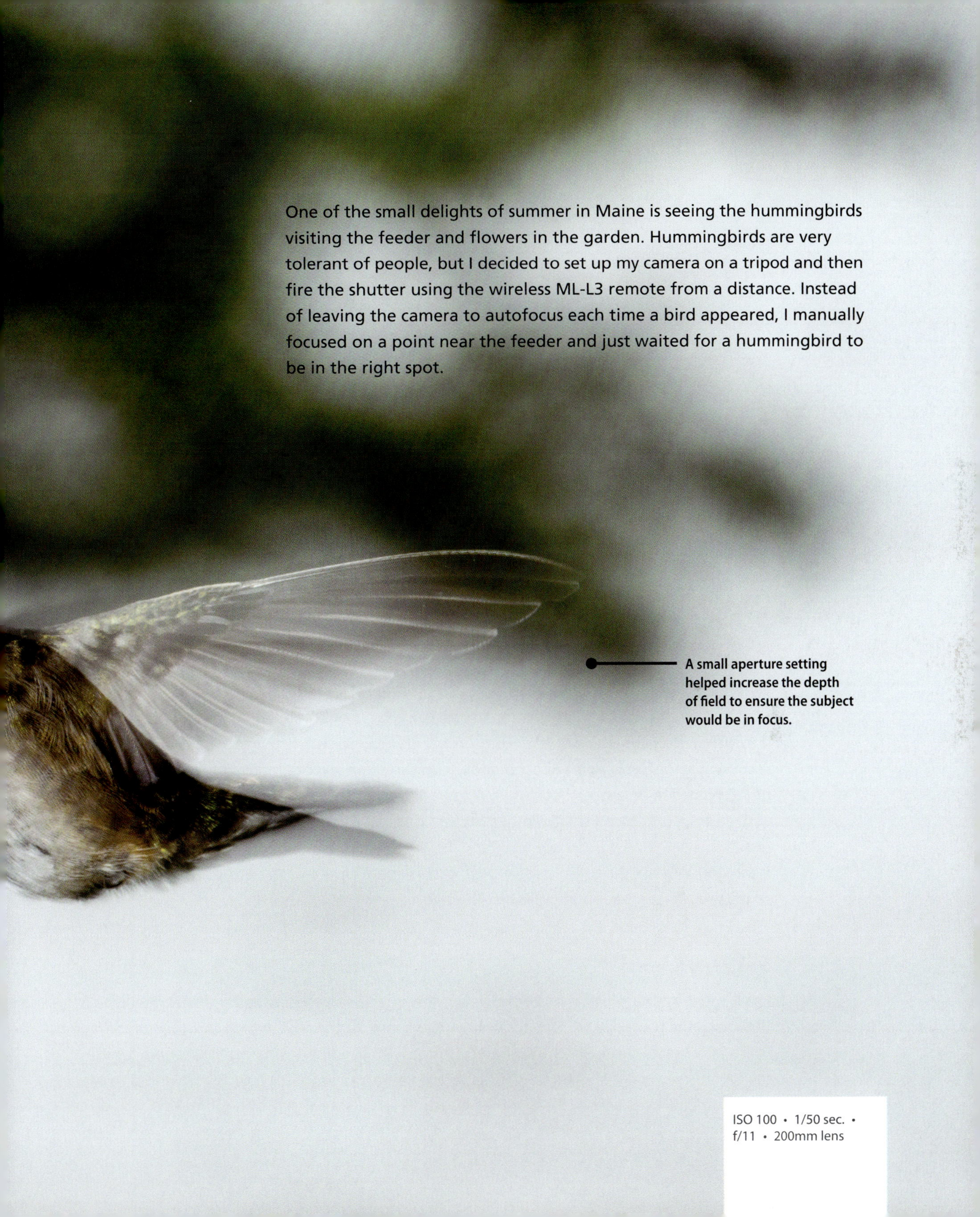

One of the small delights of summer in Maine is seeing the hummingbirds visiting the feeder and flowers in the garden. Hummingbirds are very tolerant of people, but I decided to set up my camera on a tripod and then fire the shutter using the wireless ML-L3 remote from a distance. Instead of leaving the camera to autofocus each time a bird appeared, I manually focused on a point near the feeder and just waited for a hummingbird to be in the right spot.

A small aperture setting helped increase the depth of field to ensure the subject would be in focus.

ISO 100 • 1/50 sec. • f/11 • 200mm lens

Stop Right There!

Shutter speed is the main tool in the photographer's arsenal for capturing great action shots. The ability to freeze a moment in time is often the difference between a good shot and a great one. To take advantage of this concept, you need to have a good grasp of the relationship between shutter speed and movement. When you press the shutter release button, your camera goes into action by opening the shutter curtain and then closing it after a predetermined length of time. The longer you leave your shutter open, the more your subject will move across the frame, so common sense dictates that the first thing to consider is just how fast your subject is moving.

Typically, you will be working in fractions of a second. How many fractions depends on several factors. Subject movement, while simple in concept, is actually based on three factors: The first is the direction of travel. Is the subject moving across your field of view (left to right) or traveling toward or away from you? The second consideration is the actual speed at which the subject is moving. There is a big difference between a moving sports car and a child on a bicycle. Finally, the distance from you to the subject has a direct bearing on how fast the action seems to be taking place. Let's take a brief look at each of these factors to see how they might affect your shooting.

Direction of travel

Typically, the first thing people think about when taking an action shot is how fast the subject is moving, but in reality the first consideration should be the direction of travel. Where you are positioned in relation to the subject's direction of travel is critically important in selecting the proper shutter speed. When you open your shutter, the lens gathers light from your subject and records it on the camera sensor. If the subject is moving across your viewfinder, you need a faster shutter speed to keep that lateral movement from being recorded as a streak across your image. Subjects that are moving perpendicular to your shooting location do not move across your viewfinder and appear to be more stationary. This allows you to use a slightly slower shutter speed (**Figure 5.1**). A subject that is moving in a diagonal direction—both across the frame and toward or away from you—requires a shutter speed in between the two.

Subject speed

Once the angle of motion has been determined, you can then assess the speed at which the subject is traveling. The faster your subject moves, the faster your shutter speed needs to be in order to "freeze" that subject (**Figure 5.2**). A person walking across your frame might only require a shutter speed of 1/60 of a second, whereas a cyclist traveling in the same direction would call for 1/500 of a second. That same cyclist traveling toward you at the same rate of speed, rather than across the frame, might only require a shutter speed of 1/125 of a second. You can start to see how the relationship of speed and direction comes into play in your decision-making process.

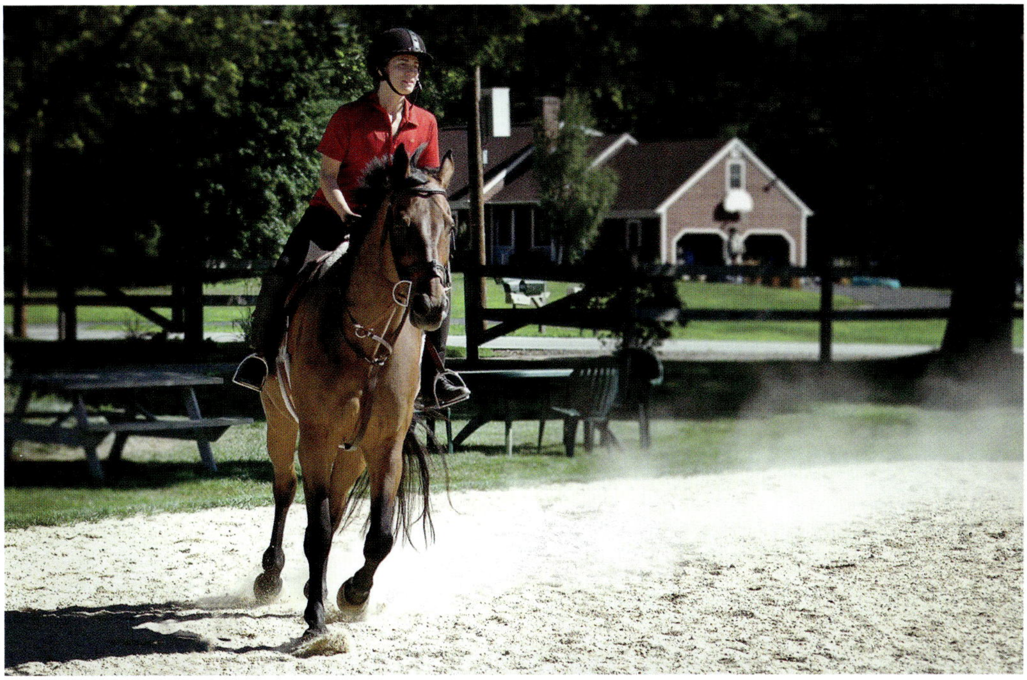

Figure 5.1
Action coming toward the camera can be captured with slower shutter speeds.

ISO 200 • 1/640 sec. • f/4 • 70mm lens

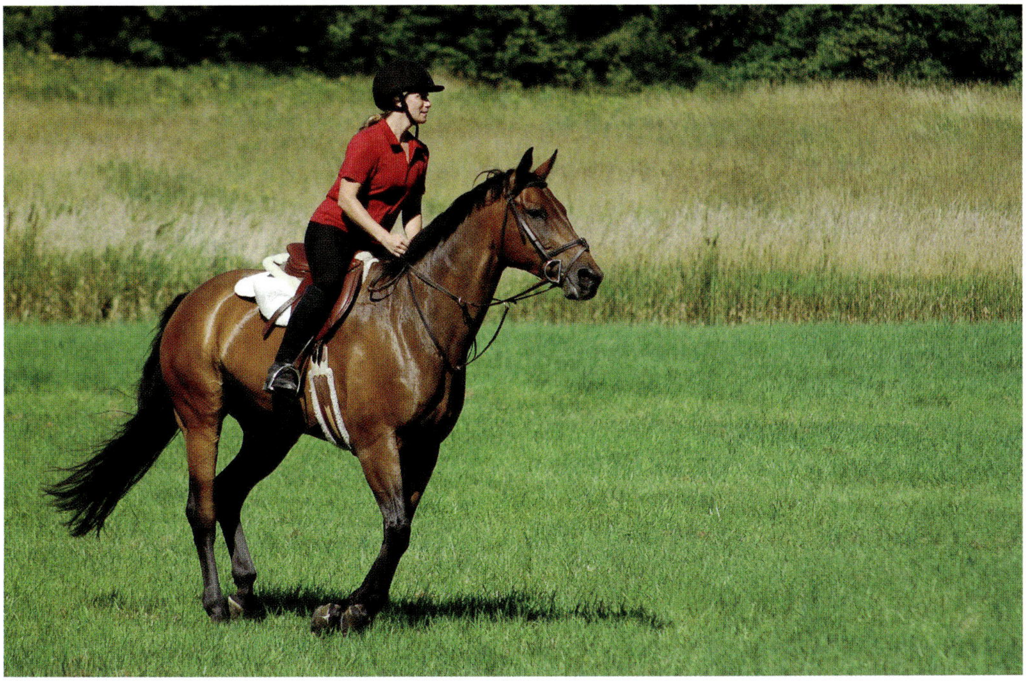

Figure 5.2
A fast-moving subject who is crossing your path will require a faster shutter speed.

ISO 200 • 1/800 sec. • f/5.3 • 200mm lens

Subject-to-camera distance

So now we know both the direction and the speed of your subject. The final factor to address is the distance between you and the action. Picture yourself looking at a highway full of cars from up in a tall building a quarter of a mile from the road. As you stare down at the traffic moving along at 55 miles per hour, the cars and trucks seem to be moving slowly along the roadway. Now picture yourself standing in the median of that same road as the same traffic flies by at the same rate of speed.

Although the traffic is moving at the same speed, the shorter distance between you and the traffic makes the cars look like they are moving much faster. This is because your field of view is much narrower; therefore, the subjects are not going to present themselves within the frame for the same length of time. The concept of distance applies to the length of your lens as well (**Figure 5.3**). If you are using a wide-angle lens, you can probably get away with a slower shutter speed than if you are using a telephoto, which puts you in the heart of the action. It all has to do with your field of view. That telephoto gets you "closer" to the action—and the closer you are, the faster your subject will be moving across your viewfinder.

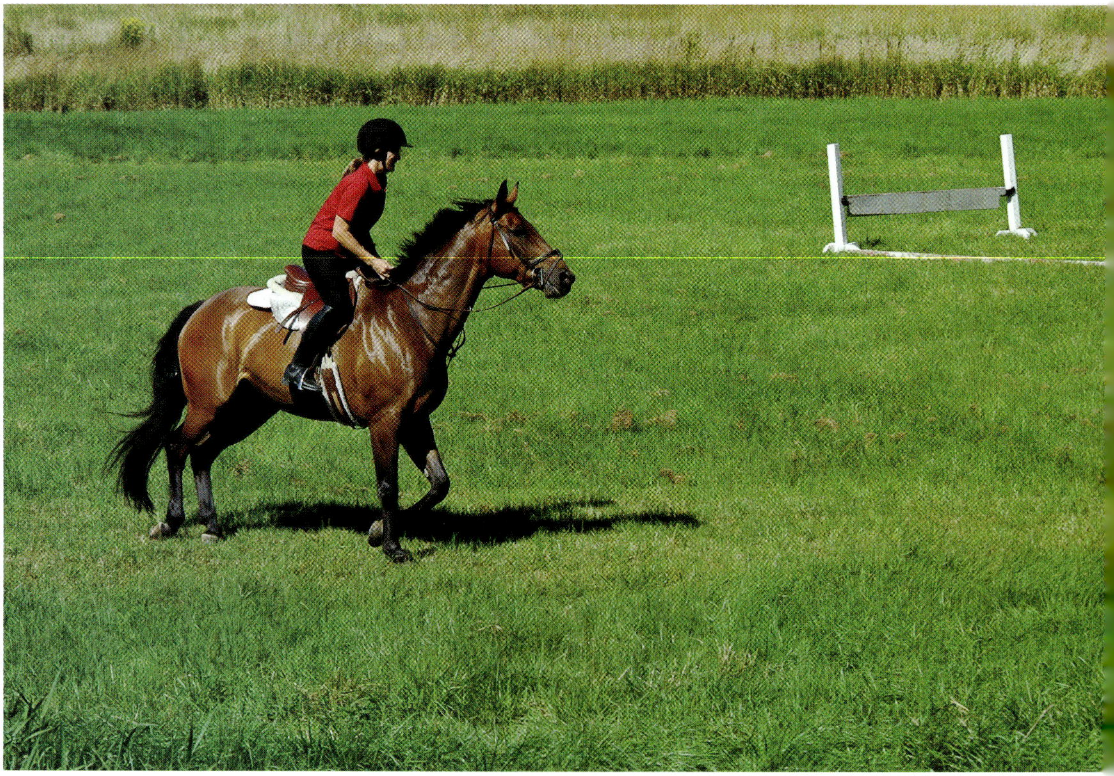

Figure 5.3
Because of the distance of the subject from the camera, a slower shutter speed could be used to capture this action.
ISO 200 • 1/400 sec. • f/8 • 75mm lens

Using Shutter Priority (S) Mode to Stop Motion

In Chapter 4, you were introduced to the professional shooting modes. You'll remember that the mode that gives you ultimate control over shutter speed is Shutter Priority, or S, mode, where you are responsible for selecting the shutter speed while handing over the aperture selection to the camera. The ability to concentrate on just one exposure factor helps you quickly make changes on the fly while staying glued to your viewfinder and your subject.

There are a couple of things to consider when using Shutter Priority mode, both of which have to do with the amount of light that is available when shooting. While you have control over which shutter speed you select in Shutter Priority mode, the range of shutter speeds available to you depends largely on how well your subject is lit.

Typically, when shooting fast-paced action, you will be working with very fast shutter speeds. This means that your lens will probably be set to its largest aperture. If the light is not sufficient for the shutter speed selected, you will need to do one of two things: select a lens that offers a larger working aperture or raise the ISO of the camera. Working off the assumption that you have only one lens available, let's concentrate on balancing your exposure using the ISO.

Let's say you are shooting a soccer game at night, and you want to get some great action shots. You set your camera to Shutter Priority mode and, after testing out some shutter speeds, determine that you need to shoot at 1/500 of a second to freeze the action on the field. When you place the viewfinder to your eye and press the shutter button halfway, you notice that the aperture value is blinking. This is your camera's way of telling you that the lens has now reached its maximum aperture and your shots are going to be underexposed if you take them at the currently selected shutter speed. You could slow your shutter speed down until the blinking goes away, but then you would get images with too much motion blur.

The alternative is to raise your ISO to a level that is fast enough for a proper exposure. The key here is to always use the lowest ISO you can get away with. That might mean ISO 100 in bright, sunny conditions or ISO 6400 for an indoor or night situation (**Figure 5.4**). Just remember that the higher the ISO, the greater the amount of noise in your image. This is the reason you see professional sports photographers using those mammoth lenses perched atop monopods. They could use a smaller lens, but to get those very large apertures they need a huge piece of glass on the front of the lens. The larger the glass on the front of the lens, the more light it gathers and the larger the aperture for shooting. For the working pro, the large aperture translates into low ISO (and thus low noise), fast shutter speeds, and razor-sharp action.

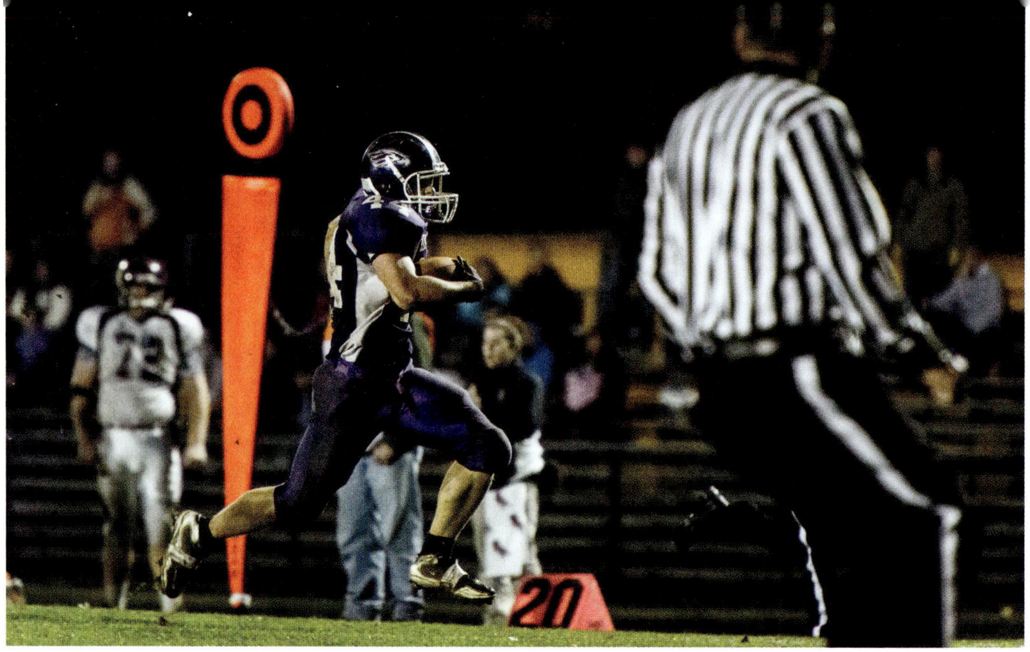

Figure 5.4
Sometimes the only way to stop action is to crank up your ISO.
ISO 25600 • 1/1000 sec. • f/5.6 • 400mm lens

Adjusting your ISO on the fly

1. Look at the exposure values (the shutter speed and aperture settings) in the lower portion of your viewfinder.
2. If the aperture setting is blinking, press the **i** button on the back of the camera.
3. Use the Multi-selector to highlight the ISO option, and then press OK (**A**).
4. Use the Multi-selector to select a higher ISO setting, and press OK to lock in the change (**B**).
5. If you now see an aperture setting in the display, shoot away. If you still see the aperture blinking, repeat steps 2 to 4 until it is set correctly.

A

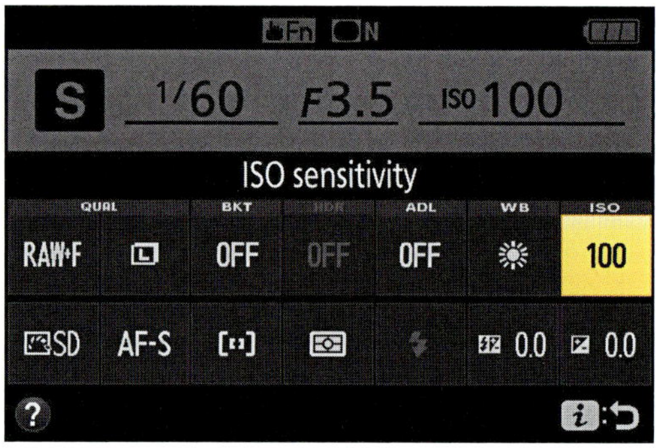

B

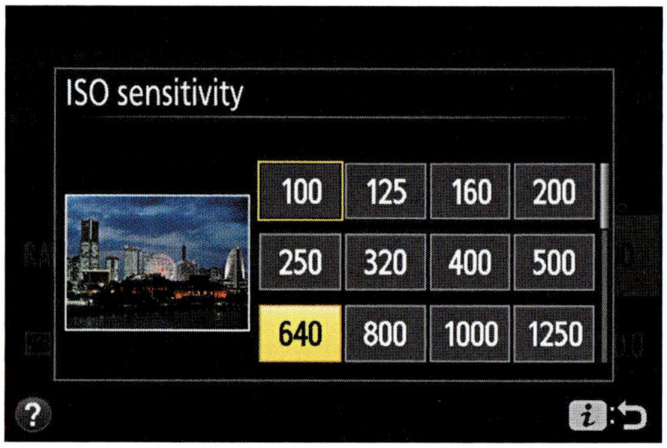

Zoom in to be sure

When reviewing your shots on the LCD, don't be fooled by the display. The smaller your image is, the sharper it will look. To ensure that you are getting sharp, blur-free images, make sure you zoom in on your LCD.

To zoom in on your images, press the Playback button located on the rear of the camera, and then press the Zoom In button (**Figure 5.5**). Continue pressing the Zoom In button to increase the zoom ratio.

To zoom back out, simply press the Zoom Out button (the magnifying glass with the minus sign on it) or press the Playback button again.

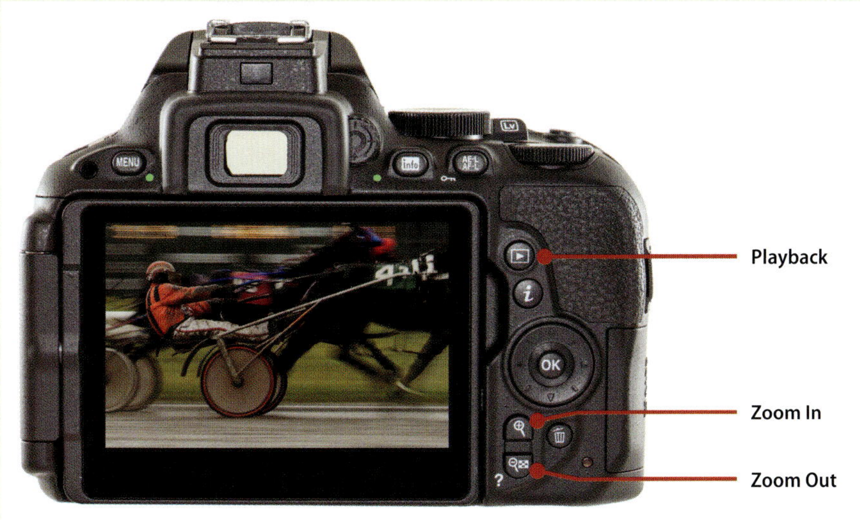

Figure 5.5 Zooming in on your image helps you confirm that the image is really sharp.

Using Aperture Priority (A) Mode to Isolate Your Subject

One of the benefits of working in Shutter Priority mode with fast shutter speeds is that, more often than not, you will be shooting with the largest aperture available on your lens. Shooting with a large aperture allows you to use faster shutter speeds, but it also narrows your depth of field.

To isolate your subject in order to focus your viewer's attention on it, a larger aperture is required. The larger aperture reduces the foreground and background sharpness. The larger the aperture, the more blurred they will be.

The reason I bring this up here is that when you are shooting most sporting events, the idea is to isolate your main subject by having it in focus while the rest of the image has some amount of blur. This sharp focus draws your viewer right to the subject. Studies have shown that the eye is drawn to sharp areas before moving on to the blurry areas. Also, depending on what your subject matter is, there can be a tendency to get distracted by a busy background if everything in the photo is equally sharp. Without a narrow depth of field, it might be difficult for the viewer to establish exactly what the main subject is in your picture.

Let's look at how to use depth of field to bring focus to your subject. In the previous section, I told you that you should use Shutter Priority mode for getting those really fast shutter speeds to stop action. Generally speaking, Shutter Priority mode will be the one you most often use for shooting sports and other action, but at times you'll want to ensure that you are getting the narrowest depth of field possible in your image. The way to do this is by using Aperture Priority mode.

So how do you know when you should use Aperture Priority mode as opposed to Shutter Priority mode? The answer isn't always obvious, but your LCD can help you make this determination. The best scenario for using Aperture Priority mode is a brightly lit scene where maximum apertures will still give you plenty of shutter speed to stop the action.

Let's say you are shooting a game in the midday sun. If you have determined that you need something between 1/500 and 1/1250 of a second for stopping the action, you could just set your camera to a high shutter speed in Shutter Priority mode and start shooting. But you also want to be using an aperture of, say, f/4.5 to get that narrow depth of field. Here's the problem: If you set your camera to Shutter Priority mode and select 1/1000 of a second as a nice compromise, you might get that desired f-stop—but you might not. As the meter is trained on your moving subject, the light levels could rise or fall, which might actually change that desired f-stop to something higher, like f/5.6 or even f/8. Now the depth of field is extended, and you will no longer get that nice isolation and separation you wanted.

To rectify this, switch the camera to Aperture Priority mode and select f/4.5 as your aperture. Now, as you begin shooting, the camera holds that aperture and makes exposure adjustments with the shutter speed. As I said before, this works well when you have lots of light—enough light so you can have a high-enough shutter speed without introducing motion blur.

The Auto ISO Sensitivity Control Trick

There is a very cool trick that can get you the best of both worlds and that won't sacrifice your shutter speed or aperture. By setting up the Auto ISO Sensitivity Control feature, you can set the camera to automatically select an ISO that keeps you at your preferred shutter speed while using the largest aperture and lowest ISO possible. It will also put an upper limit on the ISO to keep you from getting too much noise in your images.

Here's the way it works: If I am shooting an activity that requires a shutter speed of 1/250 of a second, I set that as the minimum in the Auto control settings. Then I decide that I can deal with the noise that is produced with an ISO up to 3200, so I set that as my maximum sensitivity. Since I would always like to use the lowest ISO, I set the ISO Sensitivity setting to 100. Once everything is set, the camera will now adjust my ISO without any interaction from me, letting me shoot at my desired shutter speed at the lowest possible ISO and largest aperture setting possible.

Setting up the Auto ISO Sensitivity Control feature

1. Press the Menu button, and then use the Multi-selector to get to Shooting Menu.
2. Press the Multi-selector to the right to enter the menu, and then locate the ISO Sensitivity Settings feature (**A**).
3. Press the Multi-selector to the right to enter the setup screen.
4. Press the Multi-selector to the right, select the lowest ISO that you wish to use (ISO Sensitivity), and press the OK button (**B**).

A

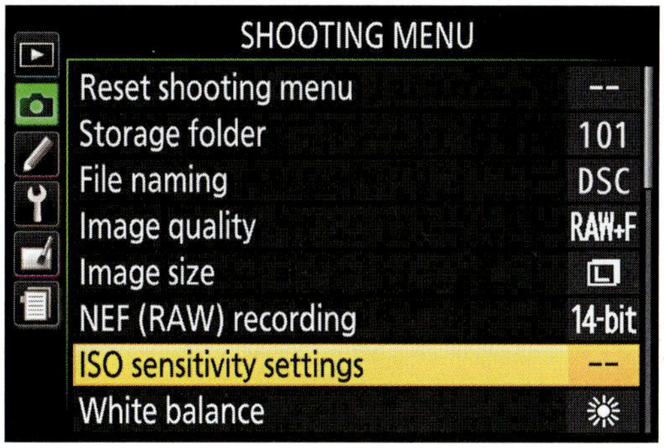

5. Press the Multi-selector down to highlight Auto ISO Sensitivity Control, and then move the selector to the right and select On to activate the feature (**C**).

B

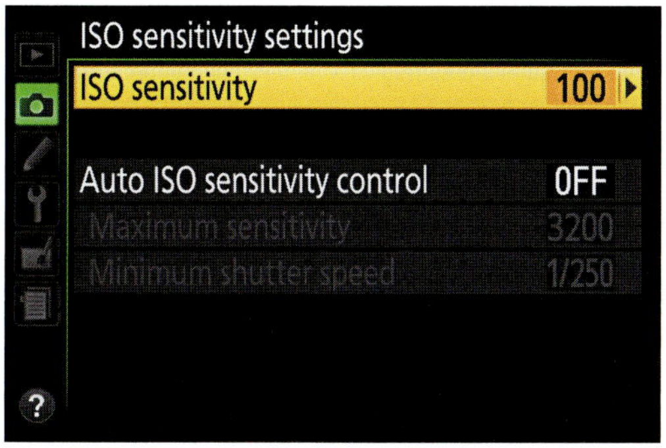

C

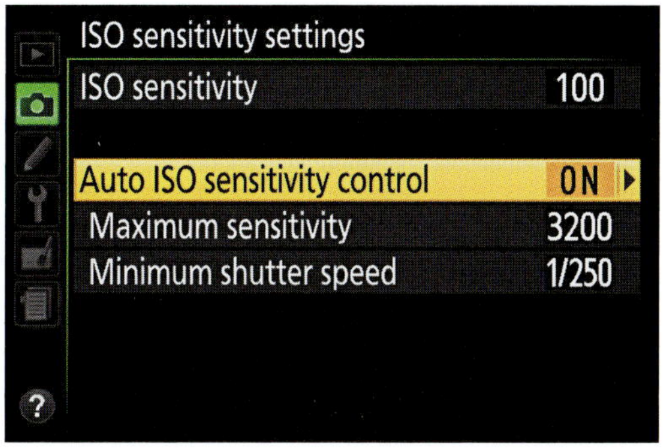

6. Use the Multi-selector to choose the Maximum Sensitivity option (**D**). This allows you to set the upper limit of your ISO.
7. Finally, select the minimum shutter speed that you want to use while shooting (**E**). This will be completely dependent on the speed necessary to stop the action you are shooting.

D

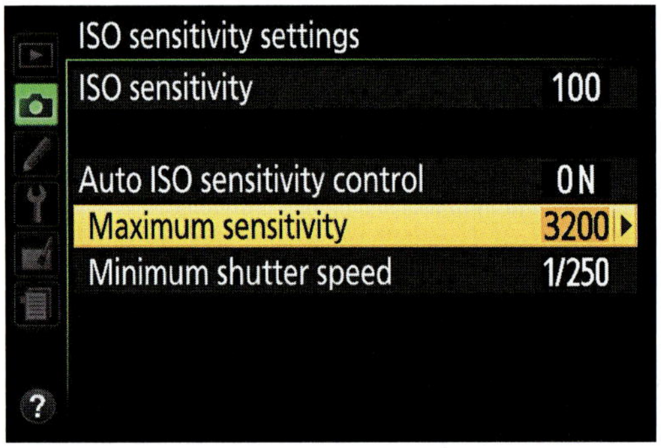

E

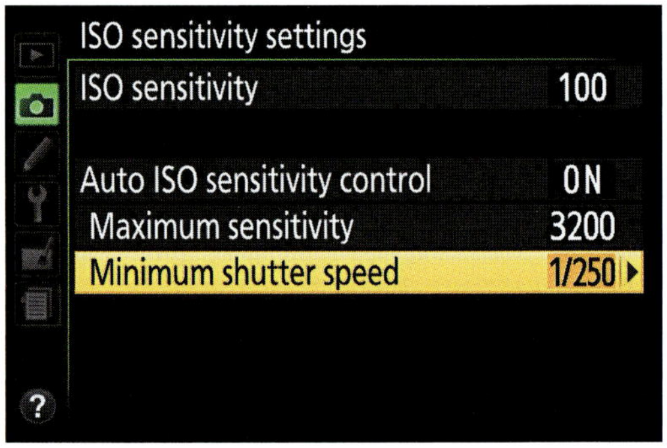

With everything set up, you can begin shooting without fear of constantly having to change the ISO. This technique is also quite helpful when working in varying light conditions. As you are shooting, you will notice the ISO Auto warning in the lower portion of the viewfinder.

Manual Callout

For more information about the Auto ISO Sensitivity Control feature, go to page 241 in the D5500 Reference Manual PDF.

Keep Them in Focus with Continuous-Servo Focus and AF Focus Point Selection

With the exposure issue handled for the moment, let's move on to an area that is equally important: focusing. If you have browsed your manual, you know that there are several focus modes to choose from in the D5500. To get the greatest benefit from each of them, it is important to understand how they work and the situations where each mode will give you the best opportunity to grab a great shot. Because we are discussing subject movement, our first choice is going to be Continuous-Servo AF mode (AF-C). AF-C mode uses the focus points in the camera to track a moving subject and then lock in the focus when the shutter button is completely depressed. As the subject moves, the camera uses something called predictive focus tracking to anticipate where the subject will be moving and then adjust focus accordingly.

Selecting and shooting in Continuous-Servo AF focus mode

1. Press the **i** button on the back of the camera.
2. Use the Multi-selector to highlight Focus mode, and then press the OK button.
3. Use the Multi-selector to select AF-C, and press OK (**A**).
4. Locate your subject in the viewfinder, and then press and hold the shutter button halfway to activate the focus mechanism.
5. The camera will maintain the subject's focus as long as it remains within one of the focus points in the viewfinder, or until you release the shutter button or take a picture.

A

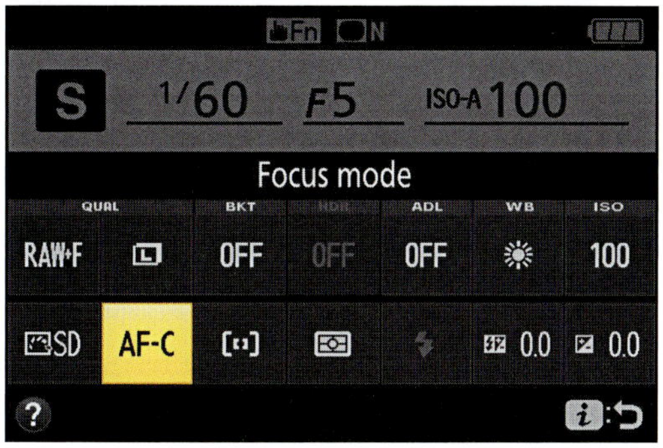

Note that holding down the shutter button for long periods of time will cause your battery to drain much faster because the camera will be constantly focusing on the subject.

When using the AF-C mode, you can change the AF-Area mode to specify how the focus points are used. There are two modes to choose from:

- **Single-Point AF.** This mode allows you to select a single focus point. The camera will ignore all other points and use only the point you specify.
- **Dynamic-Area AF.** This mode uses a focus point of your choosing as the primary focus but uses information from the surrounding points if your subject happens to move away from the point. You can select from three different areas: 9-point, 21-point, and 39-point. The area you use depends on how much movement there will be.

Setting the AF-Area mode to Dynamic

1. To set the AF-Area mode, press the **i** button on the back of the camera.
2. Use the Multi-selector to highlight the AF-Area mode, and then press the OK button (**A**).
3. Use the Multi-selector to choose the desired Dynamic-Area AF mode, and press OK (**B**).

A

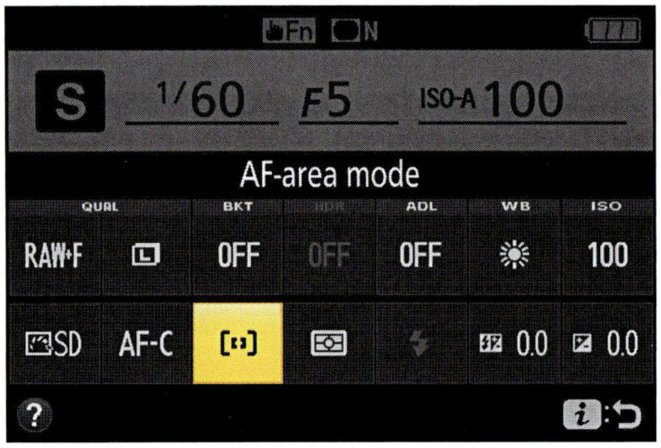

B

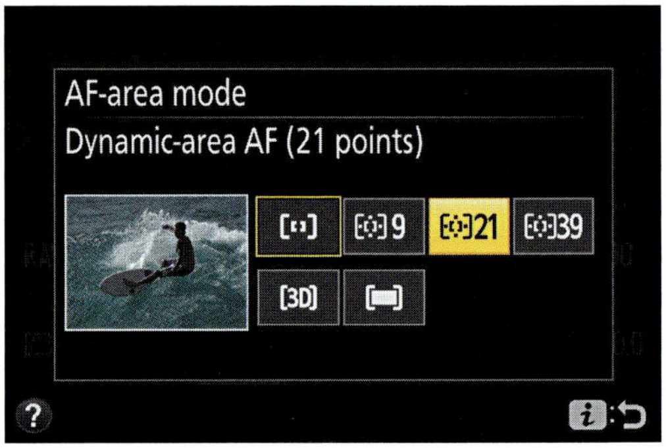

To select a focus point you want to use, simply move the Multi-selector up, down, left, or right until the desired point is highlighted in your viewfinder. Pressing the OK button in the center of the Multi-selector will reset your focus point to the center position. The touch screen has a cool function called Touch Fn, which essentially turns the touch screen into an additional function button. Check out page 268 of the Reference Manual PDF to see how to configure Touch Fn for focus-point selection.

Note that the AF-Area mode is used to select the method with which the camera will focus the lens. This is different from the AF points, which are a cluster of small points visible in the viewfinder that are used to determine where you want the lens to focus (**Figure 5.6**). If you don't see Dynamic as an option, go back and choose the AF-C focus mode.

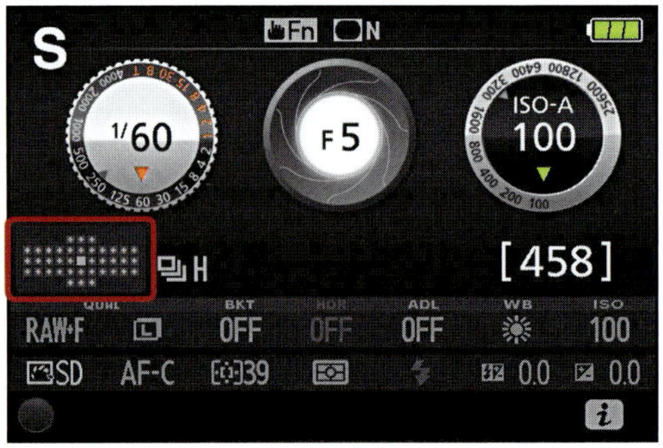

Figure 5.6 The Automatic Focus (AF) points are the 39 small boxes arranged in your viewfinder and represented by the icon in the lower-left area of the info screen.

Stop and Go with 3D-Tracking AF

If you are going to be changing between a moving target and one that is still, consider using the 3D-Tracking AF mode. This mode mixes both the AF-S and Dynamic modes for shooting a subject that goes from stationary to moving, without having to adjust your focus mode.

When you have a stationary subject, simply place your selected focus point on your subject and the camera will focus on it. If your subject begins to move out of focus, the camera will track the movement, keeping a sharp focus.

For example, suppose you are shooting a football game. The quarterback has brought the team to the line and is standing behind the center, waiting for the ball to be hiked. If you are using the 3D-Tracking AF mode, you can place your focus point on the quarterback and start taking pictures of him as he stands at the line. As soon as the ball is hiked and the action starts, the camera will switch to tracking mode and follow his movement within the frame. This technique can be a little tricky at first, but once you master it, it will make your action shooting effortless.

To select 3D-Tracking, simply follow the same steps listed for selecting Dynamic AF-Area mode earlier, but instead select the 3D-Tracking mode. It is important to know that the 3D-Tracking AF mode uses color and contrast to locate and then follow the subject, so this mode might be less effective when everything is similar in tone or color.

Choosing a focus mode

Selecting the proper focus mode depends largely on what type of subject you are photographing. Single-Point is typically best for stationary subjects. It allows you to determine exactly where you want your focus to be and then recompose your image while holding the focus in place. If you are taking pictures of an active subject that is moving quickly, trying to set a focus point with Single-Point can be difficult, if not impossible. This is when you want to rely on the Dynamic and 3D-Tracking modes to quickly assess the subject distance and set your lens focus. This can be especially helpful if the subject distance is varying constantly.

Manual Focus for Anticipated Action

While I use the automatic focus modes for the majority of my shooting, there are times when I like to fall back on manual focus. This is usually when I know when and where the action will occur and I want to capture the subject as it crosses a certain plane of focus. For example, in sports like motocross or auto racing, the subjects are on a defined track and I know exactly where I want to capture the action. I could try tracking the subject, but sometimes the view is obscured by a curve. By prefocusing the camera, all I have to do is wait for the subject to approach my point of focus and then start firing the camera.

Take a look at **Figure 5.7**. If you want to get up close and personal shooting baseball, I strongly suggest attending a local Minor League Baseball game. My friend Dave Cleaveland had a press pass to shoot the Portland Sea Dogs and was kind enough to invite me along. We spent most of the game inside the home team dugout and had a blast. Unfortunately, the game got called due to fog (Portland, Maine, is a port town after all) but not before we got some awesome action shots. We were pretty close to first base, so with the falling light level and increasing fog, I used the single-focus-point method to focus on the exact spot I wanted and then switched the lens to manual focus and waited for the play. As soon as the runner started moving, I started firing in Continuous mode to try to nail the peak of the action (he was safe). Many thanks to Dave and the Sea Dogs for a great night!

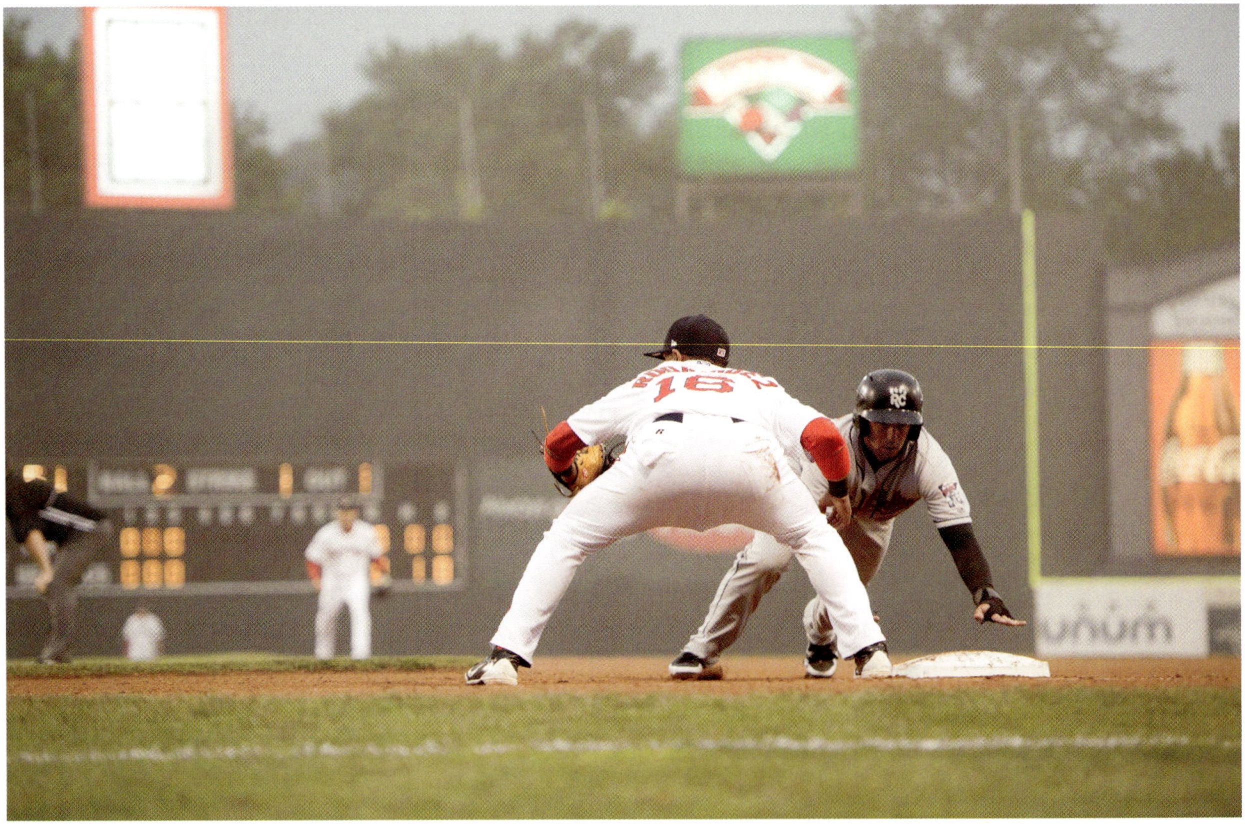

Figure 5.7 **Prefocus the camera to a point where you know the subject will be and wait for the action.**

ISO 1800 • 1/500 sec. • f/2.8 • 140mm lens

Drive modes

The drive mode determines how fast your camera will take pictures. Single-Frame is for taking one photograph at a time. With every full press of the shutter release button, the camera will take a single image. Continuous mode allows for a more rapid capture rate. Think of it like a machine gun. When you are using Continuous mode, the camera will continue to take pictures as long as the shutter release button is held down.

Keeping Up with the Continuous Shooting Mode

Getting great focus is one thing, but capturing the best moment on the sensor can be difficult if you are shooting just one frame at a time. In the world of sports, and in life in general, things move pretty fast. If you blink, you might miss it. The same can be said for shooting in Single-Frame mode. Fortunately, your D5500 comes equipped with a Continuous shooting—or burst—mode that lets you capture a series of images at up to 5 frames a second (**Figure 5.8**).

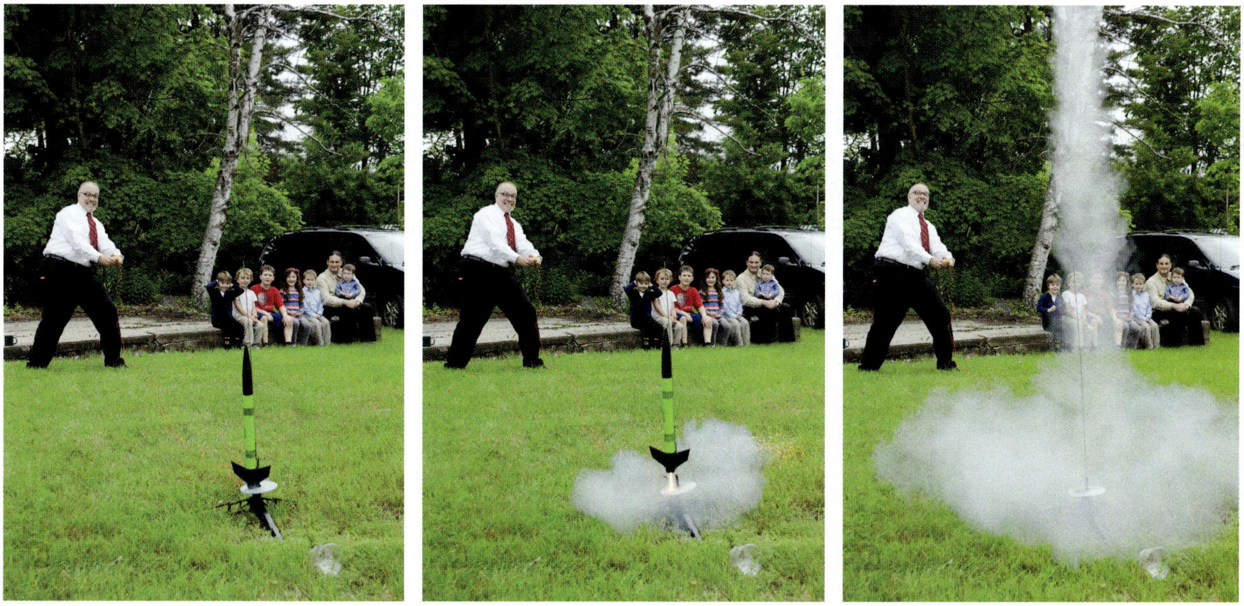

Figure 5.8 Using the Continuous shooting mode means that you are sure to capture the peak of the action.

ISO 400 • 1/500 sec. • f/4.5 • 28mm lens

Setting up and shooting in the Continuous shooting mode

1. Press the Release Mode button on the front of the camera (under the lens release button).
2. Use the Multi-selector to highlight Continuous H (High), and then press OK (**A**).

A

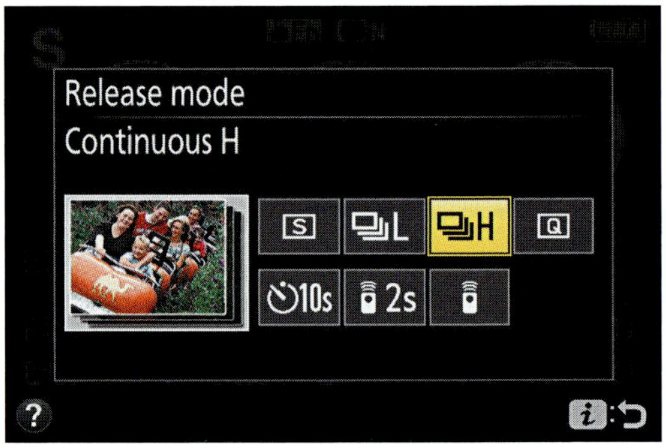

Your camera has an internal memory, called a buffer, where images are stored while they are being processed prior to being moved to your memory card. Depending on the image format you are using, the buffer might fill up, and the camera will stop shooting until space is made in the buffer for new images. The camera readout in the viewfinder tells you how many frames you have available in burst mode. As you shoot, the number will go down and then back up as the images are written to the memory card.

A Sense of Motion

Shooting action isn't always about freezing the action. At times you want to convey a sense of motion so that the viewer can get a feel for the movement and flow of an event. Two techniques you can use to achieve this effect are panning and motion blur.

Panning

Panning has been used for decades to capture the speed of a moving object as it moves across the frame. It doesn't work well for subjects that are moving toward or away from you. Panning is achieved by following your subject across your frame, moving your camera along with the subject, and using a slower-than-normal shutter speed so the background (and sometimes even a bit of the subject) has a sideways blur but the main portion of your subject is sharp and blur-free. The key to a great panning shot is selecting the right shutter speed: Too fast and you won't get the desired blurring of the background; too slow and the subject will have too much blur and will not be recognizable. Practice the technique until you can achieve a smooth motion with your camera that follows along with your subject. The other thing to remember when panning is to follow through even after the shutter has closed. This will keep the motion smooth and give you better images.

In **Figure 5.9**, I used the panning technique to follow the jockey as he raced down the track. I set the camera to the Continuous shooting mode, and I used Shutter Priority mode to select a shutter speed of 1/25 of a second while the focus mode was on Dynamic. I wasn't worried about the depth of field because I knew that the movement of my camera at the slow shutter speed would blur the background.

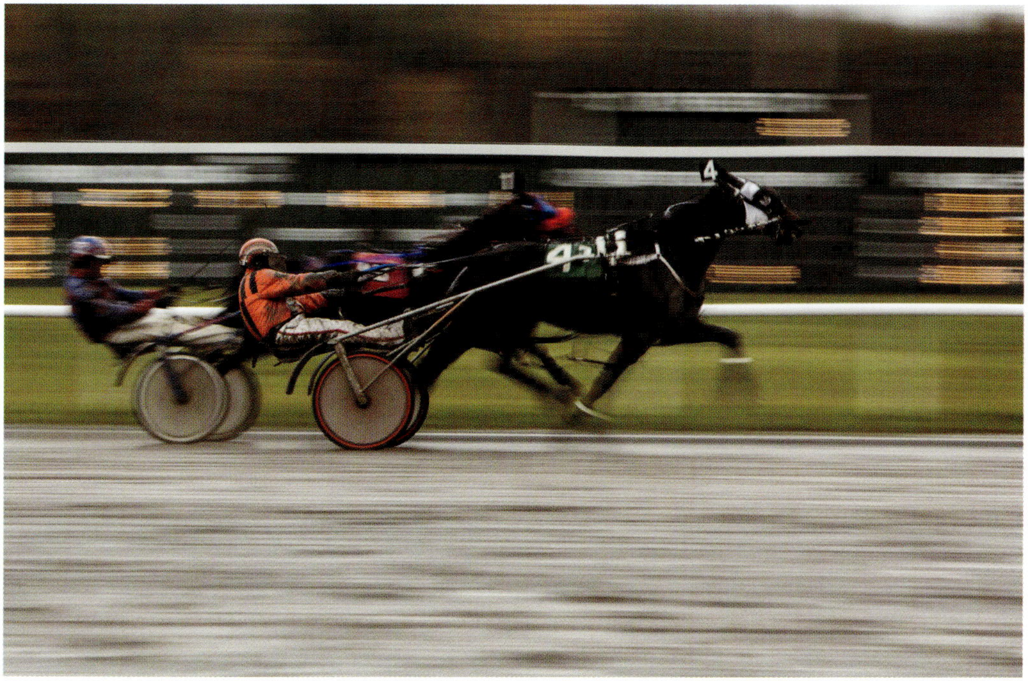

Figure 5.9
Following the subject as it moves across the field of view allows for a slower shutter speed and adds a sense of motion.

ISO 100 • 1/25 sec. • f/8 • 105mm lens

Motion blur

Another way to let the viewer in on the feel of the action is to simply include some blur in the image. This isn't accidental blur from choosing the wrong shutter speed. This blur is more exaggerated, and it tells a story. In **Figure 5.10**, I was interested in capturing the feeling of motion as the kids went around the track, so I set the shutter speed to 1/30 of a second to ensure that there would be motion blur as they rode past.

Just as in panning, there is no preordained shutter speed to use for this effect. It is simply a matter of trial and error until you have a look that conveys the action. You'll also want to make sure some area of the subject is frozen. The key to this technique is the correct shutter speed combined with keeping the camera still during the exposure. You are trying to capture the motion of the subject, not of the photographer or the camera, so use a good shooting stance or even a tripod.

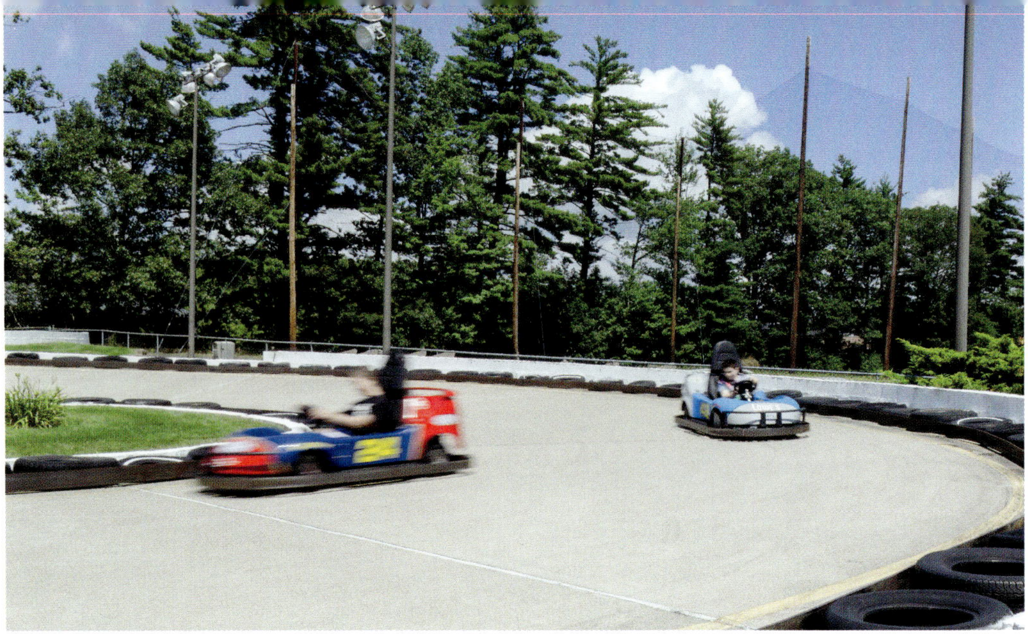

Figure 5.10
The movement of the cars, coupled with the slow shutter speed, conveys a sense of motion.

ISO 100 • 1/30 sec. • f/22 • 20mm lens

Tips for Shooting Action

Give them somewhere to go

Whether you are shooting something as simple as your child's soccer match or as complex as the aerial acrobatics of a motorcycle jumper, where you place the subject in the frame is as important as how well you expose the image. A poorly composed shot can ruin a great moment by not holding the viewer's attention.

The one mistake I see many times in action photography is that the photographer doesn't use the frame properly. If you are dealing with a subject that is moving horizontally across your field of view, give the subject somewhere to go by placing him to the side of the frame, with his motion leading toward the middle of the frame (**Figure 5.11**). This offsetting of the subject will introduce a sense of direction and anticipation for the viewer. Unless you are going to completely fill the image with the action, try to avoid placing your subject in the middle of the frame.

Get in front of the action

Here's another one. When shooting action, show the action coming toward you (**Figure 5.12**), not going away from you. People want to see faces. Faces convey the action, the drive, the sense of urgency, and the emotion of the moment. So if you are shooting action involving people, always position yourself so that the action is either coming at you or is at least perpendicular to your position.

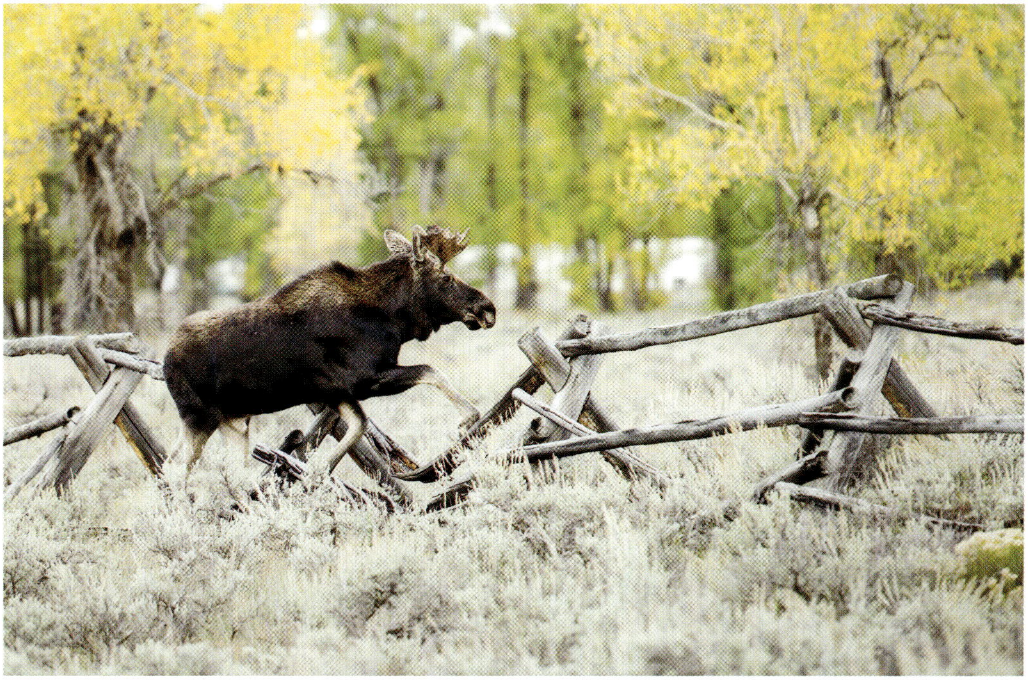

Figure 5.11
Try to leave space in front of your subject to lead the action in a direction.

ISO 450 • 1/250 sec. • f/2.8 • 200mm lens

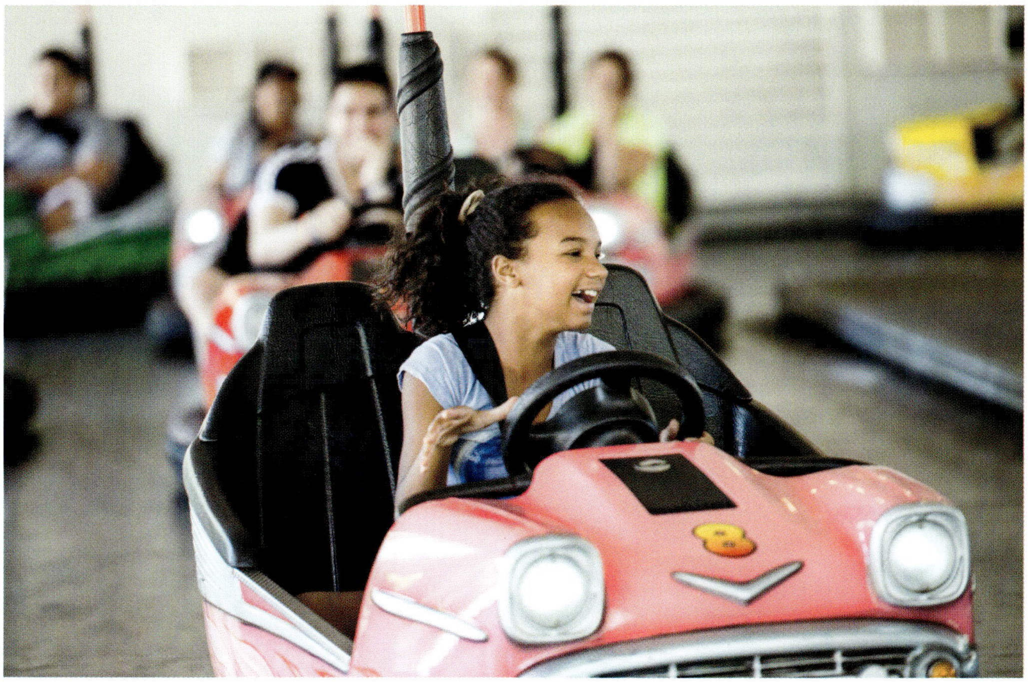

Figure 5.12
Shooting from the front with a telephoto lens gives a feeling that the action is coming right at you.

ISO 2500 • 1/1000 sec. • f/2.8 • 200mm lens

Shoot in Manual mode to lock in your exposure

Aperture Priority and Shutter Priority modes are great, but sometimes it pays to just do things yourself. If you find yourself shooting in an environment where the action is moving across backgrounds that will play havoc with your meter readings, it might be best to set up your shot in Manual mode.

Photographing kids playing in the surf on a bright, sunny day can be problematic for the camera meter due to the dark water and fluctuating amount of white foam. After some trial and error in Manual mode, I settled on a combination of settings that would freeze the action, blur the background, and not blow out the highlights on the breaking waves (**Figure 5.13**).

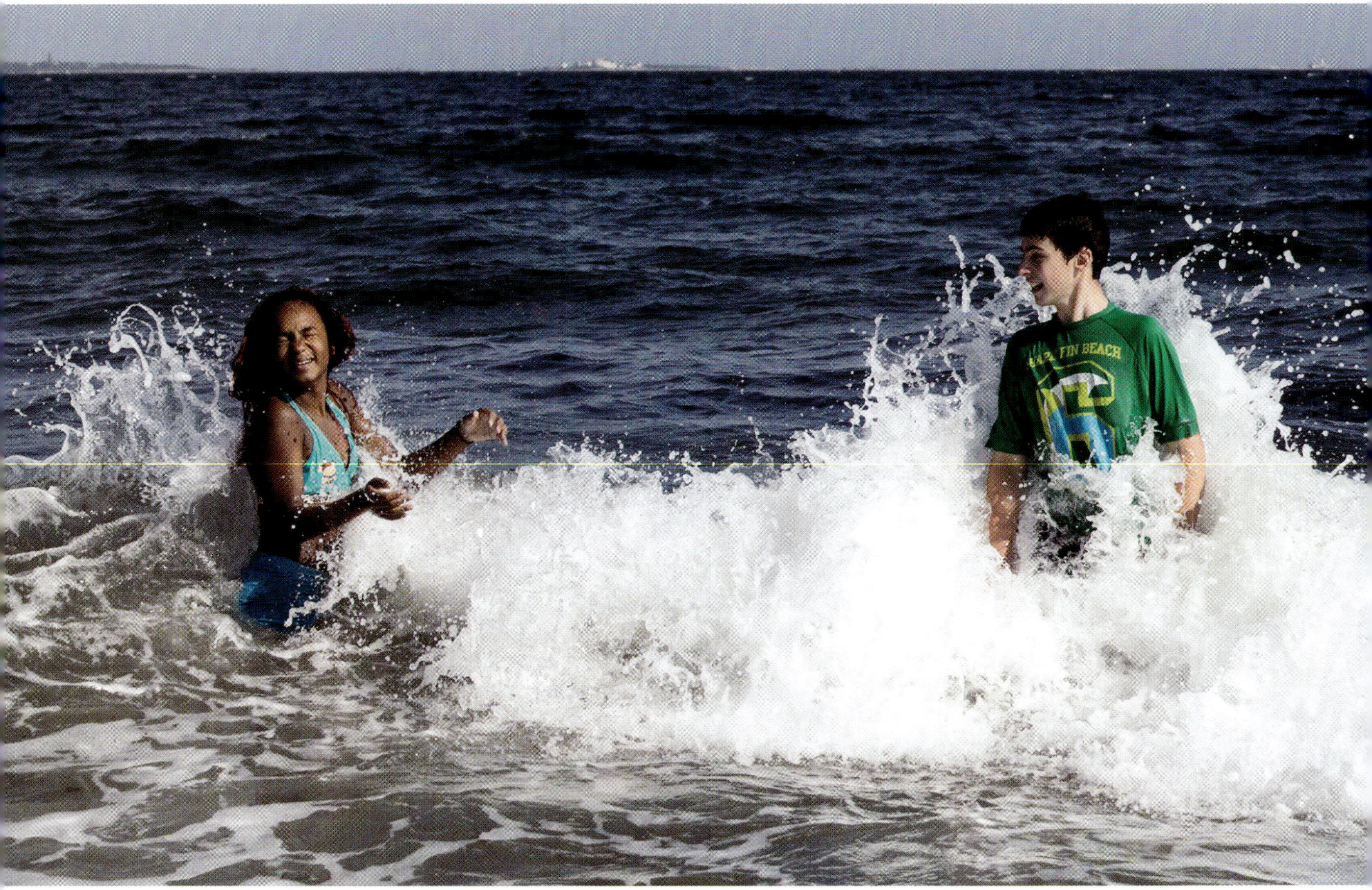

Figure 5.13 Sometimes it pays to shoot in Manual mode.

ISO 100 • 1/1250 sec. • f/7.1 • 85mm lens

Chapter 5 Assignments

These assignments will give you practice with different ways of capturing subjects in motion and keeping them in focus.

Studying the mechanics of motion

For this first assignment, you need to find some action. Explore the relationship between the speed of an object and its direction of travel. Use the same shutter speed to record your subject moving toward you and across your view. By using the same shutter speed for both, you can compare the difference made by the direction of travel.

Experimenting with wide vs. telephoto

Find a moving subject, but this time, use a wide-angle lens and then a telephoto. See how the telephoto setting on the zoom lens requires faster shutter speeds than the lens at its wide-angle setting.

Getting a feel for focusing modes

Starting with Dynamic mode, find a moving subject and get familiar with the way the mode works. Now repeat the process using the 3D-Tracking AF mode. The point of the exercise is to become familiar enough with the two modes to decide which one to use for a photographic situation.

Anticipating the spot using manual focus

Find a subject you know will cross a specific line on which you can prefocus. A street with moderate traffic works well. Focus on a spot on the street that the cars will travel across (don't forget to set your lens for Manual focus). To do this right, you need to set the drive mode on the camera to the Continuous mode. Now, when a car approaches the spot, start shooting. Try shooting in 3- or 4-frame bursts.

Following the action

Panning is a great way to show motion. To begin, find a subject that will move across your path at a steady speed and practice following it in your viewfinder from side to side. Now, with the camera in Shutter Priority mode, set your shutter speed to 1/30 of a second and the focus mode to Dynamic. Pan along with the subject and shoot as it moves across your view. Experiment with different shutter speeds and focal lengths. Panning is one of those skills that takes some time to master, so try it with different types of subjects moving at different speeds.

Feeling the movement

Instead of panning with the motion, use a stationary camera position and adjust the shutter speed until you get a blurred effect that gives the sense of motion while still allowing you to identify the subject. There is a big difference between a slightly blurred photo that looks like you picked the wrong shutter speed and one that looks as if it's intentionally showing motion. As with panning, it will take some experimentation to find just the right shutter speed to achieve the desired effect.

Share your results with the book's Flickr group!
Join the group here: flickr.com/groups/nikond5500_fromsnapshotstogreatshots

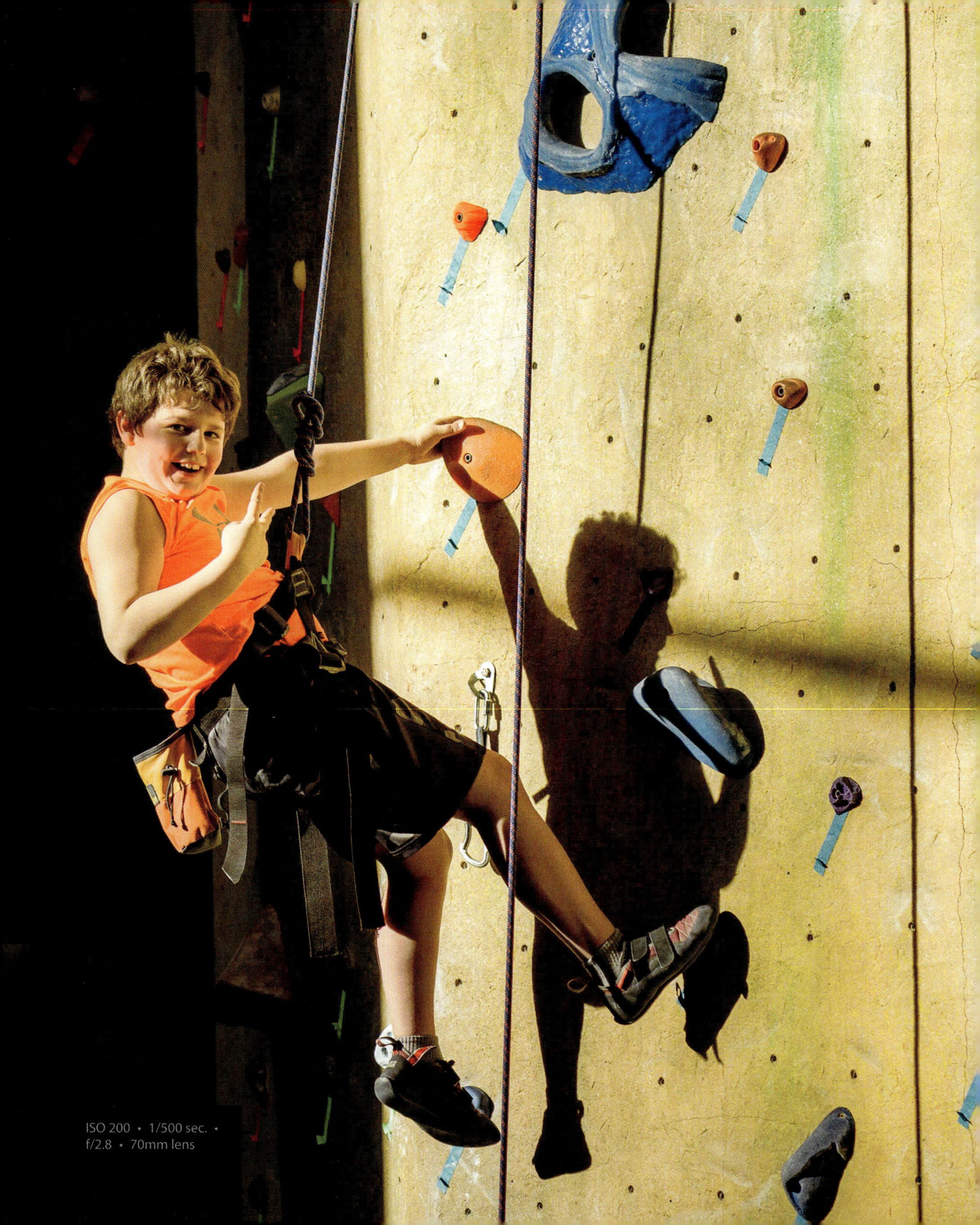

ISO 200 • 1/500 sec. •
f/2.8 • 70mm lens

6

Say Cheese!

Settings and Features to Make Great Portraits

Taking pictures of people is one of the great joys of photography. You will experience a tremendous sense of accomplishment when you capture the spirit and personality of someone in a photograph. At the same time, you have a big responsibility, because the person in front of the camera is depending on you to make him look good. You can't always change how someone looks, but you can control the way you photograph that individual. In this chapter, we will explore some camera features and techniques that can help you create great portraits.

Poring Over the Picture

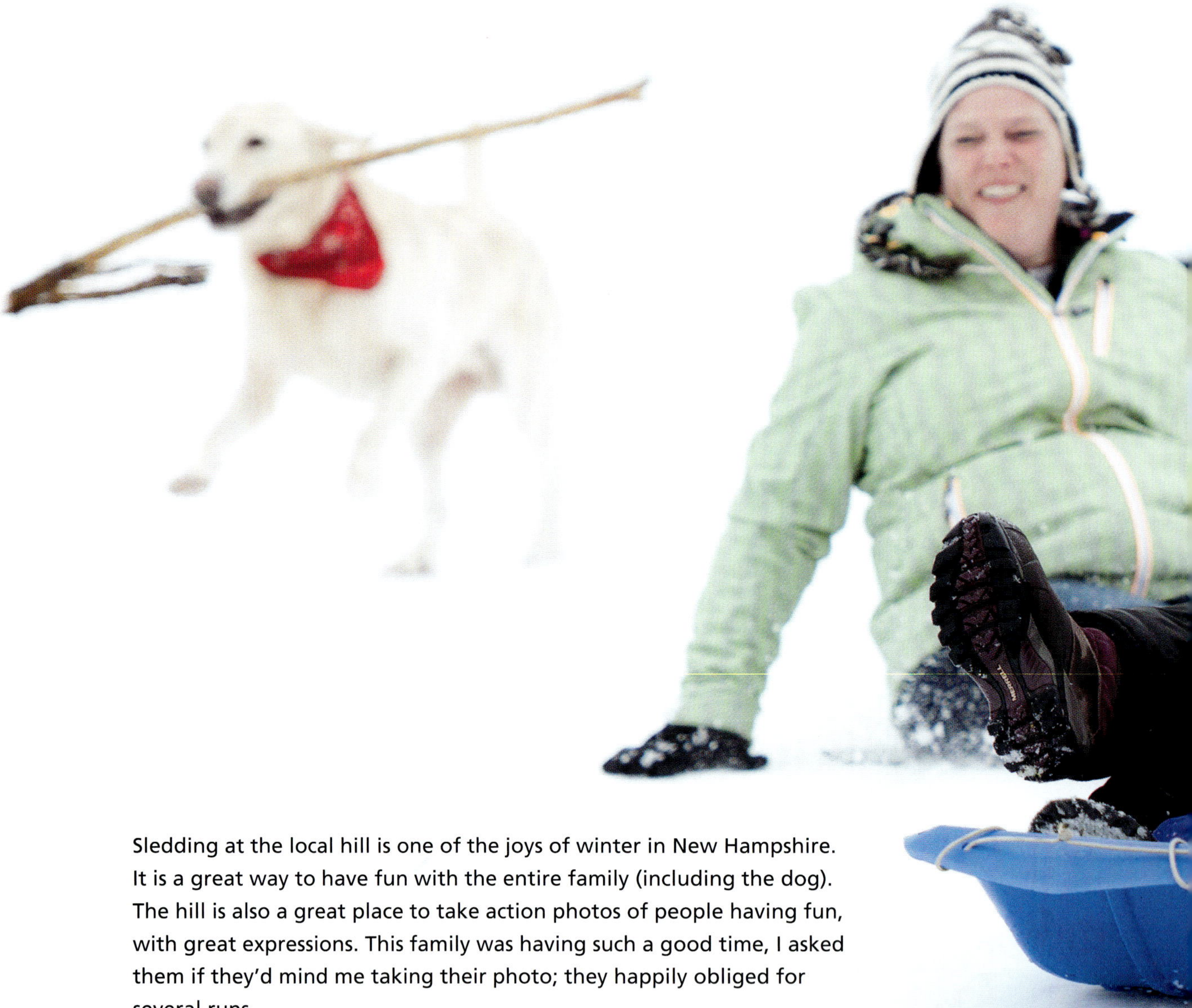

Sledding at the local hill is one of the joys of winter in New Hampshire. It is a great way to have fun with the entire family (including the dog). The hill is also a great place to take action photos of people having fun, with great expressions. This family was having such a good time, I asked them if they'd mind me taking their photo; they happily obliged for several runs.

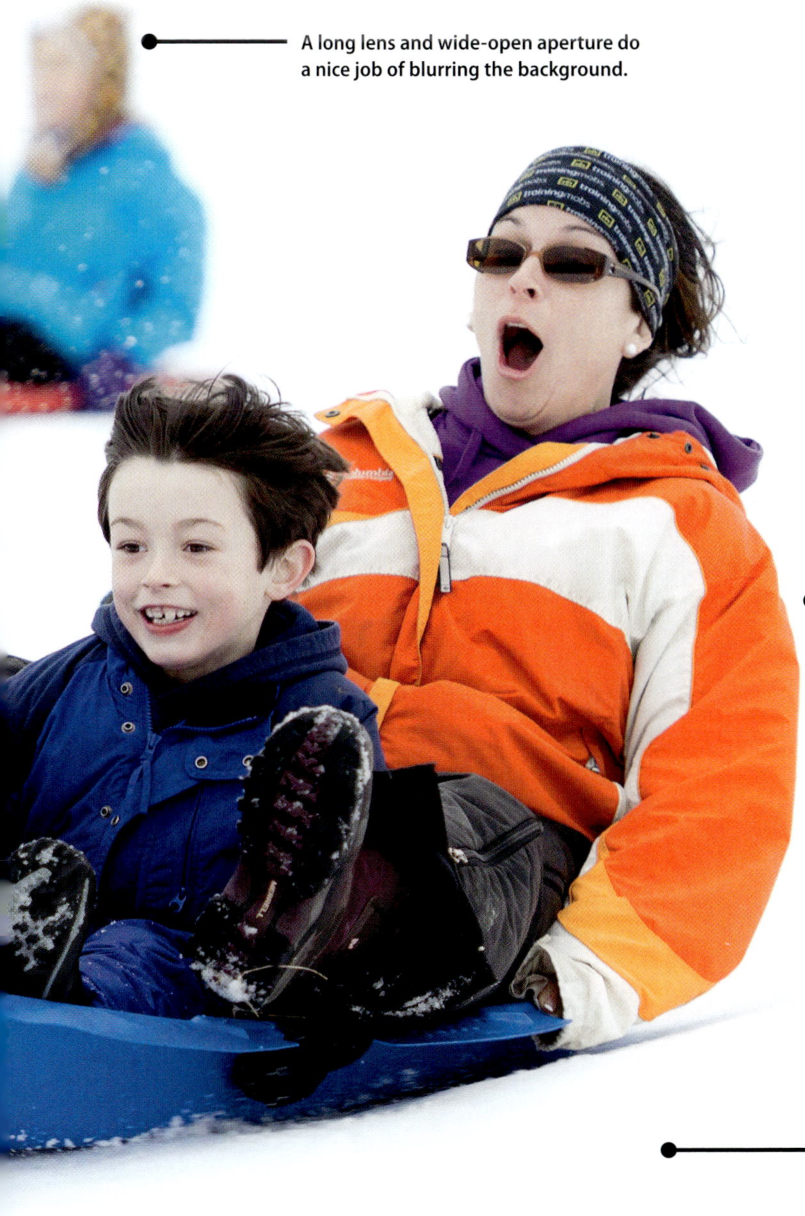

A long lens and wide-open aperture do a nice job of blurring the background.

Setting the focus mode to AF-C was critical to keeping a moving subject in focus.

I set the exposure compensation to +1 stop because the snow was causing the meter to underexpose the image.

ISO 250 • 1/500 sec. • f/2.8 • 140mm lens

Automatic Portrait Mode

In Chapter 3, we reviewed all of the automatic scene modes. One of them, Portrait mode, is dedicated to shooting portraits. While this is not my preferred camera setting, it is a great jumping-off point for those who are just starting out. The key to using this mode is to understand what is going on with the camera so when you venture farther into portrait photography, you can expand on the settings and get the most from your camera and, more importantly, your subject.

Whether you are photographing an individual or a group, the emphasis should always be on the subject. Portrait mode uses a larger aperture setting to keep the depth of field very narrow, which means the background will appear slightly blurred or out of focus. To take full advantage of this effect, use a medium- to telephoto-length lens. Also, keep a close distance to your subject. If you shoot from too far away, the narrow depth of field will not be as effective.

Aperture Priority Mode

If you took a poll of portrait photographers to see which shooting mode they use most often for portraits, the answer would certainly be Aperture Priority (**A**) mode. Selecting the right aperture is important for placing the most critically sharp area of the photo on your subject while simultaneously blurring all of the distracting background clutter (**Figure 6.1**). Not only will a large aperture give the narrowest depth of field, it will also allow you to shoot in lower light levels at lower ISO settings.

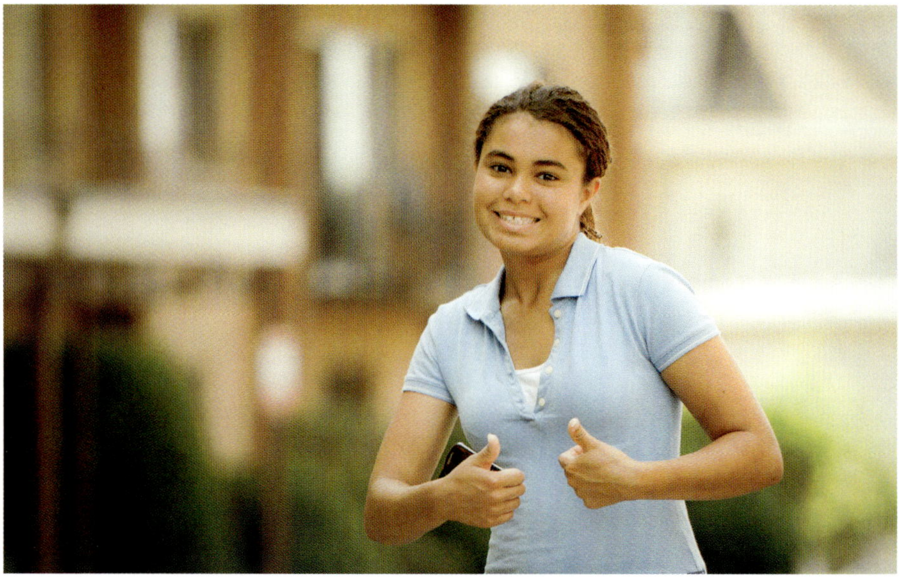

Figure 6.1
Using a wide aperture, especially with a longer lens, blurs distracting background details.

ISO 200 • 1/400 sec. • f/2.8 • 200mm lens

This isn't to say that you have to use the largest aperture on your lens. A good place to begin is f/5.6. This will give you enough depth of field to keep the entire face in focus while providing enough blur to eliminate distractions in the background. This isn't a hard-and-fast setting; f/5.6 is just a good all-around number to start with. Your aperture might change depending on the focal length of the lens you are using and on the amount of blur you want for your foreground and background elements.

Go wide for environmental portraits

There will be times when your subject's environment is of great significance to the story you want to tell. This might mean using a smaller aperture to get more detail in the background or foreground. Once again, by using Aperture Priority mode you can set your aperture to a higher f-stop, such as f/8 or f/11, and include the important details of the scene that surrounds your subject.

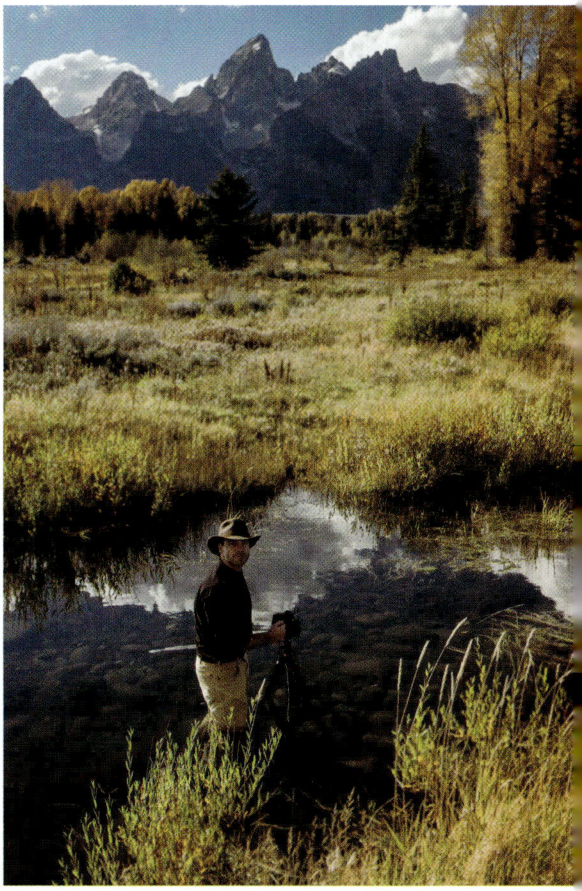

Figure 6.2 A wide-angle lens allows you to capture more of the environment in the photo without having to increase the distance between you and the subject.

ISO 100 • 1/20 sec. • f/11 • 35mm lens

Using a wider-than-normal lens can assist in getting more depth of field as well as showing the surrounding area. A wide-angle lens requires less stopping down of the aperture (making the aperture smaller) to achieve an acceptable depth of field. This is due to the fact that wide-angle lenses cover a greater area, so the depth of field appears to cover a greater percentage of the scene.

A wider lens might also be necessary to relay more information about the scenery. For example, while in Grand Teton National Park with my friend Levi Sim, I just had to photograph him making a photo while standing in the stream. I used a lens wide enough to provide context of the scene and an aperture small enough to keep it in focus (**Figure 6.2**). Select a lens length that is wide enough to tell the story but not so wide that you distort the subject. There's little in the world of portraiture quite as unflattering as giving someone a big, distorted nose (unless you are going for that sort of look). When shooting a portrait with a wide-angle lens, keep the subject away from the edge of the frame. This will reduce the distortion, especially in very wide focal lengths. As the lens length increases, distortion will be reduced. I generally don't like to go wider than about 24mm for portraits.

Metering basics

Your camera has multiple metering modes, but the way they work is very similar. A light meter measures the amount of light being reflected off your subject and then renders a suggested exposure value based on the brightness of the subject and the ISO setting of the sensor. To establish this value, the meter averages all of the brightness values to come up with a middle tone, sometimes referred to as 18 percent gray. The exposure value is then rendered based on this middle gray value. This means that a white wall would be underexposed and a black wall would be overexposed in an effort to make each one appear gray. To assist with special lighting situations, the D5500 has three metering modes: Matrix (**Figure 6.3**), which uses the entire frame; Spot (**Figure 6.4**), which takes specific readings from small areas (often used with a gray card); and Center-Weighted (**Figure 6.5**), which looks at the entire frame but places most of the exposure emphasis on the center of the frame.

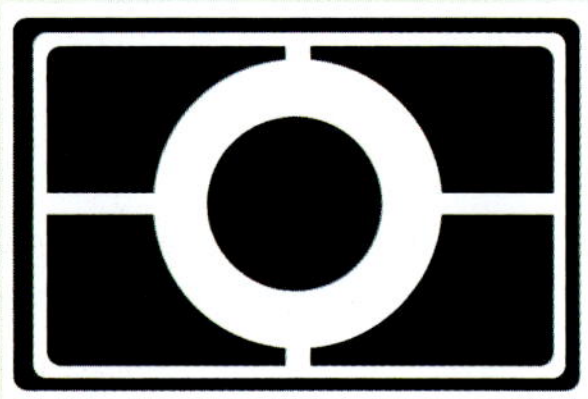

Figure 6.3 The Matrix metering mode uses the entire frame.

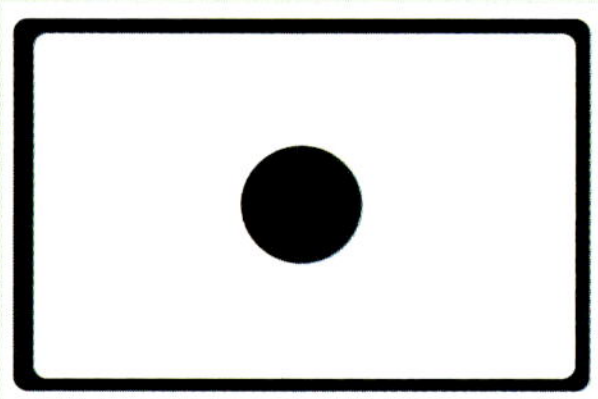

Figure 6.4 The Spot metering mode uses a very small area of the frame.

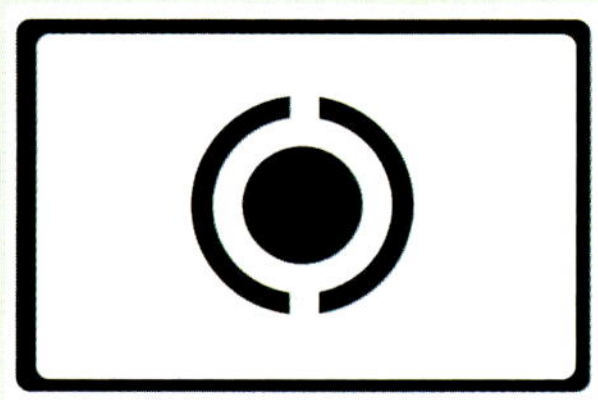

Figure 6.5 The Center-Weighted metering mode looks at the entire frame but emphasizes the center of it.

Metering Modes for Portraits

For most portrait situations, the Matrix metering mode is ideal. (For more on how metering works, see the "Metering Basics" sidebar.) This mode measures light values from all portions of the viewfinder and then establishes a proper exposure for the scene. The only problem you might encounter when using this metering mode is when you have very light or dark backgrounds in your portrait shots.

In these instances, the meter might be fooled into using the wrong exposure information because it will be trying to lighten or darken the entire scene based on the prominence of dark or light areas (**Figure 6.6**). You can deal with this in one of two ways: You can use the Exposure Compensation feature, which I cover in Chapter 7, to dial in adjustments for overexposure and underexposure. Or you can change the metering mode to Center-Weighted metering. The Center-Weighted metering mode uses only the center area of the viewfinder (about 9 percent) to get its exposure information. This is the best way to achieve proper exposure for most portraits; metering off skin tones, averaged with hair and clothing, will often give a more accurate exposure. This metering mode is also great to use when the subject is strongly backlit (**Figure 6.7**).

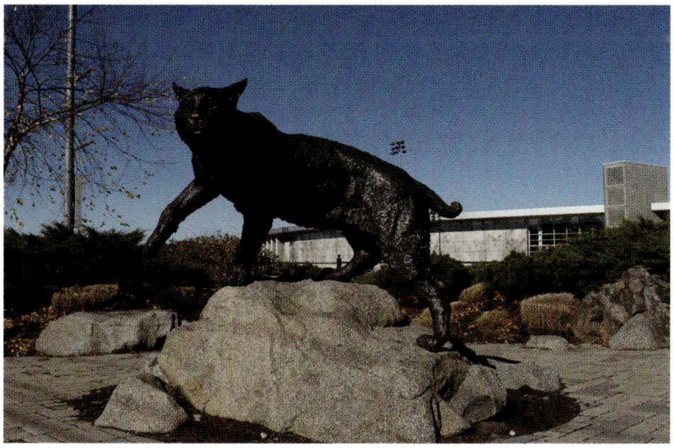

Figure 6.6 The bright background reflected a lot of light, which fooled the meter into choosing a slightly underexposed setting for the photo.

ISO 100 • 1/640 sec. • f/8 • 30mm lens

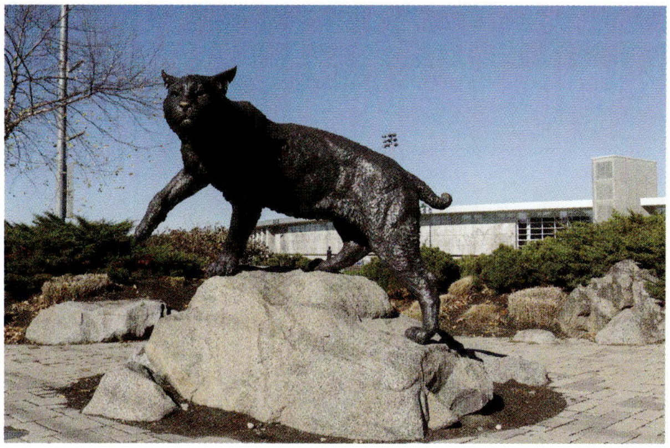

Figure 6.7 When I switched to the Center-Weighted metering mode, my camera was able to ignore much of the background and add a little more time to the exposure.

ISO 100 • 1/320 sec. • f/8 • 30mm lens

Setting your metering mode to Center-Weighted metering

1. Press the **i** button to activate the cursor in the information screen.
2. Use the Multi-selector to move the cursor to the Metering icon, and press the OK button (**A**).
3. Select the Center-Weighted icon, and press the OK button to lock in the change (**B**).

A

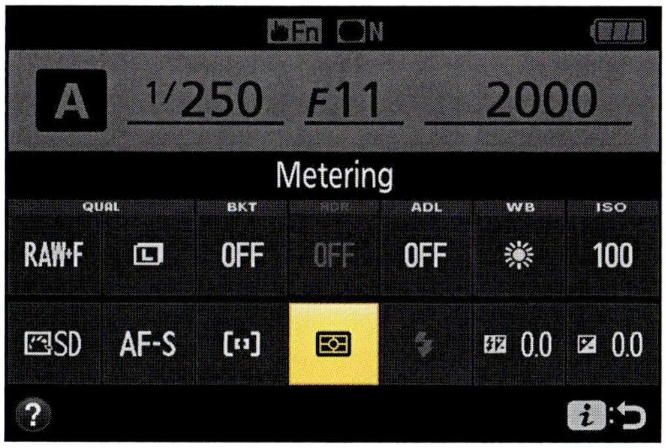

B

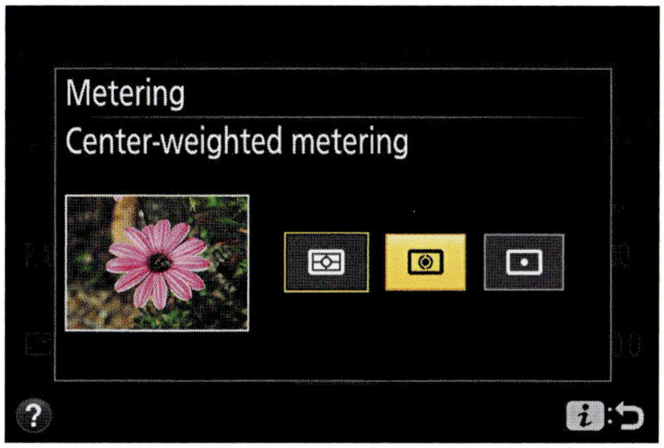

The AE-L (Auto Exposure Lock) Feature

Sometimes your subject is not in the center of the frame but you still want to use the Center-Weighted metering mode. How can you get an accurate reading if the subject isn't in the center? Try using the AE-L (Auto Exposure Lock) feature to hold the exposure setting while you recompose.

AE Lock lets you use the exposure setting from any portion of the scene that you think is appropriate and then lock that setting in regardless of how the scene looks when you recompose. An example of this is when you're shooting a photograph of someone and a large amount of blue sky appears in the picture. Normally, the meter might be fooled by all that bright sky and try to reduce the exposure. Using AE Lock, you can establish the correct metering by zooming in on the subject (or even pointing the camera toward the ground), taking the meter reading and locking it in with the AE-L feature, and then recomposing and taking your photo with the locked-in exposure.

Shooting with the Auto Exposure Lock feature

1. Find the AE-L button on the back of the camera, and place your thumb on it.
2. While looking through the viewfinder, place the focus point on your subject, press the shutter release button halfway to get a meter reading, and focus the camera.
3. Press and hold the AE-L button to lock in the meter reading. You should see the AE-L indicator in the viewfinder.
4. While pressing in the AE-L button, recompose your shot, and take the photo.
5. To take more than one photo without having to take another meter reading, just hold down the AE-L button until you are done using the meter setting.

Manual Callout

There is a way to lock in your AE-L reading so you can continue shooting without having to hold the AE-L button. This involves changing the button function in the Custom Setting menu, but I prefer to leave this feature turned off because I would, more often than not, forget that it is on and end up using the wrong metering for a new subject. If you want to learn more about this feature, check out page 267 of the Reference Manual PDF.

Focusing: The Eyes Have It

It has been said that the eyes are the windows to the soul, and nothing could be truer when you are taking a photograph of someone (**Figure 6.8**). You could have the perfect composition and exposure, but if the eyes aren't sharp the entire image suffers. While your D5500 gives you many different focusing modes to choose from, for portrait work you can't beat AF-S (Single-Servo AF) mode using a single focusing point. AF-S focusing will establish a single focus for the lens and then hold it until you take the photograph; the other focusing modes continue focusing until the photograph is taken. The single-point selection lets you place the focusing point right on your subject's eye and set that spot as the critical focus spot. Using AF-S mode lets you get that focus and recompose all in one motion.

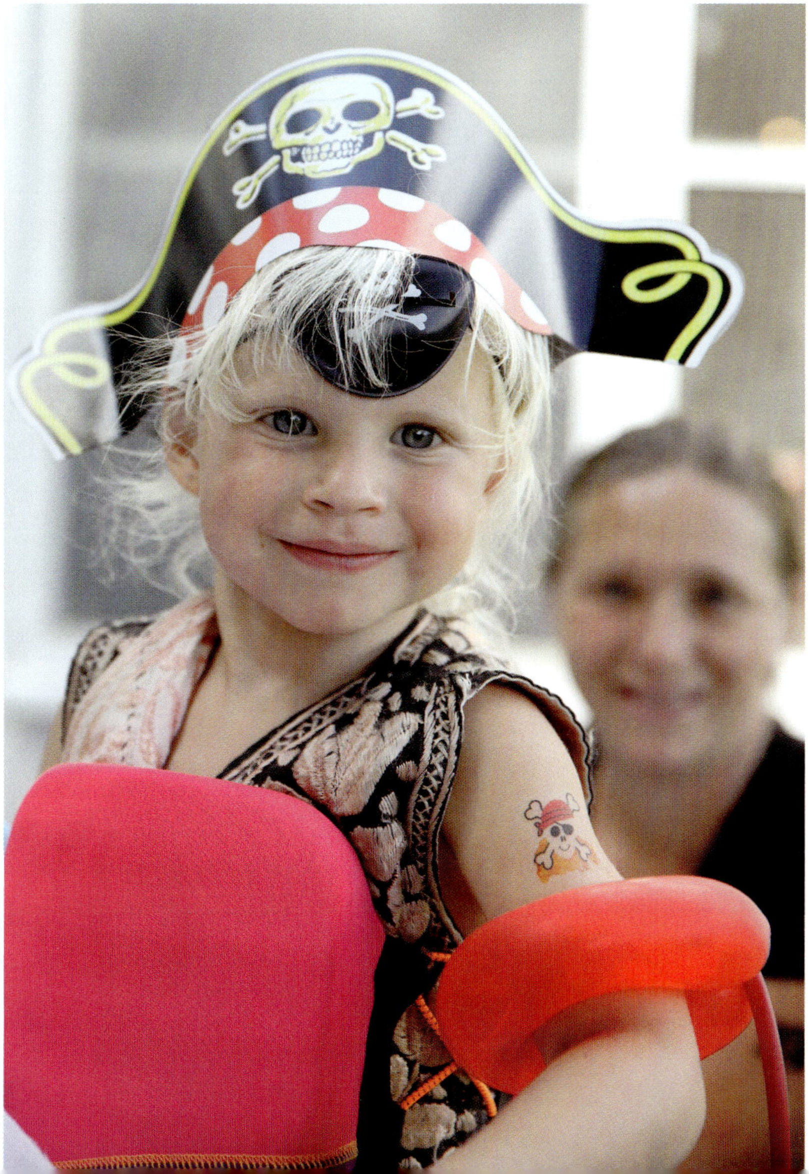

Figure 6.8
When photographing people, you should almost always place the emphasis on the eyes.

ISO 200 • 1/400 sec. • f/3.2 • 65mm lens

Setting up for AF-S focus mode

1. Press the **i** button to activate the cursor in the information screen.
2. Use the Multi-selector to move the cursor to the Focus mode icon, and press the OK button (**A**).
3. Select the AF-S setting, and then press the OK button (**B**).

A

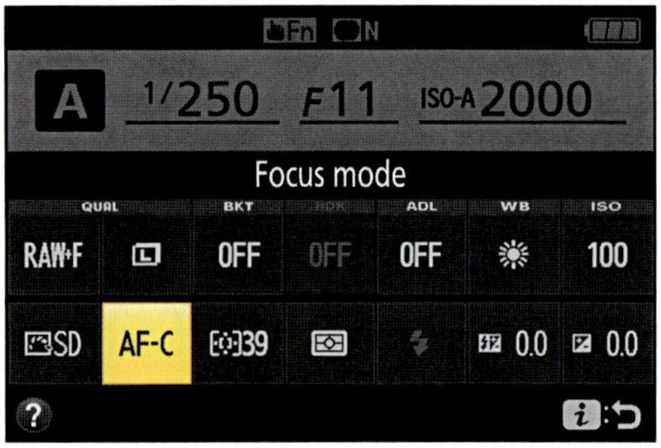

B

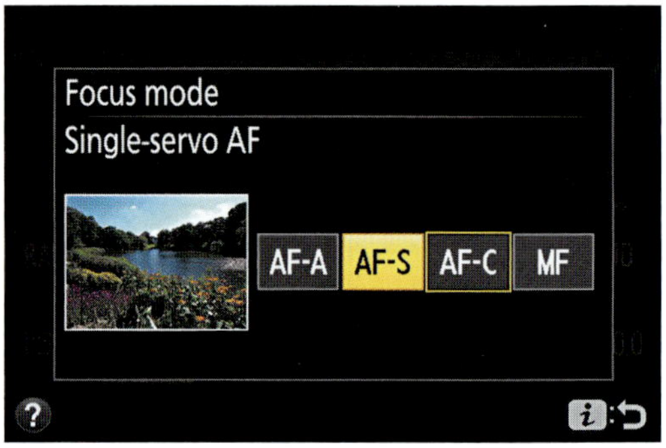

Setting your focus to a single point

1. Press the **i** button to activate the cursor in the information screen.
2. Use the Multi-selector to move the cursor to the AF-Area mode icon, and press the OK button (**C**).
3. Select the Single-Point AF icon, and press the OK button (**D**).
4. When you are back in shooting mode, use the Multi-selector to move the focus point to one of the 39 available positions. These are visible while looking through the viewfinder but also on the information screen.

C

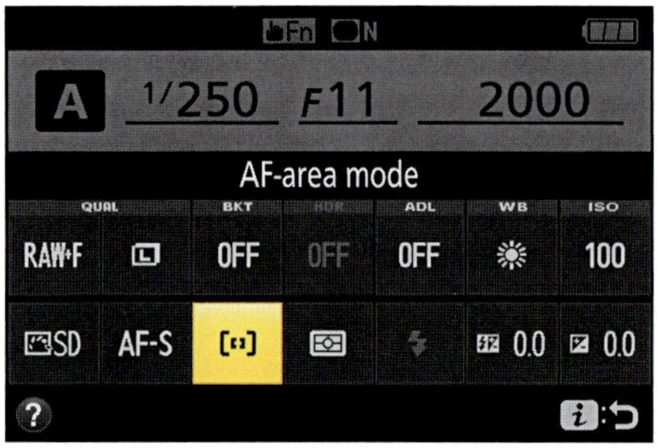

D

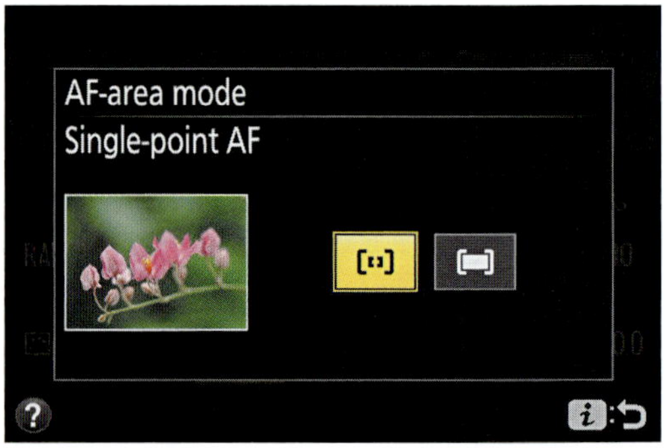

Now, to shoot using this focus point, place that point on your subject's eye, and press the shutter button halfway until focus locks (you will hear the chirp if the audible beep is turned on). While still holding the shutter button down halfway, recompose if necessary and take your shot.

I typically use the center point for focus selection. I find it easier to place that point directly on the location where my critical focus should be established and then recompose the shot. Even though the single point can be selected from other focus points, it typically takes longer to figure out where that point should be in relation to my subject. By using the center point, I can quickly establish focus and get on with my shooting.

Classic Black and White Portraits

There is something timeless about a black and white portrait. It eliminates the distraction of color and puts all the emphasis on the subject. To get great black and whites without having to resort to any image-processing software, set your picture control to Monochrome (**Figure 6.9**). You should know that the picture controls are automatically applied when shooting with the JPEG file format. If you are shooting in RAW, the picture that shows up on your rear LCD display will look black and white, but it will appear as a color image if you open it in non-Nikon RAW processing software (like Adobe Photoshop or Lightroom). This is because the nature of RAW data is that it hasn't been processed by the camera. If using Nikon's ViewNX 2 or Capture NX-D software, you'll see the assigned picture control when you first open the photo, but you can use the software to apply any picture control to your RAW image.

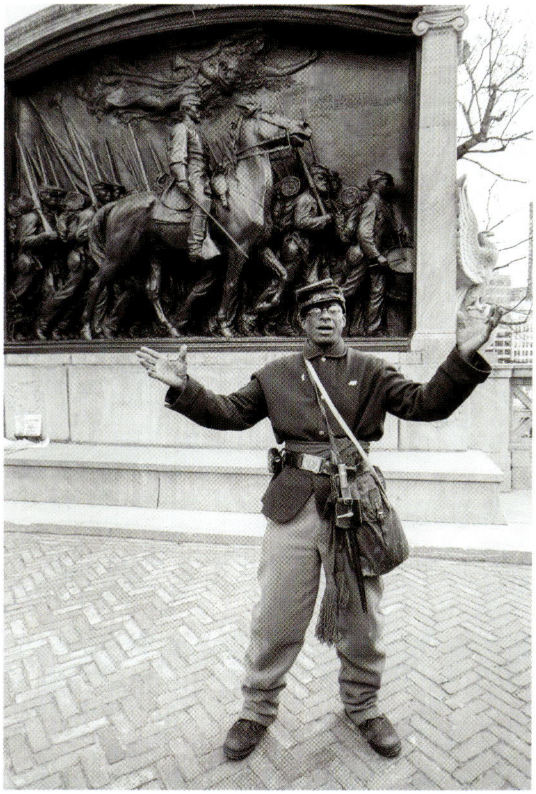

Figure 6.9 Getting great black and white portraits is as simple as setting the picture control to Monochrome.

ISO 400 • 1/400 sec. • f/3.5 • 24mm lens

The real key to using the Monochrome picture control is to customize it for your portrait subject. The control can be changed to alter the sharpness and contrast. For children and puppies, and anyone else who should look somewhat soft, set the Sharpness setting to 0 or 1. For old cowboys, longshoremen, and anyone else you want to look really detailed, try a setting of 6 or 7. I typically like to leave Contrast at a setting of around –1 or –2. This gives me a nice range of tones throughout the image.

The other adjustment you should try is changing the picture control's Filter effect from None to one of the four available settings (Yellow, Orange, Red, or Green). Using the filters will have the effect of either lightening or darkening the skin tones. The Red and Yellow filters usually lighten skin, while the Green filter can make skin appear a bit darker. Experiment to see which one works best for your subject.

Setting your picture control to Monochrome

1. Press the **i** button to activate the cursor in the information screen.
2. Use the Multi-selector to move the cursor to the Set Picture Control icon, and press the OK button.
3. Select the MC setting, and then press the OK button (**A**).

A

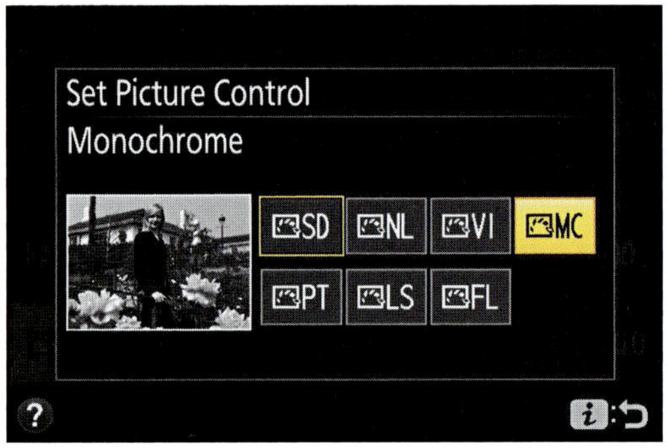

Customizing your Monochrome picture control

1. Start by pressing the Menu button.
2. Navigate to Shooting Menu, select Manage Picture Control (**B**), and press OK.
3. Select Save/Edit, and press OK again.
4. Scroll down to Monochrome (**C**), and then press the Multi-selector to the right to enter the customization screen. (Don't hit the OK button here or it will go right to the Save As screen.)

B

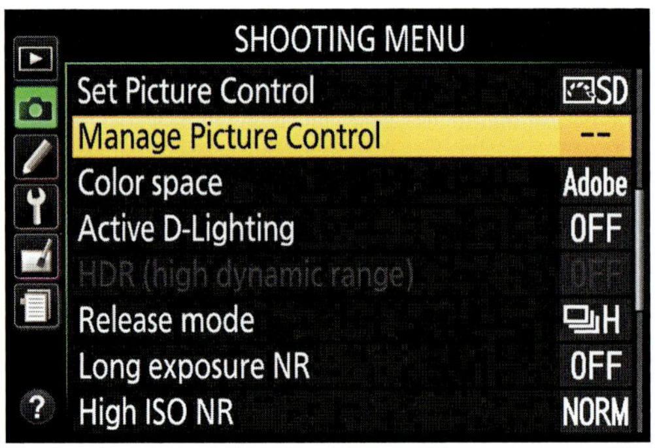

C

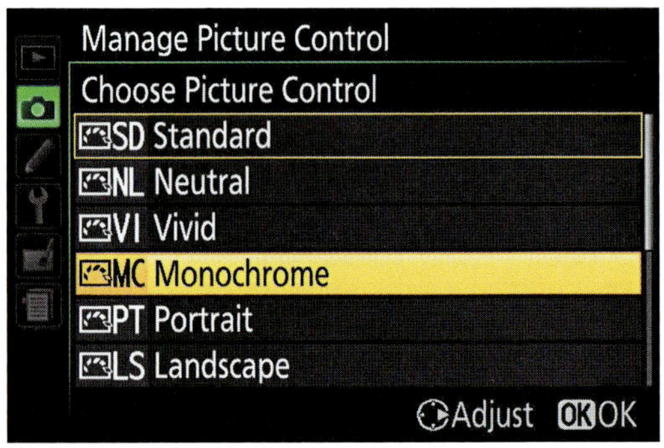

5. Now that you are in the customize screen, make the desired changes to each of the different items (move the Multi-selector up or down to select the item you want to change, and left to right to change the settings) (**D**).
6. When you have everything set the way you want, press the OK button to save your new custom settings. Select the first available slot (C-1), and press right on the Multi-selector (**E**). You can now use the default name or type in one of your own. To delete the current name, use the Command dial to select the letter location and hit the Delete (trash can) button. Then use the Multi-selector to spell the new name (**F**). When done, press the OK button.
7. To use the new setting, follow the previous set of directions for selecting a picture control, except this time choose C-1 instead of MC.

D

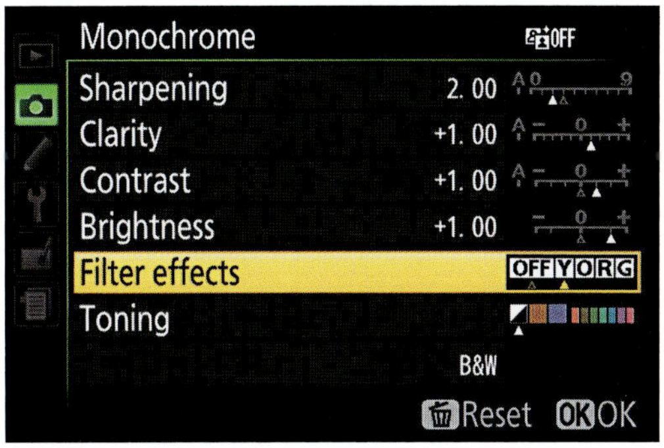

E

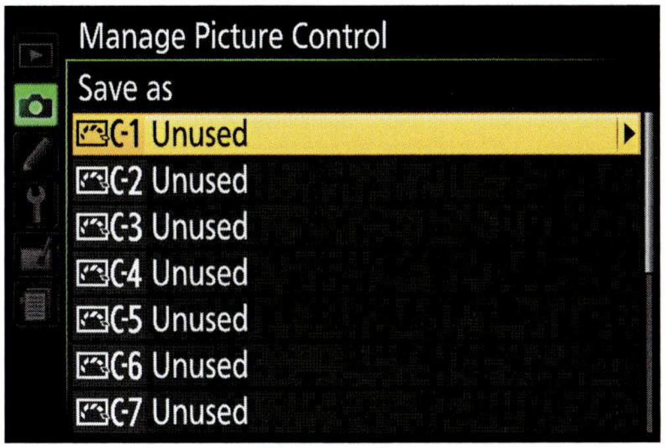

F

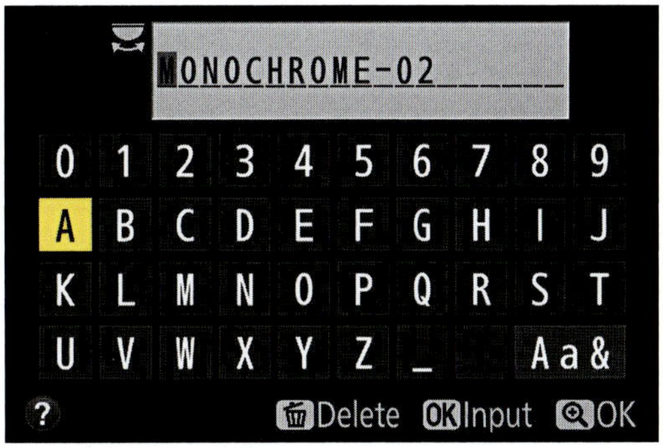

The Portrait Picture Control for Better Skin Tones

As long as we are talking about picture controls for portraits, there is another control on your D5500 that has been tuned specifically for this type of shooting. Oddly enough, it's called Portrait. To set this control on your camera, simply follow the same directions as earlier, except this time select the Portrait (PT) control instead of Monochrome. There are also individual options for the Portrait control that, as with the Monochrome control, include sharpness and contrast. You can also change the saturation (how intense the colors will be) and the hue, which lets you change the skin tones (for example, from reddish to yellowish). I prefer brighter colors, so I like to boost the Saturation setting to +2 and leave everything else at the defaults. You won't be able to use the same adjustments for everyone, especially when it comes to color tone, so do some experimenting to see what works best.

Face Detection with Live View

Face detection in digital cameras has been around for a few years, but it's still a relatively new concept in the world of the dSLR. Your D5500 has four different autofocus area modes for Live View: Wide-Area, Normal-Area, Subject-Tracking, and Face-Priority. Face-Priority mode is probably the slowest of the Live View focusing modes, so I use it mostly when I am working with a tripod or my subjects are going to remain fairly still. When you turn on Live View with Face-Priority focusing, the camera does an amazing thing: It zeroes in on any face appearing on the LCD and places a box around it (**Figure 6.10**). I'm not sure how it works; it just does.

If there is more than one face in the frame, a box will appear over each of them, but the camera will use only one to focus. The box that has the small inside corners outlined is the one the camera is currently using for focus (this is usually the closest face to the camera).

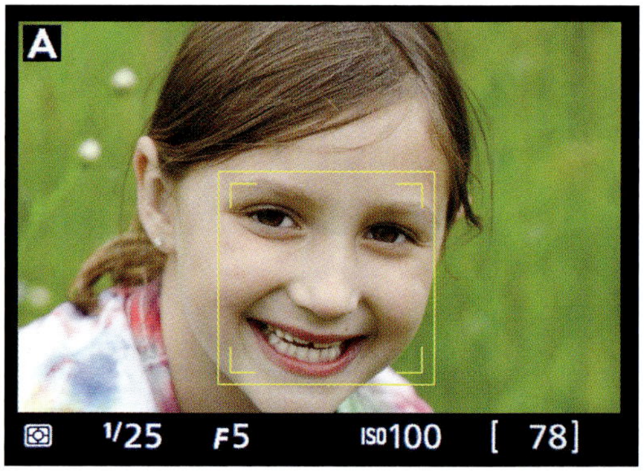

Figure 6.10 In the Live View Face-Priority mode, the camera locks in on your subject's face for easy focusing.

Setting up and shooting with Live View and Face-Priority focusing

1. Activate the Live View function by moving the Lv switch under the Mode dial on top of the camera.
2. Press the **i** button to enter the information screen, and use the Multi-selector to navigate to the AF-Area mode icon.
3. Press the OK button to enter the AF-Area mode selection screen.
4. Use the Multi-selector to choose Face-Priority AF, and press the OK button.
5. Press the shutter release button to exit the menu mode and get ready for shooting.
6. Point your camera at a person and watch as the frame appears over the face in the LCD.

7. Depress and hold the shutter release button halfway to focus on the face, and wait until you hear the confirmation chirp.
8. Press the shutter button fully to take the photograph.

Live View can be used with any of the professional modes, or you can combine it with the Portrait scene mode.

Manual Callout

There is a section in the Reference Manual PDF dedicated to using Live View mode, starting on page 162.

Using Live View's grid overlay

There is another benefit to using Live View: the grid overlay. This is a feature that actually places a grid over your image, dividing it into sectors, which can be of great benefit in properly composing your image for portraits (**Figure 6.11**). Check out Chapter 7 for full instructions on setting up and using this feature.

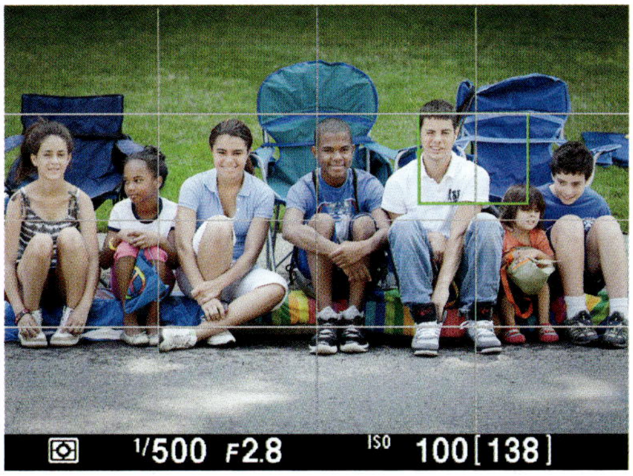

Figure 6.11 **Using Live View's grid overlay can help you compose your shots.**

Using Fill Flash to Reduce Shadows

A common problem when taking pictures of people outside, especially during the midday hours, is that the overhead sun can create dark shadows under the eyes and chin. You could have your subject turn his or her face to the sun, but that is usually considered cruel and unusual punishment. So how can you have your subject's back to the sun and still get a decent exposure of the face? Try turning on your flash to fill in the shadows (**Figure 6.12**). This also works well when you are photographing someone wearing a ball cap. The bill of the hat tends to create heavy shadows over the eyes, and the fill flash will lighten up those areas while providing a really nice catch light in the eyes.

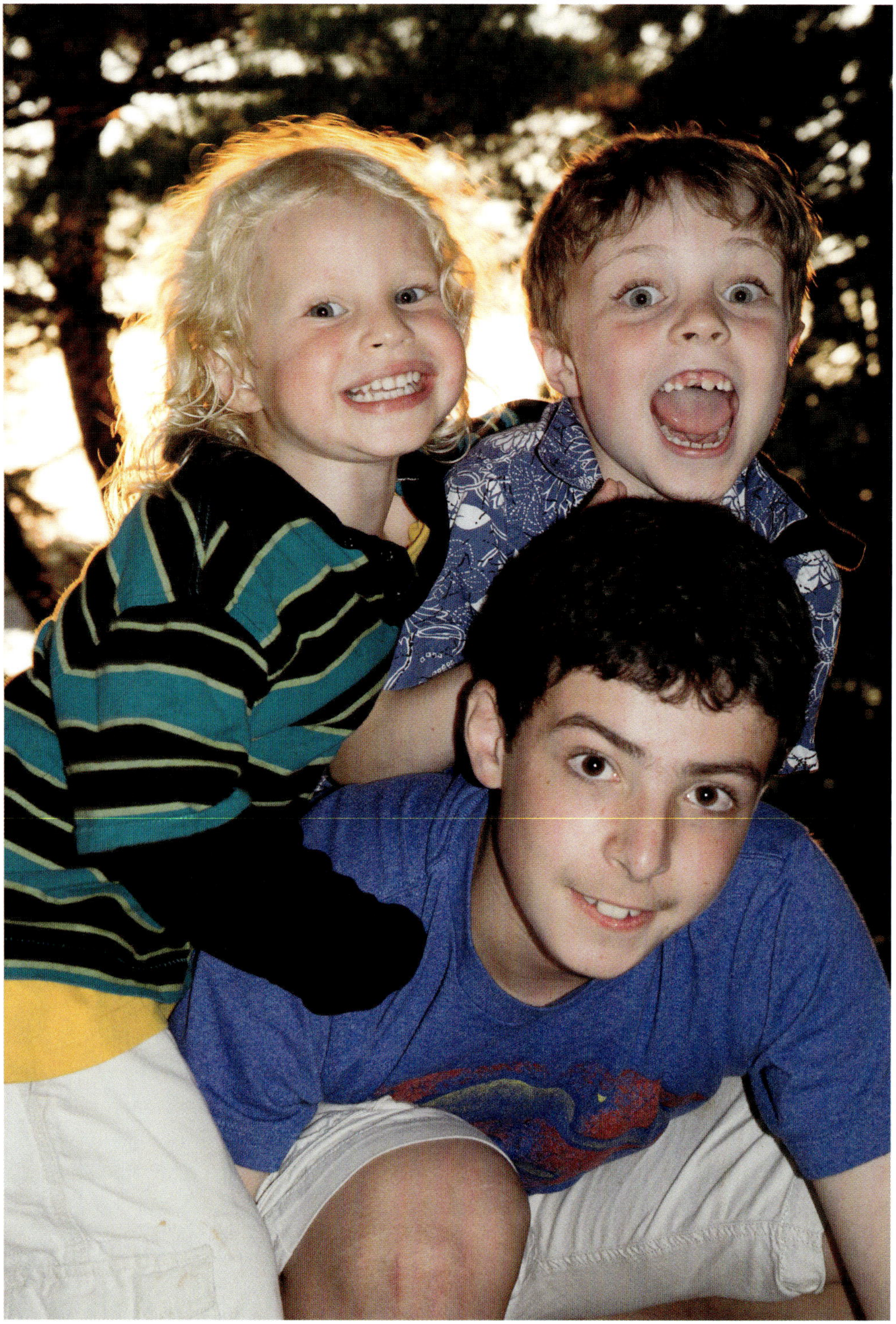

Figure 6.12
I used fill flash to lighten the faces of these kids, who were on a porch with the setting sun right behind them.

ISO 400 • 1/25 sec. • f/8 • 70mm lens

Catch Light

A *catch light* is that little sparkle that adds life to the eyes. When you are photographing a person with a light source in front of her, you will usually get a reflection of that light—be it your flash, the sun, or something else brightly reflecting—in her eyes. The light bounces off the surface of eyes as bright highlights and serves to bring attention to them.

The key to using the flash as a fill is to not use it on full power. If you do, the camera will try to balance the flash with the available light, and you will get a flat and featureless face.

Setting up and shooting with fill flash

1. Press the pop-up flash button to raise your pop-up flash into the ready position.
2. Press the **i** button to activate the cursor in the information screen.
3. Use the Multi-selector to navigate to the Flash Compensation icon, and press the OK button (**A**).
4. Select a Flash Compensation setting of –0.3, and press OK (**B**).
5. Take a photograph and check your playback LCD to see if it looks good. If not, try reducing power in one-third stop increments.

A

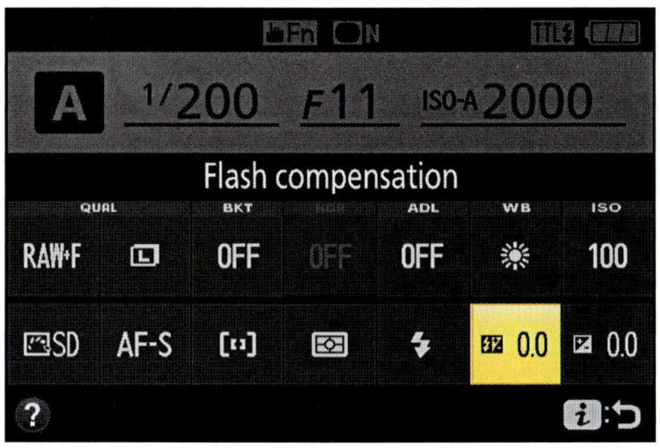

B

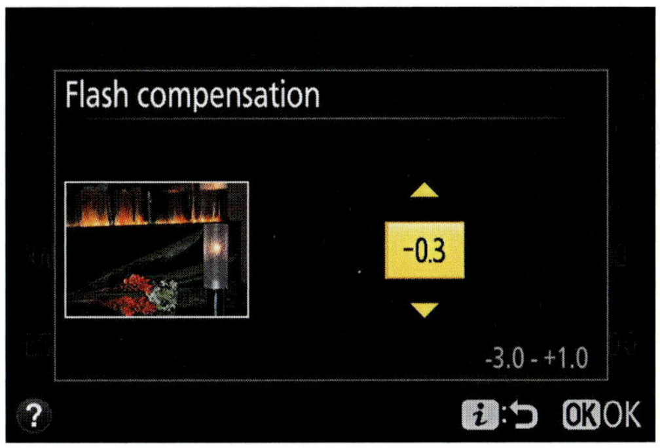

One problem that can quickly surface when using the on-camera flash is red-eye. Not to worry, though—we will talk about that in Chapter 8.

Portraits on the Move

Not all portraits are shot with the subject sitting in a chair, posed and ready for the picture. Sometimes you might want to get an action shot that says something about the person, similar to an environmental portrait. Children, especially, just like to move. Why fight it? Set up an action portrait instead.

For the photo in **Figure 6.13**, I set my camera to Aperture Priority mode, the focus mode to AF-C, and the release mode to Continuous High. Then I followed the subject down the hill and took photos all the way.

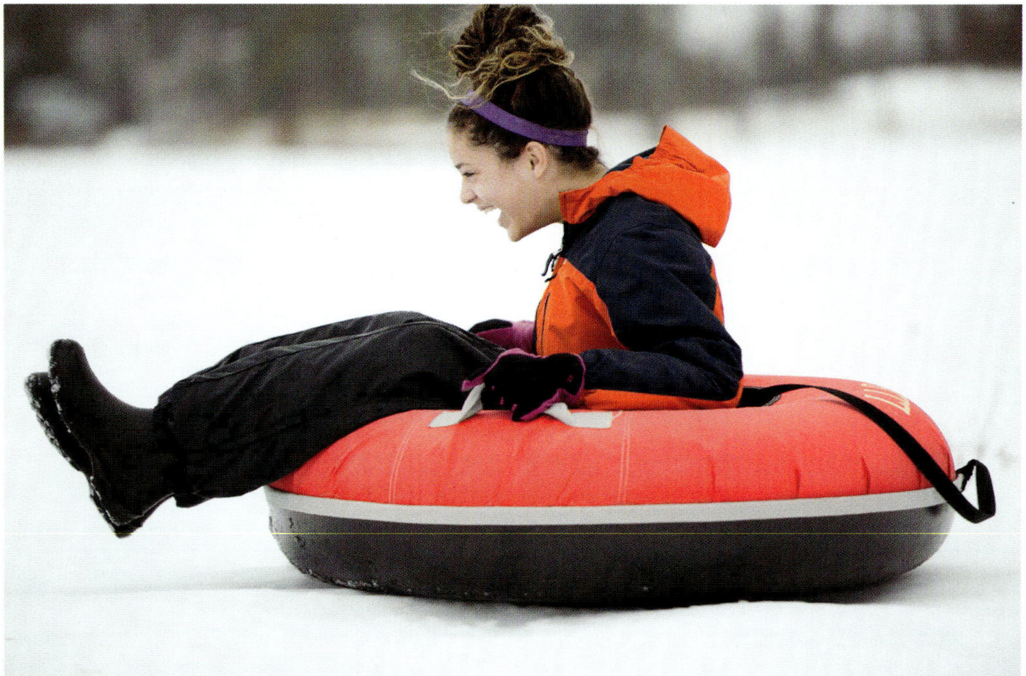

Figure 6.13
I used a fast shutter speed to stop the action, along with a large aperture to decrease depth of field.

ISO 250 • 1/400 sec. • f/2.8 • 200mm lens

Tips for Shooting Better Portraits

Before we get to the assignments for this chapter, I thought it might be a good idea to give you a few extra pointers on shooting portraits—tips that aren't necessarily related to your camera features. There are entire books that cover things like portrait lighting, posing, and so on. But here are a few ideas for making your people pics look a lot better.

Avoid the center of the frame

This falls under the category of composition. Place your subject to the side of the frame (**Figure 6.14**)—it just looks more interesting than plunking the person smack dab in the middle (**Figure 6.15**).

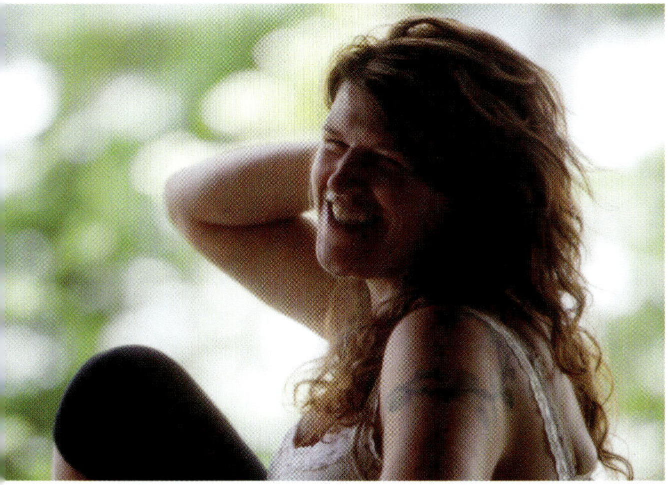

Figure 6.14 Try cropping in a bit, and place the subject's face off center to improve the shot.

ISO 400 • 1/500 sec. • f/2.8 • 170mm len

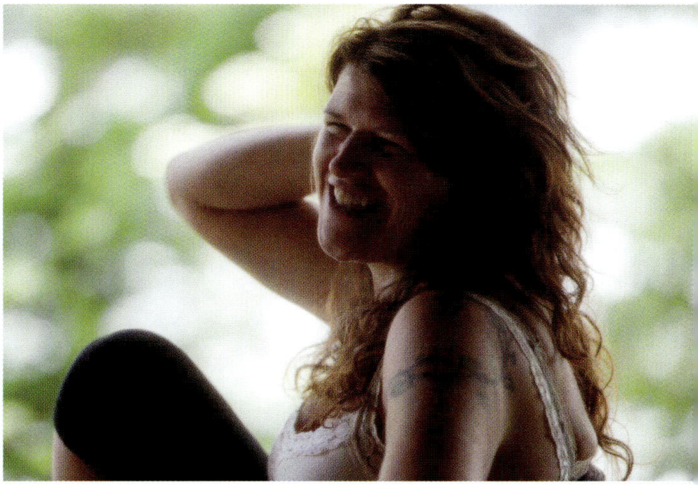

Figure 6.15 Having the subject in the middle of the frame with so much empty space on the sides can make for a less-than-interesting portrait.

ISO 400 • 1/500 sec. • f/2.8 • 170mm lens

Don't cut them off at the joint

There is an old rule about photographing people: Never crop the picture at a joint. This means no cropping at the ankles, knees, elbows, or wrists (**Figure 6.16**). If you need to crop at the legs, the proper place to crop is mid-shin or mid-thigh. For the arms, try to keep them in the frame, or crop just above or below the elbow.

Use the frame

Have you ever noticed that most people are taller than they are wide? Turn your camera vertically for a more pleasing composition (**Figure 6.17**).

Figure 6.16 (left)
A good crop for people is mid-thigh or mid-shin.

ISO 100 • 1/1000 sec. • f/2.8 • 145mm lens

Figure 6.17 (right)
Get in the habit of turning your camera to a vertical position when shooting portraits. This is also referred to as portrait orientation.

ISO 100 • 1/2000 sec. • f/2.0 • 50mm lens

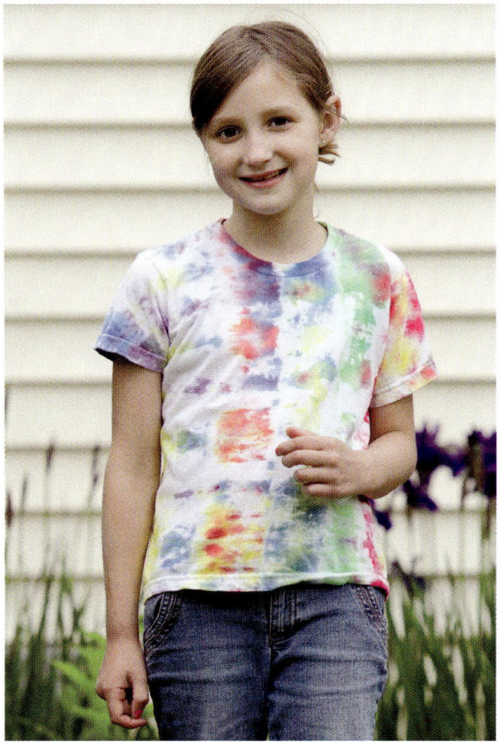

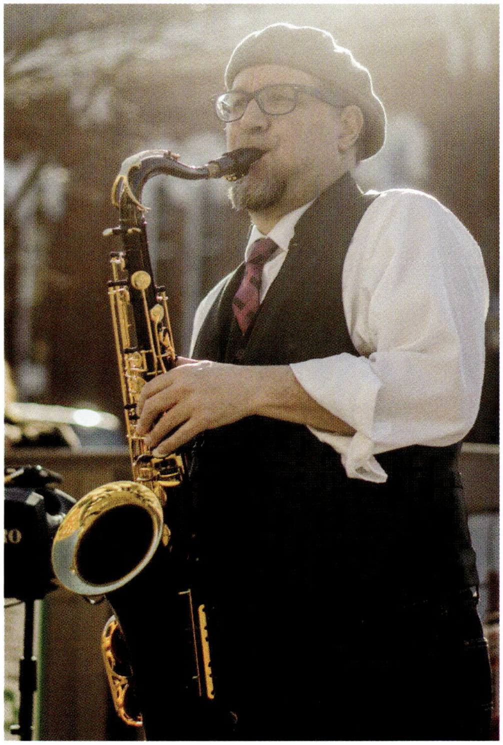

Sunblock for portraits

The midday sun can be harsh and can do unflattering things to people's faces (**Figure 6.18**). If you can, find a shady spot out of the direct sunlight. You will get softer shadows, smoother skin tones, and better detail (**Figure 6.19**). This holds true for overcast skies as well. Just be sure to adjust your white balance accordingly.

Frame the scene

Using elements in the scene to create a frame around your subject is a great way to draw the viewer in. You don't have to use a window frame to do this. Just look for elements in the foreground that could be used to force the viewer's eye toward your subject (**Figure 6.20**).

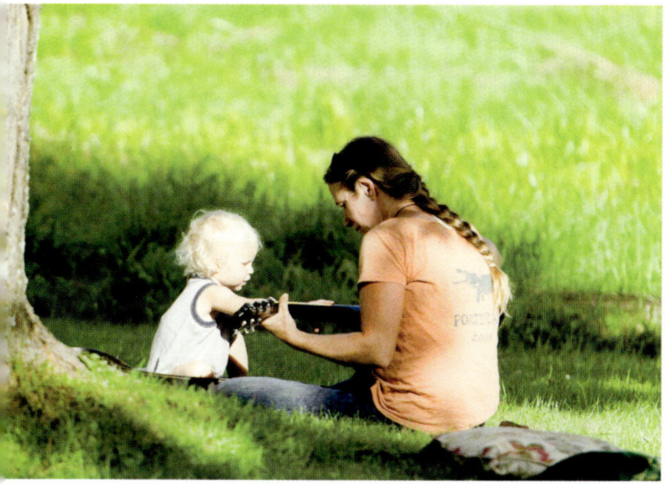

Figure 6.18 **The dappled sunlight can result in overexposure in the highlights.**

ISO 200 • 1/2000 sec. • f/2.8 • 200mm lens

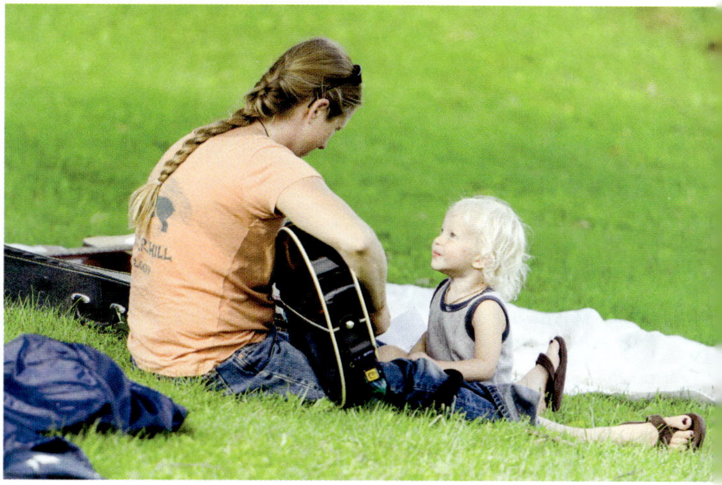

Figure 6.19 **By waiting for a cloud to pass in front of the sun and changing my position, I was able to get a much more even and pleasing result.**

ISO 200 • 1/640 sec. • f/2.8 • 200mm lens

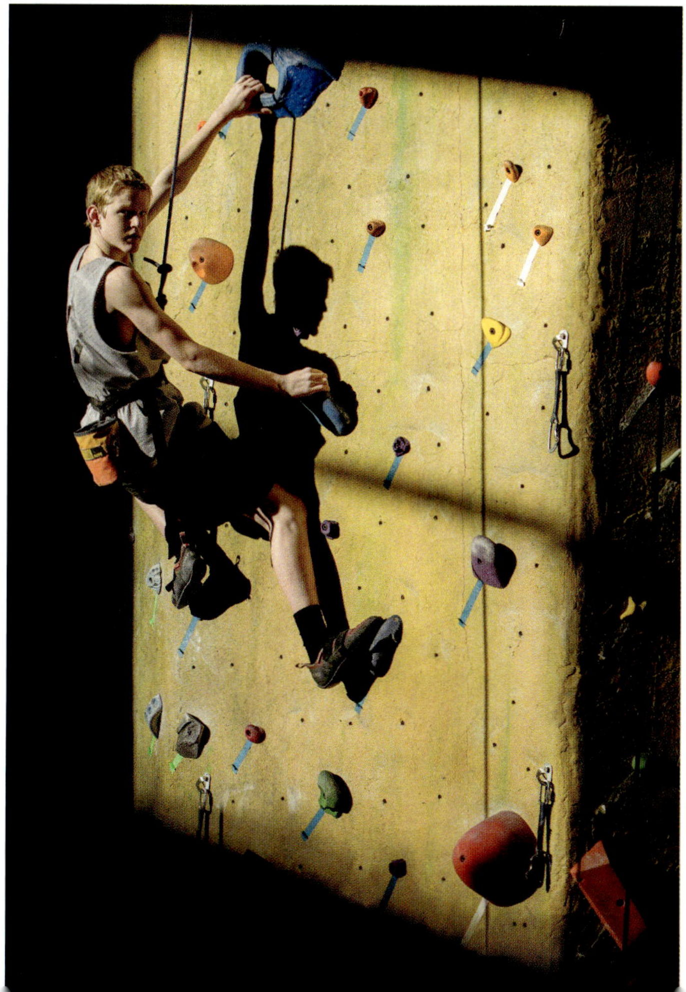

Figure 6.20 **The sunbeam from the window on the opposite wall created a frame around my subject.**

ISO 100 • 1/500 sec. • f/3.2 • 70mm lens

Keep an eye on your background

Sometimes it's so easy to get caught up in taking a great shot that you forget about the smaller details. Try to keep an eye on what is going on behind your subject so she doesn't end up with things popping out of her head (**Figures 6.21** and **6.22**).

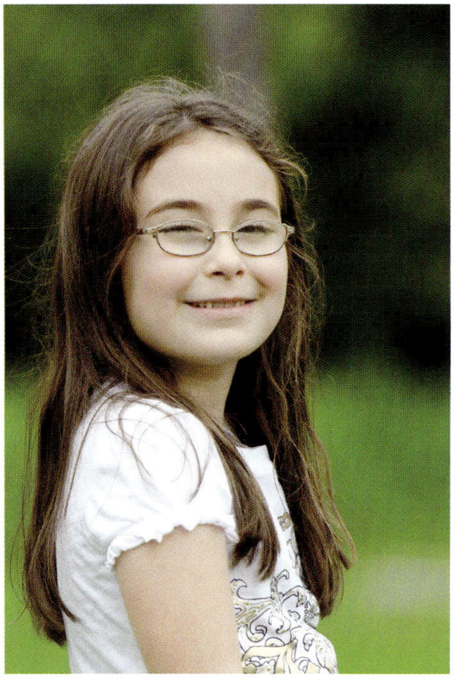

Figure 6.21 (left)
A fence post in the background is going right into the subject's head.
ISO 100 • 1/500 sec. • f/2.8 • 195mm lens

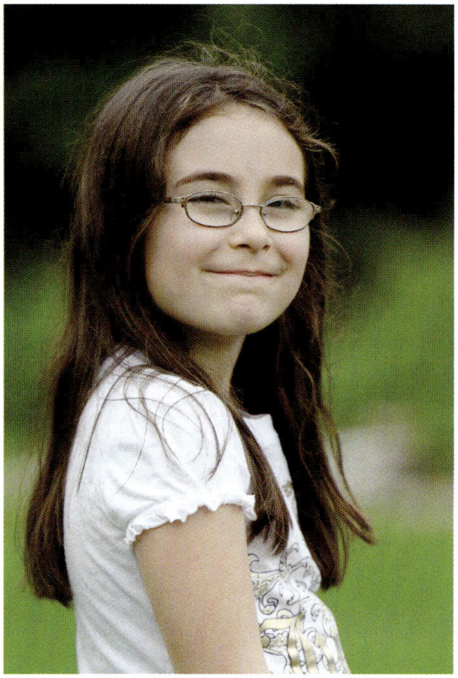

Figure 6.22 (right)
By moving the camera a little to the left, I was able to remove the distracting post from the photo.
ISO 100 • 1/500 sec. • f/2.8 • 195mm lens

Give them a healthy glow

Nearly everyone looks better with a warm, healthy glow. Some of the best light of the day happens just a little before sundown, so shoot at that time if you can (**Figure 6.23**).

More than just a pretty face

Most people think of a portrait as a photo of someone's face. Don't ignore other aspects of your subjects that reflect their personality—hands, especially, can go a long way toward describing someone (**Figure 6.24**) and capturing the moment.

Get down on their level

If you want better pictures of children, don't shoot from an adult's eye level. Getting the camera down to the child's level will make your images look more personal (**Figure 6.25**).

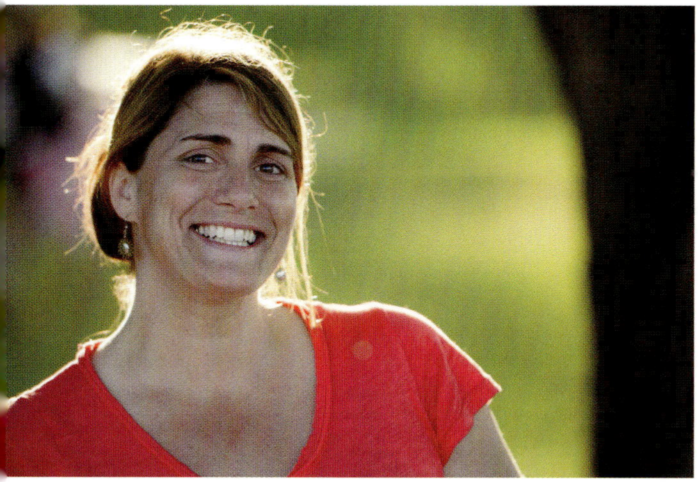

Figure 6.23 You just can't beat the glow of the late afternoon sun for adding warmth to your portraits.

ISO 400 • 1/800 sec. • f/2.8 • 200mm lens

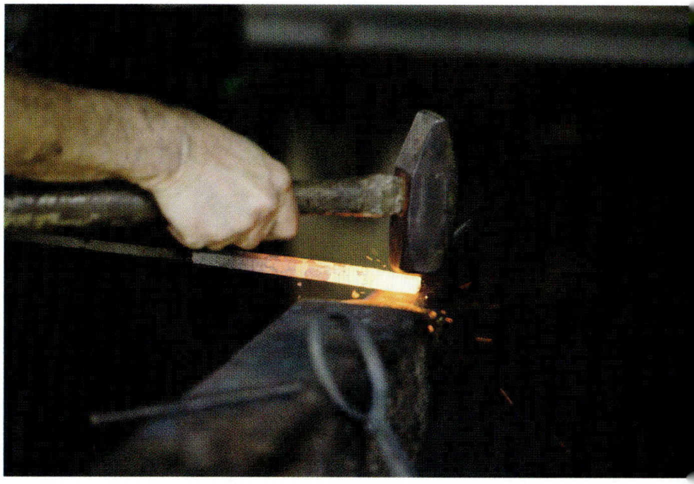

Figure 6.24 There's more to a person than just his or her face. Hands can tell a lot about what is happening in the scene.

ISO 200 • 1/320 sec. • f/2.8 • 200mm lens

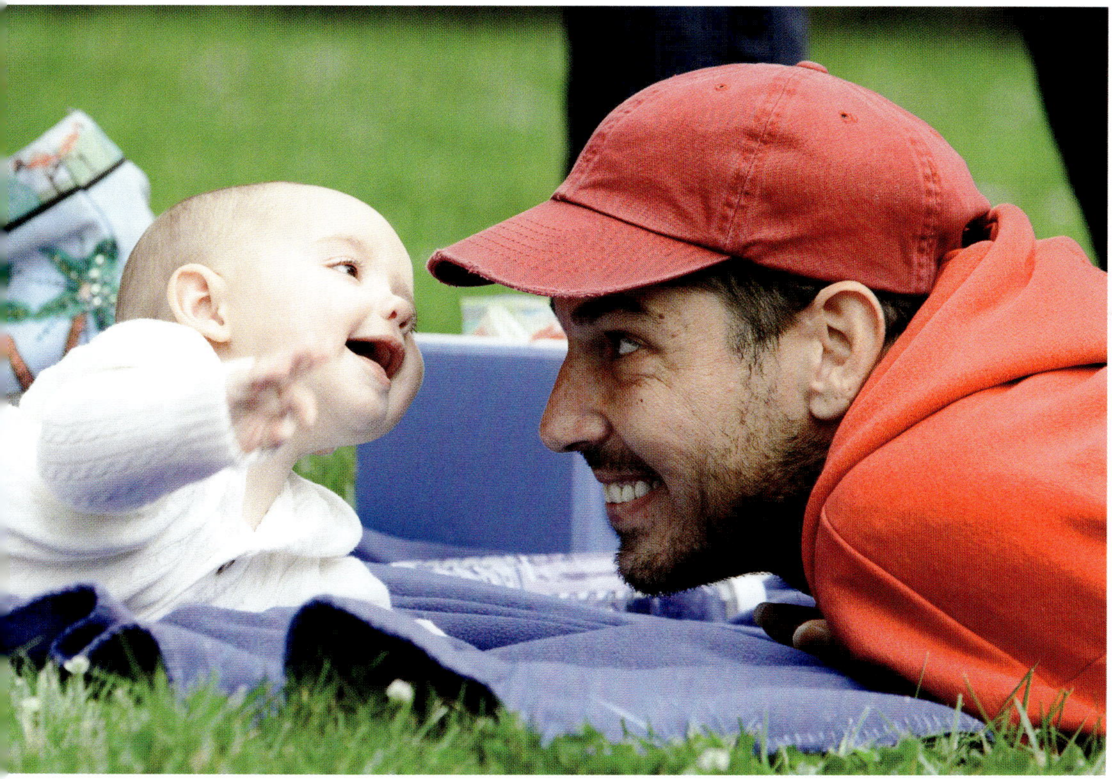

Figure 6.25 Sometimes taking photographs of children means kneeling to get the camera down on their level, but the result is a much better image.

ISO 200 • 1/320 sec. • f/5.6 • 200mm lens

Eliminate space between your subjects

One of the problems you can encounter when taking portraits of more than one person is that of personal space. What feels like a close distance to the subjects can look impersonal to the viewer. Have your subjects move close together, eliminating any open space between them (**Figure 6.26**).

Don't be afraid to get close

When you are taking someone's picture, don't be afraid of getting close and filling the frame (**Figure 6.27**). This doesn't mean you have to shoot from a foot away; try zooming in and capture the details.

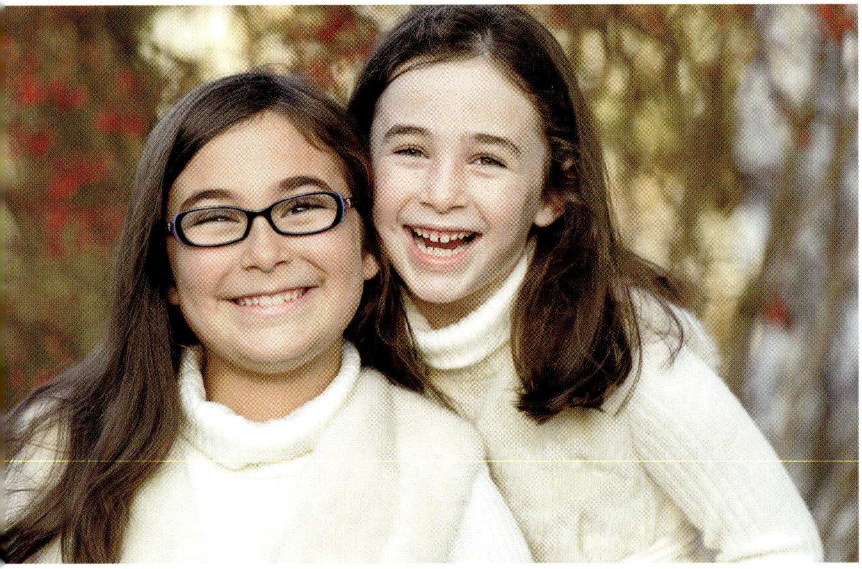

Figure 6.26 Getting kids to squish together will usually result in great smiles and laughter.

ISO 100 • 1/100 sec. • f/2.8 • 200mm lens

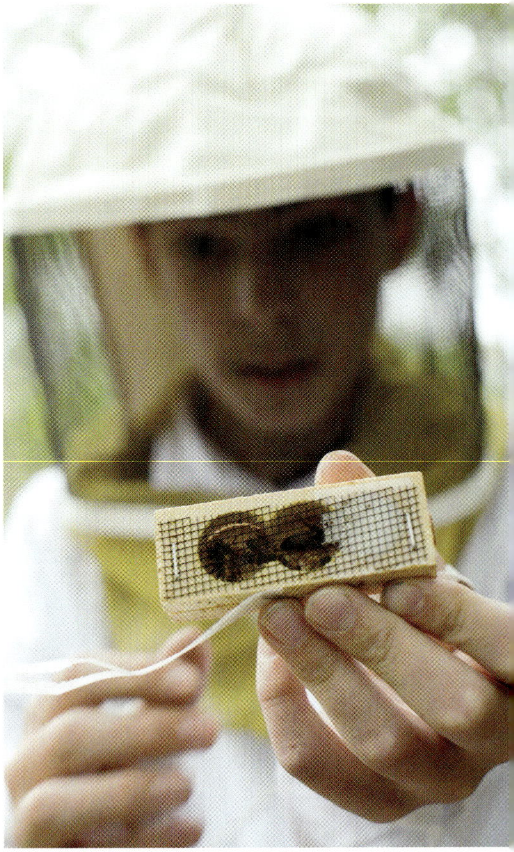

Figure 6.27 Filling the frame with the subject can lead to a much more intimate portrait.

ISO 400 • 1/60 sec. • f/4 • 50mm lens

Chapter 6 Assignments

You'll need to find some willing subjects (though even not so willing subjects can work, too) to help you with these assignments. The goal here is to experiment with depth of field, quality of light, metering modes, and picture controls.

Experimenting with depth of field in portraits

Let's start with something simple: Grab your favorite person and start playing with different aperture settings. Shoot wide open (the widest your lens goes, such as f/3.5 or f/5.6) and then really stopped down (like f/22). Look at the difference in the depth of field and how it plays an important role in placing the attention on your subject. (Make sure you don't have your subject standing against the background. Give some distance so there is a good blurring effect of the background at the wide f-stop setting.)

Discovering the qualities of natural light

Pick a nice sunny day and try shooting some portraits in the midday sun. If your subject is willing, have him turn so the sun is in his face. If he is still speaking to you after being blinded, have him turn his back to the sun. Try this with and without the fill flash so you can see the difference. Finally, move him into a completely shaded spot and take a few more shots.

Picking the right metering method

Find a very dark or light background and place your subject in front of it. Now take a couple of shots, giving a lot of space around her for the background to show. Switch metering modes and use the AE Lock feature to get a more accurate reading of your subject. Notice the differences in exposure between the metering methods.

Using picture controls for portraits

Have some fun playing with the different picture controls. Try the Portrait control as compared to the Standard (SD) control. Then try out Monochrome and play with the different color filter options to see how they affect skin tones.

Share your results with the book's Flickr group!
Join the group here: flickr.com/groups/nikond5500_fromsnapshotstogreatshots

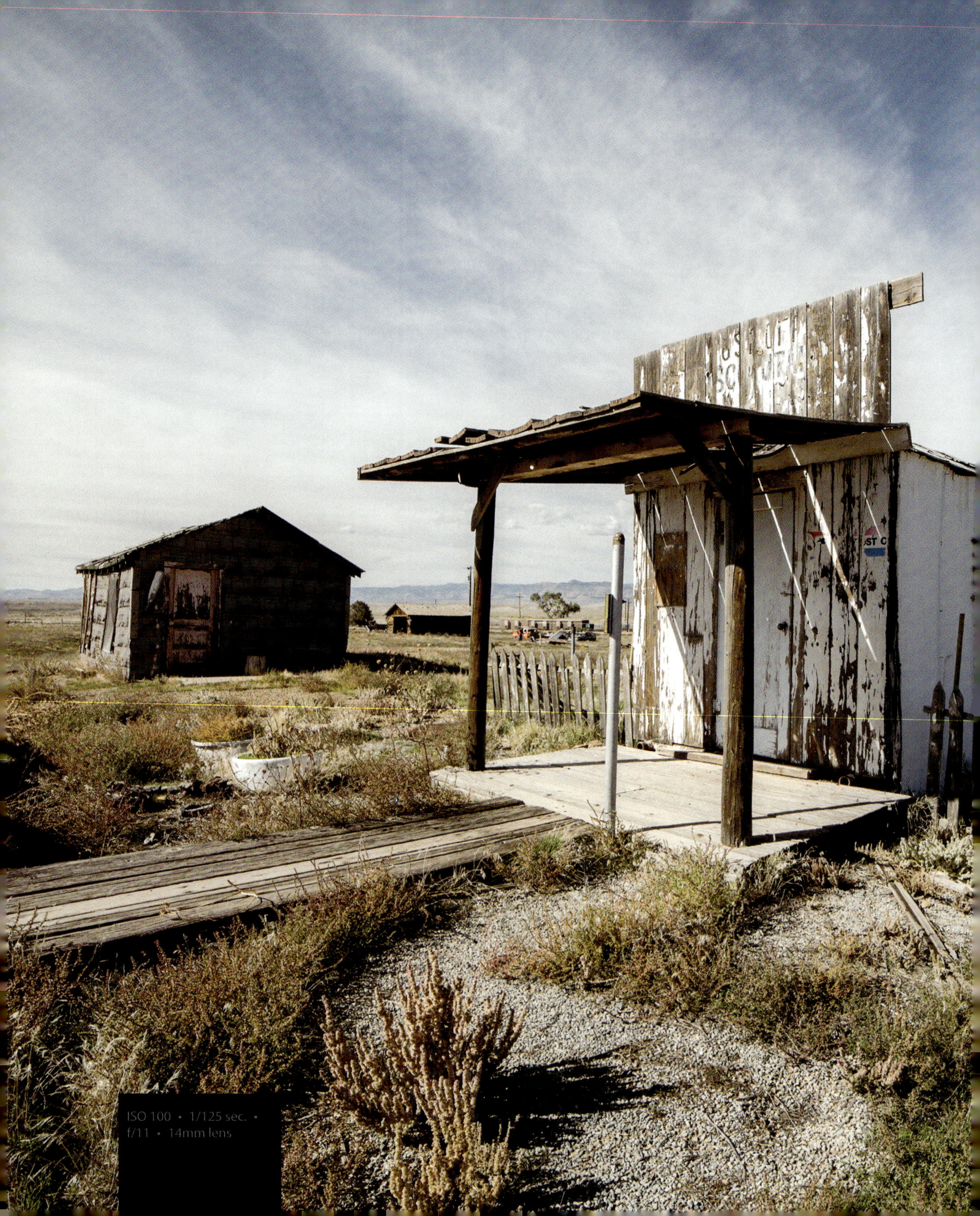

ISO 100 • 1/125 sec. • f/11 • 14mm lens

7

Landscape Photography

Tips, Tools, and Techniques to Get the Most Out of Your Landscape Photography

Shooting landscapes has always brought joy to my photography. It might have to do with being outdoors and working at the mercy of Mother Nature. Maybe it's the way it challenges me to visualize the landscape and try to capture it with my camera. It truly is a celebration of light, composition, and the world we live in.

In this chapter, we will explore some of the features of the D5500 that not only improve the look of your landscape photography but also make it easier to take great shots. We will also explore some typical scenarios and discuss methods to bring out the best in your landscape work.

Poring Over the Picture

You always need a Plan B. On a recent trip to Canyonlands National Park, we had planned to photograph sunrise at the famous Mesa Arch, but even though we arrived early, we failed to beat the crowd. Luckily, we had an alternative plan to photograph at the (relatively) nearby Dead Horse Point State Park. We arrived before the sun broke the horizon and had plenty of time to find new vantage points for capturing the canyon in the beautiful dawn light.

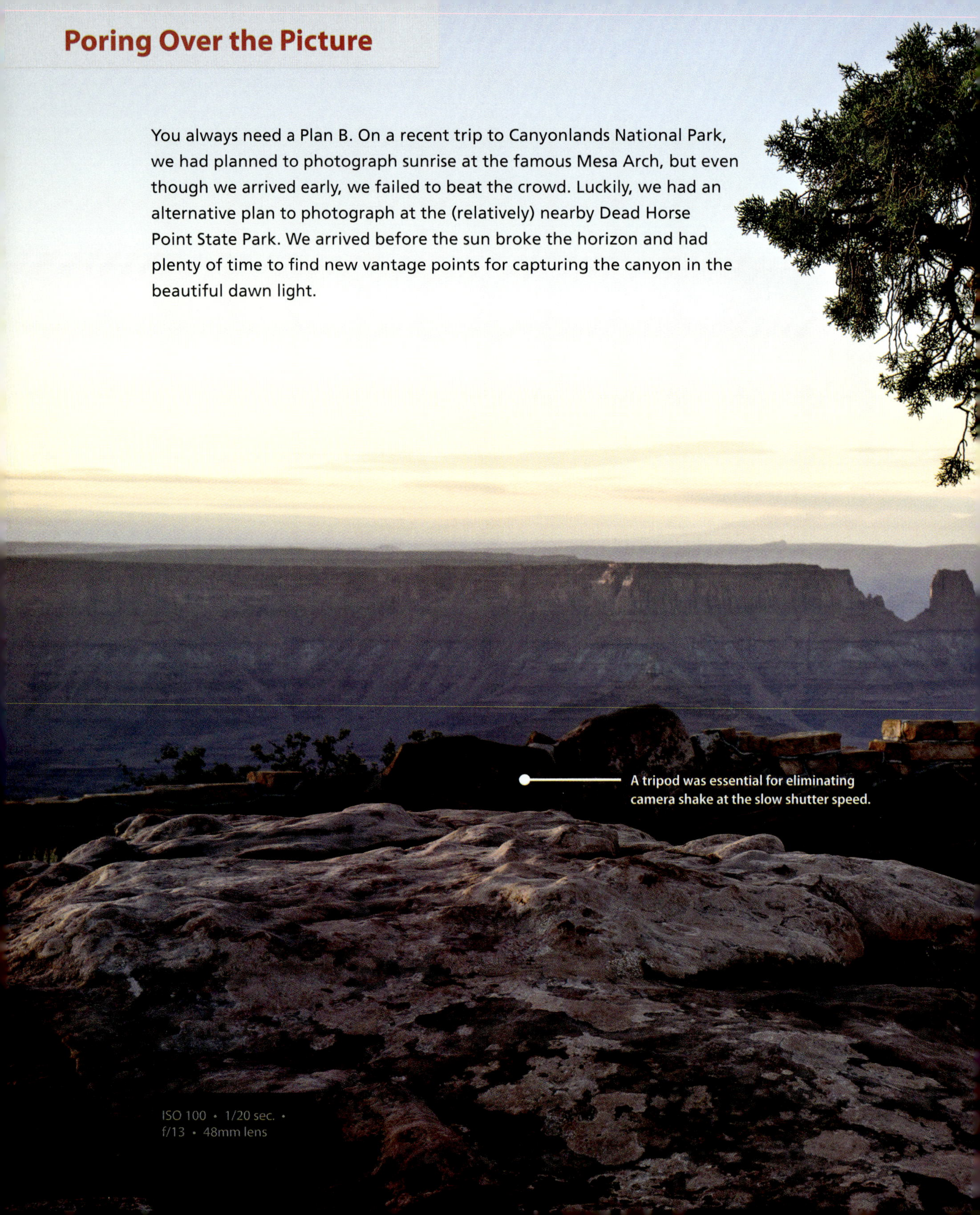

ISO 100 • 1/20 sec. • f/13 • 48mm lens

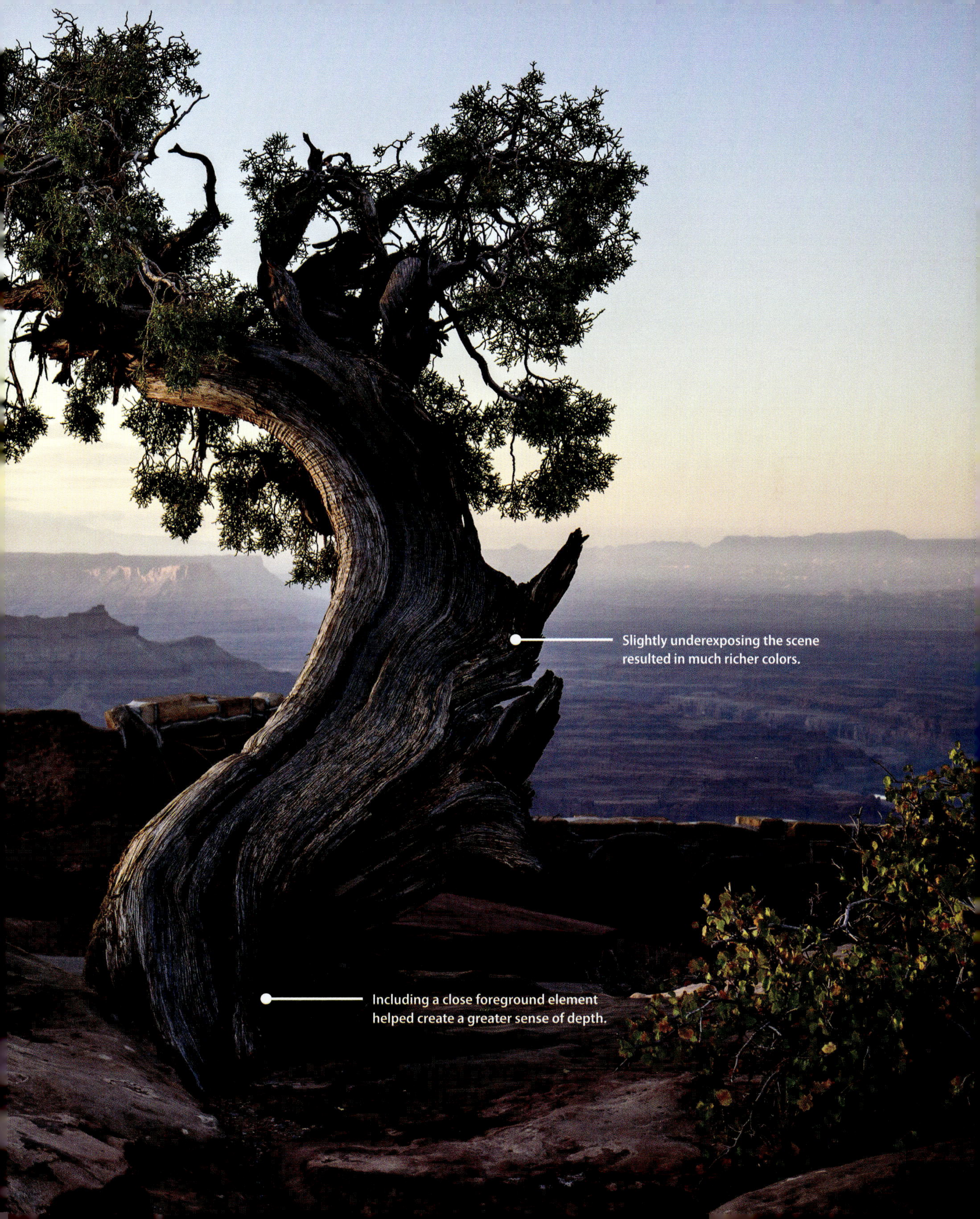
Slightly underexposing the scene resulted in much richer colors.
Including a close foreground element helped create a greater sense of depth.

Sharp and In Focus: Using Tripods

Throughout the previous chapters we have concentrated on using the camera to create great images. We will continue that focus through this chapter, but we need to consider one additional piece of equipment that is crucial in the world of landscape shooting: the tripod. There are a couple of reasons tripods are so critical to your landscape work, the first of which involves the time of day you will be working. For reasons discussed later, the best light for most landscape work happens at sunrise and just before sunset. While these are the best times to shoot, they're also kind of dark. That means you'll be working with slow shutter speeds. Slow shutter speeds mean camera shake. Camera shake equals bad photos.

The second reason is also related to the amount of light you're gathering with your camera. When taking landscape photos, you will usually want to work with very small apertures, as they give you lots of depth of field. This means that, once again, you will be working with slower-than-normal shutter speeds.

Slow shutter = camera shake = bad photos.

Do you see the pattern here? The one tool in your arsenal that will truly defeat the camera shake issue and ensure tack-sharp photos is a good tripod (**Figure 7.1**).

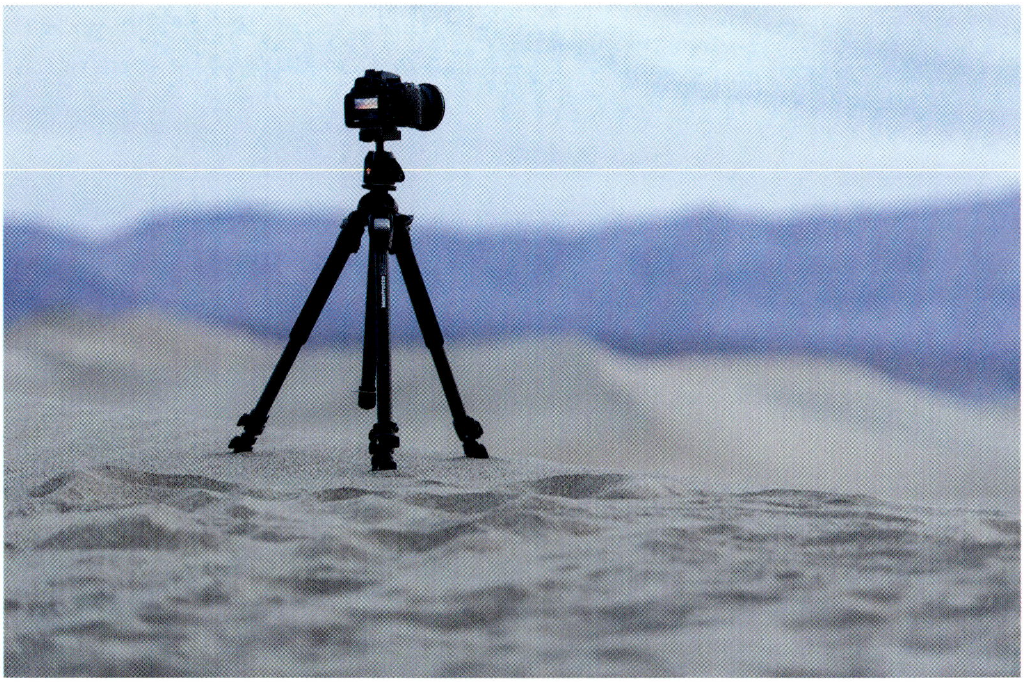

Figure 7.1
A sturdy tripod is the key to sharp landscape photos.

ISO 800 • 1/250 sec. • f/2.8 • 130mm lens

So what should you look for in a tripod? Well, first make sure it is sturdy enough to support your camera and any lens you might want to use. Next, check the height of the tripod. Bending over all day to look through the viewfinder of a camera on a short tripod can wreak havoc on your back. Finally, think about getting a tripod that uses a quick-release head. This usually employs a plate that screws into the bottom of the camera and then quickly snaps into place on the tripod—especially helpful when you are moving between shooting by hand and using the tripod. There's more information about tripods in Chapter 11.

Tripod stability

Most tripods have a center column that allows the user to extend the height of the camera above the point where the tripod legs join together. This might seem like a great idea, but the reality is that the farther you raise that column, the less stable your tripod becomes. Think of a tall building that sways near the top. To get the most solid base for your camera, always try to use it with the center column at its lowest point so your camera is right at the apex of the tripod legs.

VR lenses and tripods don't mix

If you are using Vibration Reduction (VR) lenses on your camera, you need to remember to turn off this feature when you use a tripod (**Figure 7.2**). This is because Vibration Reduction can, while trying to minimize camera movement, actually create movement when the camera is already stable. To turn off the VR feature, just slide the VR selector switch on the side of the lens to the Off position.

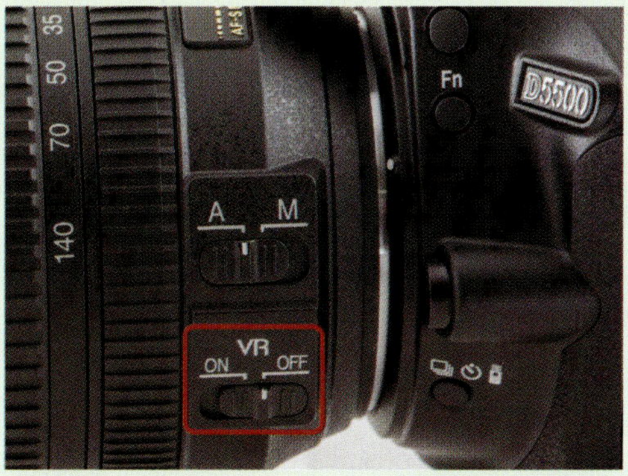

Figure 7.2 Turn off the Vibration Reduction feature when using a tripod.

Selecting the Proper ISO

When you are shooting most landscape scenes, the ISO should be increased only as a last resort. While it is easy to select a higher ISO to get a smaller aperture, the noise it can introduce into your images can be quite harmful. The noise is visible not only as large grainy artifacts but sometimes as multiple colors, which further degrades the image quality.

Take a look at **Figures 7.3** and **7.4**, which show a photograph taken with an ISO of 10,000. The purpose was to shorten the shutter speed and still use a small aperture setting of f/16. The problem is that the noise level is so high that, in addition to being distracting, it is obscuring the fine details.

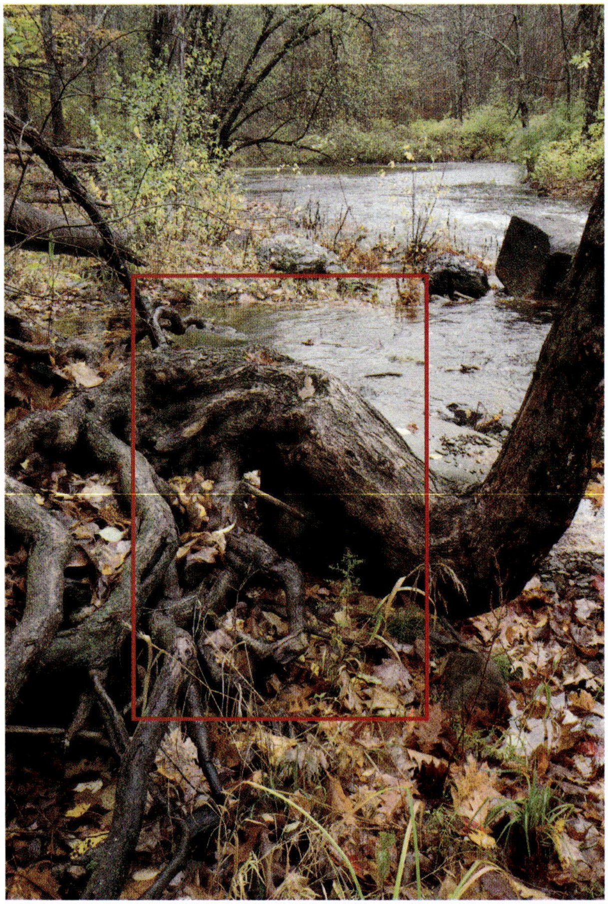

Figure 7.3 **A high ISO setting created a lot of digital noise in the shadows.**

ISO 10,000 • 1/200 sec. • f/16 • 38mm lens

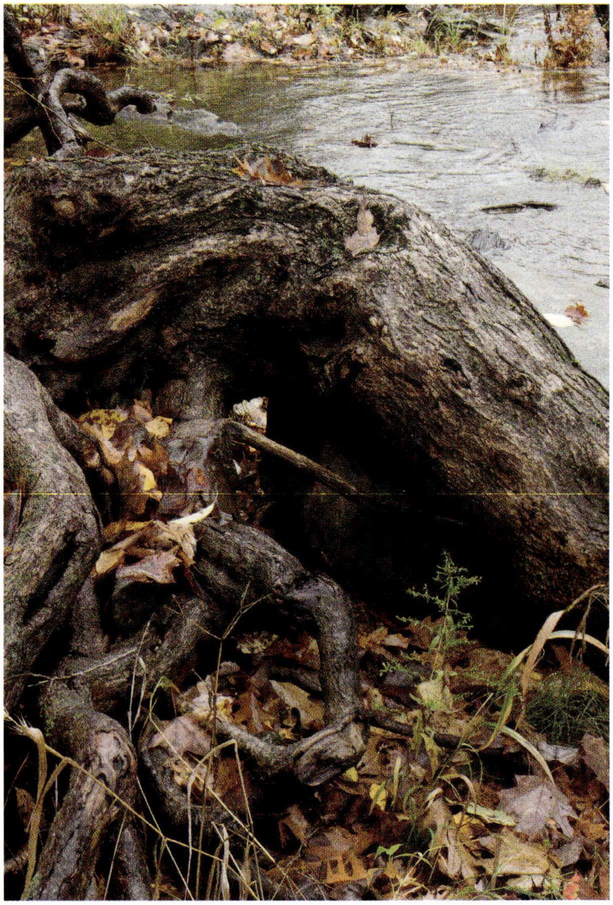

Figure 7.4 **When the image is enlarged, the noise is even more apparent (look for the grainy texture).**

Now check out another image that was taken in the same dim light but with a much lower ISO setting (**Figures 7.5** and **7.6**). As you can see, the noise levels are much lower, which means that my blacks look black, and the fine details are beautifully captured.

When shooting landscapes, set your ISO to the lowest possible setting at all times. Between the use of Vibration Reduction lenses (if you are handholding the camera) and a good tripod, there should be few circumstances where you would need to shoot landscapes with anything above an ISO of 400.

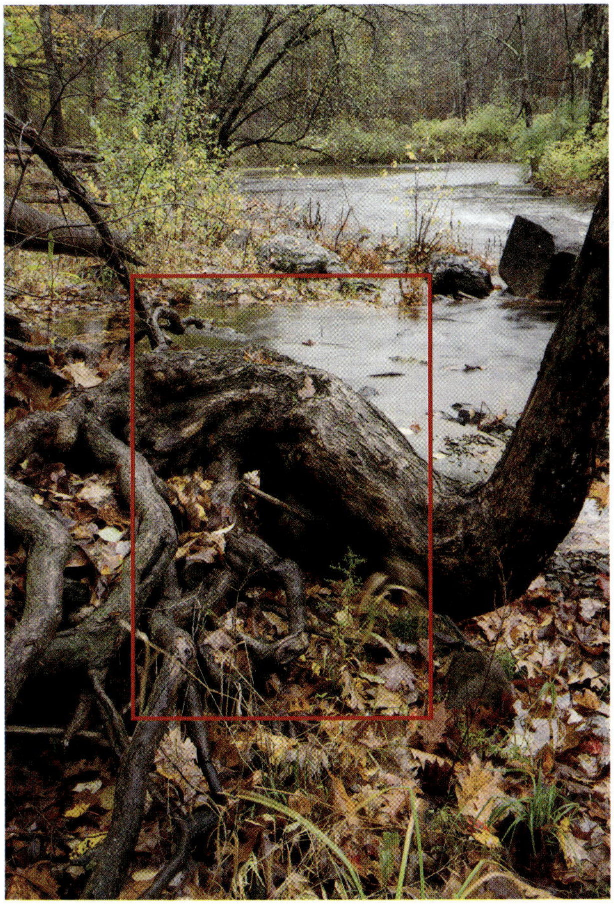

Figure 7.5 By lowering the ISO to 100, I was able to avoid the noise and capture a clean image.

ISO 100 • 1/2 sec. • f/16 • 38mm lens

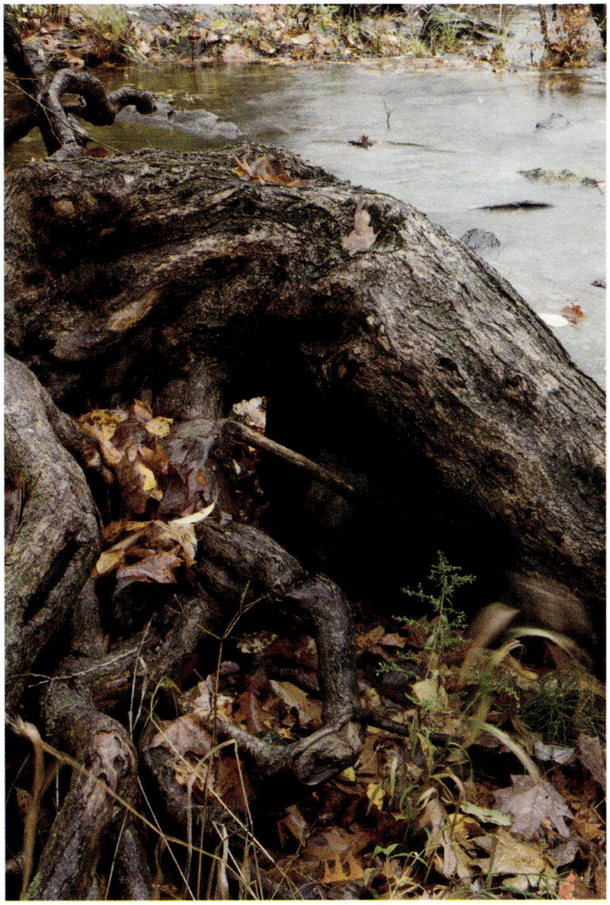

Figure 7.6 Zooming in shows that the noise levels for this image are almost nonexistent.

Using Noise Reduction

Both of the images above were taken with a tripod, but the image set to an ISO of 100 required a much longer shutter speed (1/2 of a second at ISO 100) compared with the high-ISO image (1/200 of a second at ISO 10,000).

A word of warning about using a low ISO setting: The sometimes-lengthy shutter speeds can also introduce noise. This noise is a result of the camera sensor heating up as it is being exposed to light. This effect is not visible in short exposures, but as you start shooting with shutter speeds that exceed 1 second, the level of image noise can increase. Your camera has a couple of features you can turn on to combat noise from long exposures and high ISOs.

Setting up noise reduction

1. Press the Menu button, and then use the Multi-selector to get to Shooting Menu.
2. Using the Multi-selector, select Long Exposure NR, and then press OK. Change this option to On, and press the OK button (**A**).
3. Now use the Multi-selector to get to the High ISO NR (**B**) setting (just under Long Exposure NR), and press OK.
4. High ISO noise reduction comes in four flavors: High, Normal, Low, and Off. Set this to Normal for everyday shooting or to High for those instances where you have to significantly raise your ISO (**C**).

A

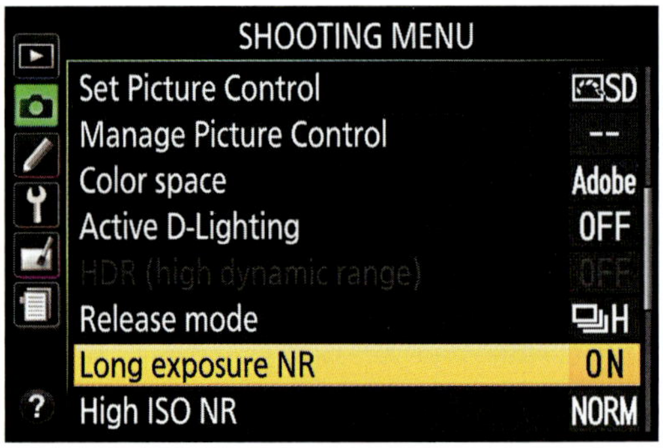

B

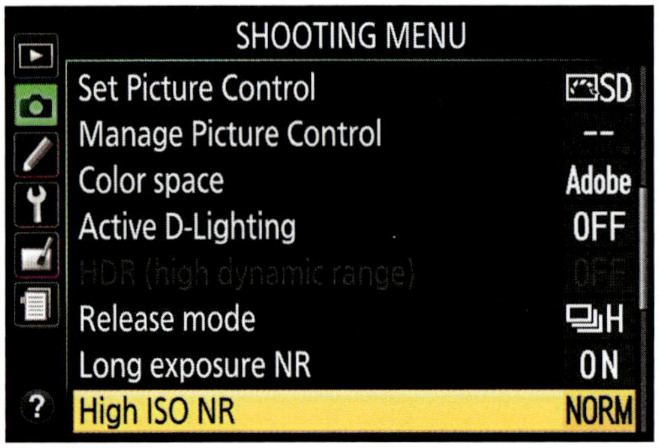

C

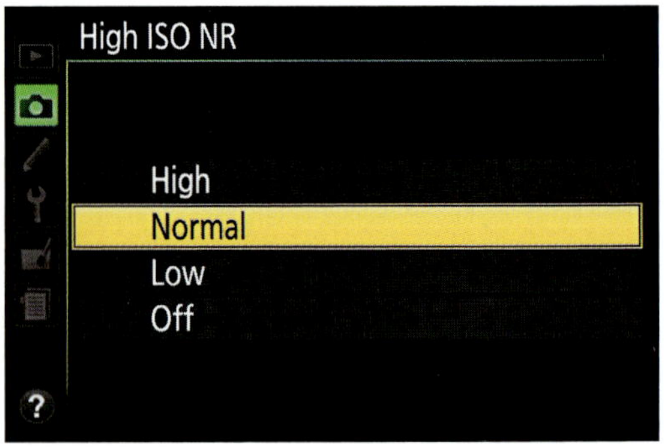

Selecting a White Balance

This probably seems like a no-brainer. If it's sunny, select Daylight. If it's overcast, choose the Shade or Cloudy setting. Those choices wouldn't be wrong for those circumstances, but why limit yourself? Sometimes you can actually change the mood of the photo by selecting a white balance that doesn't quite fit the light for the scene you are shooting.

Figure 7.7 is an example of a correct white balance. It was late afternoon and the sun was starting to move low in the sky, giving everything that warm afternoon glow. The white balance for this image was set to Daylight.

But what if I want to make the scene look as if it had been shot in the early morning hours? Simple, I just change the white balance to Fluorescent, which is a much cooler setting (**Figure 7.8**).

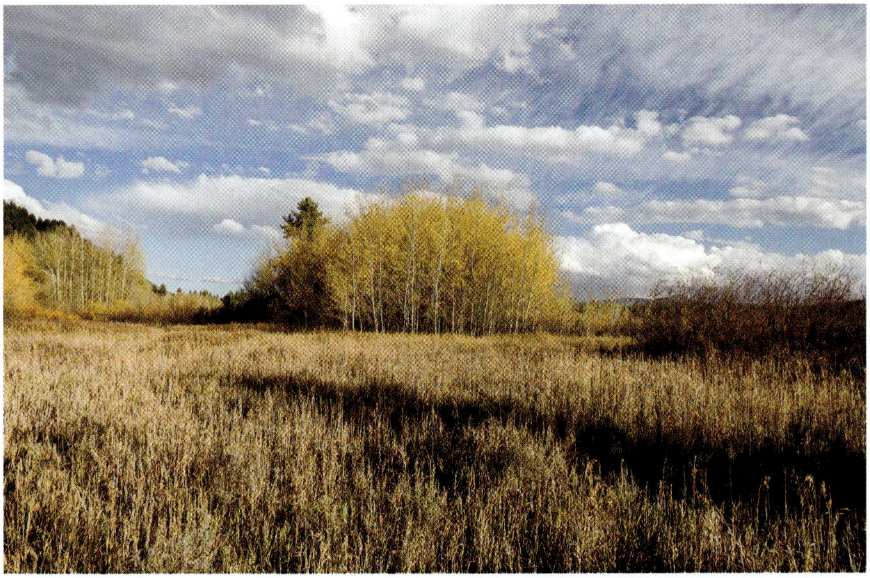

Figure 7.7
Using the "proper" white balance yields predictable results.

ISO 100 • 1/30 sec. • f/11 • 24mm lens

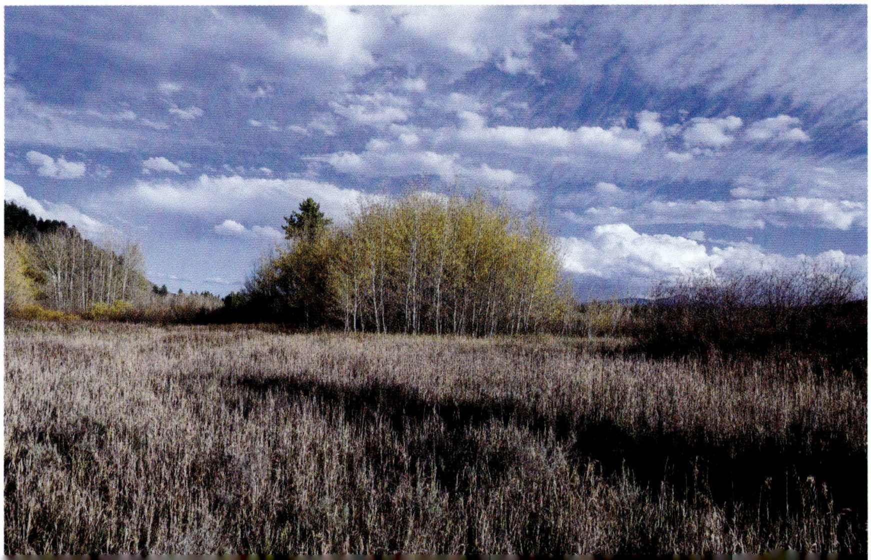

Figure 7.8
Changing the white balance to Fluorescent gives the impression that the picture was taken at a different time of day than it really was.

ISO 100 • 1/30 sec. • f/11 • 24mm lens

You can select the most appropriate white balance for your shooting conditions in a couple of ways. The first is to take some shots, review them on the LCD, and keep the one you like. Of course, you would need to take one for each white balance setting, which means you have to take about seven shots to see which is most pleasing.

The second method, and my personal favorite, doesn't require taking a single shot: Use Live View to get perfectly selected white balances. Live View gives instant feedback as you scroll through all of the white balance settings and displays them for you right on the LCD. Even better, you can choose a custom setting that will let you dial in exactly the right look for your image.

To use Live View to preview the white balance, first you have to customize the Function button.

Customizing the Function button for white balance

1. Press the Menu button, and use the Multi-selector to get to Custom Setting Menu.
2. Now highlight menu item f: Controls, and press OK (**A**).
3. Select item f1: Assign Fn Button, and press OK (**B**).
4. Now select WB: White Balance, and press OK (**C**). This will give you quick access to the white balance options by pressing the Function button.

A

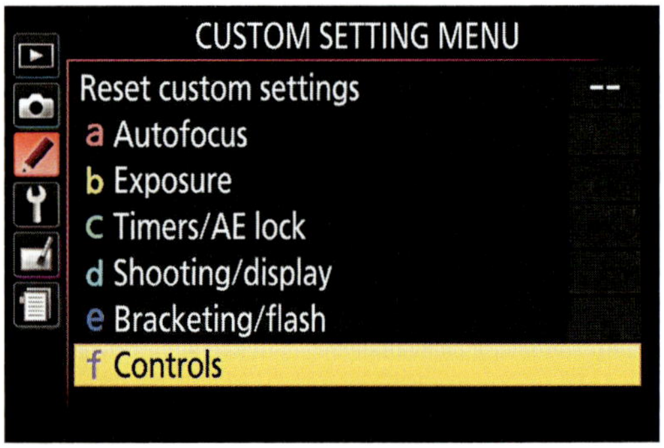

B

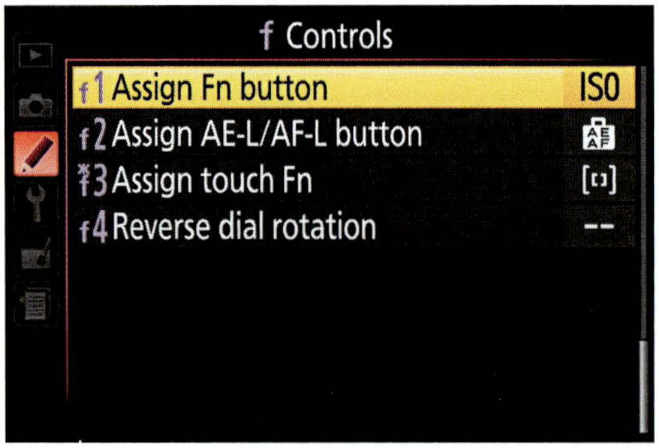

C

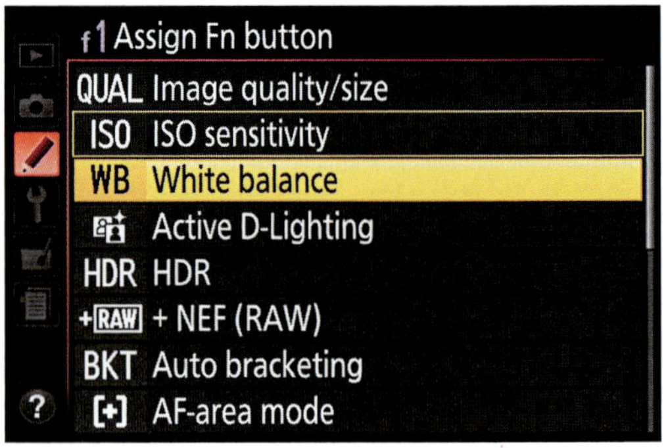

Using Live View to preview different white balance settings

1. Rotate the Live View (Lv) switch located under the Mode dial on top of the camera.
2. With Live View activated, press the Function button on the front of the camera (it's located between the lens release and flash buttons).
3. While holding the Function button, use the Command dial to select from among the different white balance choices while viewing the effect on the rear LCD.
4. To lock in your change, just release the Function button, and then rotate the Lv switch to exit Live View mode.

Using the Landscape Picture Control

When shooting landscapes, I always look for great color and contrast. This is one of the reasons that so many landscape shots are taken in the early morning or during sunset, also known as the golden hours. The light is much more vibrant and colorful at these times of day and adds a sense of drama to an image.

> **Manual Callout**
>
> Check out page 152 in the Reference Manual PDF for more information on setting picture controls.

You can help boost this effect, especially in the less-than-golden hours of the day, by using the Landscape picture control (**Figure 7.9**). Just as in the Landscape mode found in the automatic scene modes, you can set up your landscape shooting so you capture images with increased sharpness and a slight boost in blues and greens. This control will add some pop to your landscapes without the need for additional processing in any software.

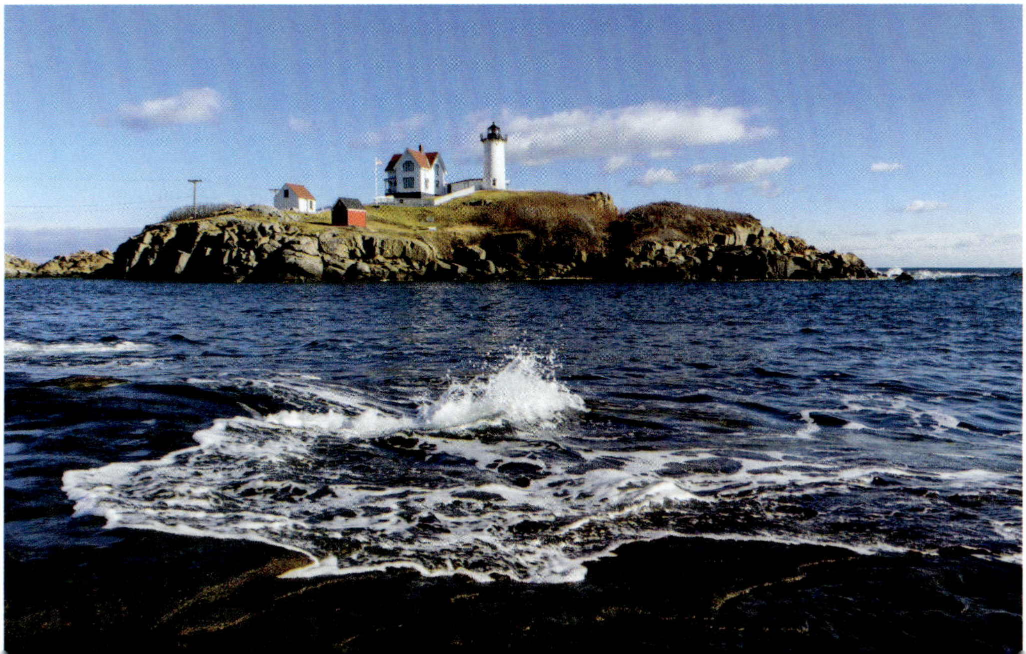

Figure 7.9
Using the Landscape picture control can add sharpness and more vivid color to skies and vegetation.

ISO 400 • 1/400 sec. • f/11 • 18mm lens

Taming Overexposure with Exposure Compensation

Balancing exposure in scenes that have a wide contrast in tonal ranges can be extremely challenging. The one thing you should never do is overexpose your photos (skies are especially vulnerable) to the point of blowing out your highlights (unless, of course, that is the look you are going for). It's one thing to have white clouds, but it's a completely different, and bad, thing to have no detail at all in those clouds. This usually happens when the camera is trying to gain exposure in the darker areas of the image (**Figure 7.10**). The one way to tell if you have blown out your highlights is to turn on the Highlight Alert, or "blinkies," feature on your camera (see the "How I Shoot" section in Chapter 4). When you take a shot where the highlights are exposed beyond the point of having any detail, that area will blink in your LCD display. It is up to you to determine if that particular area is important enough to regain detail by altering your exposure. If the answer is yes, the easiest way to go about it is to use some exposure compensation.

With this feature, you can force your camera to choose an exposure that ranges, in 1/3-stop increments, from five stops over to five stops under the metered exposure (**Figure 7.11**).

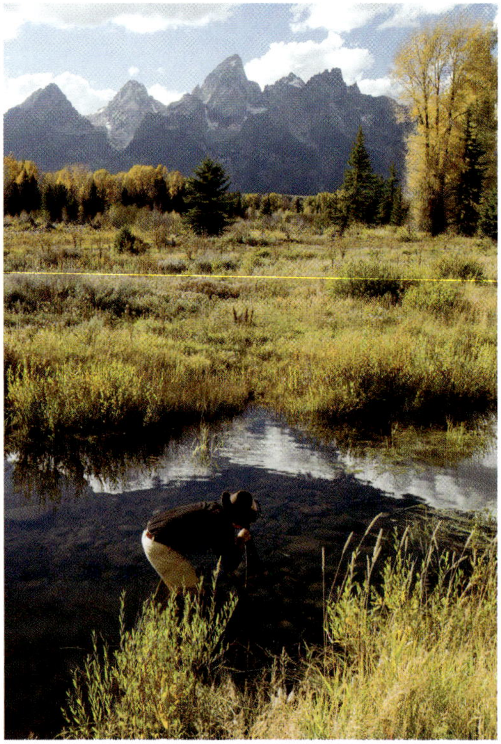

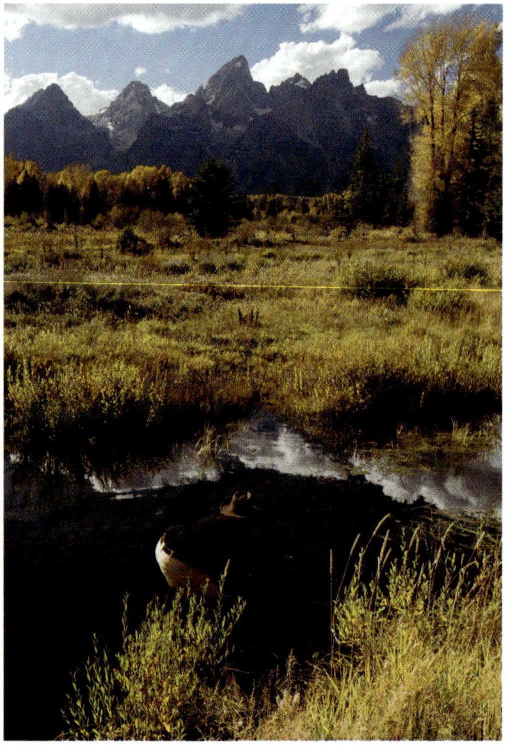

Figure 7.10 (left)
The darker colors in the foreground caused the meter to overexpose slightly, which washes out color and loses detail in the highlights.

ISO 100 • 1/25 sec. • f/11 • 36mm lens

Figure 7.11 (right)
A compensation of one stop of underexposure brought back the detail in the highlights and produced a more vibrant photo.

ISO 100 • 1/50 sec. • f/11 • 18mm lens

High-key and low-key images

When you hear someone refer to a subject as being *high key*, it usually means that the entire image is composed of a very bright subject with very few shadow areas—think snow or beach. It makes sense, then, that a *low-key* subject has very few highlight areas and a predominance of shadow areas. Think of a cityscape at night as an example of a low-key photo.

Using exposure compensation to regain detail in highlights

1. Activate the camera meter by lightly pressing the shutter release button.
2. Using your index finger, press and hold the Exposure Compensation button to change the over-/underexposure setting by rotating the Command dial.
3. Rotate the Command dial to the left one click and take another picture (each click of the Command dial is a 1/3-stop change).
4. If the blinkies are gone, you are good to go. If not, keep subtracting from your exposure by 1/3 of a stop until you have a good exposure in the highlights.

I generally keep my camera set to –1/3 stop for most of my landscape work unless I am working with a location that is very dark or low key.

You can also change the Exposure Compensation setting by using the **i** button on the rear of the camera.

Adjusting exposure compensation using the i button

1. Press the **i** button to activate the cursor in the information display.
2. Use the Multi-selector to move the cursor to the Exposure Compensation position, and press OK.
3. Now press in a downward direction on the Multi-selector to lower the compensation by 1/3 of a stop. Each press downward will continue to reduce the exposure in 1/3-stop increments for up to five stops (although I rarely need to go past one stop).

It should be noted that any exposure compensation will remain in place even after turning the camera off and then on again. Don't forget to reset it once you have successfully captured your image. Also, exposure compensation only works in the Program, Shutter Priority, and Aperture Priority modes. Changing between these three modes will hold the compensation you set while switching from one to the other. When you change the Mode dial to one of the automatic scene modes or to Manual, the compensation will set itself to zero.

Shooting Beautiful Black and White Landscapes

There is almost nothing as timeless as a beautiful black and white landscape photo. For many, it is the purest form of photography. The genre conjures up thoughts of Ansel Adams out in Yosemite Valley, capturing stunning monoliths with his 8x10 view camera. Well, just because you are shooting with a digital camera doesn't mean you can't create your own stunning photos using the power of the Monochrome picture control. (See the "Classic Black and White Portraits" section of Chapter 6 for instructions on setting up this feature.) Not only can you shoot in black and white, you can also customize the camera to apply built-in filters to lighten or darken different elements within your scene, as well as add contrast and definition.

The four filter colors are red, yellow, green, and orange. The most typically used filters in black and white photography are red and yellow. This is because the color of these filters will darken opposite colors and lighten similar colors. So if you want to darken a blue sky, you would use a yellow filter because blue is the opposite of yellow. To darken green foliage, you would use a red filter. Check out the series of shots with different filters applied in **Figure 7.12**.

You can see that there is no real difference in contrast between the color and the black and white image with no filter. The red filter has the effect of darkening the skies slightly, while lightening the grasses in the foreground. The yellow filter doesn't darken the sky or lighten the grasses as much as the red. For this particular shot, I much prefer the look of the red filter.

Other options in the Monochrome picture control enable you to adjust the sharpness and contrast and even add some color toning to the final image. This information is also in the "Classic Black and White Portraits" section of Chapter 6. I like to have Sharpness set to 5 and Contrast set to +1 for my landscape images. This gives an overall look to the black and white image that is reminiscent of classic black and white films. Experiment with the various settings to find the combination that is most pleasing to you.

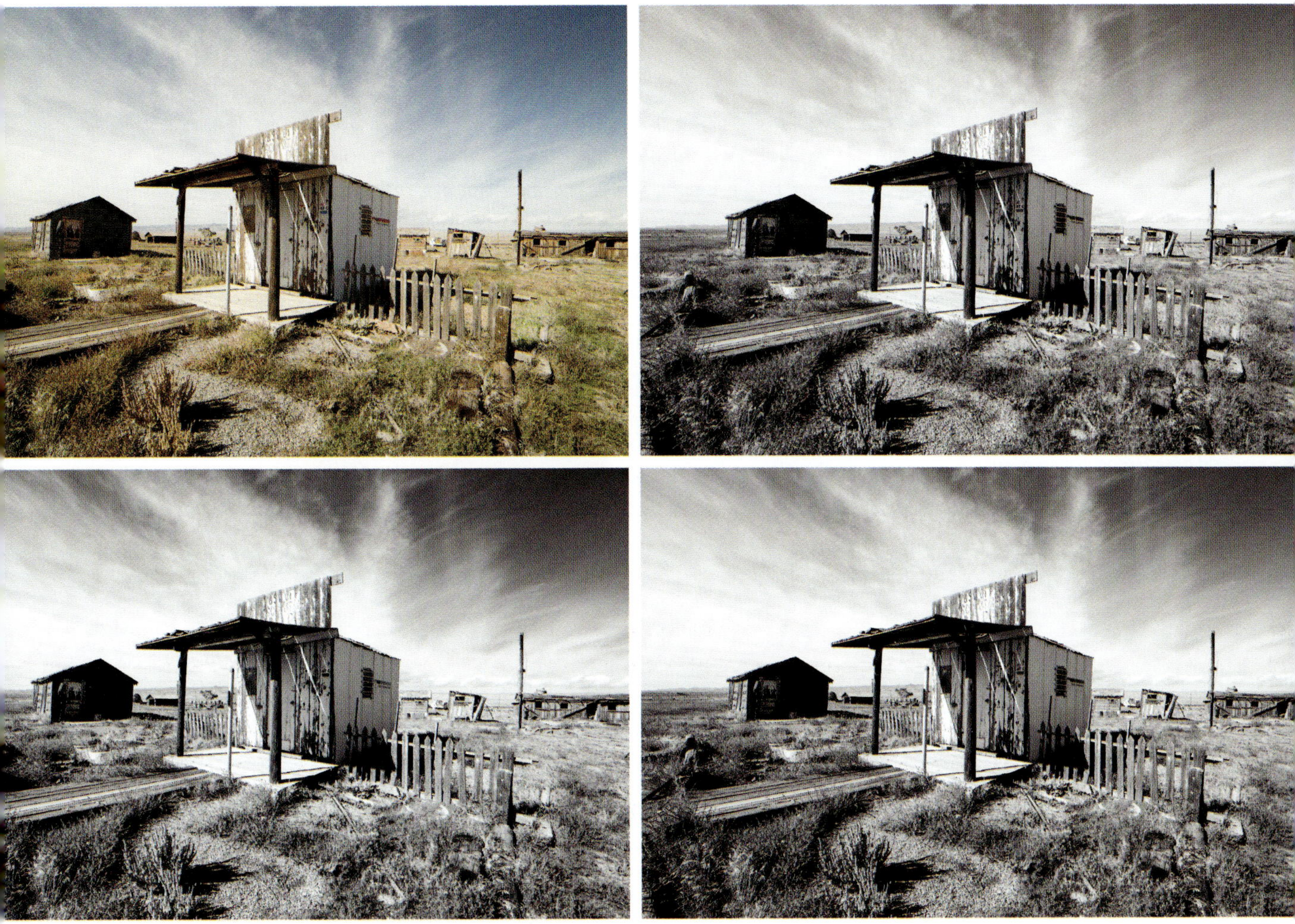

Figure 7.12 Adding color-filter settings to the Monochrome picture control allows you to lighten or darken elements in your scene. The top right image has no filter applied to it. The bottom left has a red filter, and the bottom right has a yellow filter.

ISO 100 • 1/125 sec. • f/11 • 14mm lens

The Golden Light

If you ask professional landscape photographers what their favorite time to shoot is, chances are they'll tell you it's the hours surrounding daybreak and sunset (**Figures 7.13** and **7.14**). This is because the light is coming from a very low angle to the landscape, which creates shadows and gives depth and character. There is also a quality to the light that seems cleaner and more colorful than the light you get when shooting at midday. One thing that can dramatically improve any morning or evening shot is the presence of clouds. The sun will fill the underside of the clouds with a palette of colors and add drama to your skies.

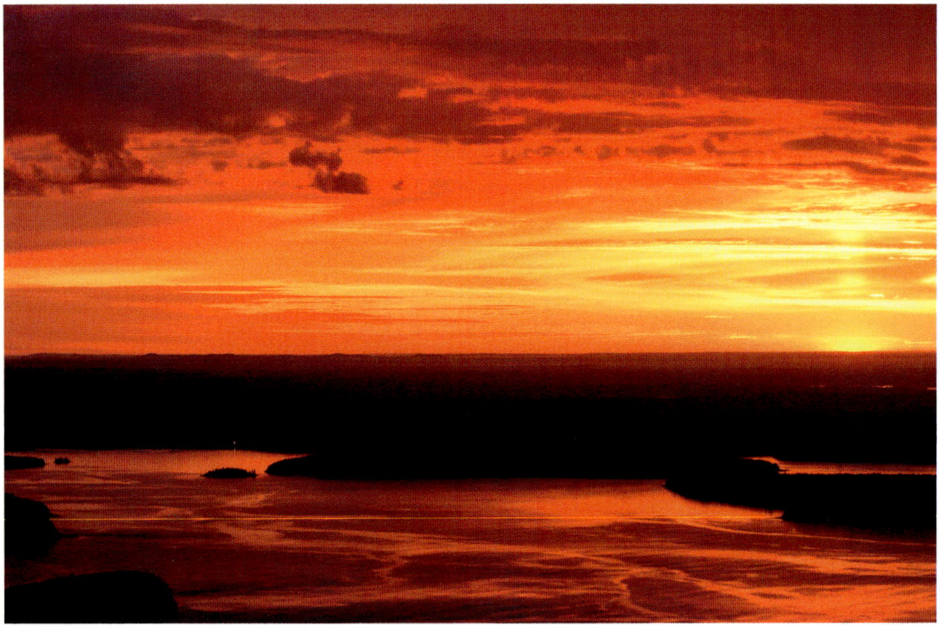

Figure 7.13
The few minutes just prior to sunrise can add great colors to a partly cloudy sky.

ISO 200 • 1/13 sec. • f/8 • 80mm lens

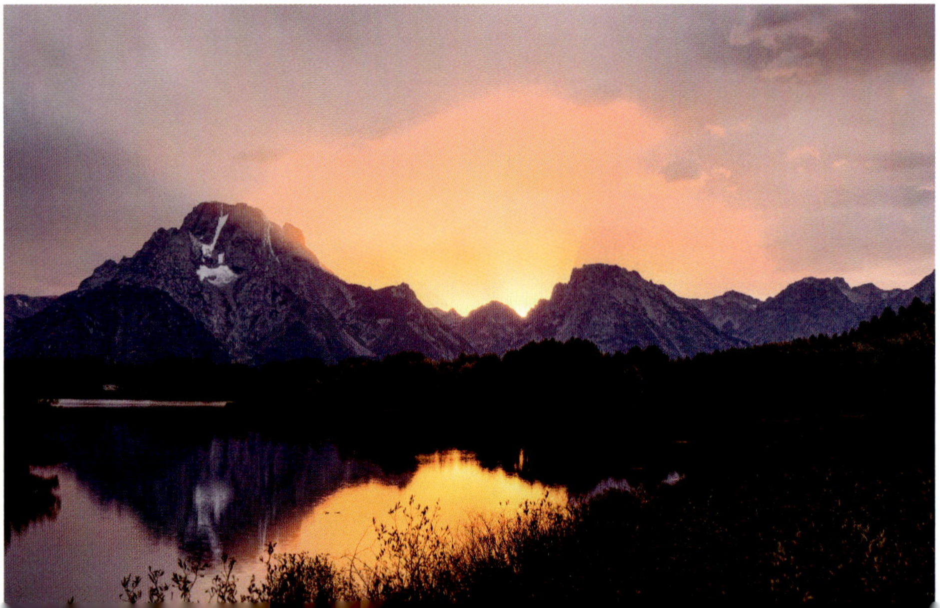

Figure 7.14
Late afternoon sun is usually warmer and adds drama and warmth to the scene.

ISO 100 • 0.4 sec. • f/11 • 70mm lens

Where to Focus

Large landscape scenes are great fun to photograph, but they can present a problem: Where exactly do you focus when you want everything to be sharp? Since our goal is to create a great landscape photo, we will need to concentrate on how to best create an image that is tack sharp, with a depth of field that renders great focus throughout the scene.

I have already stressed the importance of a good tripod when shooting landscapes. The tripod lets you concentrate on the aperture portion of the exposure without worrying about how long your shutter will be open. This is because the tripod provides the stability to handle any shutter speed you might need when shooting at small apertures. I find that for most of my landscape work, I set my camera to Aperture Priority mode and the ISO to 100–200 (for a clean, noise-free image).

However, shooting with the smallest aperture on your lens doesn't necessarily mean you will get the proper sharpness throughout your image. The real key is knowing where in the scene to focus your lens to maximize the depth of field for your chosen aperture. To do this, you must use something called the "hyper focal distance" of your lens.

Hyper focal distance, also referred to as HFD, is the point of focus that will give you the greatest acceptable sharpness from a point near your camera all the way out to infinity. If you combine good HFD practice in combination with a small aperture, you will get images that are sharp to infinity.

There are a couple of ways to do this, and the one that is probably the easiest, as you might guess, is the one most widely used by working pros. When you have your shot all set up and composed, focus on an object that is about one-third of the distance into your frame. It is usually pretty close to the proper distance and will render favorable results. When you have the focus set, take a photograph, and then zoom in on the preview on your LCD to check the sharpness of your image. In **Figure 7.15**, an aperture of f/11 gave me a sharply focused image all the way back to the distant peak. This was an excellent opportunity to use the AF-S focus mode as well.

One thing to remember is that as your lens gets wider in focal length, your HFD will be closer to the camera position. This is because the wider the lens, the greater the depth of field you can achieve—yet another reason why a good wide-angle lens is indispensable to the landscape shooter.

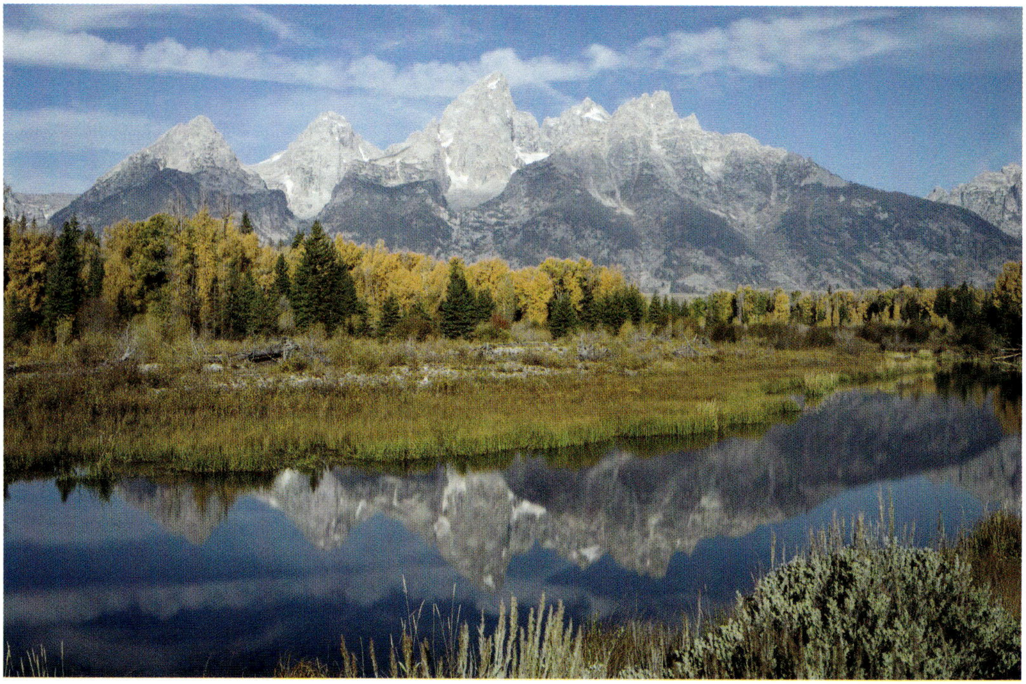

Figure 7.15
To get maximum focus from near to far, I set the focus about one-third of the way into the scene, and then recomposed before taking the picture.
ISO 100 • 30 sec. • f/11 • 42mm lens

You can have the best of both worlds, though, by having the camera focus for you, then switching to Manual focus to comfortably recompose your shot (**Figure 7.16**).

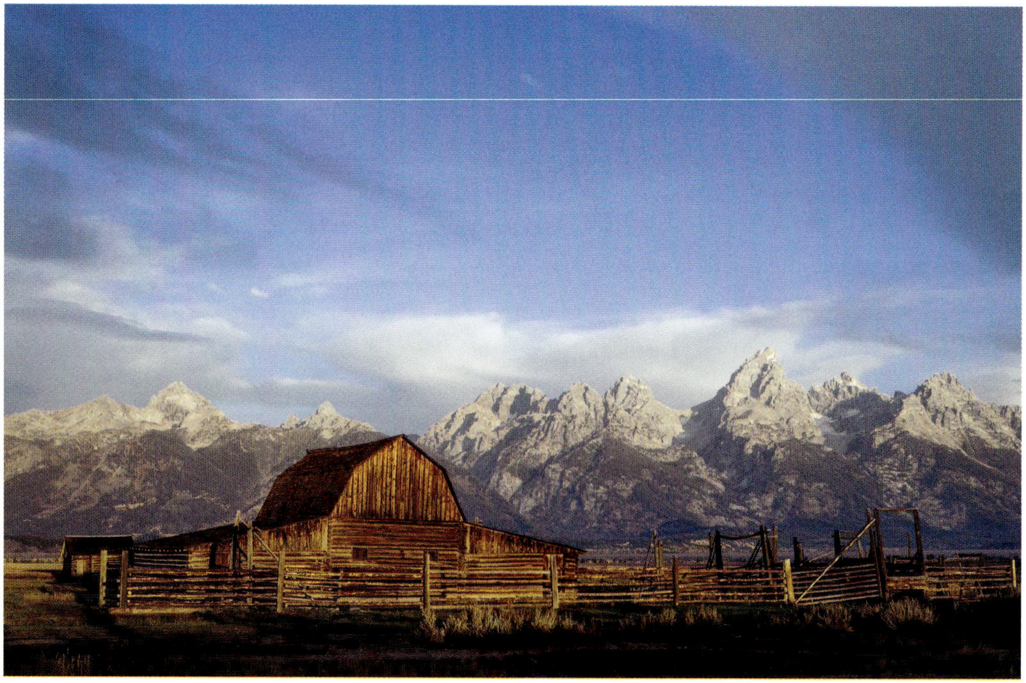

Figure 7.16
Using the DOF (depth of field) one-third rule, I focused on the barn and then switched the lens to Manual focus before recomposing for the final shot.
ISO 100 • 1/15 sec. • f/11 • 45mm lens

Getting focused while using a tripod

1. Set up your shot and find the area you want to focus on.
2. Pan your tripod head so your active focus point is on that spot.
3. Press the shutter button halfway to focus the camera.
4. Switch the camera to Manual focus by sliding the switch on the lens barrel from A to M.
5. Recompose on the tripod, and then take the shot.

The camera will fire without trying to refocus the lens. This works especially well for wide-angle lenses, which can be difficult to focus in Manual mode.

Making Water Fluid

There's little else quite as satisfying for the landscape shooter as capturing a silky waterfall shot. Creating the smooth-flowing effect is as simple as adjusting your shutter speed to allow the water to be in motion while the shutter is open. The key is to have your camera on a stable platform (such as a tripod) so you can use a shutter speed that's long enough to work. To achieve a great effect, use a shutter speed that is at least 1/15 of a second or longer.

Setting up for a waterfall shot

1. Attach the camera to your tripod, and then compose and focus your shot.
2. Make sure the ISO is set to 200 (or lower).
3. Using Aperture Priority mode, set your aperture to the smallest opening (such as f/22 or f/36) to slow down the shutter speed.
4. Press the shutter button halfway so the camera takes a meter reading.
5. Check to see if the shutter speed is 1/15 of a second or slower.
6. Take a photo, and then check the image on the LCD.

You can also use Shutter Priority mode for this effect by dialing in the desired shutter speed and having the camera set the aperture for you. I prefer to use Aperture Priority to ensure that I have the greatest depth of field possible.

If the water is blinking on the LCD, indicating a loss of detail in the highlights, use the Exposure Compensation feature (as discussed earlier in this chapter) to bring details back into the waterfall. You will need to have the Highlight Alert feature turned on to check for overexposure (see "How I Shoot" in Chapter 4).

There is a possibility that you will not be able to have a shutter speed that is long enough to capture a smooth effect, especially if you are shooting in bright daylight conditions. To overcome this obstacle, you need a filter for your lens—either a polarizing filter or a neutral density filter. The polarizing filter redirects waves of light to create more vibrant colors, reduce reflections, and darken blue skies, as well as lengthen exposure times by two stops due to the darkness of the filter. It is a handy filter for landscape work. The neutral density filter is typically just a dark piece of glass that serves to darken the scene by one, two, or more stops (**Figure 7.17**). This allows you to use slower shutter speeds during bright conditions. Think of it as sunglasses for your camera lens. You will find more discussion on filters in Chapter 11.

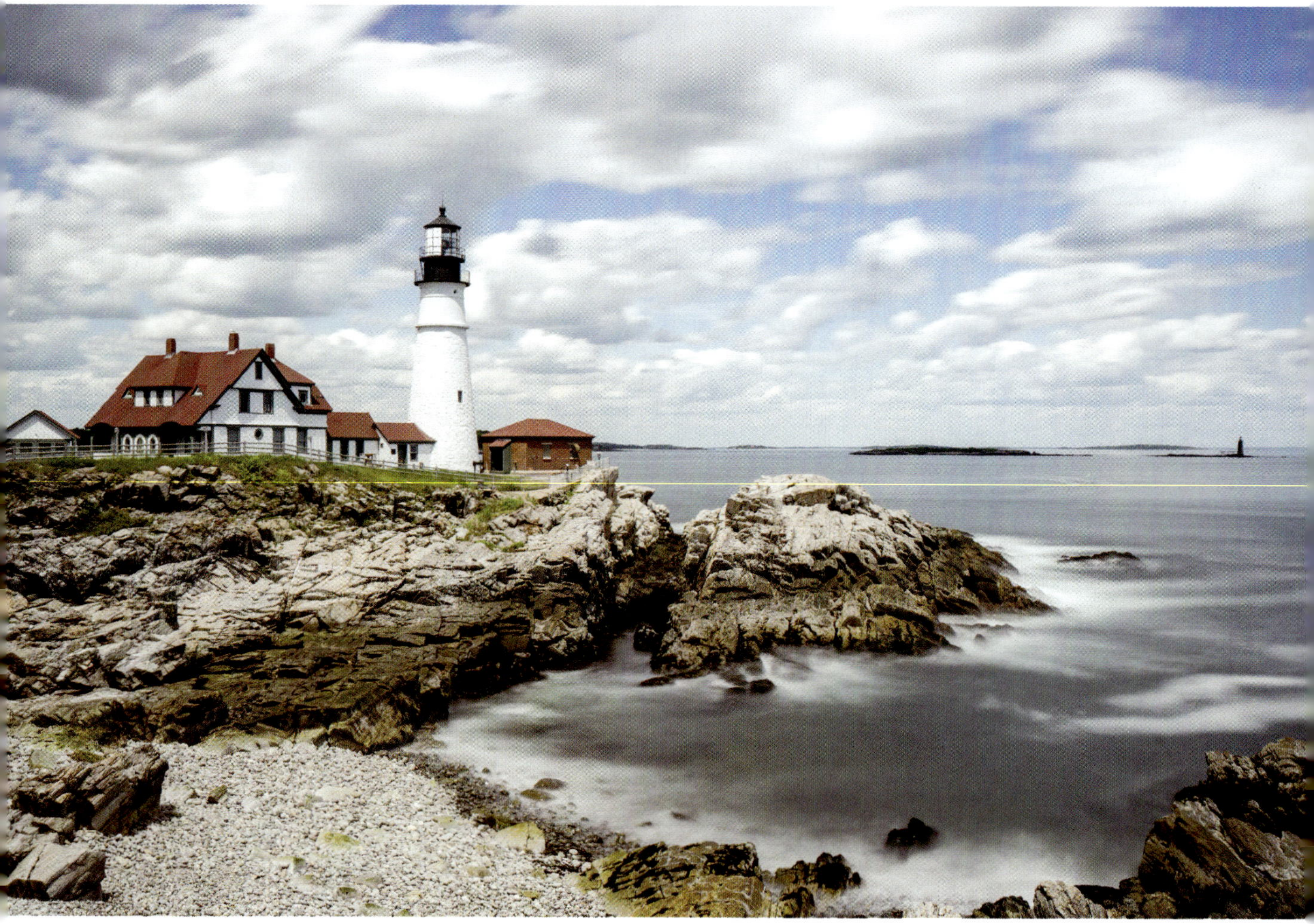

Figure 7.17 I used a neutral density filter to add 10 stops of exposure, thus allowing for a longer exposure time and transforming the water into mist and the clouds into a streaming blur.

ISO 100 • 30 sec. • f/22 • 32mm lens

Directing the Viewer: A Word About Composition

As a photographer, it's your job to lead the viewer through your image. You accomplish this by using the principles of composition, which is the arrangement of elements in the scene that draws the viewer's eyes through your image and holds their attention. As the director of this viewing, you need to understand how people see, and then use that information to focus their attention on the most important elements in your image.

We look at elements in a photograph in a general order. The first thing we notice is brightness. The eye wants to travel to the brightest object within a scene. So if you have a bright sky, it's probably the first place the eye will go. The second thing is sharpness. Sharp, detailed elements will get more attention than soft, blurry areas. Finally, the eye will move to vivid colors while leaving the dull, flat colors for last. It is important to know these essentials in order to grab—and keep—viewers' attention and then direct them through the frame.

In **Figure 7.18**, the eye is drawn to the bright moon in the upper third of the frame. From there, it is pulled toward the color and details of the foliage that is anchoring the lower portion of the image. The eye moves along the bottom of the frame, then is lifted back up to the distant mountains, and then right back to the beginning. The elements within the image all help keep the eye moving but never leaving the frame.

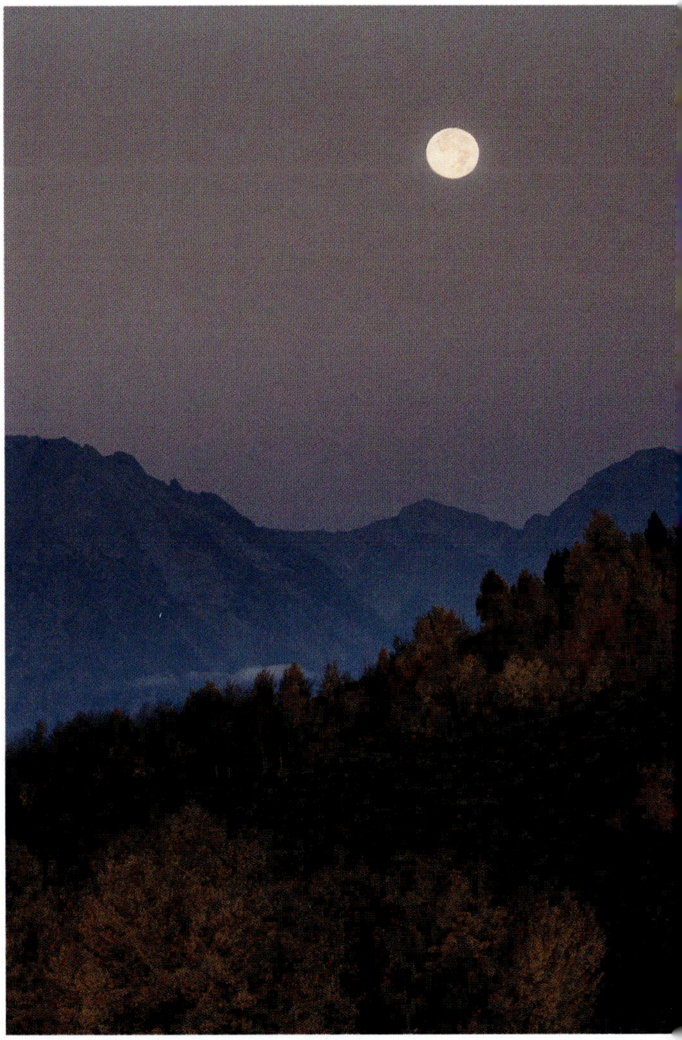

Figure 7.18 The composition of the elements pulls the viewer's eyes around the image, leading from one element to the next in a circular pattern.

ISO 200 • 1/30 sec. • f/8 • 200mm lens

Rule of thirds

There are quite a few philosophies concerning composition. The easiest one to begin with is known as the rule of thirds. Using this principle, you simply divide your viewfinder into thirds by imagining two horizontal and two vertical lines that divide the frame equally.

The key to using this method of composition is to have your main subject located at or near one of the intersecting points (**Figure 7.19**).

By placing your subject near these intersecting lines, you are giving the viewer space to move within the frame. The one thing you don't want to do is place your subject smack dab in the middle of the frame. This is sometimes referred to as bull's-eye composition, and it works only with the right subject matter. It's not always wrong, but it will usually be less appealing and may not hold the viewer's attention.

Speaking of the middle of the frame: The other main rule of thirds deals with horizon lines. Generally speaking, you should position the horizon one-third of the way up or down in the frame. Splitting the frame in half by placing your horizon in the middle of the picture is akin to placing the subject in the middle of the frame; it doesn't lend a sense of importance to either the sky or the ground.

In **Figure 7.20**, I incorporated the rule of thirds by keeping my horizon in the top third of the frame. I have also placed the prominent rock in the foreground near the intersecting

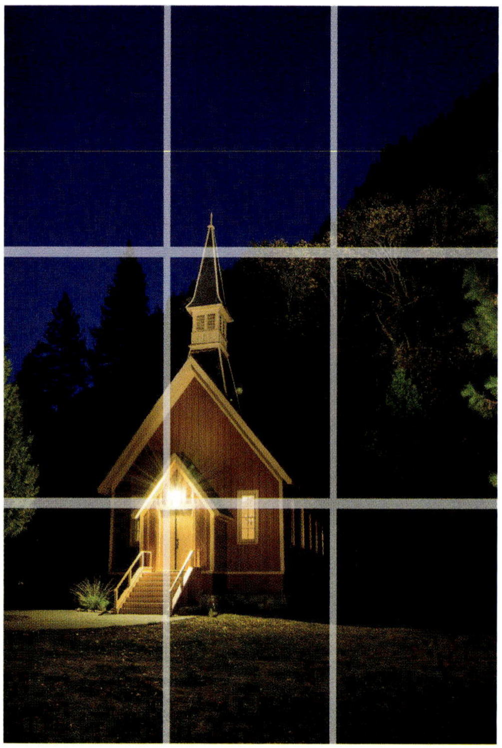

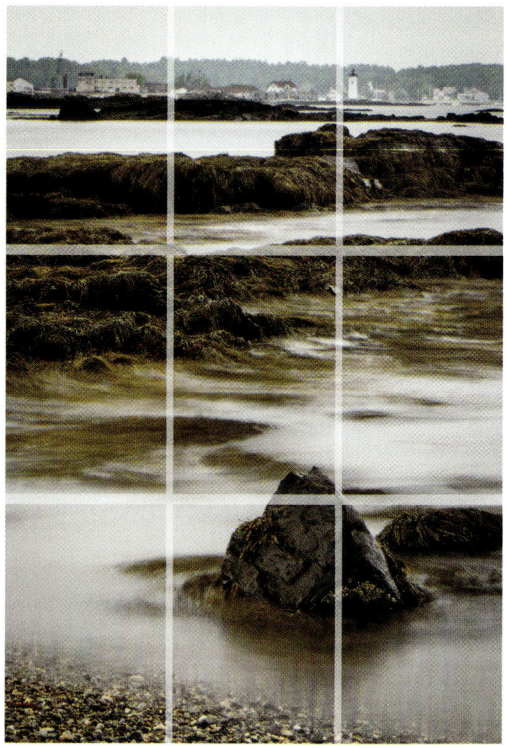

Figure 7.19 (left) Placing the chapel door in the left third of the image creates a much more interesting composition than having it dead center in the frame.

ISO 400 • 30 sec. • f/13 • 20mm lens

Figure 7.20 (right) Placing the horizon of this image in the top third of the frame places emphasis on the subjects below it—the sea and the interesting stones.

ISO 100 • 6 sec. • f/22 • 85mm lens

lines on the right side of the frame. I achieved this by choosing the right focal length (in this case, it was 85mm) and by moving my camera position until I had all of the key elements in the right place.

The D5500 has a visual tool for assisting you in composing your photo, in the form of a grid overlay in Live View.

Using a grid overlay in Live View

1. Rotate the Lv switch under the Mode dial to activate Live View.
2. Press the Info button on the back of the camera to cycle through the Live View display options until you see the grid overlay.

Although the grid in the Live View screen isn't equally divided into thirds, it will give you an approximation for where you should be aligning your subjects in the frame, and it can help you keep your horizon straight. You can also enable the grid overlay inside the viewfinder by setting d3: Viewfinder Grid Display to On in the Custom Setting menu.

Creating depth

Because a photograph is a flat, two-dimensional space, you need to create a sense of depth by using the elements in the scene to create a three-dimensional feel. This is accomplished by including different and distinct spaces for the eye to travel through: a foreground, a middle ground, and a background. By using these three spaces, you draw the viewer in and render depth to your image.

The sunrise scene shown in **Figure 7.21** illustrates this well. The boulder on the near shore defines the foreground area. The reflecting pond defines the middle ground, and the sky creates a perfect backdrop for the scene.

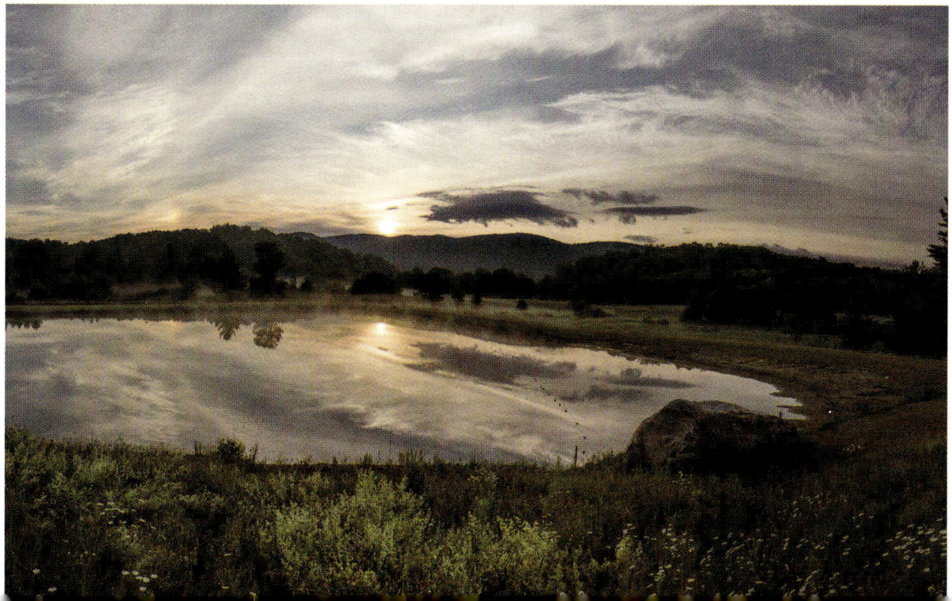

Figure 7.21
The boulder in the foreground, the pond, and the sky all add to the feeling of depth in the image.

ISO 100 • 1/125 sec. • f/11 • 18mm lens

Advanced Techniques to Explore

This section comes with a warning attached. All of the techniques and topics up to this point have been centered on your camera. The following two sections, covering panoramas and high dynamic range (HDR) images, require you to use image-processing software to complete the photograph. They are, however, important enough that you should know how to correctly shoot for success, if you choose to explore these two popular techniques. But wait, what about the in-camera HDR function of the D5500? Don't worry, we'll cover that, too, but as you'll soon see, it has its limitations. I want to show you an alternative HDR method that will give you more data in your captures and more control over the finished product.

Shooting panoramas

If you have ever visited the Grand Canyon, you know just how large and wide open it truly is—it's difficult to capture its splendor in just one frame. The same can be said for a mountain range, a cityscape, or any extremely wide vista. There are two methods you can use to capture the feeling of this type of scene.

The "fake" panorama

The first method is to shoot with your lens set to its widest focal length and then crop out the top and bottom portion of the frame in your imaging software. Panoramic images are generally two or three times wider than a normal image.

Creating a fake panorama

1. To create the look of the panorama, find your widest lens focal length. The 18mm setting on the 18–140mm AF-S kit lens is a great starting point.
2. Using the guidelines discussed earlier in the chapter, compose and focus your scene, and select the smallest aperture possible.
3. Shoot your image. That's all there is to it, from a photography standpoint.
4. Now, open the image in your favorite image-processing software and crop the extraneous foreground and sky from the image, leaving you with a wide panorama of the scene. A typical panoramic aspect ratio is 3:1, where the longest side is three times longer than the short side.

Figure 7.22 shows an example using a photo taken at Grand Teton National Park.

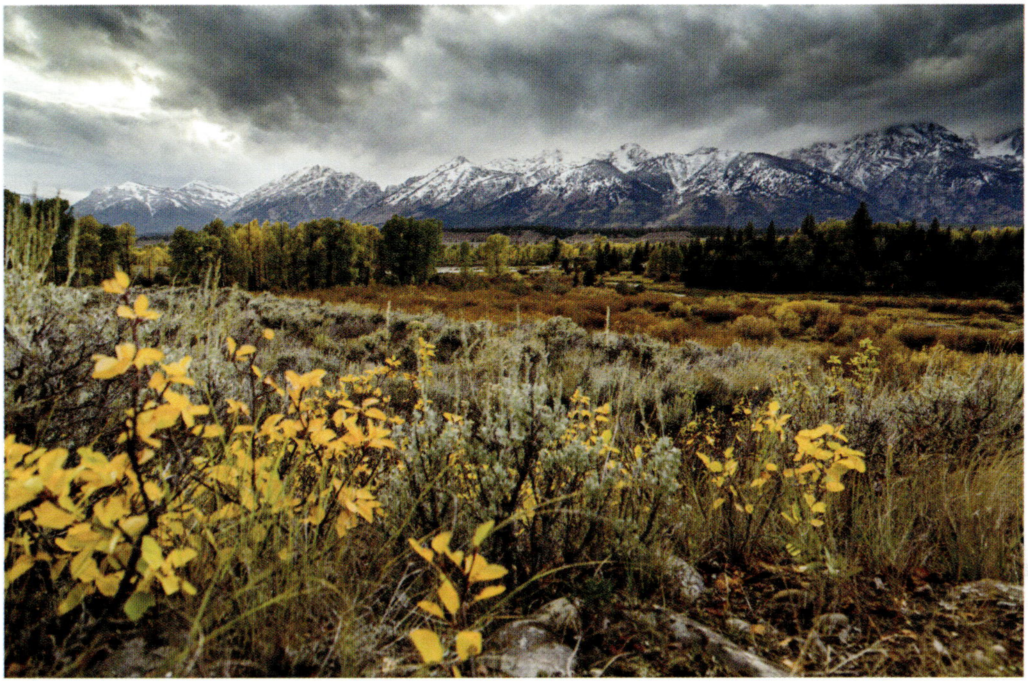

Figure 7.22 **This image could look good as a panorama, too.**

ISO 100 • 1/20 sec. • f/8 • 24mm lens

As you can see, the image was shot with a wide perspective, using a 24mm lens. While it is not a bad photo, it has the potential to have more of an impact with the right crop. Now look at the same image, cropped for panoramic view (**Figure 7.23**). As you can see, it makes a huge difference in the image and gives much higher visual impact by drawing your eyes across the length of the horizon and allowing you to better see the details in the foreground.

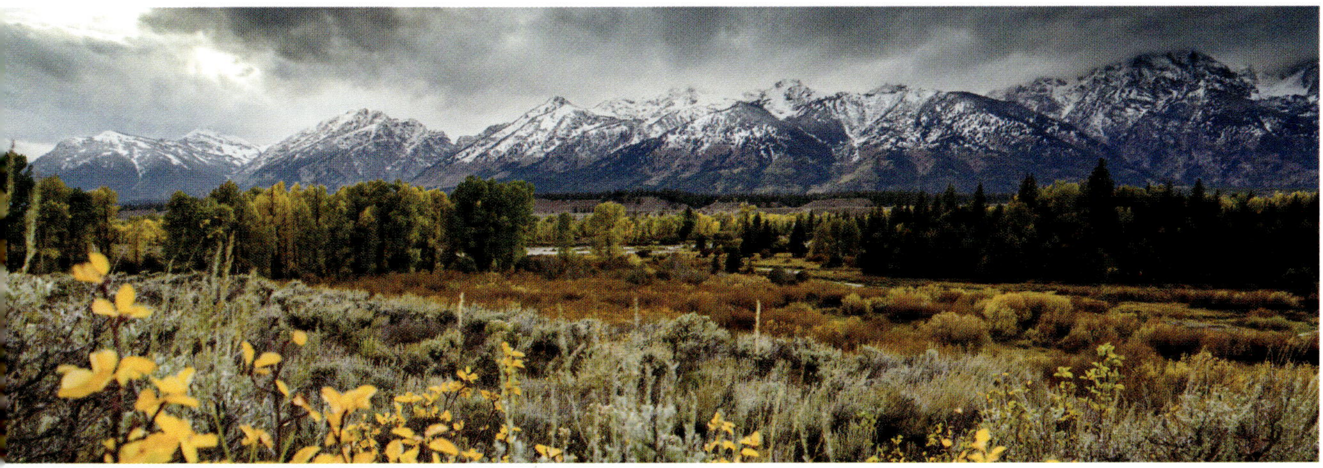

Figure 7.23 **Cropping gives the feeling of a sweeping vista and makes the shot visually appealing.**

The multiple-image panorama

The previous method is sometimes referred to as a "fake" panorama because it is made with a standard-size frame and then cropped down to a narrow perspective. To shoot a true panorama, you need to either use a special panorama camera that shoots a very wide frame or employ the following method, which requires the combining of multiple frames.

The multiple-image pano has gained in popularity in the past few years; this is principally due to advances in image-processing software. Many software options are available now that will take multiple images, align them, and then "stitch" them into a single panoramic image. The real key to shooting a multiple-image pano is to overlap your shots by about 30 percent from one frame to the next (**Figures 7.24** and **7.25**). It is possible to handhold the camera while capturing your images, but the best method for capturing great panoramic images is to use a tripod. Rotating the camera to portrait orientation provides a nice tall image for cropping out your final panoramic image, and helps you avoid the distortions at the edges of the frame that are caused by using a wide-angle lens.

Now that you have your series of overlapping images, you can import them into your image-processing software to stitch them together and create a single panoramic image.

Shooting properly for a multiple-image panorama

1. Mount your camera on your tripod, and make sure it is level.
2. Choose a focal length for your lens that is somewhere between 24mm and 80mm (depending on the distance between you and your subject).
3. In Aperture Priority mode, use a very small aperture for the greatest depth of field. Take a meter reading of a bright part of the scene and make note of it.
4. Now change your camera to Manual mode (M), and dial in the aperture and shutter speed that you obtained in the previous step.
5. Set your lens to Manual focus, and then focus your lens for the area of interest using the HFD method of finding a point one-third of the way into the scene. (If you use autofocus, you risk getting different points of focus from image to image, which will make the image stitching more difficult for the software.)
6. While carefully panning your camera, shoot your images to cover the entire area of the scene from one end to the other, leaving a 30 percent overlap from one frame to the next.
7. Use your favorite imaging software to combine all of the photographs into a single panoramic image, and then crop off any excess areas to achieve the desired aspect ratio.

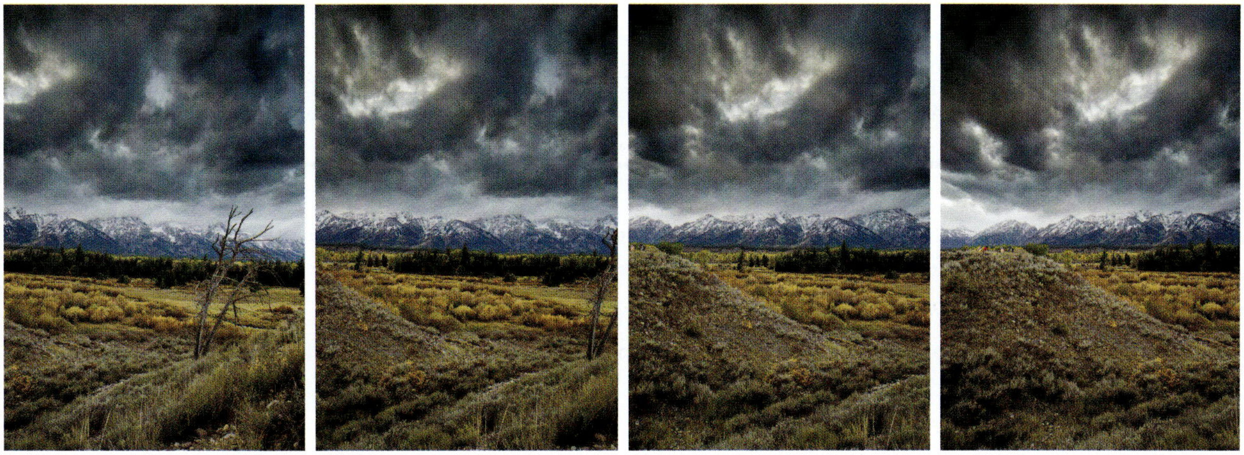

Figure 7.24 **Here you see the makings of a panorama, with four shots overlapping by about 30 percent from frame to frame.**

ISO 100 • 1/8 sec. • f/8 • 24mm lens

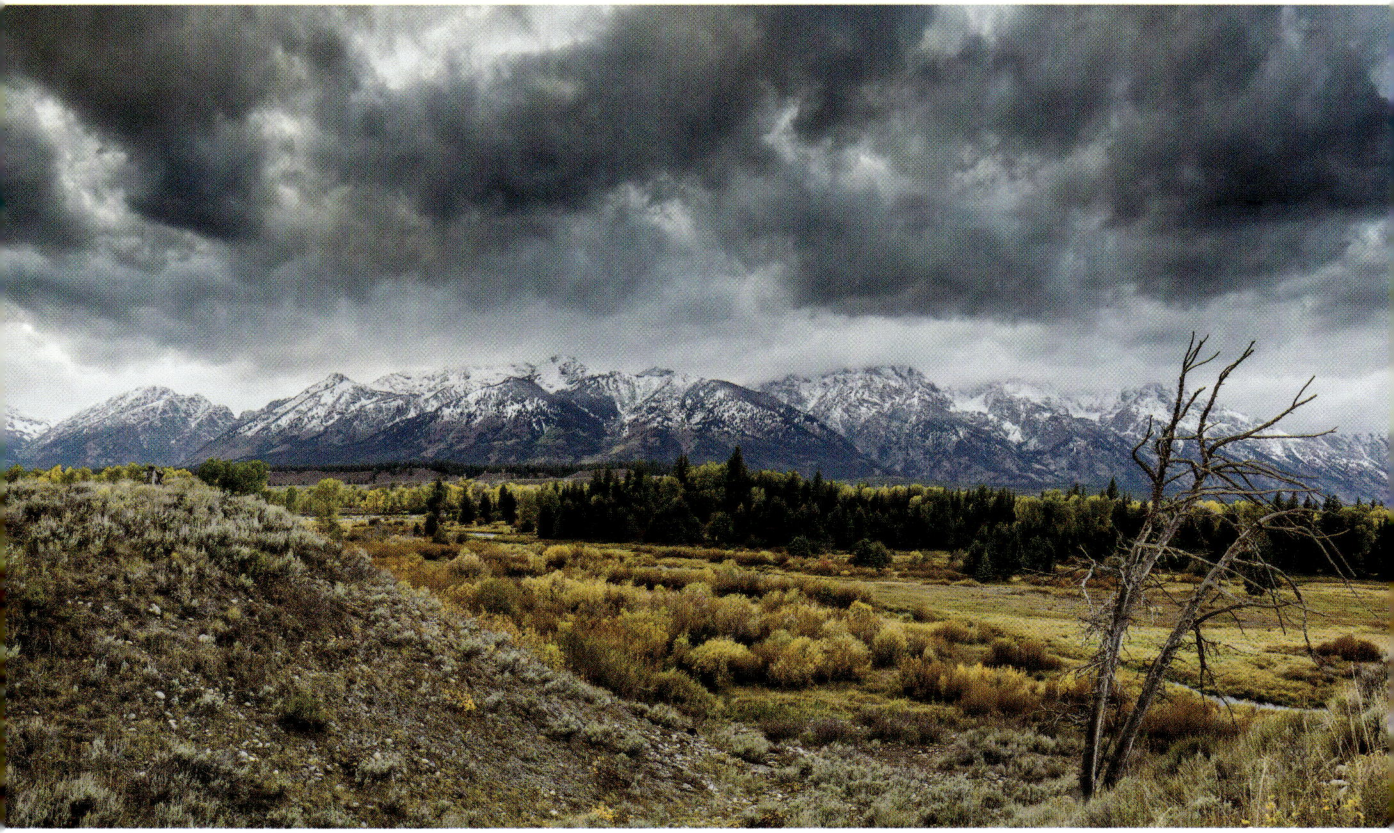

Figure 7.25 **I used Adobe Photoshop to combine all of the exposures into one large panoramic image.**

Sorting your shots for the multi-image panorama

If you shoot more than one series of shots for your panoramas, it can sometimes be difficult to know when one series of images ends and the other begins. Here is a quick tip for separating your images.

Set up your camera using the steps listed here. Now before you take your first good exposure in the series, hold up one finger in front of the camera and take a shot. Now move your hand away and begin taking your overlapping images. When you have taken your last shot, hold two fingers in front of the camera and take another shot.

Now when you go to review your images, use the series of shots that falls between the frames with one and two fingers in them. Then just repeat the process for your next panorama series.

Shooting high dynamic range (HDR) images

One of the more recent trends in digital photography is the use of high dynamic range (HDR) to capture the full range of tonal values in your final image. Typically, when you photograph a scene that has a wide range of tones from shadows to highlights, you have to make a decision regarding which tonal values you are going to emphasize and then adjust your exposure accordingly. This is because your camera has a limited dynamic range, at least as compared with the human eye. HDR photography allows you to capture multiple exposures for the highlights, shadows, and midtones and then combine them into a single image using software. A number of software applications allow you to combine the images and then perform a process called tone mapping, whereby the complete range of exposures is represented in a single image. I will not be covering how to use the various software applications, but I will explore the process of shooting a scene to help you render properly captured images for the HDR process. Note that using a tripod is absolutely necessary for this technique, since you need to have perfect alignment of each image when they are combined.

Before we look at how to shoot for HDR photos to be processed in specialized software, let's take a look at the HDR function built into the D5500. The in-camera HDR function on the D5500 takes two exposures—one slightly underexposed and one slightly overexposed—and then blends the two photos together automatically in the camera to create a new photo that contains a wider dynamic range (meaning more detail in the highlights and shadows) than a single exposure does. This is not far off from the Active D-Lighting function, which automatically reduces the exposure and then uses software in the camera to increase the brightness in the shadows while preserving more detail in the highlights. Both functions have their place, and you should know how to use them.

That said, the downside of the in-camera HDR function is that it combines the data from only two captures (many photographers shooting HDR images combine three to seven exposures' worth of data) and it works only in JPEG mode. You also have limited control over the blending process, and you have to make your decision before you shoot. Of course you can massage the final JPEG image a little to tease out more detail, but if you are going to do that, you lose one of the benefits of the in-camera process.

Shooting an in-camera HDR photo

1. Mount your camera on your tripod, and make sure it is level.
2. Press the **i** button, and set the image quality to JPEG (Fine) and the ISO to 100.
3. With the info edit screen still active, use the Multi-selector to highlight HDR (High Dynamic Range) (**A**).
4. Press OK to go to the HDR (High Dynamic Range) settings screen (**B**).
5. For testing purposes, choose Auto and let the camera decide how to create the HDR based on the scene. Generally speaking, the greater the contrast in the scene, the higher the setting you would choose. Press OK to set the value.
6. Press the shutter button halfway to leave the menu.
7. Set your program mode to Aperture Priority so you can control the depth of field while the camera does everything else.

A

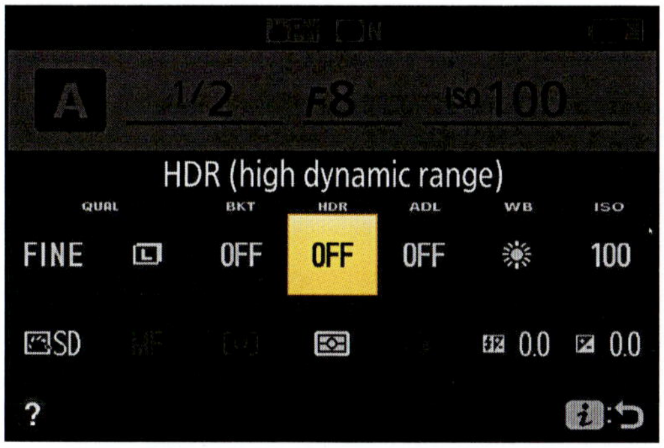

B

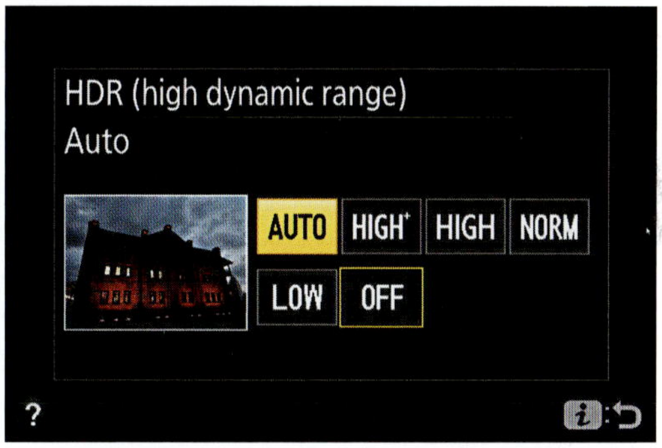

Note that HDR will be displayed in the viewfinder as a reminder that you are in HDR mode. Compose your photo and press the shutter button once. You'll hear the shutter fire twice, and then the camera will churn away for a few seconds as it processes the images and blends them together into the final HDR photo. What you should see is a photo with slightly more detail in the highlights and shadows than a typical capture would have (**Figure 7.26**). In my testing, the difference was often rather subtle, but I did see more detail in the HDR version. For comparison's sake, I created a second HDR image of the same scene from three exposures that were shot in RAW, assembled in Photoshop, and processed in Lightroom.

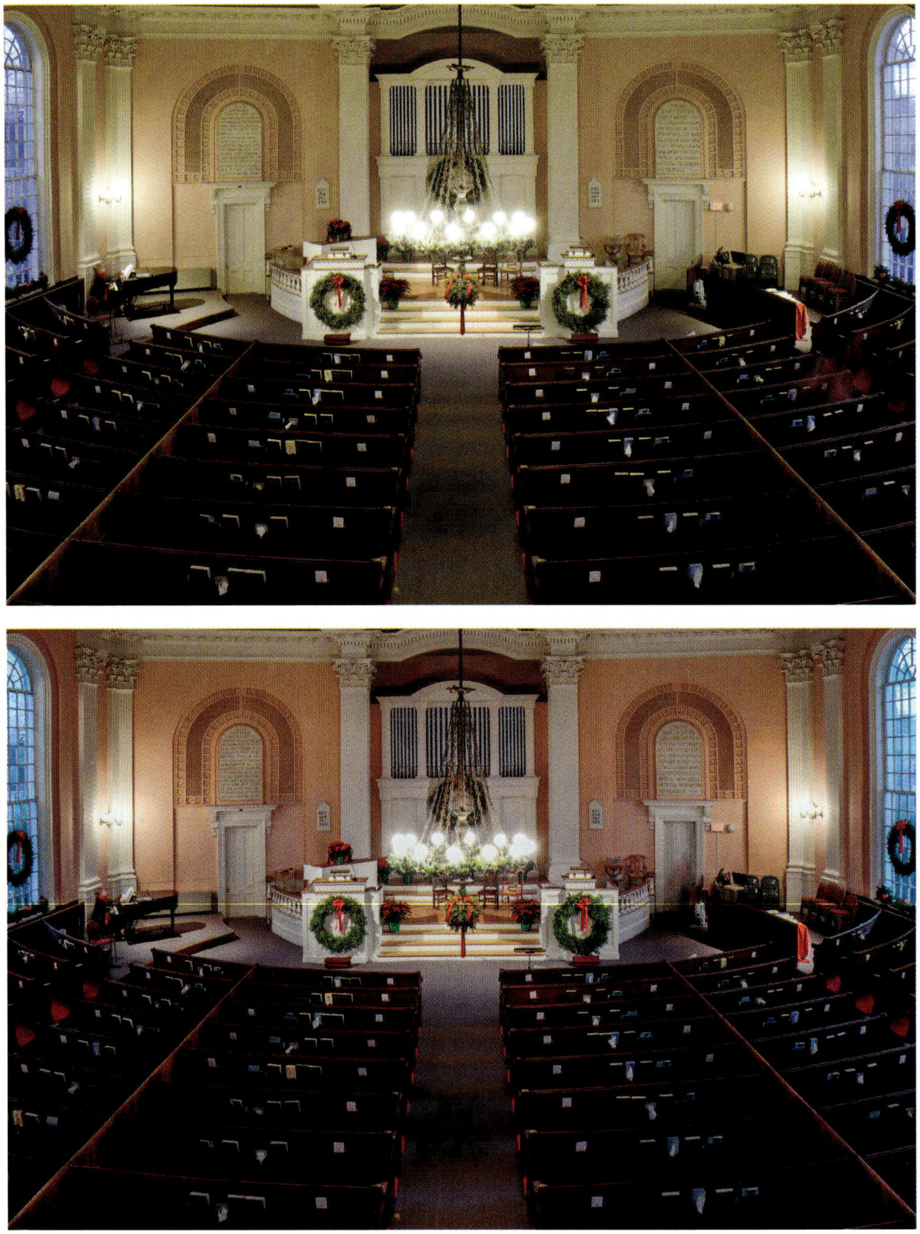

Figure 7.26
The photo on the top is from an in-camera HDR process. The photo on the bottom is the result of a manual HDR image I created from three exposures shot in RAW and assembled in post-processing.

ISO 100 • 1/80 sec. • f/8 • 12mm lens

Manual Callout

Check out page 135 in the Reference Manual PDF for more information on the HDR function.

By all means, give this feature a good test drive to get a feel for the conditions under which it will deliver the best results. If you are shooting in JPEG already, it is a nice trick to have in your back pocket (again, much like Active D-Lighting). That said, if you are interested in delving a little further into HDR photography, you can take advantage of the D5500's Auto Exposure Bracket function to take three different exposures (in RAW mode, even) and combine them in dedicated HDR software. I think you'll be impressed by how much more detail you are able to capture (**Figures 7.27** to **7.30**).

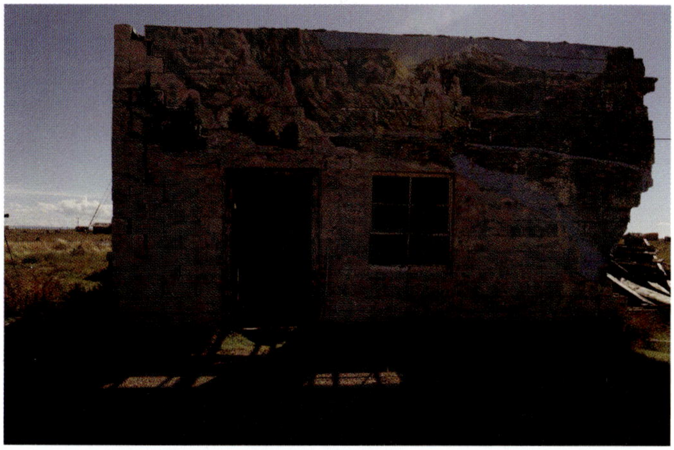

Figure 7.27 Underexposing two stops will render more detail in the highlight areas of the sky.

ISO 100 • 1/320 sec. • f/11 • 24mm lens

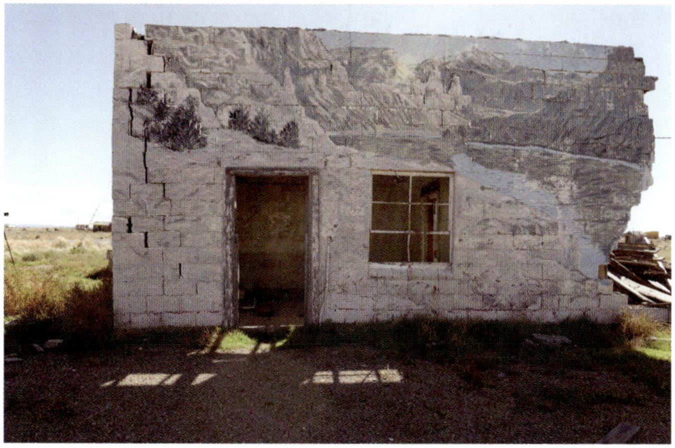

Figure 7.28 This is the normal exposure as dictated by the camera meter.

ISO 100 • 1/80 sec. • f/11 • 24mm lens

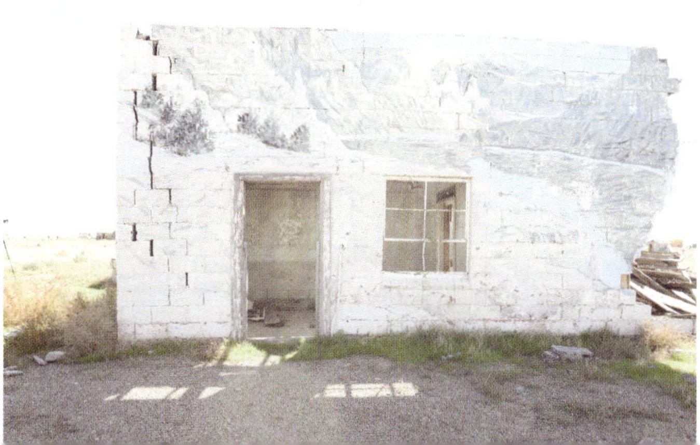

Figure 7.29 Overexposing by two stops ensures that the darker areas are exposed for detail in the shadows.

ISO 100 • 1/20 sec. • f/11 • 24mm lens

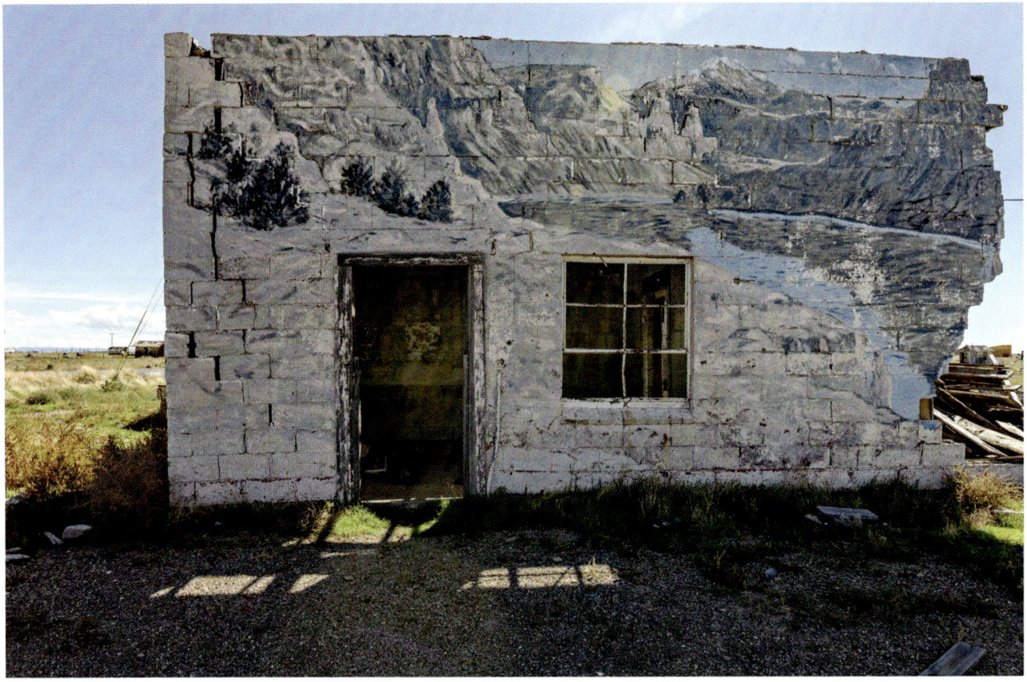

Figure 7.30
This is the final HDR image that was rendered from the three other exposures on the previous page.

As you can see, the final tone-mapped result from this process (I used Adobe Lightroom CC to create this HDR image) contains a lot more visual data than the in-camera HDR photo could. Did it take more work? Yes, undoubtedly, but I want you to have these tools in your repertoire so that you can choose what fits best with your style and workflow. The other benefit of this technique is that you have total control over the look of the final image, and you can even reprocess the same RAW captures in a myriad of ways depending on your style and taste.

Setting up for shooting an HDR image

1. Set your ISO to 100 to ensure clean, noise-free images.
2. Set your program mode to Aperture Priority. During the shooting process, you will be taking three shots of the same scene, creating an overexposed image, an underexposed image, and a normal exposure. Since the camera is going to be adjusting the exposure, you want it to make changes to the shutter speed, not the aperture, so that your depth of field is consistent.
3. Set your camera file format to RAW. This is extremely important because the RAW format contains a much larger range of exposure values than a JPEG file, and the HDR software needs this information.

4. Change your shooting mode to Continuous. This will allow you to capture your exposures quickly. Even though you will be using a tripod, there is always a chance that something within your scene will be moving (like clouds or leaves). Shooting in the Continuous mode minimizes any subject movement between frames.
5. Adjust the Auto Exposure Bracket (BKT) mode to shoot three exposures in two-stop increments. To do this, you will first need to set the BKT function for AE bracketing.
6. Press the Menu button, navigate to Custom Setting Menu, and then enter item e: Bracketing/Flash.
7. Locate item e2: Auto Bracketing Set, and press OK. In the next menu screen, select AE Bracketing, and then press the OK button.
8. Press the Menu button twice to exit the menu. Press the **i** button to enter the Function setup screen on the rear LCD, use the Multi-selector to highlight BKT, and press OK. Using the Multi-selector, change the option from Off to AE2.0, and press OK.
9. Focus the camera using the Manual focus method discussed earlier in the chapter, compose your shot, secure the tripod, and hold down the shutter button until the camera has fired three consecutive times. The result will be one normal exposure as well as one underexposed and one overexposed image.

A software program such as Adobe Photoshop CC, Lightroom CC, or HDRsoft Photomatix Pro can now process your exposure-bracketed images into a single HDR file. You can find more information on HDR photography and creating HDR images in the HDR Learning Center on Photofocus (photofocus.com/hdr-learning-center).

Remember to turn the BKT function back to Off when you are done, or the camera will continue to shoot bracketed images.

Bracketing your exposures

In HDR, *bracketing* is the process of capturing a series of exposures at different stop intervals. You can bracket your exposures even if you aren't going to be using HDR. Sometimes this is helpful when you have a tricky lighting situation and you want to ensure that you have just the right exposure to capture the look you're after. In HDR, you bracket to the plus and minus side of a "normal" exposure, but you can also bracket all of your exposures to the over or under side of normal. It all depends on what you are after. If you aren't sure whether you are getting enough shadow detail, you can bracket a little toward the overexposed side. The same is true for highlights. You can bracket in increments as small as a third of a stop. This means that you can capture several images with very subtle exposure variances and then decide later which one is best. If you want to bracket just to one side of a normal exposure, set your exposure compensation to +1 or –1, depending on your needs, and then use the bracketing feature to automatically bracket your exposures.

Chapter 7 Assignments

We've covered a lot of ground in this chapter, so it's definitely time to put this knowledge to work in order to get familiar with these new camera settings and techniques.

Comparing depth of field: Wide-angle vs. telephoto

Practice using the hyper focal distance of your lens to maximize the depth of field. You can do this by picking a focal length to work with on your lens. If you have a zoom lens, try using the longest length. Compose your image and find an object to focus on. Set your aperture to f/22 and take a photo. Now do the same thing with the zoom lens at its widest focal length. Use the same aperture and focus point. Review the images and compare the depth of field when using a wide-angle as opposed to telephoto focal length. Try this again but with a large aperture.

Applying hyper focal distance to your landscapes

Pick a scene that has objects that are near the camera position and something that is clearly defined in the background. Try using a wide to medium-wide focal length for this (18–35mm). Use a small aperture and focus on the object in the foreground; then recompose and take a shot. Without moving the camera position, use the object in the background as your point of focus and take another shot. Finally, find a point that is one-third of the way into the frame from near to far and use that as the focus point. Compare all of the images to see which method delivered the greatest range of depth of field from near to infinity.

Using Live View and the rule of thirds

Now let's get some practice using the rule of thirds for improving composition. To do this, you need to employ Live View with the grid overlay turned on for a little visual assistance. Using the Live View grid, practice shooting while placing your main subject in one of the intersecting line locations. Take some comparison shots with the subject at one of the intersecting locations, and then shoot the same subject in the middle of the frame.

Placing your horizons

Finally, find a location with a defined horizon and, using the Live View grid, shoot the horizon along the top third of the frame, in the middle of the frame, and along the bottom third of the frame.

Test driving the in-camera HDR function

Now that you know the feature exists, look for high-contrast scenes (where there are areas of bright highlight with detail and dark shadow with detail), and put that HDR function through its paces. You may not like all the images, but learning to recognize the situations where HDR comes in handy is worth the practice.

Share your results with the book's Flickr group!
Join the group here: flickr.com/groups/nikond5500_fromsnapshotstogreatshots

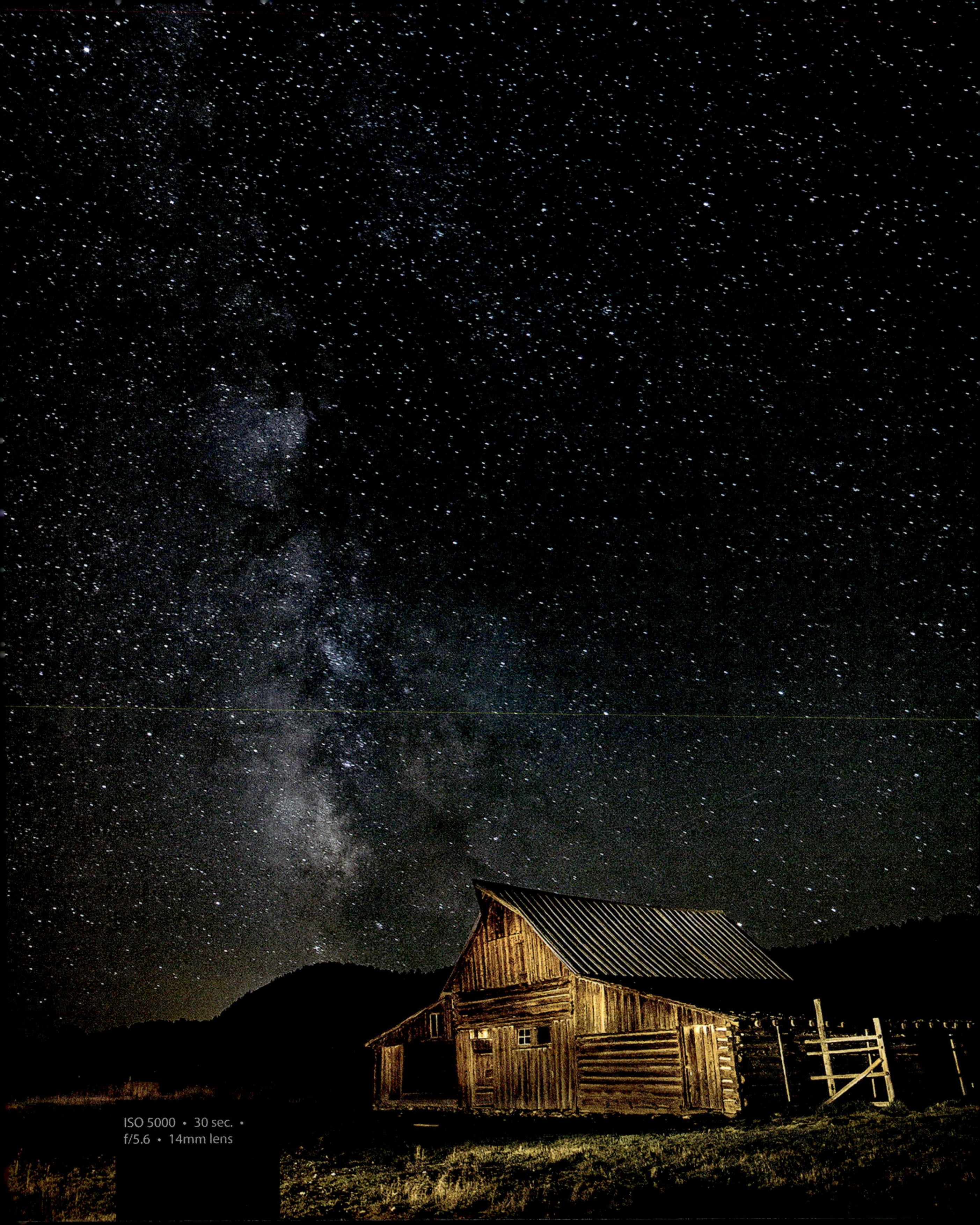

ISO 5000 • 30 sec. • f/5.6 • 14mm lens

8

Mood Lighting

Shooting When the Lights Get Low

There is no reason to put away your camera when the sun goes down. Your D5500 has some great features that let you work with available light as well as the built-in flash. In this chapter, we will explore ways to push your camera's technology to the limit in order to capture great photos in difficult lighting situations. We will also explore the use of flash and how best to use your built-in flash features to improve your photography. But first let's look at working with low-level available light.

Poring Over the Picture

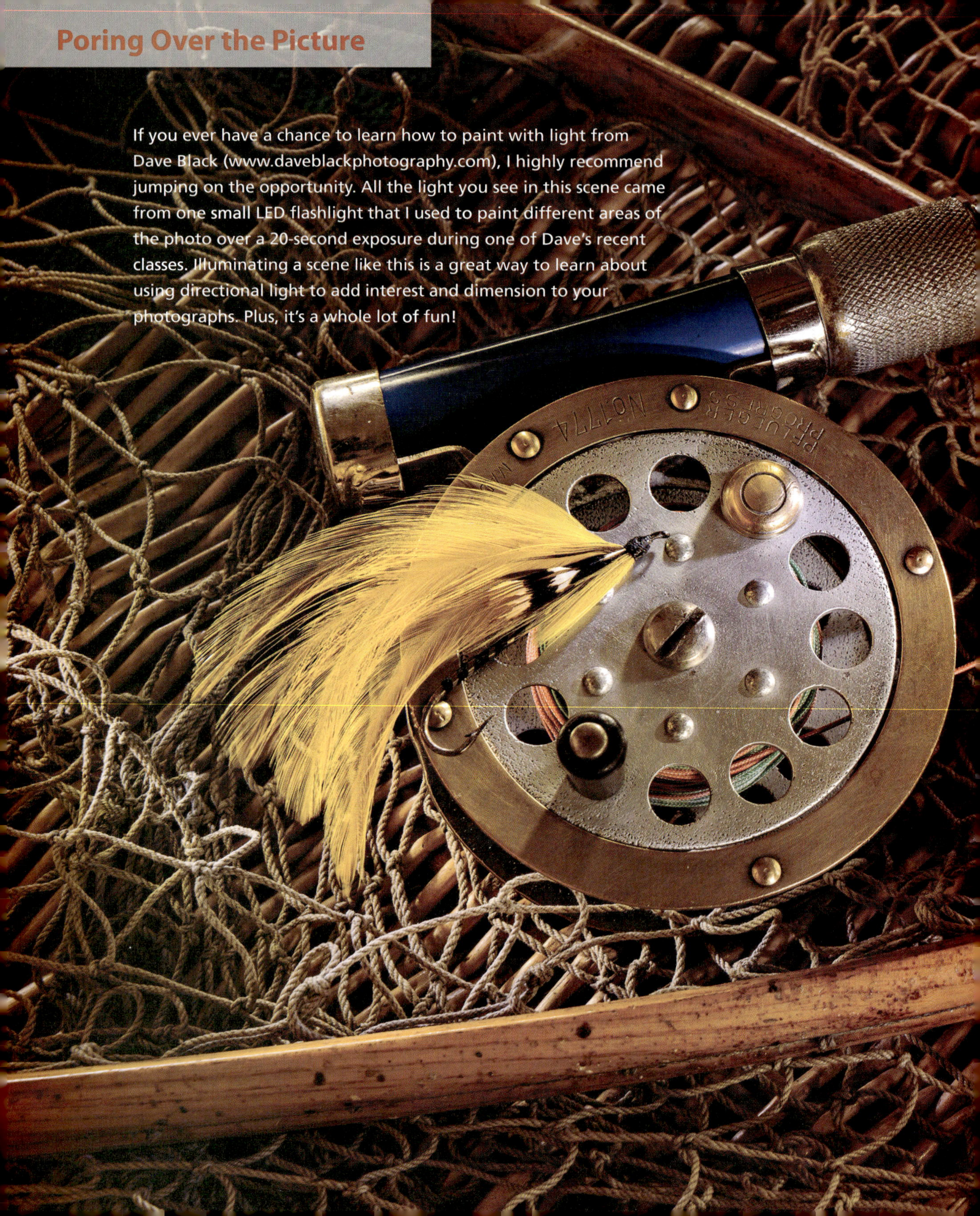

If you ever have a chance to learn how to paint with light from Dave Black (www.daveblackphotography.com), I highly recommend jumping on the opportunity. All the light you see in this scene came from one small LED flashlight that I used to paint different areas of the photo over a 20-second exposure during one of Dave's recent classes. Illuminating a scene like this is a great way to learn about using directional light to add interest and dimension to your photographs. Plus, it's a whole lot of fun!

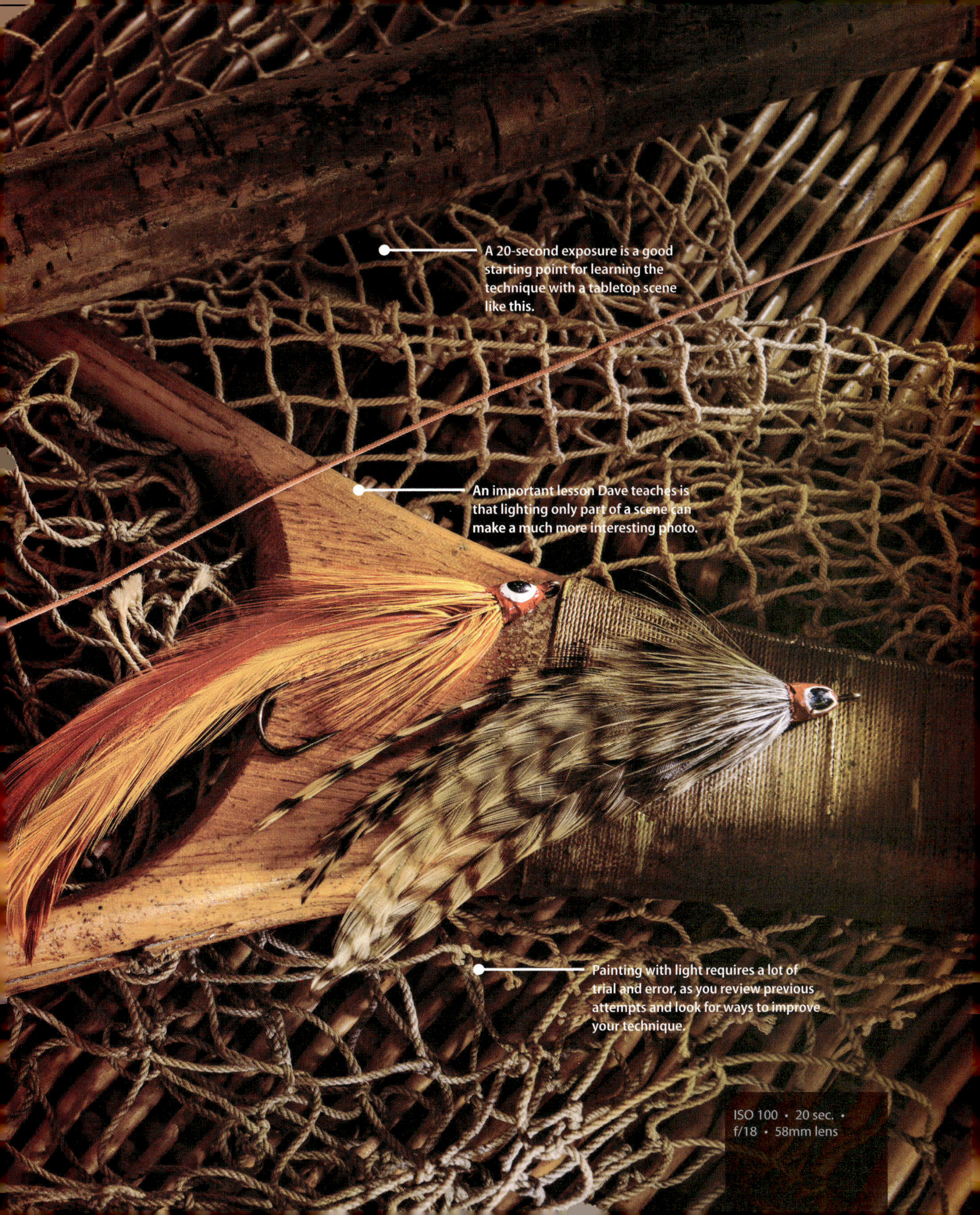
A 20-second exposure is a good starting point for learning the technique with a tabletop scene like this.
An important lesson Dave teaches is that lighting only part of a scene can make a much more interesting photo.
Painting with light requires a lot of trial and error, as you review previous attempts and look for ways to improve your technique.
ISO 100 • 20 sec. • f/18 • 58mm lens

Raising the ISO: The Simple Solution

Let's begin with the obvious way to keep shooting when the lights get low: raising the ISO (**Figure 8.1**). By now you know how to change the ISO by using the **i** button and the Multi-selector. In typical shooting situations, you should keep the ISO in the 100–800 range. This will keep your pictures nice and clean by minimizing the digital noise. But as the available light gets low, you might find yourself working in the higher ranges of the ISO scale, which could lead to more noise in your image.

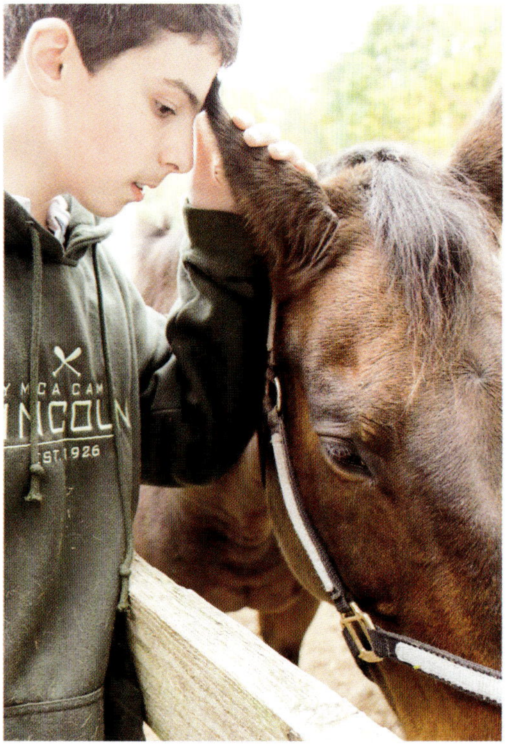

Figure 8.1 **Some moments just need to be captured in the available light, no matter how little light is available.**

ISO 3200 • 1/125 sec. • f/4 • 24mm lens

You could use the flash, but it has a limited range (15–20 feet) that might not work for you. Also, you could be in a situation where flash is prohibited, or at least frowned upon—for instance, at a wedding or in a museum. Sometimes the flash just kills the mood of the scene you are trying to capture.

And what about a tripod with a long shutter speed? That is also an option, and we'll cover it a little later. The problem with this combination is it works well only when subjects aren't moving. Besides, try to set up a tripod in a museum and see how quickly you grab the attention of the security guards.

So if the only choice to get the shot is to raise the ISO to 800 or higher, make sure you turn on the High ISO Noise Reduction feature (**Figure 8.2**). This Shooting menu function is set to Normal by default, but as you start using higher ISO values, you should consider changing it to the High setting. (Chapter 7 explains how to set the Noise Reduction features.) If you move on to shooting in RAW mode, you will have other tools in the RAW processing software for dealing with noise.

To see the effect of High ISO Noise Reduction, you need to zoom in and take a closer look (**Figures 8.3** and **8.4**).

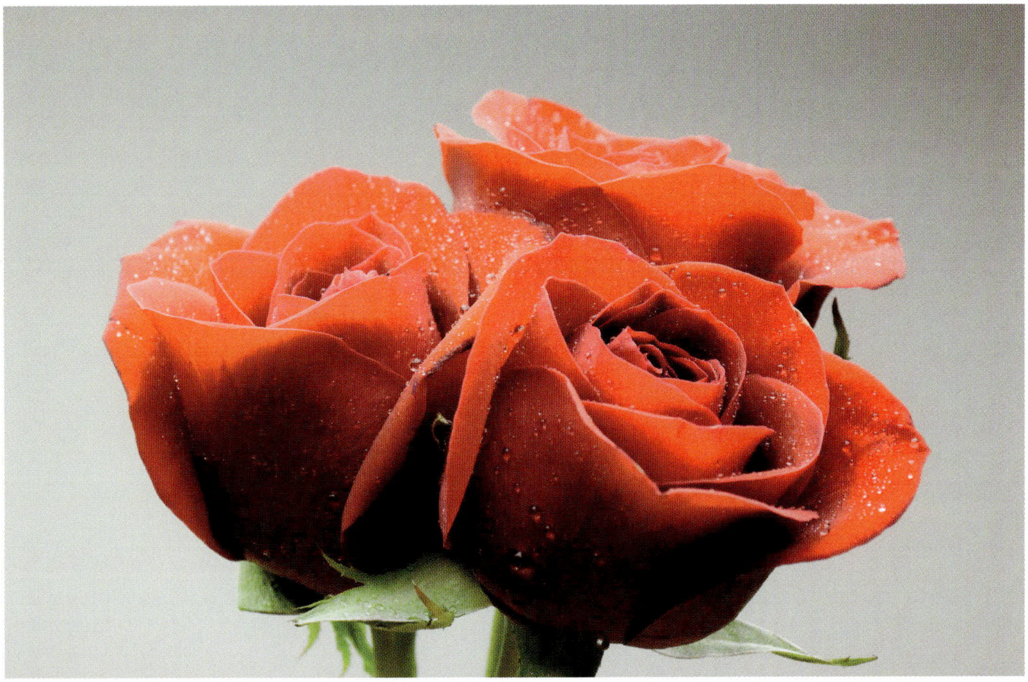

Figure 8.2 **Although this looks like a well-lit shot, it was made possible through the use of a very high ISO and the High ISO Noise Reduction feature.**

ISO 6400 • 1/60 sec. • f/11 • 95mm lens

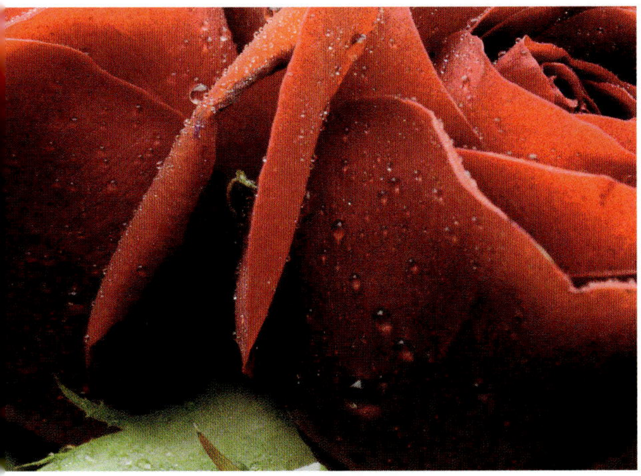

Figure 8.3 **Here is a close-up of the same flower, so you can get an idea of how things look with High ISO Noise Reduction turned off.**

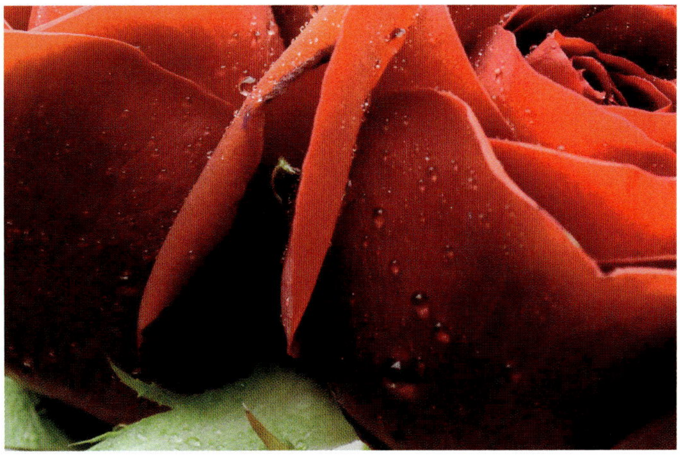

Figure 8.4 **Here is the same flower photographed with High ISO Noise Reduction set to Normal. While it doesn't get rid of all the noise, it reduces the effect.**

Raising the noise reduction to the High setting slightly increases the processing time for your images, so if you are shooting in the Continuous drive mode, you might see a reduction in the speed of your frames per second.

> **Noise reduction saves space**
>
> When shooting at very high ISO settings, running High ISO Noise Reduction at the Normal or High setting can save you space on your memory card. If you are saving your photos as JPEGs, the camera will compress the information in the image to take up less space. When you have excessive noise, you can literally add megabytes to the file size. This is because the camera has to deal with more information: It views the noise in the image as photo information and therefore tries not to lose that information during the compression process. More noise equals bigger files. So not only will turning on the High ISO Noise Reduction feature improve the look of your images, it will also save you some space so you can take a few more shots.

Using Very High ISOs

Is ISO 6400 just not enough for you? Well, in that case, you will need to set your camera to one of the higher ISO settings. The ISO settings on the D5500 can go all the way up to 25600.

Using the higher ISO settings

1. With the information screen active, press the **i** button to activate the cursor.
2. Use the Multi-selector to move the cursor to the ISO Sensitivity setting, and press the OK button (**A**).
3. Use the Multi-selector to scroll through the ISO settings until you reach the higher settings. Select the ISO of choice, and press the OK button (**B**).
4. Press the shutter release button to return to active shooting mode.

A

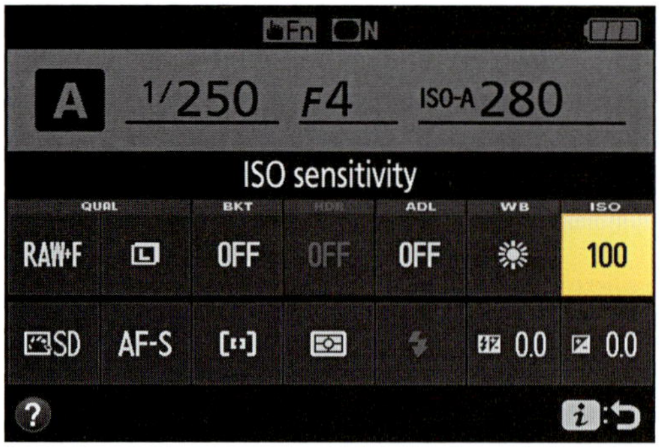

B

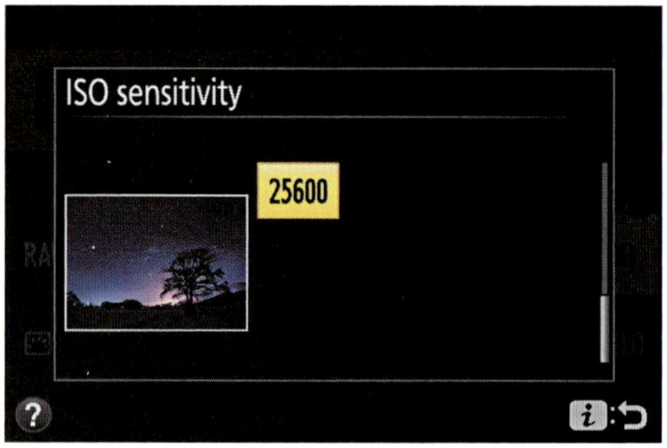

A word of warning about the highest ISO settings: Although it is great to have these high ISO settings available during low-light shooting, they should always be your last resort. Even with High ISO Noise Reduction turned on, the amount of visible noise will be extremely high. If you are going to be shooting frequently in low-light situations, I urge you to consider investing in a faster lens (with a wide aperture), which, when coupled with ISOs between 3200 and 6400, will allow you to increase your shutter speed fast enough to stop the action under poor lighting conditions (**Figure 8.5**).

Don't forget about the D5500's Night Vision effect (refer to Chapter 3) when there's almost no light and you can live with the grainy black and white image the effect produces (**Figure 8.6**).

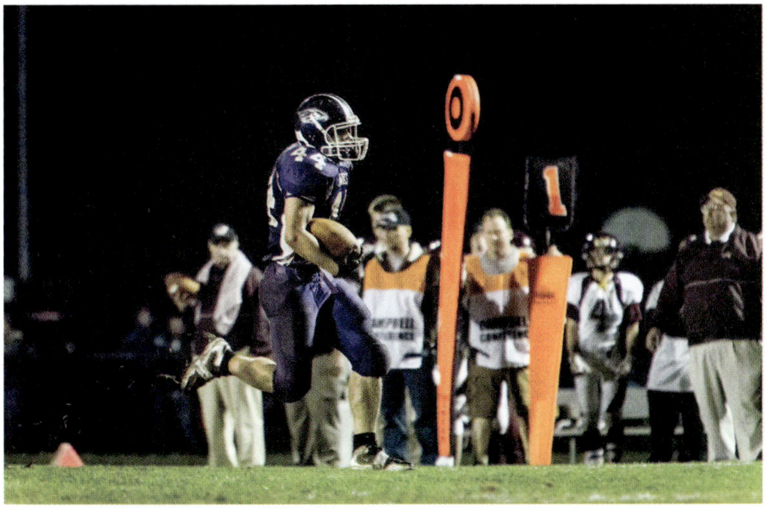

Figure 8.5
The only way to get a fast-enough shutter speed during this evening game was to raise the ISO to 25600.
ISO 25600 • 1/1000 sec. • f/5.6 • 400mm lens

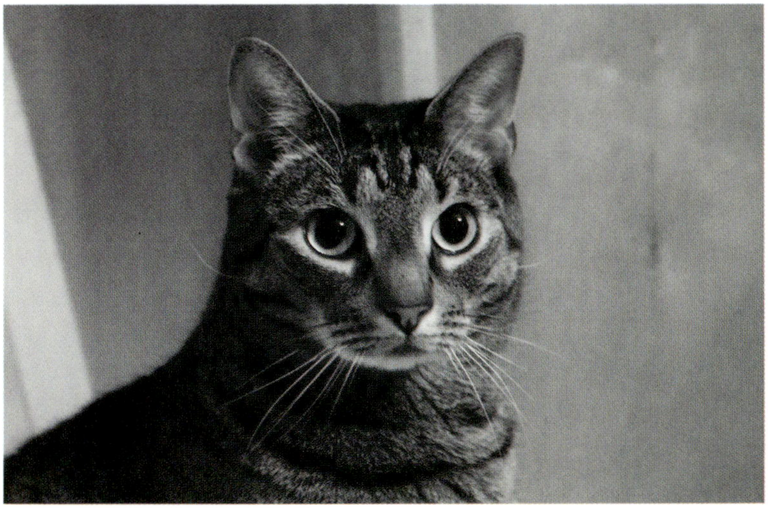

Figure 8.6
I used the Night Vision effect to capture my cat stalking the food bowl for a late-night snack.
ISO 32254 • 1/125 sec. • f/5.6 • 70mm lens

Stabilizing the Situation

If you purchased your camera with the Vibration Reduction (VR) lens, you already own a great tool for squeezing two stops of exposure out of your camera when shooting without a tripod. The average person can handhold her camera down to about 1/60 of a second before blurriness results due to hand shake. As the length of the lens is increased (or zoomed), the ability to handhold at slow shutter speeds (1/60 of a second and slower) and still get sharp images is further reduced (**Figure 8.7**).

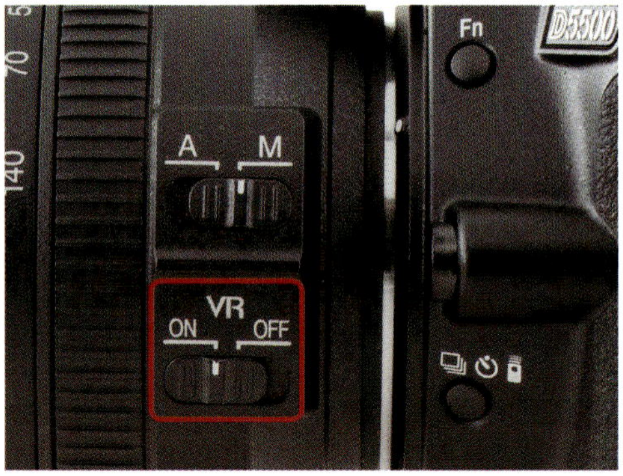

Figure 8.7 **Turning on the VR switch will allow you to shoot in lower lighting conditions.**

The Nikon VR lenses contain small gyro sensors and servo-actuated optical elements, which correct for camera shake and stabilize the image. The VR function is so good that it is possible to improve your handheld photography by two or three stops, meaning if you are pretty solid at a shutter speed of 1/60 of a second, the VR feature lets you shoot at 1/15, and possibly even 1/8, of a second (**Figures 8.8** and **8.9**). When shooting in low-light situations, make sure you set the VR switch on the side of your lens to the On position.

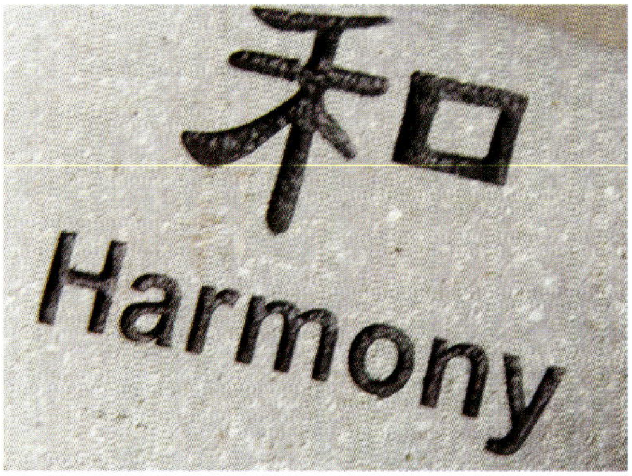

Figure 8.8 **This photo was taken handheld with VR turned off.**

ISO 200 • 1/10 sec. • f/11 • 85mm lens

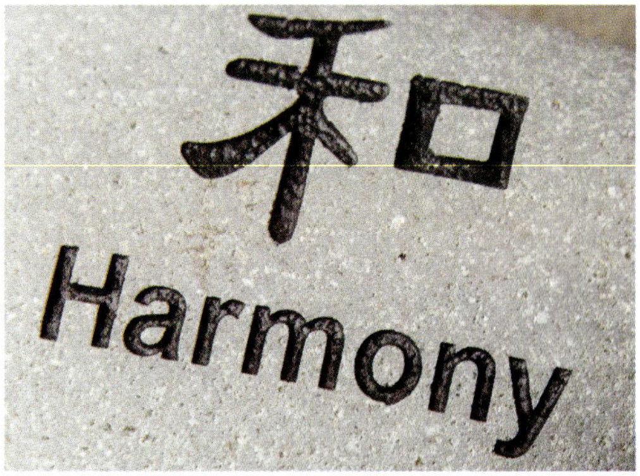

Figure 8.9 **This photo was taken handheld with VR turned on and all the same camera settings.**

Self-time your way to sharper images

Whether you are shooting with a tripod or resting your camera on a wall, you can increase the sharpness of your pictures by taking your hands out of the equation. Whenever you use your finger to depress the shutter release button, you are increasing the chance that there will be a little bit of shake in your image. To eliminate this possibility, try setting your camera up to use the self-timer. To turn on the self-timer, just press the Release Mode button (directly beneath the lens release button) and select it from the available options. There are four self-timer modes: 2, 5, 10, and 20 seconds. I generally use the 2-second mode to cut down on time between exposures. If you want to use one of the other modes, you will need to change this in the Custom Setting menu (select Timers/AE Lock and choose the c3: Self-Timer setting).

Focusing in Low Light

The D5500 has a great focusing system, but occasionally the light levels might be too low for the camera to achieve an accurate focus. You can do a few things to overcome this obstacle.

First, you should know that the camera uses contrast in the viewfinder to establish a point of focus. This is why your camera will not be able to focus when you point it at a white wall or a cloudless sky. It simply can't find any contrast in the scene to work with. Knowing this, you might be able to use a single focus point in AF-S mode to find an area of contrast that is of the same distance as your subject. You can then maintain that focus by holding down the shutter button halfway and recomposing your image.

Then there are those times when the camera just doesn't have anything to focus on. A perfect example of this would be a fireworks display. If you point your lens to the night sky in any automatic focus (AF) mode, it will just keep searching for—and not finding—a focus point. On these occasions, you can simply turn off the autofocus feature and manually focus the lens. Look for the A/M switch on the side of the lens and slide it to the M position. Don't forget to put it back in A mode at the end of your shoot.

Don't stop shooting just because the sun goes down. On my last trip to Arches National Park, I took a small group out for some long-exposure night shooting and light painting, and we got some nice shots of Balanced Rock (**Figure 8.10**). Although the moon was bright, it was too dark to focus using autofocus. Flipping the switch to Manual allowed me to take the shot, then check focus on the LCD.

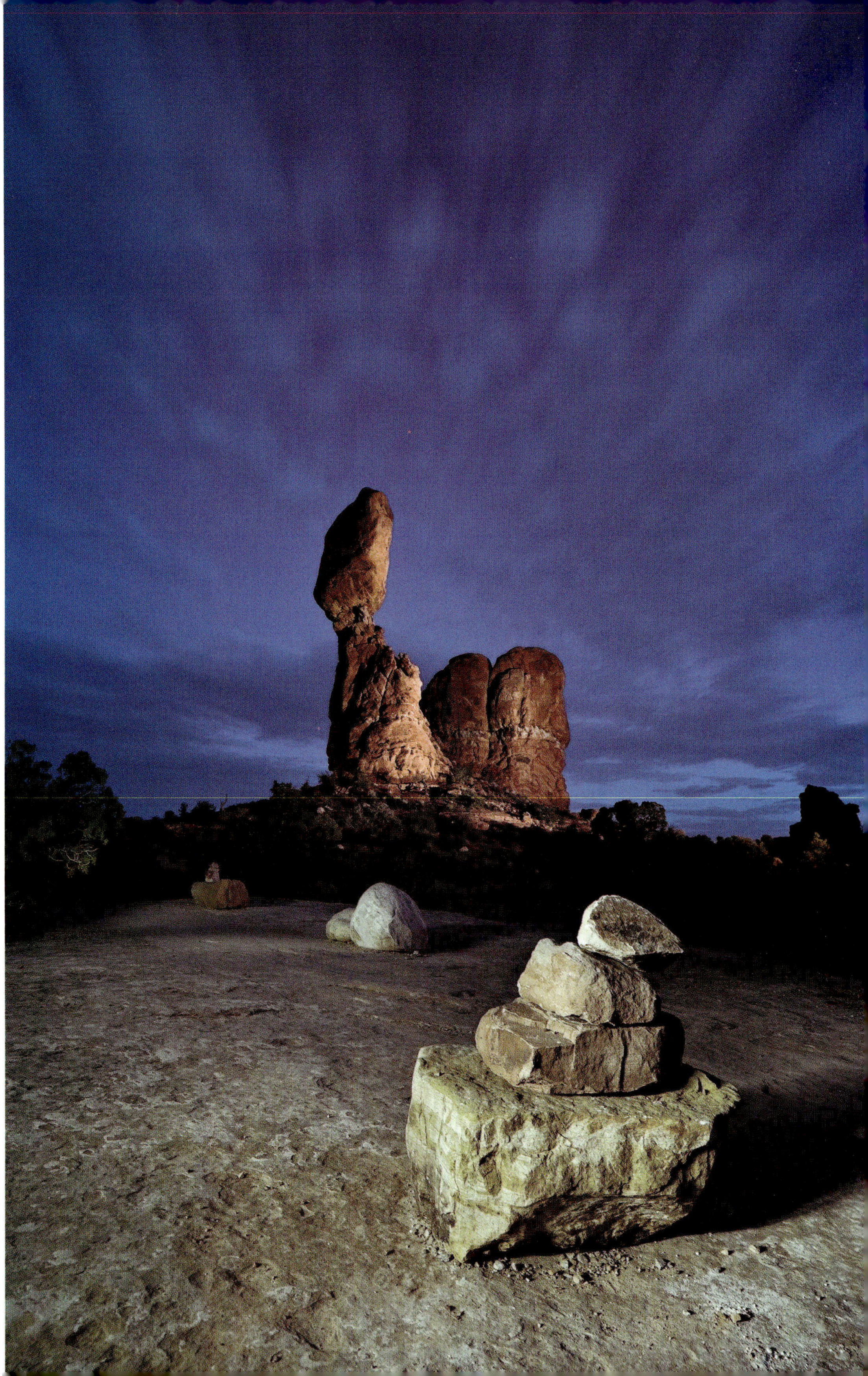

Figure 8.10
A long exposure under moonlight can turn the night to day, but there is not enough light for autofocus.

ISO 800 • 30 sec. • f/9 • 14mm lens

AF-Assist Illuminator

Another way to ensure good focus is to use the D5500's AF-Assist Illuminator. AF-Assist uses a small, bright beam of light from the front of the camera to shine some light on the scene, which assists the autofocus system in locating more detail. This feature is automatically activated when you use the flash, except in Landscape, Sports, and Flash Off modes (in Landscape mode, the subject is usually too far away; in Sports mode, the subject is probably moving; and in Flash Off mode, you've disabled the flash entirely). Also, the Illuminator will be disabled when you are shooting in the AF-C or Manual focus mode, as well as when the Illuminator is turned off in the camera menu. AF-Assist should be enabled by default, but you can check the menu just to make sure.

Turning on the AF-Assist feature

1. Press the Menu button, and go to Custom Setting Menu.
2. Navigate to the item called a: Autofocus, and press the OK button (**A**).
3. Highlight the menu item called a3: Built-In AF-Assist Illuminator, and press the OK button (**B**).
4. Set the option to On, and press the OK button to complete the setup.

A

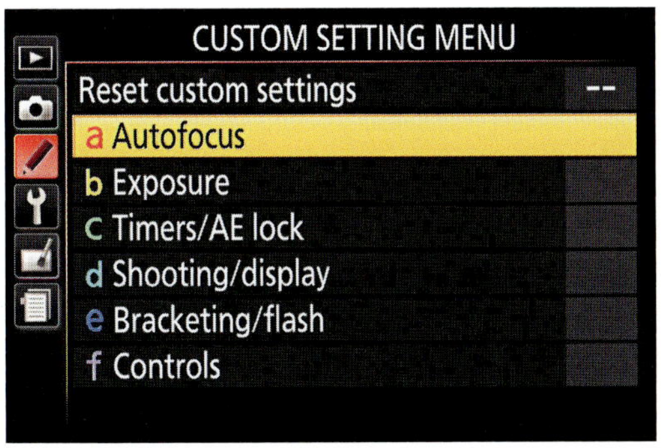

B

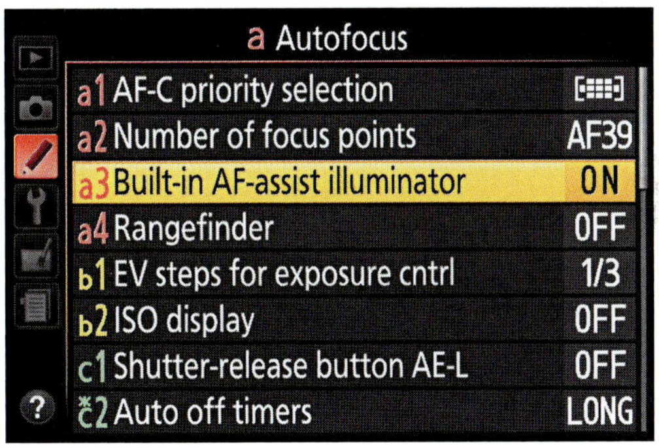

Working without the flash

If you are shooting in one of the automatic scene modes, the flash might be set to activate automatically. If you don't wish to operate the flash, you will have to turn it off in the information screen.

Disabling the flash

1. Press the **i** button to activate the cursor in the information screen.
2. Use the Multi-selector to select the Flash Mode item, and press the OK button (**A**).
3. Use the Multi-selector to find the option to turn off the flash (look for the lightning bolt with the circle and slash), and press the OK button (**B**).
4. Make sure the pop-up flash is in the down position before shooting.

A

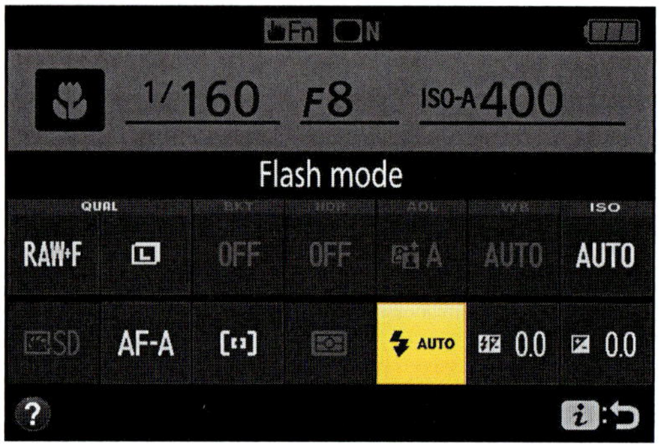

B

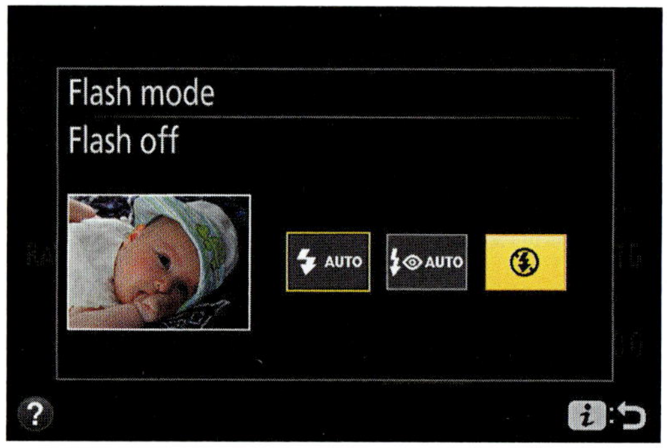

To disable the flash in the professional modes, simply keep the flash head in the lowered position. It will not be active unless you raise it.

Shooting Long Exposures

We have covered some of the techniques for shooting in low light, so let's go through the process of capturing a night or low-light scene for maximum image quality. The first thing to consider is that in order to shoot in low light with a low ISO, you will need to use shutter speeds that are longer than you could possibly handhold (longer than 1/15 of a second). This will require the use of a tripod or stable surface for you to place your camera on. For maximum quality, the ISO should be low—somewhere below 800. The Long Exposure Noise Reduction feature should be turned on to minimize the effects of exposing for longer durations (to set this up, see Chapter 7).

The time just after sunset, when there is still light in the sky, is a great time to capture the transition from day to night. In **Figure 8.11**, I had the camera on a tripod and had locked in focus on El Capitan (Yosemite) while there was plenty of light. I used the self-timer to trip the shutter and avoid moving my camera during the shot.

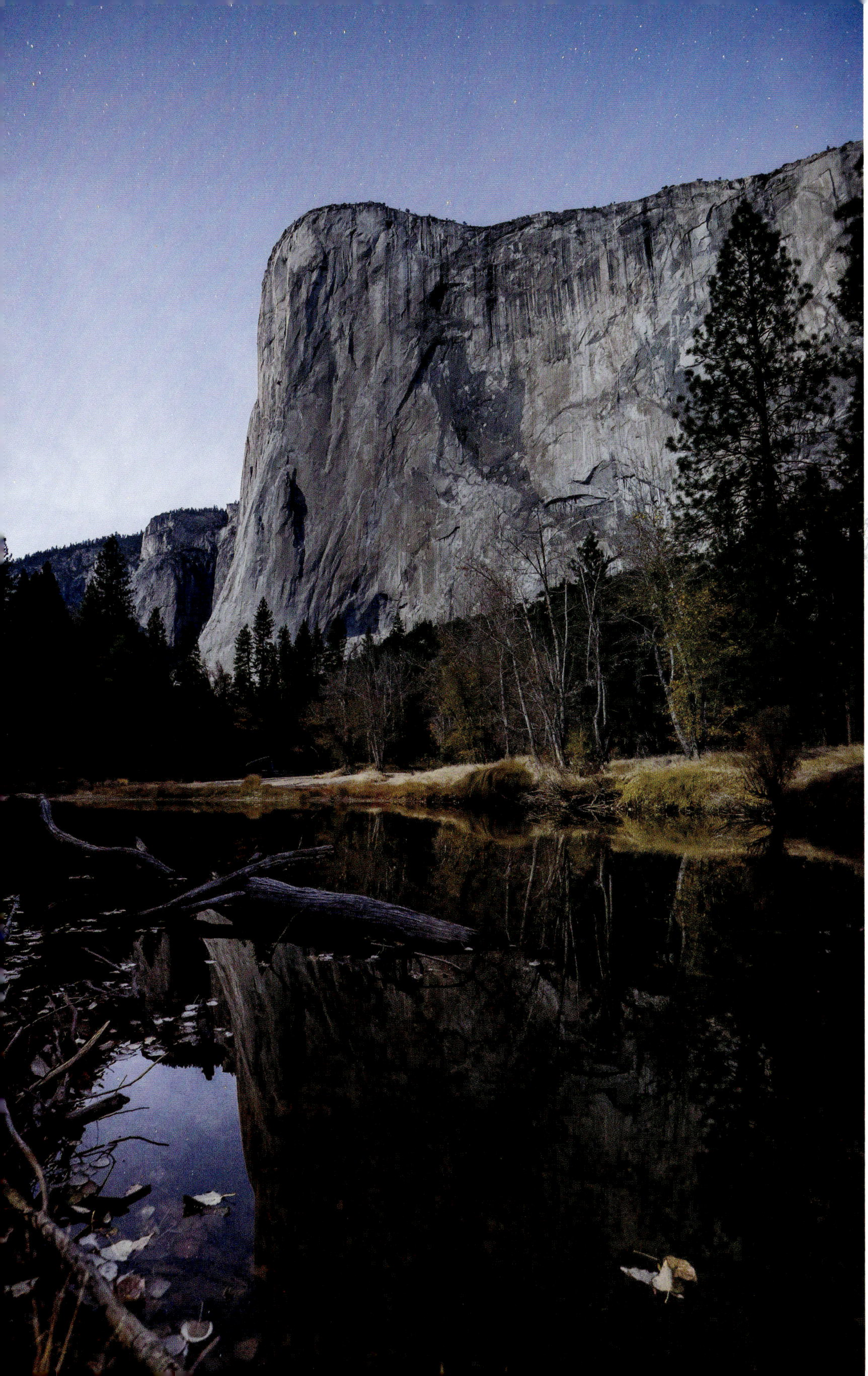

Figure 8.11
The time just after sunset, when the sun is below the horizon and the stars are beginning to appear, is magical.

ISO 400 • 30 sec. • f/4 • 16mm lens

Once you have the noise reduction turned on, set your camera to Aperture Priority (A) mode. That way, you can concentrate on the aperture that you believe is most appropriate and let the camera determine the best shutter speed. If it is too dark for the autofocus to function properly, try manually focusing. Finally, consider using a remote release (see Chapter 11) to activate the shutter. If you don't have one, check out the sidebar "Self-Time Your Way to Sharper Images." Once you shoot the image, you may notice some lag time before it is displayed on the rear LCD. This is due to the noise-reduction process, which can take anywhere from a fraction of a second up to 30 seconds, depending on the length of the exposure.

Flash sync

The shutter needs to be fully open while the flash is going off, called *flash synchronization (flash sync* for short) This is not an issue if you are using a long shutter speed, such as 1/15 of a second, but flash sync does become more critical for fast shutter speeds. To ensure that the flash and shutter are synchronized, the D5500 implements a top sync speed of 1/200 of a second. This means that when you are using the flash, you will not be able to use a shutter speed any faster than 1/200. If you did use a faster shutter speed, the shutter would actually start closing before the flash fired, which would cause a black area to appear in the frame where the light from the flash was blocked by the shutter.

Using the Built-In Flash

There are going to be times when you have to turn to your camera's built-in flash to get the shot. The pop-up flash on the D5500 is not extremely powerful, but with the camera's advanced metering system, it does a pretty good job of lighting up the night...or just filling in the shadows.

If you are working with one of the automatic scene modes, the flash should automatically activate when needed. If, however, you are working in one of the professional modes, you will have to turn the flash on for yourself. To do this, just press the pop-up flash button located on the front of the camera (**Figure 8.12**). Once the flash is up, it is ready to go (**Figure 8.13**). It's that simple.

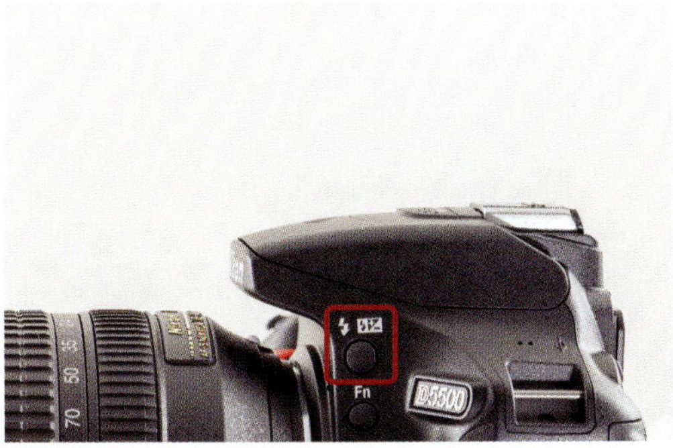

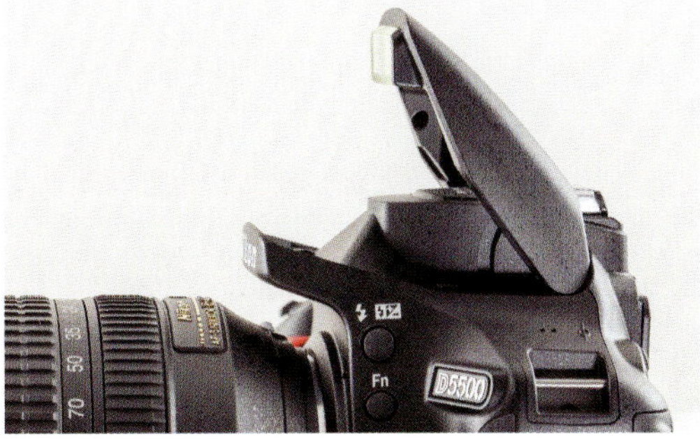

Figure 8.12 (left) A quick press of the pop-up flash button will release the built-in flash up to its ready position.

Figure 8.13 (right) The pop-up flash in its ready position

Flash range

Because the pop-up flash is fairly small, it does not have enough power to illuminate a large space. The effective distance varies, depending on the aperture and ISO setting. At ISO 200 and f/4, the range is about 14 feet. This range can be extended to as far as 27 feet when the camera is set to an ISO of 800. Check out page 98 of the Reference Manual PDF for a chart that shows the effective flash range for differing ISO and aperture settings.

Shutter speeds

The standard flash synchronization speed for your camera is between 1/60 and 1/200 of a second. When you are working with the built-in flash in the automatic and scene modes, the camera will typically use a shutter speed of 1/60 of a second. The exception to this is when you use the Night Portrait mode, which will fire the flash with a slower shutter speed so that some of the ambient light in the scene has time to record in the image.

Controlling the shutter speed is the real key to using the flash to get great pictures. The goal is to balance the light from the flash with the existing light so that everything in the picture has an even illumination. Let's take a look at the shutter speeds for the professional modes.

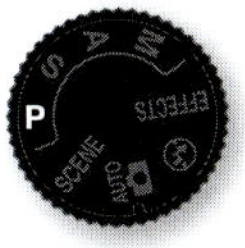

Program (P): The shutter speed stays at 1/60 of a second. The only adjustment you can make in this mode is overexposure or underexposure using the Exposure Compensation or Flash Compensation settings.

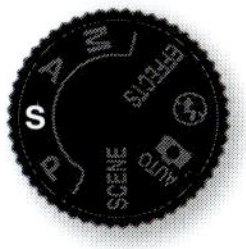

Shutter Priority (S): You can adjust the shutter speed to as fast as 1/200 of a second all the way down to 30 seconds. The lens aperture will adjust accordingly, but typically at long exposures the lens will be set to its largest aperture.

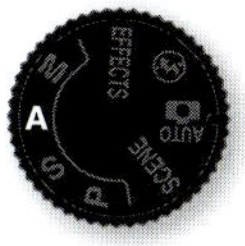

Aperture Priority (A): This mode will allow you to adjust the aperture but will adjust the shutter speed between 1/200 and 1/60 of a second in the standard flash mode.

Metering modes

The built-in flash uses a technology called TTL (Through the Lens) metering to determine the appropriate amount of flash power to output for a good exposure. When you depress the shutter button, the camera quickly adjusts focus while gathering information from the entire scene to measure the amount of ambient light. As you press the shutter button down completely, the flash uses that exposure information and fires a predetermined amount of light at your subject during the exposure.

The default setting for the flash meter mode is TTL. The flash can be set to Manual mode. In Manual flash mode, you can determine how much power you want coming out of the flash, ranging from full power all the way down to 1/32 power. Each setting from full power on down will cut the power by half. This is the equivalent of reducing flash exposure by one stop with each power reduction.

Setting the flash to the Manual power setting

1. Press the Menu button, and then navigate to Custom Setting Menu.
2. Using the Multi-selector, highlight the item labeled e: Bracketing/Flash, and press the OK button (**A**).
3. Highlight item e1: Flash Cntrl for Built-In Flash, and press OK (**B**).

A

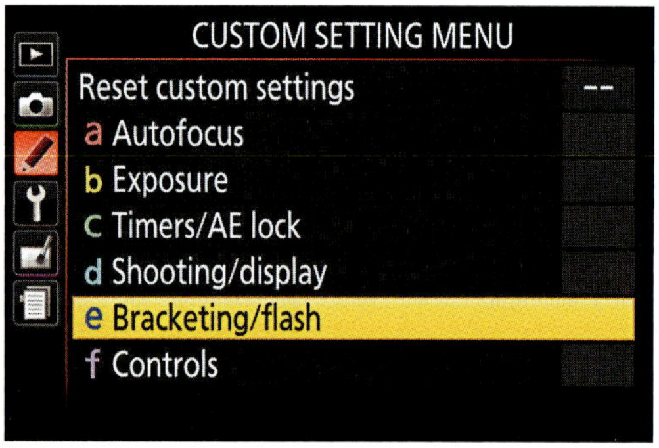

B

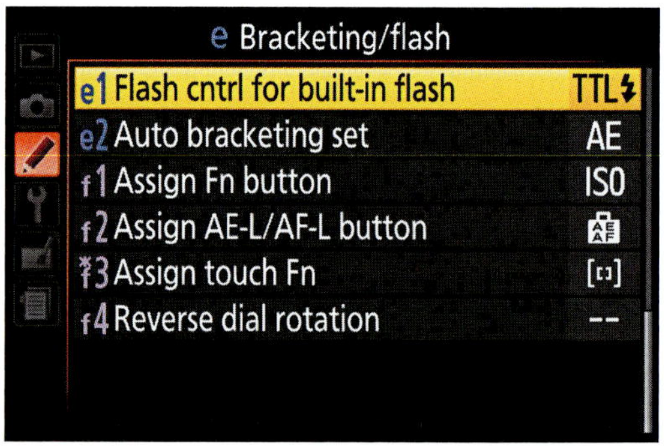

4. Change the setting to Manual (**C**), press the OK button to adjust the desired power—Full, ½, ¼, etc.—and then press the OK button again (**D**).

C

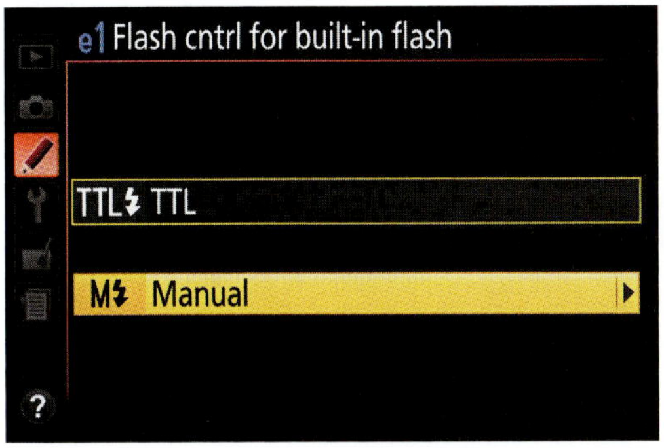

D

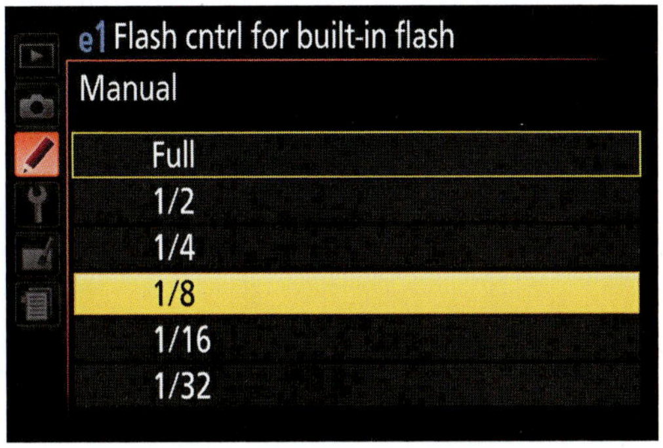

Don't forget to set the flash back to TTL when you are done, because the camera will hold this setting until you change it.

Compensating for the Flash Exposure

The TTL system will usually do an excellent job of balancing the flash and ambient light for your exposure, but it does have the limitation of not knowing what effect you want in your image. You may want more or less flash in a particular shot. You can achieve this by using the Flash Exposure Compensation feature.

Just as with exposure compensation, flash compensation allows you to dial in a change in the flash output in increments of 1/3 of a stop. You will probably use this most often to tone down the effects of your flash, especially when you are using the flash as a subtle fill light (**Figures 8.14** and **8.15**). The range of compensation goes from +1 stop down to –3 stops.

Figure 8.14 (left) This shot was taken with the pop-up flash set to normal power. There is a bright highlight on the cheeks and forehead.

ISO 200 • 1/125 sec. • f/4.5 • 80mm lens

Figure 8.15 (right) This shot was made with the same camera settings. The difference is that the flash compensation was set to –1 stop, and it did a nice job of taking the edge off the flash to help it blend into the overall exposure.

ISO 200 • 1/125 sec. • f/4.5 • 80mm lens

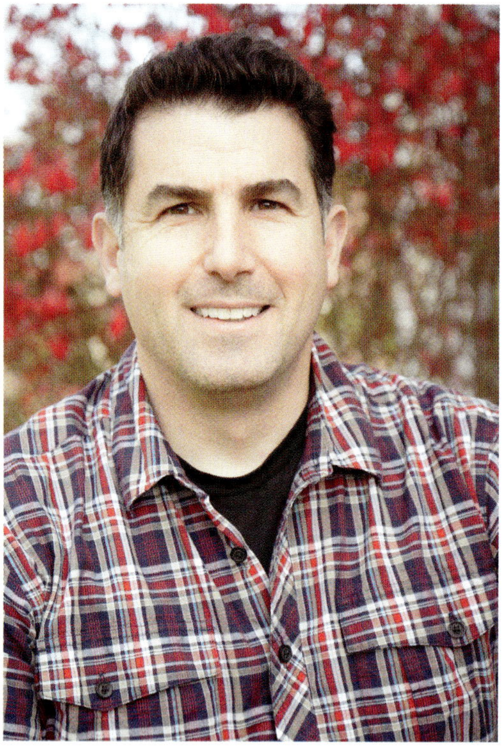

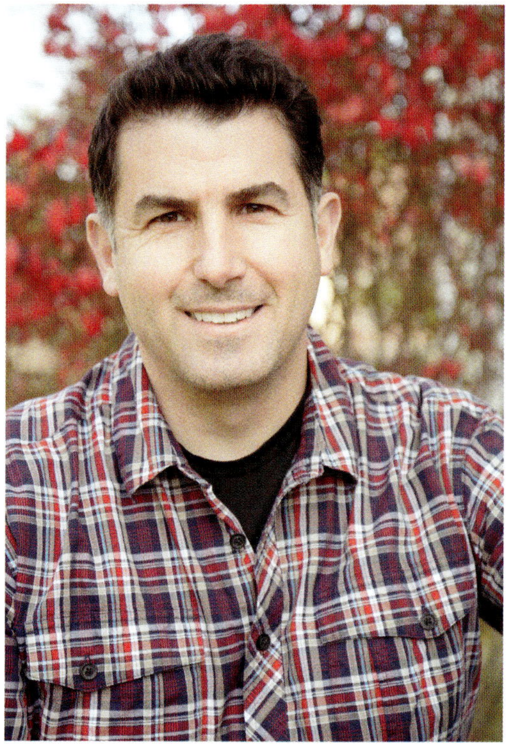

Using the Flash Exposure Compensation feature to change the flash output

1. With the flash in the upright and ready position, press and hold the Flash Compensation (the same button used to pop the flash) and Exposure Compensation (just behind the shutter) buttons at the same time.
2. While holding down these two buttons, rotate the Command dial to set the amount of compensation you desire. Turning to the left reduces the flash power 1/3 of a stop with each click of the dial. Turning right increases the flash power.
3. Press the shutter button halfway to return to shooting mode, and then take the picture.
4. Review your image to see if more or less flash compensation is required, and repeat these steps as necessary.

You can also change the flash compensation by using the information screen on the back of the camera.

Adjusting flash compensation using the information screen

1. Press the **i** button to activate the cursor in the information screen.
2. Use the Multi-selector to find the Flash Compensation item (located along the bottom portion of the screen), and press the OK button (**A**).
3. Use the Multi-selector to select the amount of compensation, and then press the OK button (**B**).

A

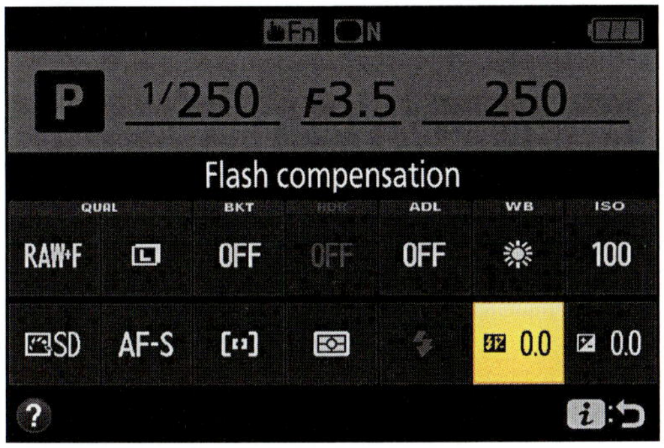

B

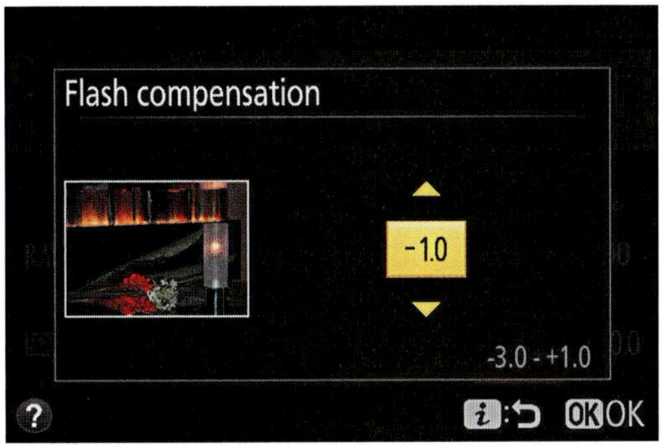

The Flash Exposure Compensation feature does not reset itself when the camera is turned off, so whatever compensation you have set will remain in effect until you change it. Your only clue to knowing that the flash output has changed will be the presence of the Flash Exposure Compensation symbol in the viewfinder. It will disappear when there is zero compensation set.

Reducing Red-Eye

We've all seen the result of using on-camera flashes when photographing people: the dreaded red-eye! This demonic effect is the result of the light from the flash entering the pupil and then reflecting back as an eerie red glow. The closer the flash is to the lens, the greater the chance you will get red-eye. This is especially true when it is dark and the subject's pupils are fully dilated. There are two ways to combat this problem. The first is to get the flash away from the lens. That's not really an option, though, if you are using the pop-up flash. Therefore, you will need to turn to the Red-Eye Reduction feature.

This is a simple feature that shines a light from the camera at the subject, causing their pupils to shrink, thus eliminating or reducing the effects of red-eye (**Figure 8.16**).

The feature is set to Off by default and needs to be turned on by using the information screen or by using a combination of the flash button and the Command dial.

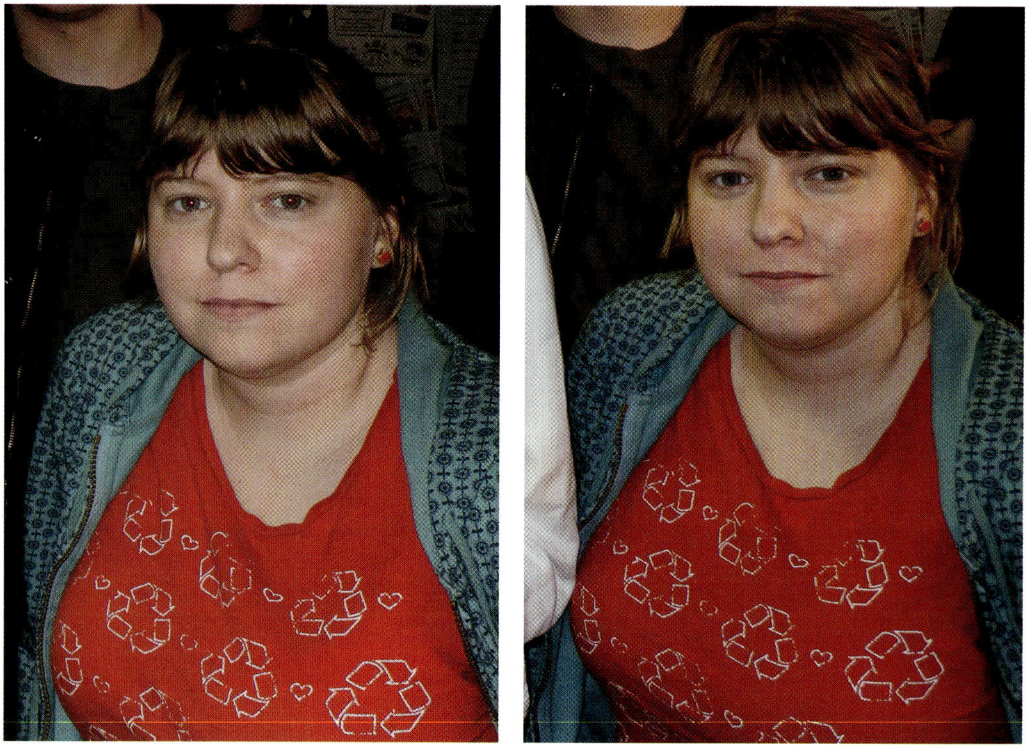

Figure 8.16
Red-eye be gone!
ISO 800 • 1/60 sec. • f/5.6 • 200mm lens

Turn on the lights!

When shooting indoors another way to reduce red-eye, or just shorten the length of time that the reduction lamp needs to be shining into your subject's eyes, is to turn on a lot of lights. The brighter the ambient light levels, the smaller the subject's pupils will be. This will reduce the time necessary for the red-eye reduction lamp to shine. It will also allow you to take more candid pictures because your subjects won't be required to stare at the red-eye lamp while waiting for their pupils to reduce.

Turning on the Red-Eye Reduction feature

1. Press the **i** button to activate the cursor in the information screen.
2. Use the Multi-selector to find the Flash Mode item, and press the OK button (**A**).
3. Use the Multi-selector to select the Red-Eye Reduction mode, represented by an eye (**B**).
4. With Red-Eye Reduction activated, compose your photo, and then press the shutter release button to take the picture.

A

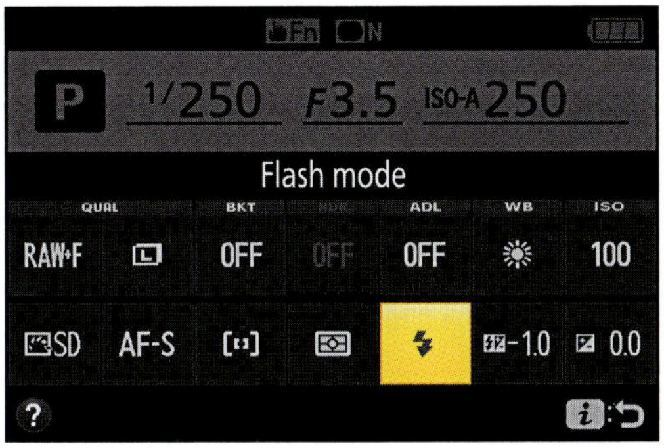

B

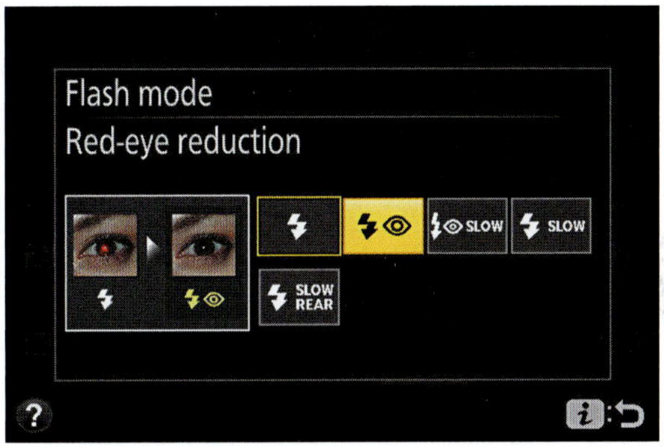

When Red-Eye Reduction is activated, the camera will not fire the instant you press the shutter release button. Instead, the Red-Eye Reduction lamp will illuminate for a second or two and then fire the flash for the exposure. This is important to remember because people have a tendency to move around, so you will need to instruct them to hold still for a moment while the lamp works its magic.

Truth be told, I rarely shoot with Red-Eye Reduction turned on because of the time it takes before allowing me to shoot. If I am after candid shots and have to use the flash, I will take my chances on red-eye and try to fix the problem in my image-processing software or even in the camera's retouching menu. The Nikon ViewNX 2 software has an Auto Red-Eye Reduction feature that works really well, too.

Rear Curtain Sync

There are two flash synchronization modes in the D5500: Front Curtain Sync and Rear Curtain Sync. You may be asking, "What in the world does synchronization do, and what's with these 'curtains'?" Good questions.

When your camera fires, there are two curtains that open and close to make up the shutter. The first, or front, curtain moves out of the way, exposing the camera sensor to the light. At the end of the exposure, the second, or rear, curtain moves in front of the sensor, ending that picture cycle. In flash photography, timing is extremely important because the flash fires in milliseconds and the shutter is usually opening in tenths or hundredths of a second. To make sure these two functions happen in order, the camera usually fires the flash just as the first curtain moves out of the way (see the "Flash Sync" sidebar, earlier in this chapter). Front Curtain Sync is labeled as Fill Flash on the camera.

In Rear Curtain Sync mode, the flash will not fire until just before the second shutter curtain ends the exposure. So, why have this mode at all? Well, there might be times when you want to have a longer exposure to balance out the light from the background to go with the subject needing the flash. Imagine taking a photograph of a friend standing in Times Square at night with all the traffic moving about and the bright streetlights overhead. If the flash fires at the beginning of the exposure and then the objects around the subject move, those objects will often blur or even obscure the subject a bit. If the camera is set to Rear Curtain Sync, though, all of the movement is recorded using the existing light first, and then the subject is "frozen" by the flash at the end by the exposure.

There is no right or wrong to it. It's just a decision on what type of effect you would like to create. Many times, Rear Curtain Sync is used for artistic purposes or to record movement in the scene without it overlapping the flash-exposed subject (**Figure 8.17**). To make sure that the main subject is always getting the final pop of the flash, I leave my camera set to Rear Curtain Sync most of the time. You can have a lot of fun with Rear Curtain Sync.

In **Figure 8.18**, I simply changed the flash mode back to the Fill Flash setting, which caused the flash to fire at the beginning of the exposure (meaning Front Curtain Sync). I was in Aperture Priority mode, and this flash-setting change resulted in the camera switching my shutter speed to 1/60 of a second. The majority of the light in the scene came from the flash since the ambient light levels were so low.

Note that if you do intend to use a longish exposure with Front Curtain Sync, you need to have your subject remain fairly still so any movement that occurs after the flash goes off will be minimized in the image. If you look carefully at Figure 8.18, you can see the slight blur of the pins as they moved after the flash fired.

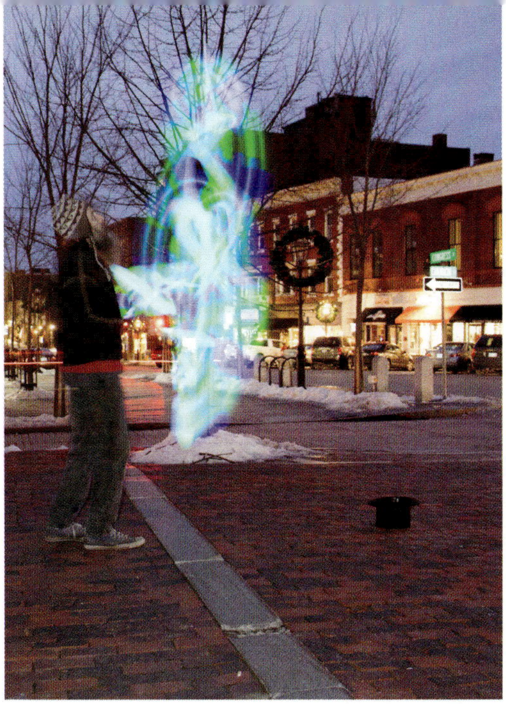

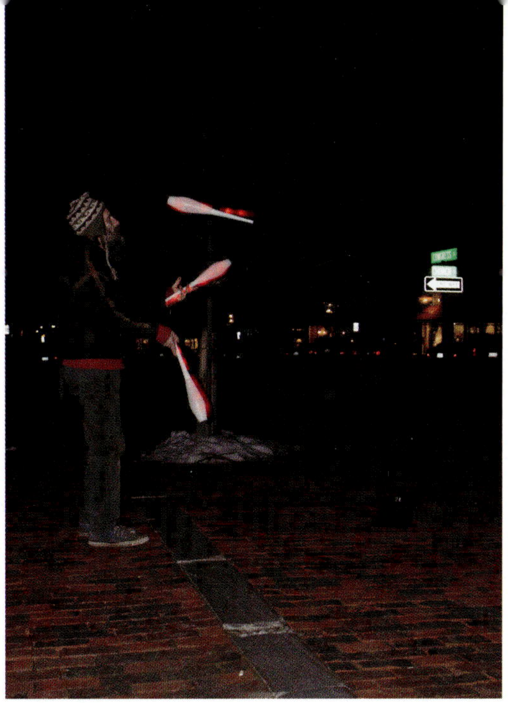

Figure 8.17 (left)
The effect of Rear Curtain Sync is most evident during long flash exposures, such as this photo of a man juggling illuminated pins.

ISO 400 • 2 sec. • f/4 • 30mm lens

Figure 8.18 (right)
This subject was illuminated at the beginning of the exposure, and little of the ambient light affected the photo.

ISO 400 • 1/60 sec. • f/4 • 30mm len

Setting your flash sync mode to Rear Curtain Sync

1. Press the **i** button to activate the cursor in the information screen.
2. Use the Multi-selector to find the Flash Mode item, and press the OK button (**A**).
3. Use the Multi-selector to select the Rear-Curtain + Slow Sync mode (**B**).
4. With Rear Curtain Sync activated, compose your photo, adjust your shutter or aperture depending on the shooting mode you are using, and then press the shutter release button to take the picture.

A

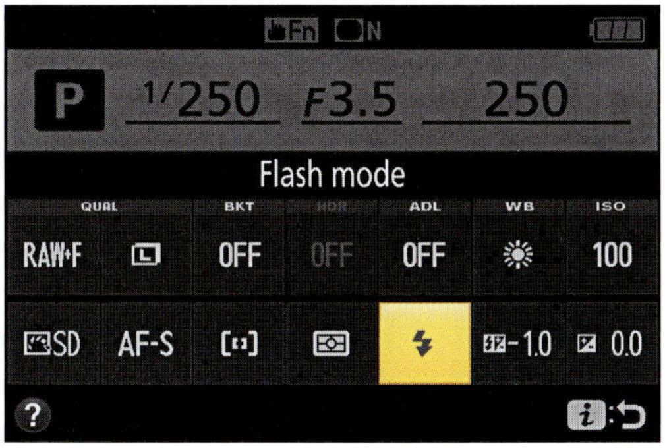

B

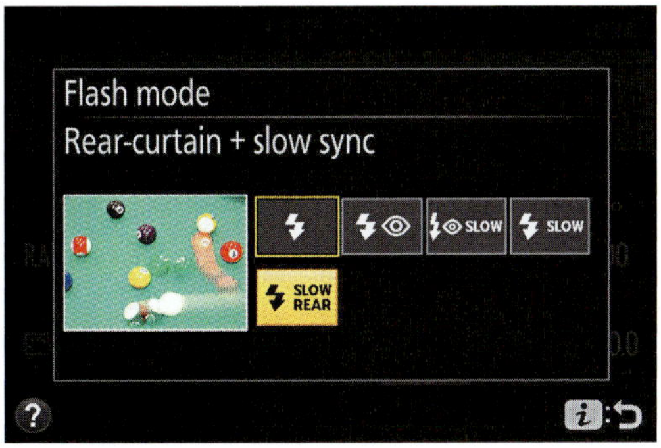

Flash and Glass

If you find yourself in a situation where you want to use your flash to shoot through a window or display case, try placing your lens right against the glass so that the reflection of the flash won't be visible in your image (**Figures 8.19** and **8.20**). This is extremely useful in museums and aquariums, and at the amusement park, when you want to capture that fortune teller.

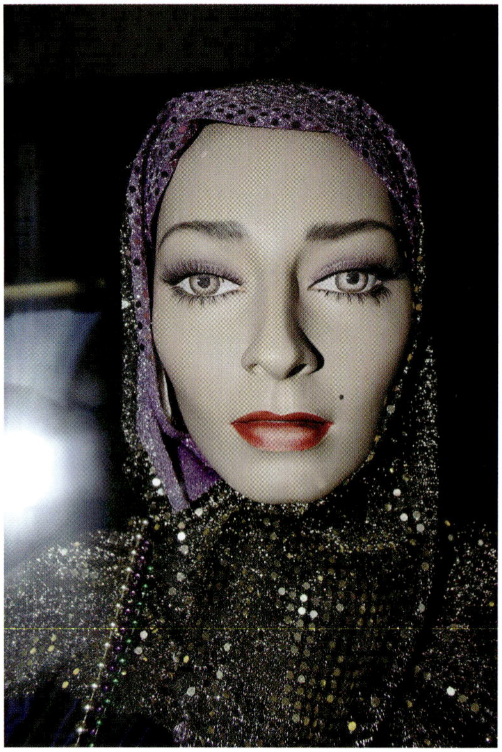

Figure 8.19 The bright spot on the left of the frame is a result of the flash reflecting off the display glass.

ISO 100 • 1/60 sec. • f/8 • 18mm lens

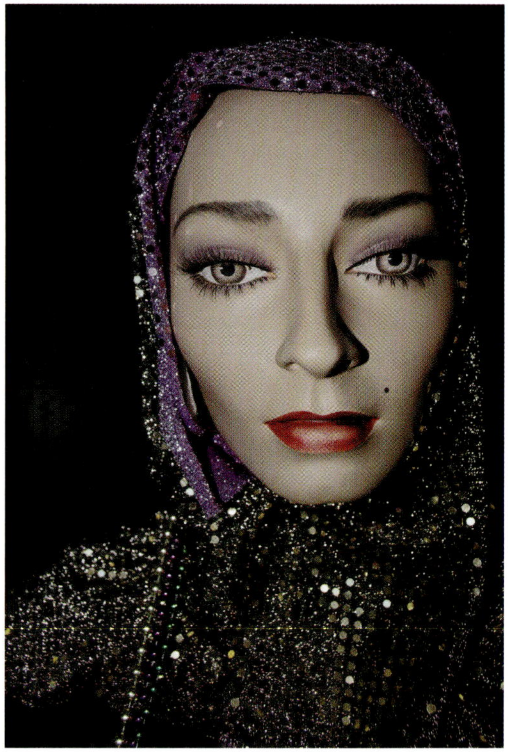

Figure 8.20 To eliminate the reflection, place the lens against the glass or as close to it as possible. This might also require zooming the lens out a little.

ISO 100 • 1/60 sec. • f/8 • 18mm lens

A Few Words About External Flash

We have discussed several ways to get control over the built-in pop-up flash on the D5500. The reality is that, as flashes go, it will only render fairly average results. For people photography, the built-in flash is probably one of the most unflattering light sources you could ever use. This isn't because the flash isn't good—it's actually very sophisticated for its size. The problem is that light should come from any direction besides the camera to best flatter a human subject. When the light emanates from directly above the lens, it gives the effect of becoming a photocopier. Imagine putting your face down on a scanner: The result would be a flatly lit, featureless photo.

To really make your flash photography come alive with possibilities, you should consider buying an external flash, such as the Nikon SB-700 AF Speedlight. The SB-700 has a swiveling flash head and more power, and it communicates with the camera and the TTL system to deliver balanced flash exposures. For more information about the Nikon Speedlight system, be sure to check out Chapter 11.

Manual Callout

For more information on the use of external Speedlight flashes on your D5500, check out page 323 of the Reference Manual PDF.

Chapter 8 Assignments

Now that we have looked at the possibilities of shooting after dark, it's time to put it all to the test. These assignments cover the full range of shooting options, both with flash and without. Let's get started.

How steady are your hands?

It's important to know just what your limits are in terms of handholding your camera and still getting sharp pictures. This will change depending on the focal length of the lens you are working with. Wider-angle lenses are more forgiving than telephoto lenses, so check this out for your longest and shortest lenses. Using the 18–140mm zoom as an example, set your lens to 140mm and then, with the camera set to ISO 200 and the mode set to Shutter Priority, turn off the VR and start taking pictures with lower and lower shutter speeds. Review each image on the LCD at a zoomed-in magnification to take note of when you start seeing visible camera shake in your images. It will probably be around 1/60 of a second for a 140mm lens.

Now do the same for the wide-angle setting on the lens. My limit is about 1/30 of a second. These shutter speeds are with the Vibration Reduction feature turned off. If you have a VR lens, try it with and without the VR feature enabled to see just how slow you can set your shutter speed while getting sharp results.

Pushing your ISO to the extreme

Find a place to shoot where the ambient light level is low. This could be at night or indoors in a darkened room. Using the mode of your choice, start increasing the ISO from 100 until you get to Hi1. Make sure you evaluate the level of noise in your image, especially in the shadow areas. Only you can decide how much noise is acceptable in your pictures. I can tell you from personal experience that I never like to stray above that ISO 1000 mark unless I absolutely need to get the shot regardless of the noise.

Eliminating the noise

Turn on High ISO Noise Reduction and repeat the previous assignment. Find your acceptable limits with Noise Reduction turned on. Also pay attention to how much detail is lost in your shadows with this function enabled.

Getting long exposures in the dark

If you don't have a tripod, find a stable place to set your camera outside and try some long exposures. Set your camera to Aperture Priority mode, and then use the self-timer to activate the camera (this will keep you from shaking the camera while pressing the shutter button).

Shoot in an area that has some level of ambient light, be it a streetlight, traffic lights, or even a full moon. The idea is to get some late-night, low-light exposures.

Reducing the noise in your long exposures

Now repeat the last assignment but with Long Exposure Noise Reduction set to On. Look at the difference in the images that were taken before and after Noise Reduction was enabled. For best results, perform this assignment and the previous assignment in the same shooting session, using the same subject.

Testing the limits of the pop-up flash

Wait for the lights to get low and then press that pop-up flash button to start using the built-in flash. Try using the different shooting modes to see how they affect your exposures. Use the Flash Exposure Compensation feature to take a series of pictures while adjusting from –3 stops all the way to +1 stop so you become familiar with how much latitude you will get from this feature.

Getting the red out

Find a friend with some patience and a tolerance for bright lights. Have him sit in a darkened room or outside at night, and then take his picture with the flash. Now turn on Red-Eye Reduction to see if you get better results. Don't forget to have him sit still while the red-eye lamp does its thing.

Getting creative with Rear Curtain Sync

Set up your camera for Rear Curtain Sync and start shooting. Moving targets are best. Experiment with Shutter Priority and Aperture Priority modes to lower the shutter speeds and exaggerate the effect. Try using a low ISO so the camera is forced to use longer shutter speeds. Be creative and have some fun!

Share your results with the book's Flickr group!
Join the group here: flickr.com/groups/nikond5500_fromsnapshotstogreatshots

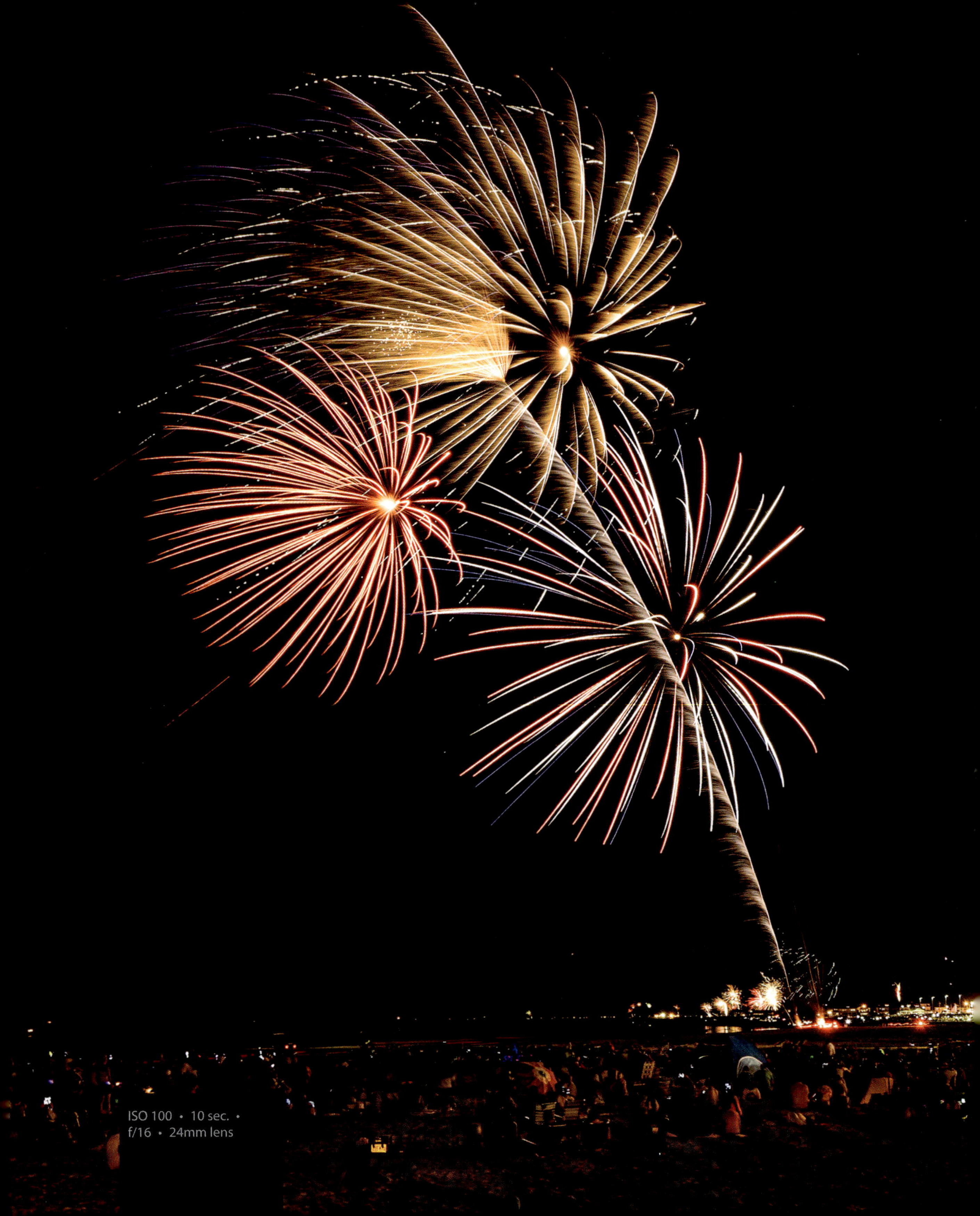

ISO 100 • 10 sec. • f/16 • 24mm lens

9

Advanced Techniques

Impress Your Family and Friends

We covered a lot of ground in the previous chapters, especially on the general photographic concepts that apply to most, if not all, shooting situations. There are, however, some specific tools and techniques that will give you an added advantage in obtaining great shots. Additionally, we will look at how to customize controls on your camera to reflect your personal shooting preferences and always have them at the ready.

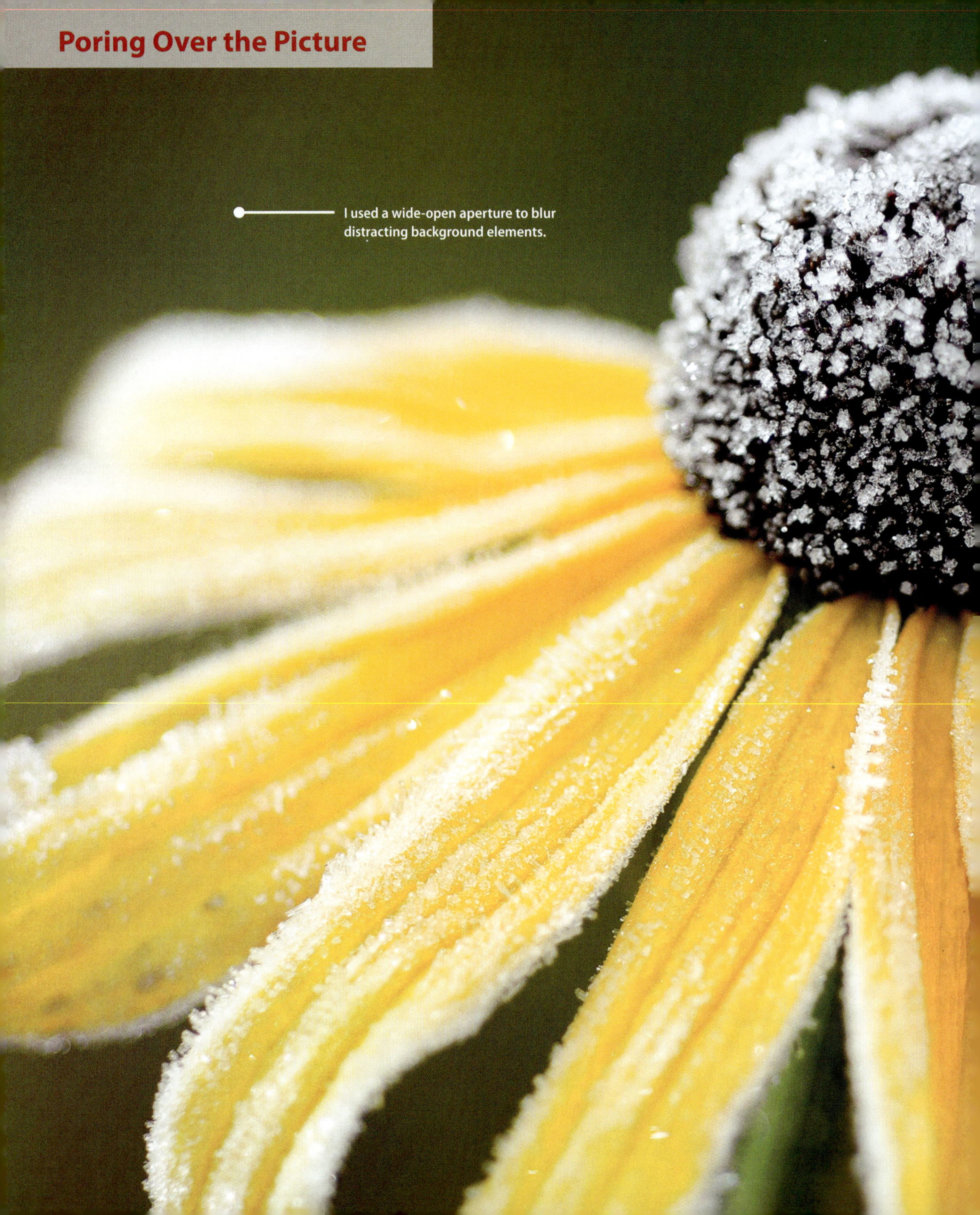
I used a wide-open aperture to blur distracting background elements.

There is something irresistible about a study of contrasts. Areas of sharp focus stand out against larger areas of blur. A yellow flower, iconic of summer and warmth, covered in frost just seems so out of place, we have to look closer. Early fall in New Hampshire is a good time to find the Black-Eyed Susans covered in a frosty dew, an excellent photo opportunity.

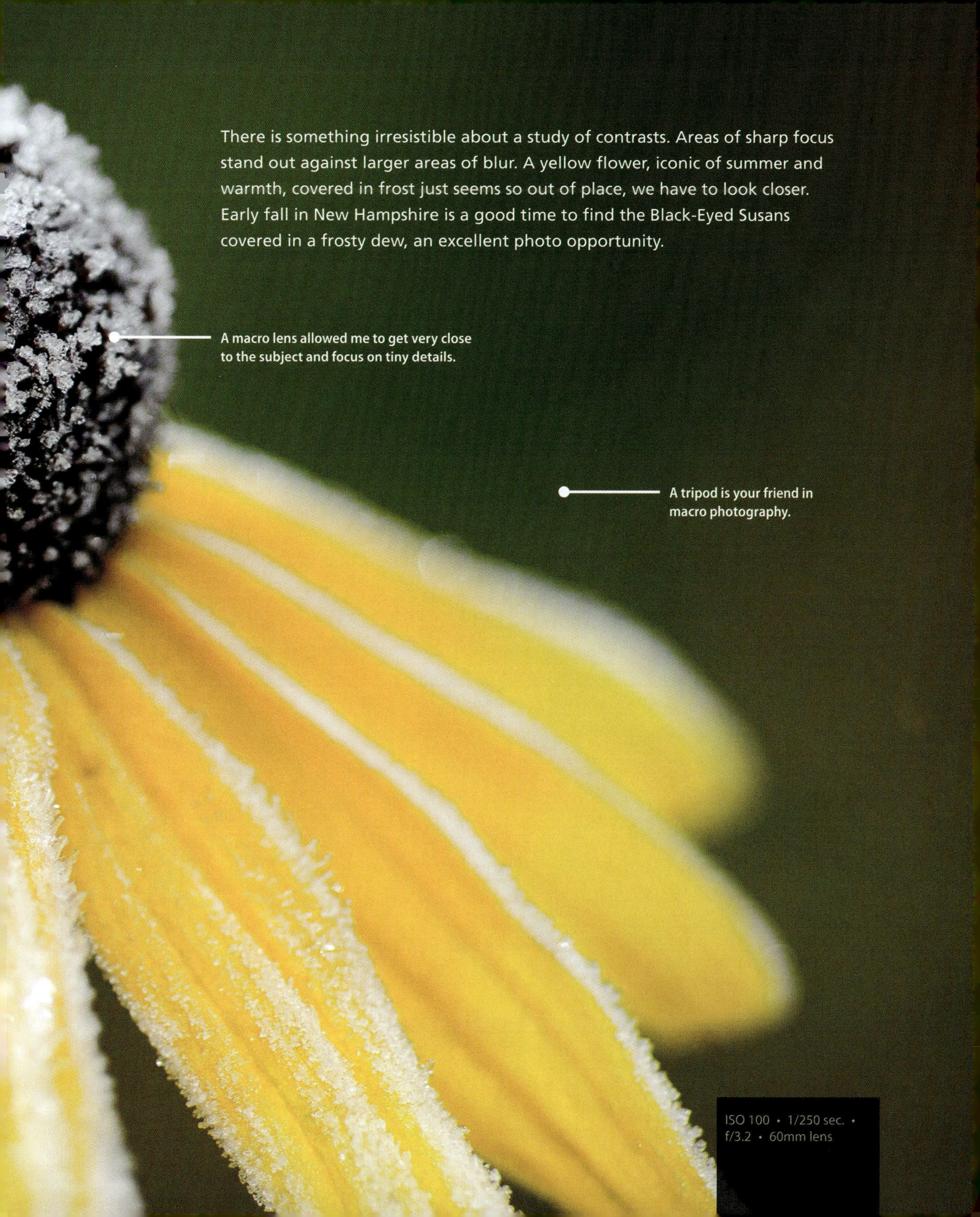

ISO 100 • 1/250 sec. • f/3.2 • 60mm lens

Spot Metering for More Exposure Control

Matrix metering mode will provide accurate metering information for the majority of your photography. It does an excellent job of evaluating the scene and then relating the proper exposure information to you. The only problem is, as with any metering mode on a camera, Matrix metering doesn't know what it is looking at. In specific circumstances, you will want to get an accurate reading from just a portion of a scene and discount all of the remaining area in the viewfinder. To give you greater control of the metering operation, you can switch the camera to Spot metering mode. This allows you to take a meter reading from a very small circle in the center of the viewfinder while ignoring the rest of the viewfinder area.

So when would you need to use this? Think of a person standing in front of a very light wall. In Matrix metering mode, the camera would see the entire scene and try to adjust the exposure information so the light background is exposed to render a darker wall in your image. This means the scene would actually be underexposed and your subject would appear too dark (**Figure 9.1**). To correct this, you can place the camera in Spot metering mode and take a meter reading right off of—and *only* off of—your subject, ignoring the light-colored wall altogether. Spot metering will read the location where you have your focus point, placing all of the exposure information right on your point of interest (**Figure 9.2**).

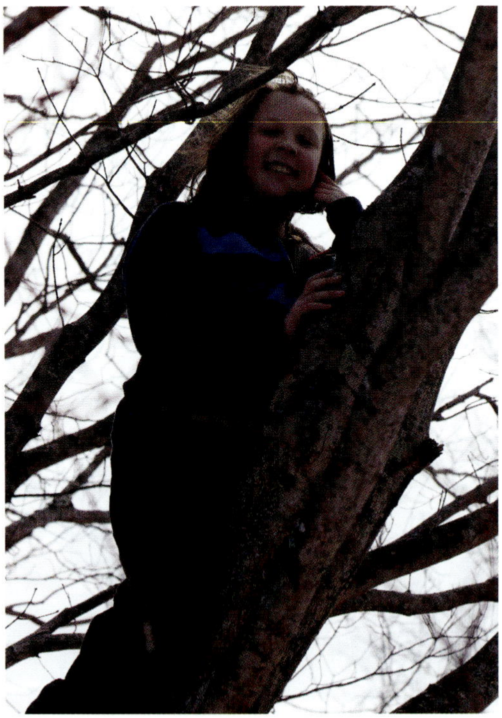

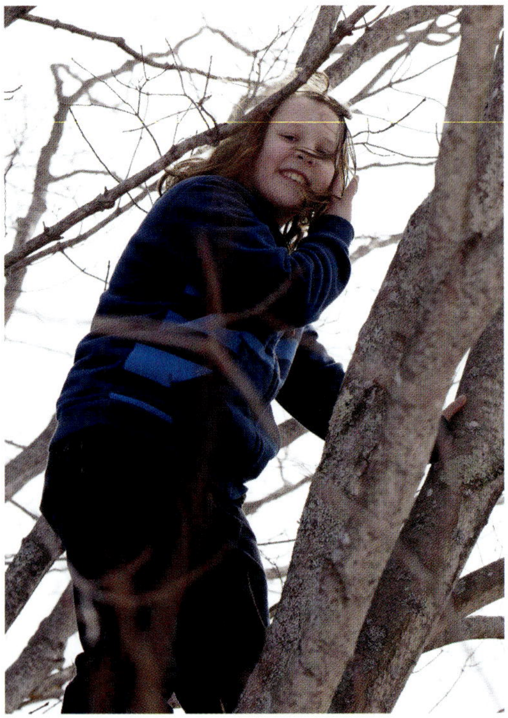

Figure 9.1 (left) A bright background can throw off your exposure.

ISO 100 • 1/1250 sec. • f/4 • 50mm lens

Figure 9.2 (right) By switching to Spot metering, I was able to get a more accurate exposure for my young friend up in the tree.

ISO 100 • 1/640 sec. • f/4 • 50mm lens

Other situations that would benefit from Spot metering include

- Snow or beach environments where the overall brightness level of the scene could fool the meter
- When a subject is strongly backlit, leaving it underexposed
- Cases where the overall feel of a photo is too light or too dark

Setting up and shooting in Spot metering mode

1. Press the **i** button to activate the cursor in the information screen.
2. Move the cursor to the current metering method, and press the OK button.
3. Use the Multi-selector to select the Spot metering option, and press the OK button to lock in your change.
4. Use the Multi-selector to move the focus point onto your subject, and take your photo. The meter reading will come directly from the location of the focus point.

Note that if you are using the Auto-Area focus mode, the camera will use the center focus point as the Spot metering location.

When using Spot metering mode, remember that the meter believes it is looking at a middle-gray value, so you might need to incorporate some exposure compensation. This will come from experience as you use the meter.

Metering for sunrise or sunset

Capturing a beautiful sunrise or sunset is all about the sky. If there is too much foreground in the viewfinder, the camera's meter will deliver an exposure setting that is accurate for the darker foreground areas but leaves the sky looking overexposed, undersaturated, and generally just not very interesting (**Figure 9.3**). To gain more emphasis on the colorful sky, point your camera at the brightest part of it and take your meter reading there. Use the AE Lock to meter for the brightest part of the sky and then recompose. The result will be an exposure setting that underexposes the foreground but provides a darker, more dramatic sky (**Figure 9.4**).

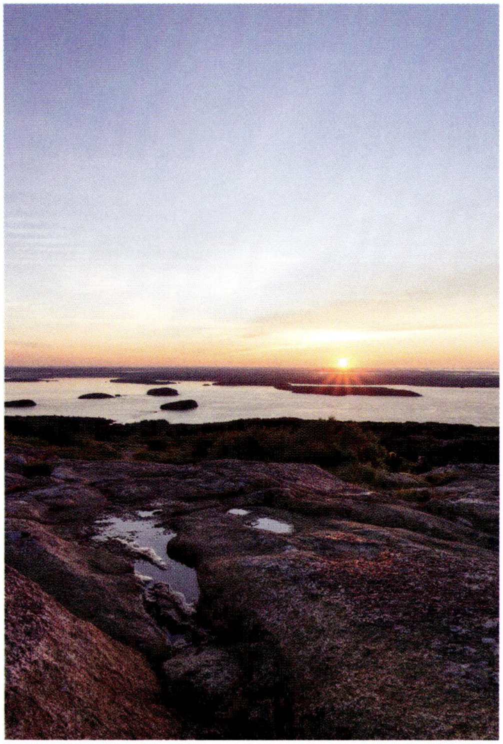

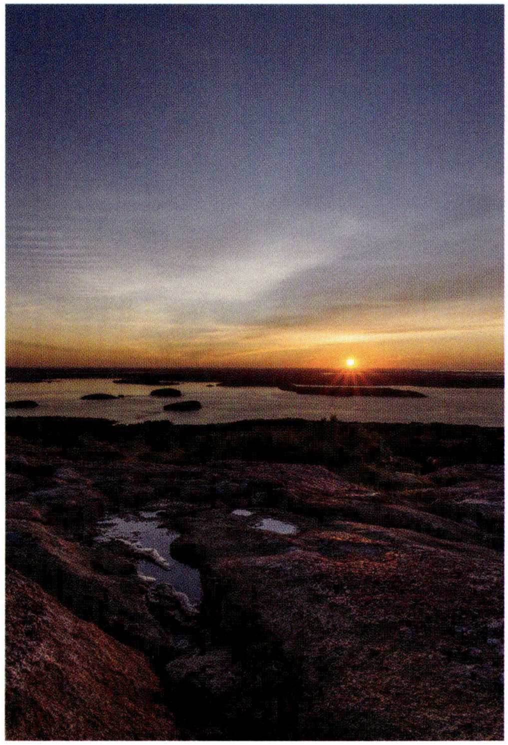

Figure 9.3 (left)
By metering with all the information in the frame, you get bright skies and more detail in the ground.

ISO 100 • 1/5 sec. • f/16 • 24mm lens

Figure 9.4 (right)
By taking the meter reading from the brightest part of the sky, you will get darker, more colorful sunsets and sunrises.

ISO 100 • 1/20 sec. • f/16 • 24mm lens

Shooting in Manual Mode

Probably one of the most advanced, and yet most basic, skills to master is shooting in Manual mode. Considering the power and utility of most of the automatic modes, Manual mode almost never sees the light of day. I have to admit that I don't select it for use very often, but there are times when no other mode will do. Studio work with external flashes is one such situation. I know that when I work with studio lights, my exposure will not change, so I use Manual to eliminate any automatic changes that might happen from shooting in Program, Shutter Priority, or Aperture Priority mode.

Since you probably aren't too concerned with studio strobes at this point, I will concentrate on one of the more likely uses for Manual mode: long nighttime exposures.

Bulb photography

If you want to work with long shutter speeds that don't quite fit into one of the selectable shutter speeds, you can select Bulb. This setting is available only in Manual mode, and its sole function is to open the shutter at your command and then close it again when you decide. I can think of two common scenarios where Bulb comes in handy: shooting fireworks and photographing lightning.

If you are photographing fireworks, you could certainly use one of the longer shutter speeds available in Shutter Priority mode, since they are available for exposure times of up to 30 seconds. But sometimes you don't need 30 seconds' worth of exposure, and sometimes you need more.

If you open the shutter and then see a great burst of fireworks, you might decide that is all you want for that particular frame, so you click the button to end the exposure (**Figure 9.5**). Set the camera to 30 seconds and you might get too many bursts, but shorten it to 10 seconds and you might not get the one you want. The same can be said for photographing a lightning storm. Lightning can be very tricky to capture, and using the Bulb setting to open and then close the shutter at will allows for more creativity as well as more opportunity to get the shot. Capturing light trails from someone moving a glow stick in a dark room or your backyard at night is an easy (and safe) way to practice Bulb photography from the comfort of your own home.

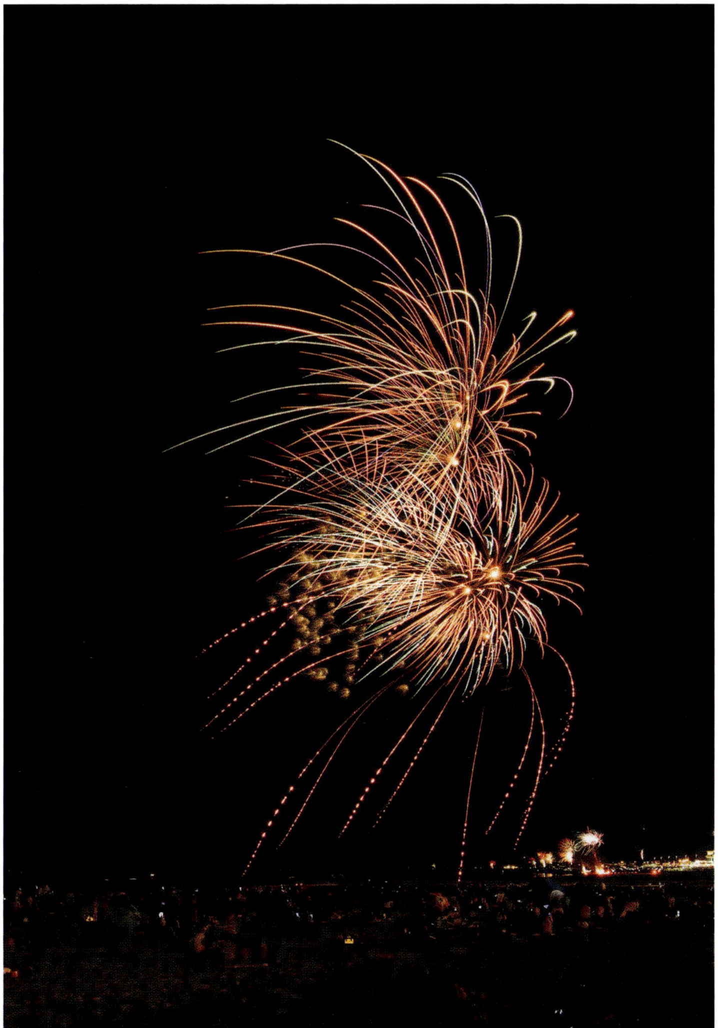

Figure 9.5
The Bulb setting is great for capturing fireworks.

ISO 100 • 9.6 sec. • f/16 • 24mm lens

To select the Bulb setting, simply place your camera in Manual mode, and then rotate the Command dial to the left until the shutter speed displays Bulb on the rear LCD screen.

When you're using the Bulb setting, the shutter will only stay open for the duration that you are holding down the shutter button. You should use a sturdy tripod or shooting surface to eliminate any self-induced vibration. Using your finger on the shutter button for a Bulb exposure will definitely increase the chances of getting some camera shake in your images. To get the most benefit from the Bulb setting, I suggest using a remote cord, such as the Nikon MC-DC2, or the ML-L3 wireless remote (see Chapter 11 for more details). You'll also want to turn on Long Exposure Noise Reduction, as covered in Chapter 7. With the wireless remote, you press once to open the shutter, and then press the button on the remote a second time to close it.

Bulb

If you are new to photography, you might be wondering where in the world the *Bulb* shutter function got its name. After all, wouldn't it make more sense to call it the Manual shutter setting? It probably would, but this is one of those terms that harks back to the origins of photography. Way back when, the shutter was actually opened through the use of a bulb-shaped device that forced air through a tube, which, in turn, pushed a plunger down, activating the camera shutter. When the bulb was released, it pulled the plunger back, letting the shutter close and ending the exposure.

Shooting lightning

If you are going to photograph lightning strikes in a thunderstorm, please exercise extreme caution. Standing in the open with a tripod is like standing over a lightning rod. Work from indoors if at all possible.

Avoiding Lens Flare

Lens flare is one of the problems you will encounter when shooting in the bright sun. Lens flare will show itself as bright circles on the image (**Figure 9.6**).

Often you will see multiple circles in a line leading from a very bright light source such as the sun. The flare is a result of the sun bouncing off the multiple pieces of optical glass in the lens and then being reflected back onto the sensor.

You can avoid the problem using one of these methods:

- Try to shoot with the sun coming from over your shoulder, not in front of you or in your scene.
- Use a lens shade to block the unwanted light from striking the lens. You don't have to have the sun in your viewfinder for lens flare to be an issue. All it has to do is strike the front glass of the lens.
- If you don't have a lens shade, try using your hand or some other element to block the light.

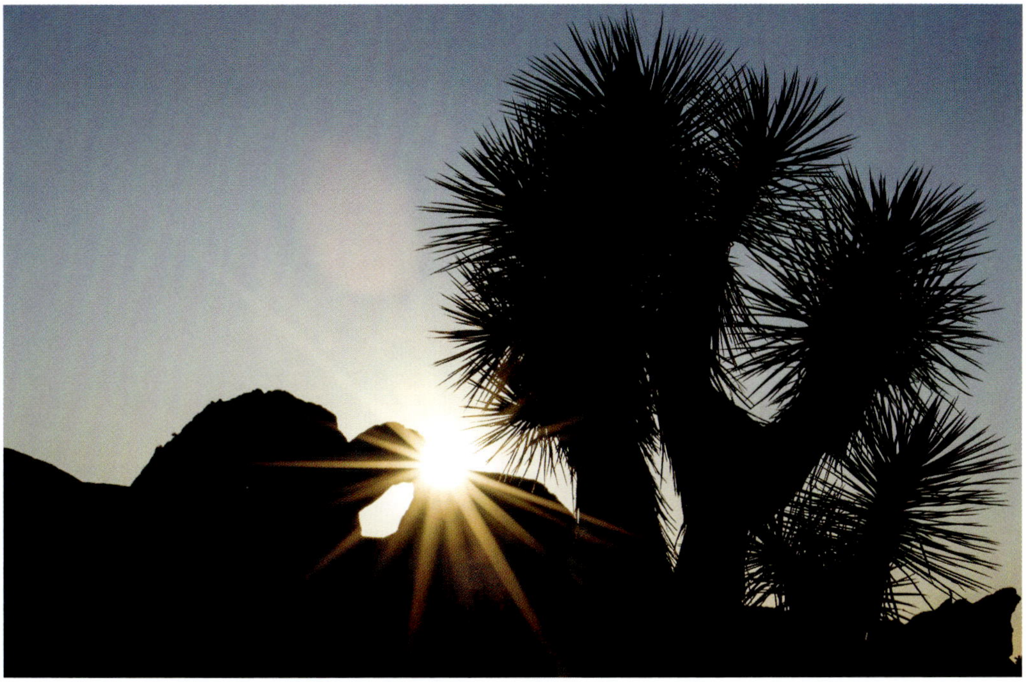

Figure 9.6
Shooting into the sun will almost always get you some lens flare.

ISO 100 • 1/60 sec. • f/22 • 100mm lens

Using the Sun Creatively

Have you ever seen photographs where the sun is peeking through a small hole and it creates a very cool starburst effect? There is actually a little trick to pulling it off, and it's fairly easy. The real key is to be shooting at f/22 (or whatever your smallest aperture is). Then you need to have just a bit of the sunlight in your frame, either peeking over an edge or through a small hole. The other thing you need to do is make sure you are properly exposing for the rest of your scene, not the bright bit of sunlight you are allowing in. With a little practice, you can make some very cool shots (**Figure 9.7**).

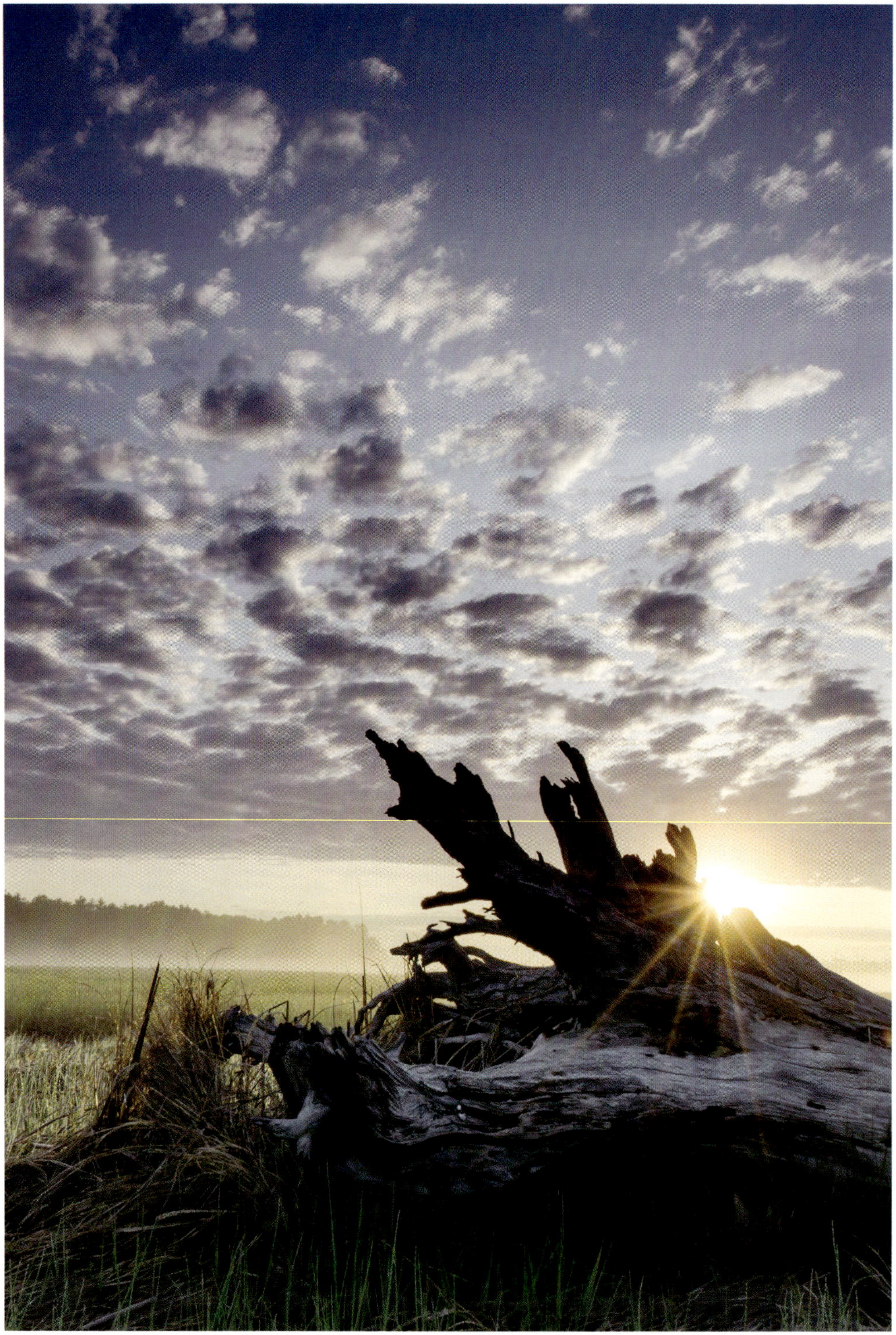

Figure 9.7
Waiting for the sun to rise in a misty marsh.

ISO 100 • 1/25 sec. • f/22 • 18mm lens

Bracketing Exposures

What if you are doing everything right in terms of metering and mode selection, yet your images still sometimes come out too light or too dark? You can use a technique called "bracketing," which will help you find the best exposure value for your scene by taking a normal exposure as well as ones that are overexposed and underexposed. Having these differing exposure values will most often present you with one frame that just looks better than the others. I use the bracketing function all the time, and I have it assigned to my Function button so I can access it quickly. You can also change the bracketing by adjusting the setting in your information screen (**Figure 9.8**).

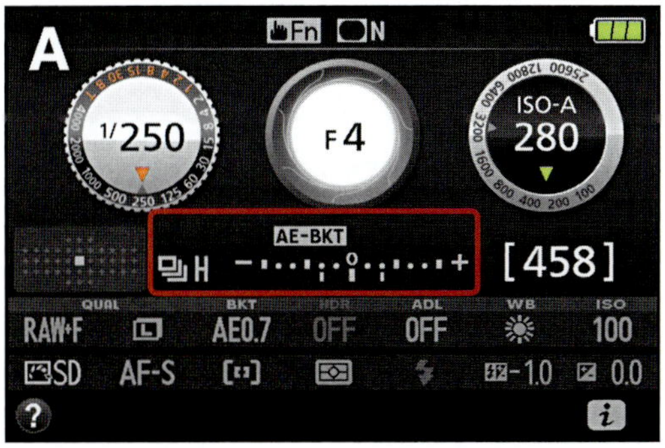

Figure 9.8 **The information screen shows you just how much bracketing is being applied on an over/under scale.**

Once you have entered the Auto Bracketing screen, you can decide how much variation you want between bracketed exposures. You can choose from one-third of a stop all the way to two full stops of exposure difference between each bracketed exposure. If I am shooting in the JPEG mode, I will typically bracket in one-stop increments to help zero in on that perfect exposure, and then just delete the photos that didn't make the grade (**Figures 9.9**, **9.10**, and **9.11**).

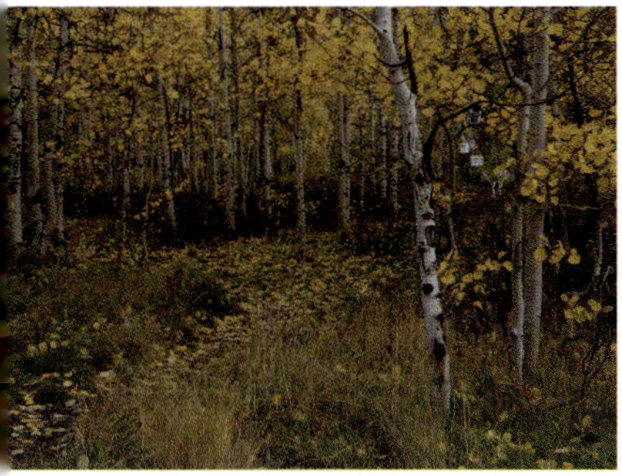

Figure 9.9 **One stop of exposure below normal.**

ISO 100 • 1 sec. • f/11 • 46mm lens

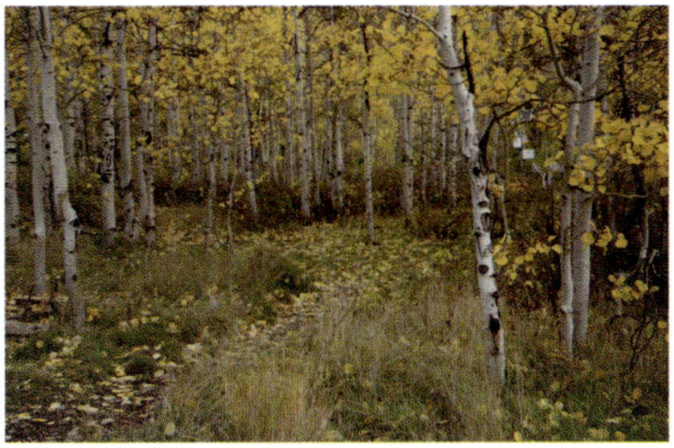

Figure 9.10 **The normal exposure as indicated by the camera meter.**

ISO 100 • 2 sec. • f/11 • 46mm lens

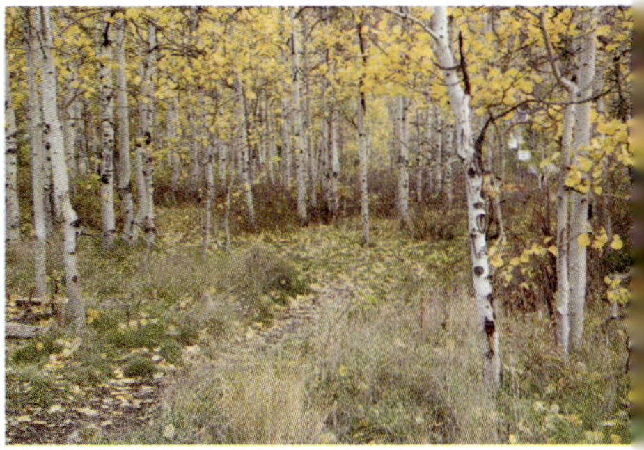

Figure 9.11 **One stop of exposure above normal.**

ISO 100 • 4 sec. • f/11 • 46mm lens

Setting Auto Exposure Bracketing

1. Press the **i** button to activate the cursor in the information screen, and move it to the BKT setting (**A**).
2. Press the OK button to enter the Auto Bracketing screen, and then use the Multi-selector to set the amount of bracketed exposure you desire (**B**). Press the OK button to lock in your change.
3. Frame your subject in the viewfinder, and then take three pictures. The result will be three differently exposed images.

A

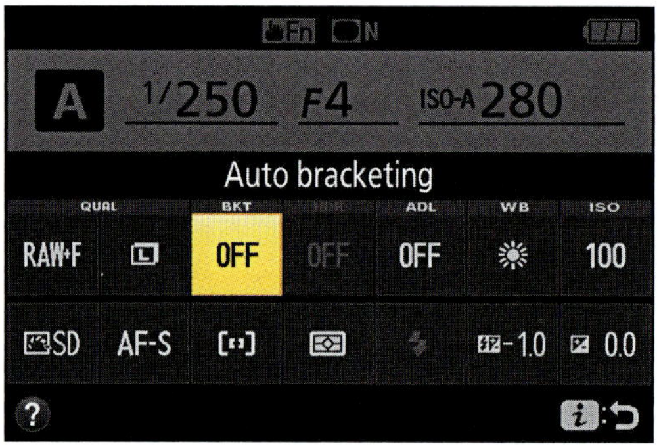

B

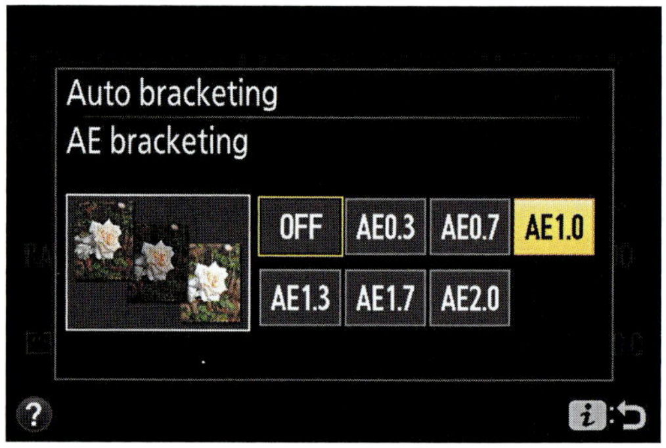

When I am out shooting in the RAW file format, I typically shoot with my camera set to an exposure compensation of –1/3 stop to protect my highlights. If I am dealing with a subject that has a lot of different tonal ranges from bright to dark, I will often bracket by one stop over and under my already compensated exposure. That means I will have exposures of –1 1/3, –1/3, and +2/3. Another thing to remember is that AE Bracketing will use the current mode for making the exposure changes. This means that if you are in Aperture Priority mode, the camera will make adjustments to your shutter speed. Likewise, if you are in Shutter Priority, the changes will be made to your aperture value. This is important to remember since it could affect certain aspects of your image, such as depth of field or camera shake. You also need to know that AE Bracketing will remain in effect until you set it back to zero, even if you turn the camera off and then on again.

Macro Photography

Put simply, macro photography is close-up photography. Depending on the lens or lenses that you got with your camera, you may have the perfect tool for macro work. Some lenses are made to shoot in a macro mode, but you don't have to feel left out if you don't have one of those. Check the spec sheet that came with your lens to see what the minimum focusing distance is for your lens.

If you have a zoom, you should work with the lens at its longest focal length. Also, work with a tripod because handholding will make focusing difficult. The easiest way to make sure your focus is precisely where you want it is to use Manual focus mode.

Since I am recommending a tripod for your macro work, I will also recommend using Aperture Priority mode so you can achieve differing levels of depth of field. Long lenses at close range can make for some very shallow depth of field, so you will need to work with apertures that are probably much smaller than what you normally use. If you are shooting outside, try shading the subject from direct sunlight by using some sort of diffusion material, such as a white sheet or diffusion panel. By diffusing the light, you will see much greater detail because you will have a lower contrast ratio (softer shadows), and detail is what macro photography is about (**Figure 9.12**).

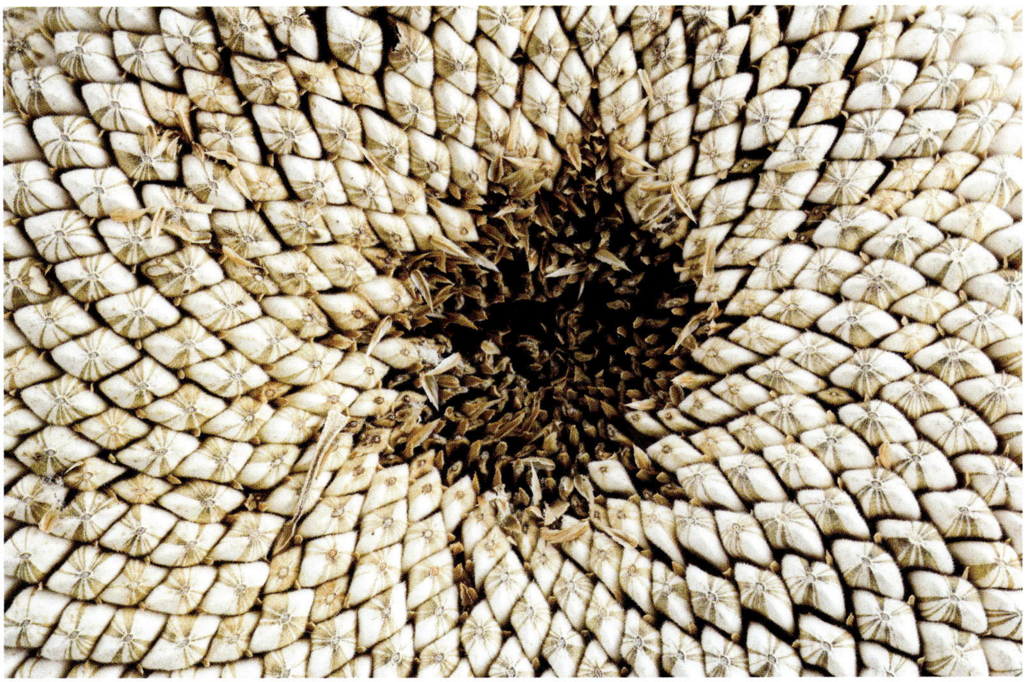

Figure 9.12
A dried sunflower head has an amazing amount of detail and a spiraling pattern.

ISO 100 • 1/2 sec. • f/11 • 85mm lens

Using Active D-Lighting

Your camera provides an automatic function called Active D-Lighting, which can make your pictures look better. It works this way: The camera evaluates the tones in your image and then underexposes for the highlight areas while lightening any areas that it believes are too dark or lacking in contrast (**Figures 9.13** and **9.14**). Active D-Lighting is automatically applied to images that are shot in any of the automatic scene modes, except for the High Key, Low Key, and Silhouette scene modes.

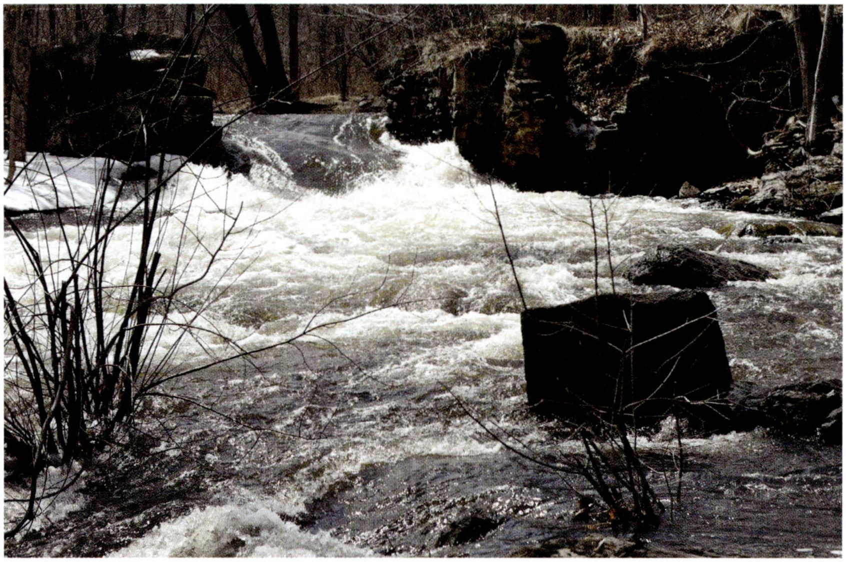

Figure 9.13
Without Active D-Lighting, the shadows in the image are dark and contrasty, while the brighter areas are a little washed out.

ISO 100 • 1/500 sec. • f/5.6 • 50mm lens

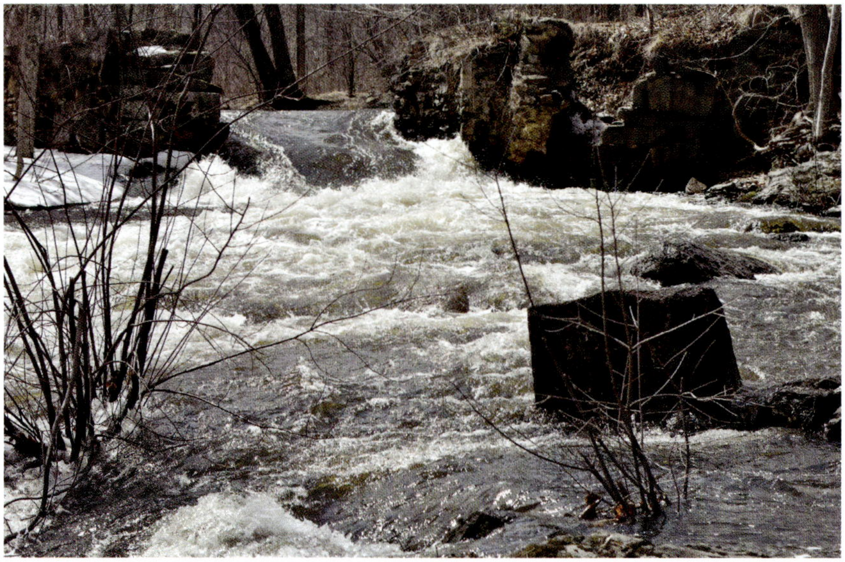

Figure 9.14
Active D-Lighting on the High setting reveals a lot more detail in the brighter areas even while managing to bring out more detail in the shadows.

ISO 100 • 1/800 sec. • f/5.6 • 50mm lens

You can choose from six levels: Off, Low (L), Normal (N), High (H), Extra High (H*), and Auto (A). You will need to evaluate the strength of the effect on your images and change the setting accordingly. If I am shooting JPEG, I will typically leave it set to Normal so I have brighter, more detailed shadow areas in my photographs while still maintaining good exposure in my skies. You should know that Active D-Lighting can be adjusted only when using one of the professional modes. Also, you will want to turn it off if you are using flash exposure compensation, since it will try to work against you when you alter the flash strength.

Because Active D-Lighting reduces exposure and then uses Nikon's own secret sauce to process the final result in-camera when shooting JPEG, I don't use Active D-Lighting when shooting in RAW mode if I am not going to process the RAW images in Nikon's software (such as ViewNX 2 or Capture NX-D). This is because third-party RAW processing software (such as Adobe Photoshop or Lightroom) sees only the slightly underexposed image and is unaware of the Active D-Lighting setting. Just keep that in the back of your mind when you decide to make the move up to shooting in RAW mode.

Setting up Active D-Lighting

1. Press the **i** button to activate the cursor in the information screen, and then use the Multi-selector to navigate to the ADL setting (**A**).
2. Press the OK button, and then move the Multi-selector up or down to select the level of Active D-Lighting you desire (**B**).
3. Press the OK button to lock in your changes, and resume shooting.

A

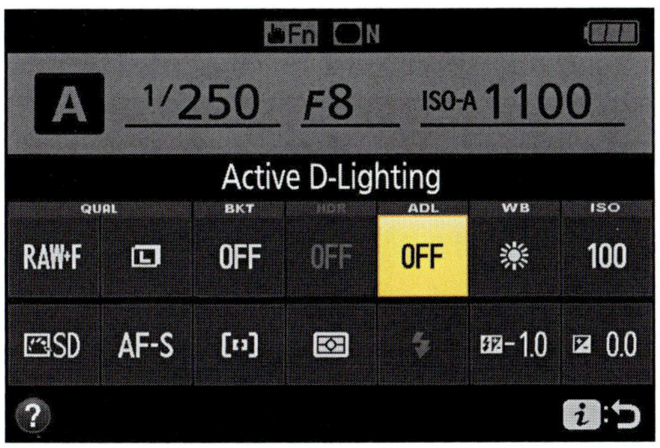

B

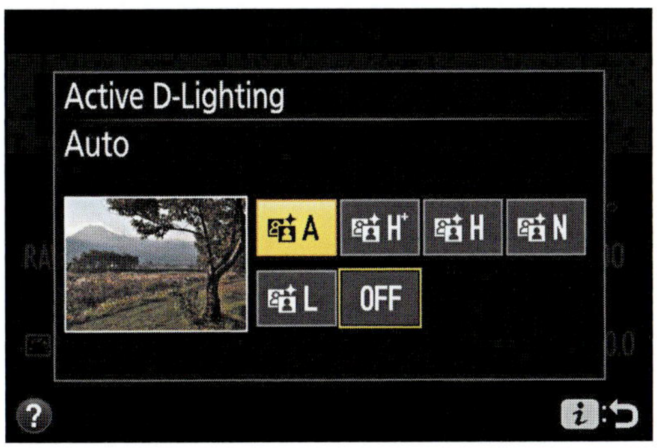

The Active D-Lighting setting can also be changed in the Shooting menu.

You can set up your camera to automatically take one shot with Active D-Lighting turned on and another with it turned off, via the Auto Bracketing menu.

Bracketing with Active D-Lighting

1. Press the Menu button, and then use the Multi-selector to go to Custom Setting Menu (**A**).
2. Highlight menu item e: Bracketing/Flash, and press OK (**B**).
3. Select item e2: Auto Bracketing Set, and press OK (**C**).
4. Highlight ADL Bracketing, and press OK (**D**).

A

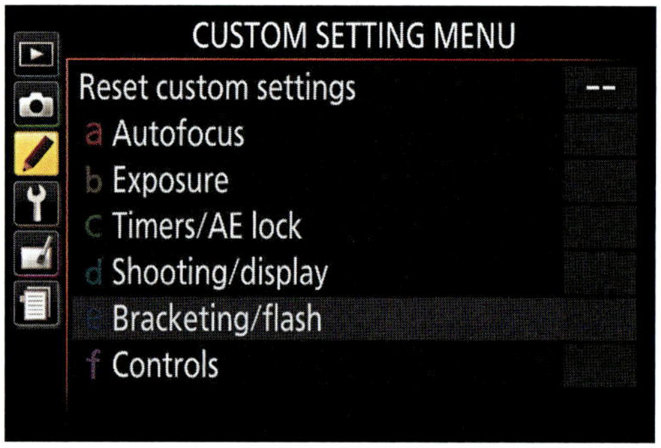

B

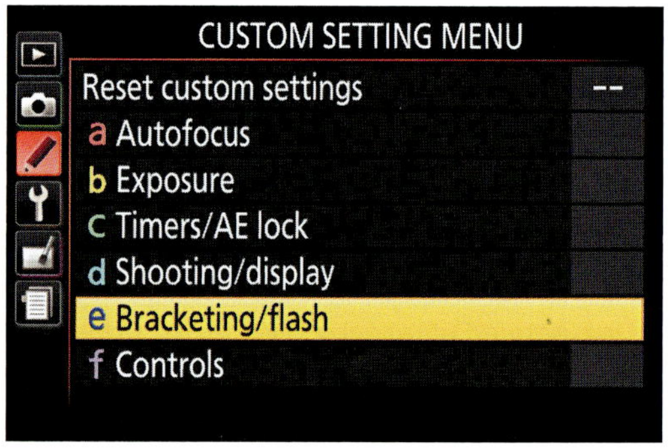

C

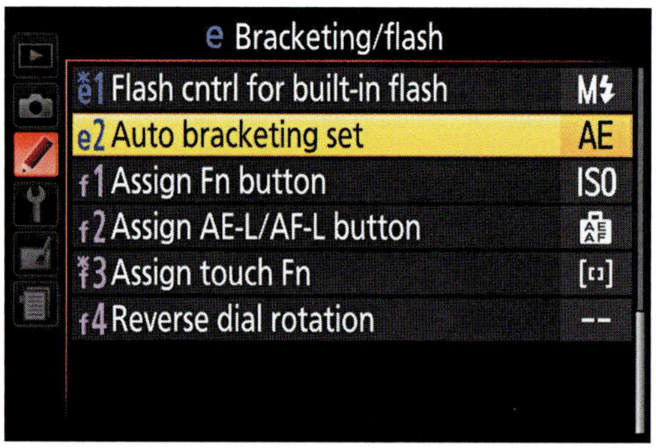

D

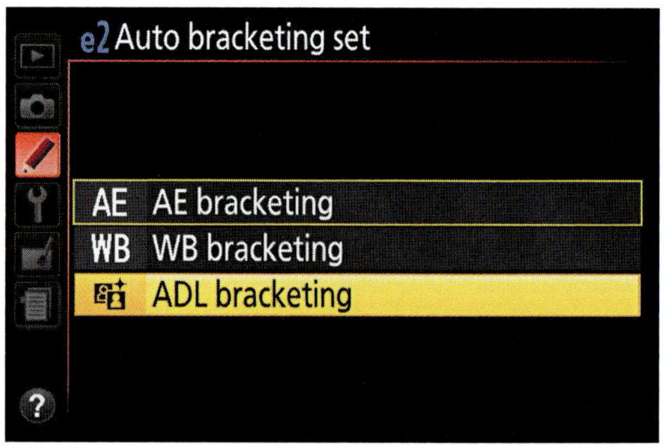

Now you can enable automatic bracketing via the **i** button (just like we did earlier for exposure) and see what Active D-Lighting has to offer while comparing shots taken with and without it. Just remember to go back to the Auto Bracketing menu to change it to AE when you want to bracket exposure.

Interval Timer Shooting

One of the coolest underutilized features in most Nikon cameras is the interval timer (found under the Shooting menu). The feature is getting more use with the rising popularity of time-lapse photography, in which a series of photos are taken over a set period of time and at set intervals between each exposure, and then made into a video. A quick online search for "time-lapse video" will provide countless examples.

While creating time-lapse videos is indeed fun, the interval timer can be a practical helper for shooting stills, too. I like to use it when I'm photographing wildlife (birds in particular) and to capture myself working with my bees (as in that photo back in Chapter 2). Using this feature, I can set up the camera to shoot a subject, trigger it to run over some period of time, and walk away. The camera dutifully fires away, and then at the end I grab the card and enjoy seeing what my camera saw (**Figure 9.15**). I also use this same technique to create star trail photos, where a series of photos are later combined into a single photo showing the earth's rotation as the movement of the stars (**Figure 9.16**).

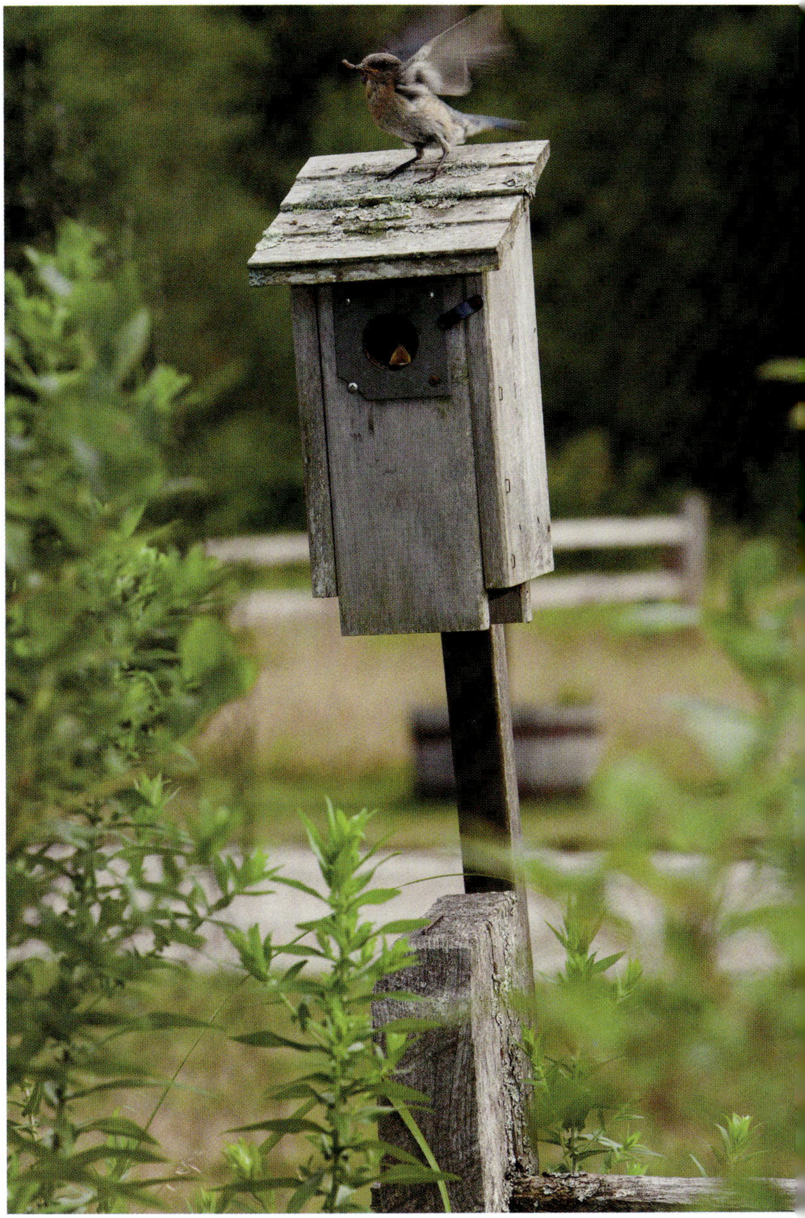

Figure 9.15 **I set up my camera in front of one of my bluebird houses and let it run for about an hour. This is one of my favorite shots.**

ISO 200 • 1/60 sec. • f/8 • 155mm lens

Manual Callout

Check out page 101 in the Reference Manual PDF to learn more about using the interval timer.

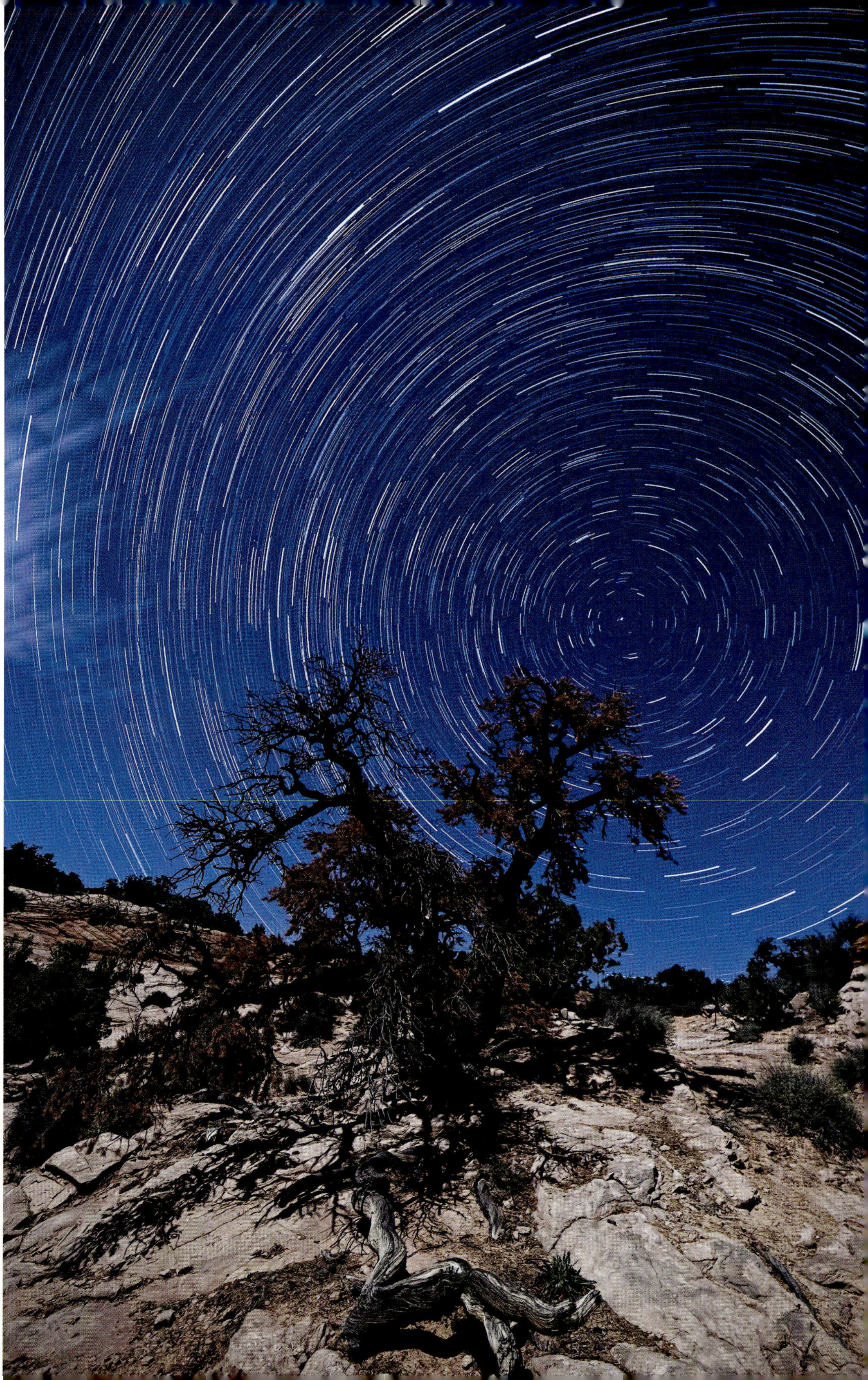

Figure 9.16
This is the result of 60 30-second exposures combined into a single photo using a program called StarStaX.

ISO 2000 • 30 sec. • f/5.6 • 14mm lens

Chapter 9 Assignments

Many of the techniques covered in this chapter are specific to certain shooting situations that may not come about very often. If you want to be a truly accomplished photographer, it's a good idea to practice them anyway so when the situation does present itself, you will be ready.

Adding some drama to the end of the day

Most sunset photos don't reflect what the photographer saw because he or she didn't meter correctly for them. The next time you see a colorful sunset, pull out your camera and take a photo, and then take a photo with a meter reading from the sky and see what a difference it makes.

Making spot-on exposures

Spot metering mode can give accurate results, but only when the camera is pointed at something that has a middle tone. Try adding something gray to the scene and taking a reading off it. Now switch back to your regular metering mode and see if the exposure is slightly different.

Using the Bulb setting to capture the moment

This is one of those settings you won't use often, but it's pretty handy when you do need it. If you have the opportunity to shoot a fireworks display or a distant storm, try setting the camera to Bulb and playing with some long exposures to capture just the moments you want.

Bracketing your way to better exposures

Why settle for just one variation of an image when you can bracket to get the best exposure choice? Set your camera up for a 1/3-bracket series, and then expand it to a one-stop series. Review the results to see if the normal setting was the best, or perhaps one of the bracketed exposures is even better.

Moving in for a close-up

Macro photography is best practiced on stationary subjects, which is why I like shooting flowers. If you have a zoom lens, check the minimum focusing distance and then try to get right to that spot to squeeze the most from your subject. Experiment with using a diffuse light source as well, to minimize shadows.

Share your results with the book's Flickr group!
Join the group here: flickr.com/groups/nikond5500_fromsnapshotstogreatshots

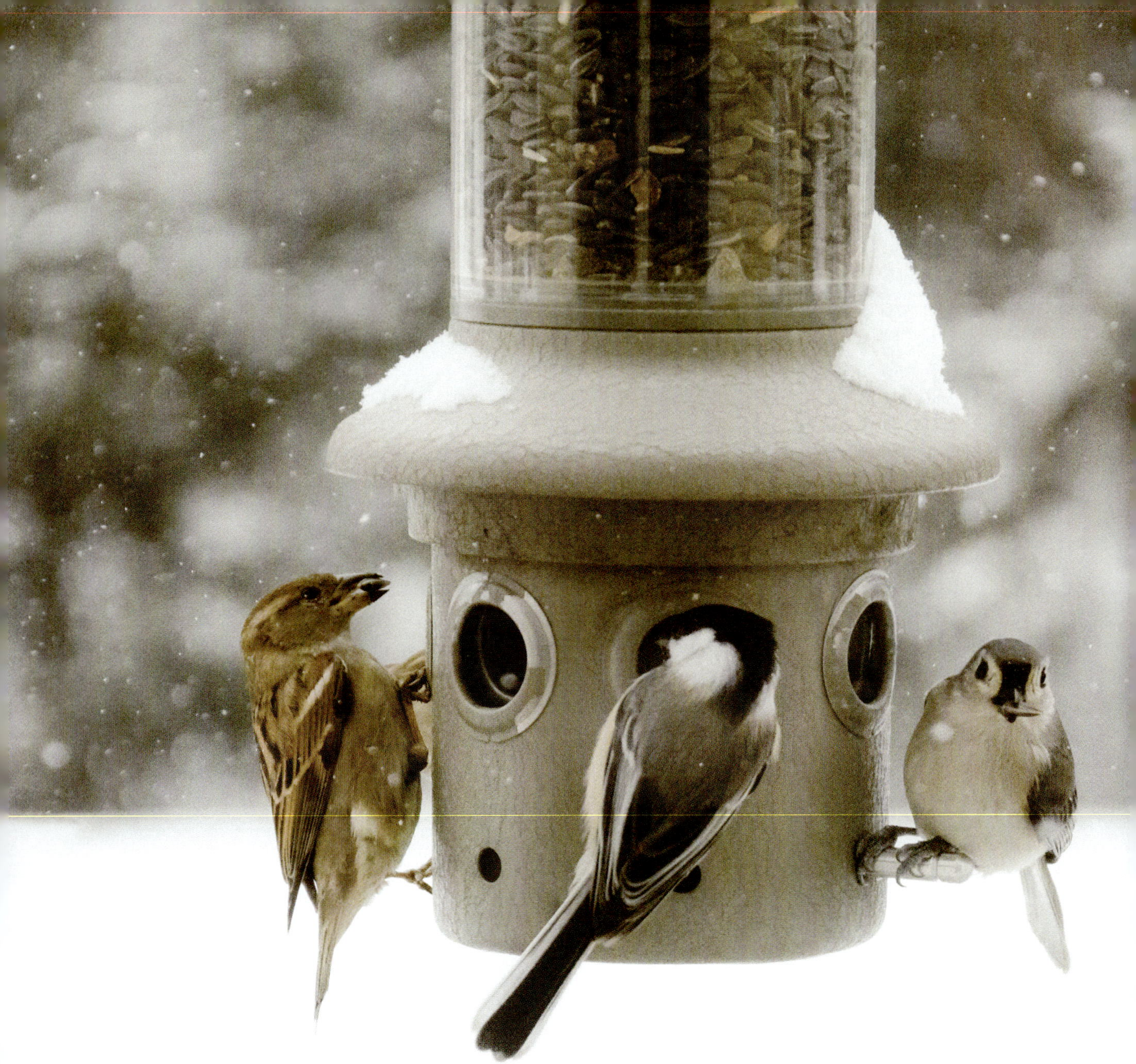

ISO 2000 • 1/3200 sec. • f/4.5 • 70mm lens

10

D5500 Video: Beyond the Basics

Video and the D5500

Probably one of the reasons you purchased the D5500 instead of a competing camera model is that it has the ability to capture video—not just regular video, but high-definition video. As I discussed in the book's introduction, I am going to keep the focus of this book on the photography aspects of the camera, but that doesn't mean I am going to ignore the video functions completely. Let's cover some of the basic facts about the movie-making features.

Video recording is a feature of the Live View capabilities of the camera, so you'll have to put the camera into the active Live View mode to begin to capture video. This is accomplished by rotating the Live View switch (**Figure 10.1**) on the top of the camera, which activates Live View on the rear display. If you want to control the aperture, you should set the aperture value while in Manual mode or Aperture Priority mode before switching to Live View. Otherwise, switch to one of the other modes and let the camera adjust it automatically.

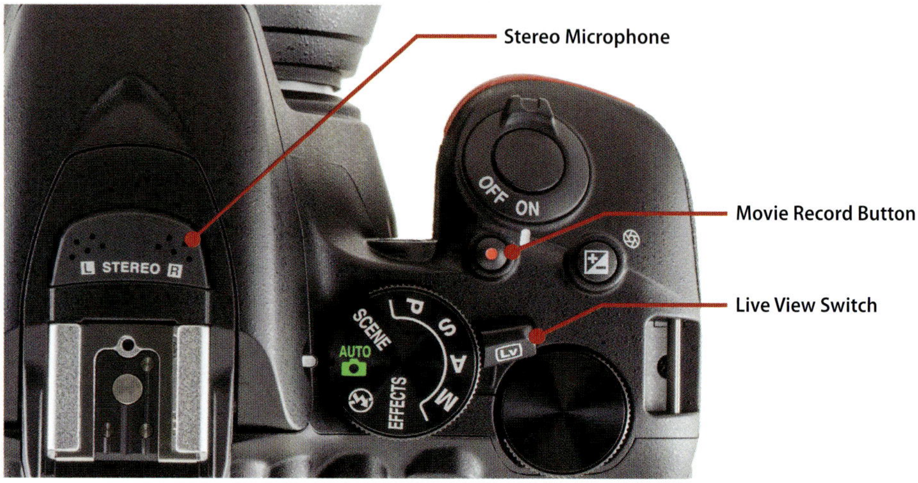

Figure 10.1
Rotate the Live View switch to start.

Once Live View is active, press the **i** button, and choose a focus mode. It is possible to use the Full-Time-Servo (AF-F) mode while recording video, and you should try it out because it does a fine job in some situations, but I strongly urge you to refine your Manual focus skills. Using Manual focus not only gives you creative control of what is in focus, it also eliminates the sound of the lens trying to maintain autofocus.

Once your subject is in focus, you can push the Movie Record button to begin the recording process (there is no special movie mode). When the camera begins recording, you will notice a few new icons show up on the LCD (**Figure 10.2**). At the top is a blinking red Record icon to let you know that the camera is in active recording mode. To the left, you'll notice the timer that is counting down your remaining recording time. This number is directly related to the quality you have selected for your video. Below is the audio recording indicator. To stop the video recording, simply press the Movie Record button a second time. This will take you back to Live View mode. To turn off Live View, rotate the Live View switch once more or turn the camera off.

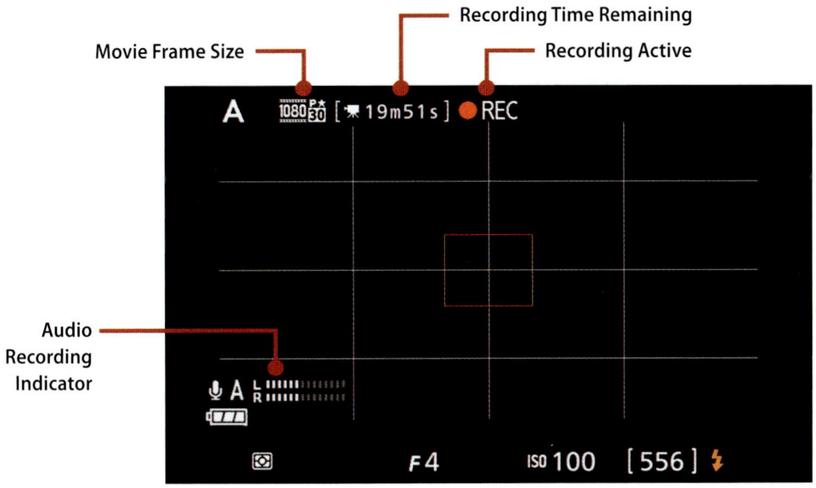

Figure 10.2 Video recording in progress.

Video quality

The highest-quality video setting on your D5500 will render high-definition video with a resolution of 1920x1080 pixels. This is also referred to as 1080p. The 1080 represents the height of the video image in pixels, and the "p" stands for progressive (see the following sidebar). You can select lower-resolution video depending on your needs. The other two video resolutions are 1280x720 and 640x424. For high-definition TV and computer or media station viewing, you will be served best by using the 1920x1080 recording resolution. If you don't need full 1080p HD, such as when recording for the Internet or mobile devices, you might want to consider using the 1280x720 or 640x424 choice, since those require less physical storage and take less time to upload to the Internet. The second variable to consider is frame rate, which is how many video frames per second (fps) are recorded. The D5500 offers three choices to consider: 60, 30, and 24. The 60p setting will provide the smoothest playback and allow for smoother slow-motion playback in post-production, but since it contains so much data it will produce a much larger file size for a given amount of recording time. Unless you absolutely know you require the higher frame rate, you should stick to the 1920x1080 30p option for everyday recording.

Progressive scan

When it comes to video, two terms are associated with the quality of the video and how it is captured and displayed on a monitor or screen: *progressive* and *interlaced.* These describe how the video is drawn by line for each frame. Video frames are not displayed all at once like a photograph. In progressive video, the lines are drawn in sequence from top to bottom. Interlaced video draws all of the odd-numbered lines and then all of the even-numbered lines. This odd-even drawing can look like screen flicker, which is why the progressive video standard is preferred, especially when viewing higher-definition images.

Setting the movie quality

1. Start by pressing the Menu button.
2. Navigate to Shooting Menu using the Multi-selector, highlight the Movie Settings option, and press OK (**A**).
3. Highlight the Frame Size/Frame Rate setting, and press OK (**B**); press OK to choose your desired setting (**C**).
4. Leave the Movie Quality setting on High (**D**).
5. Press the Menu button twice to exit the menu mode and return to shooting, or rotate the Live View switch to jump right into the Live View video recording mode.

A

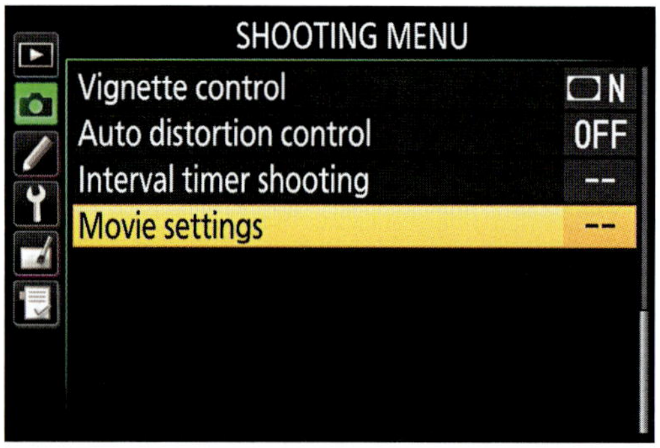

B

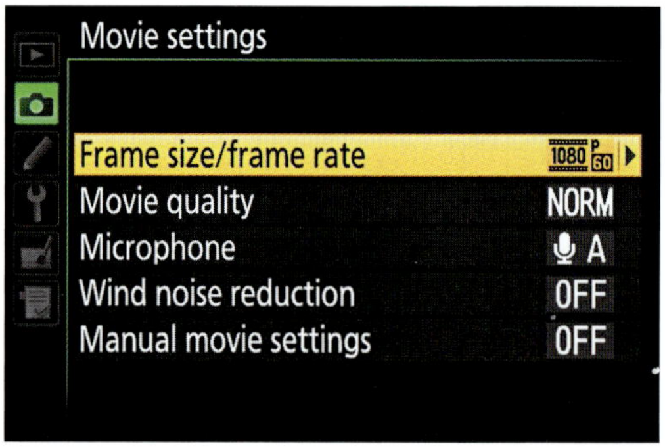

C

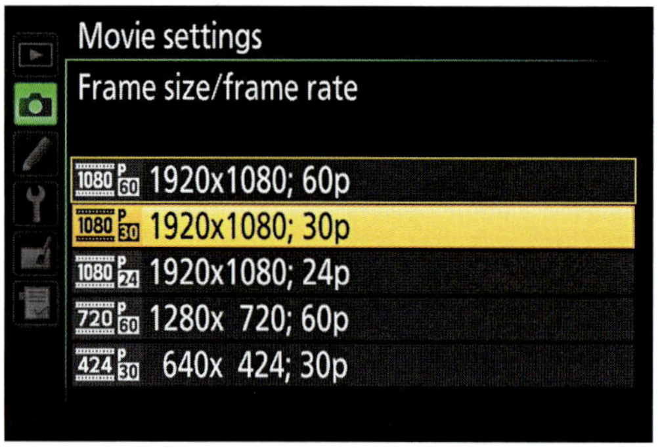

D

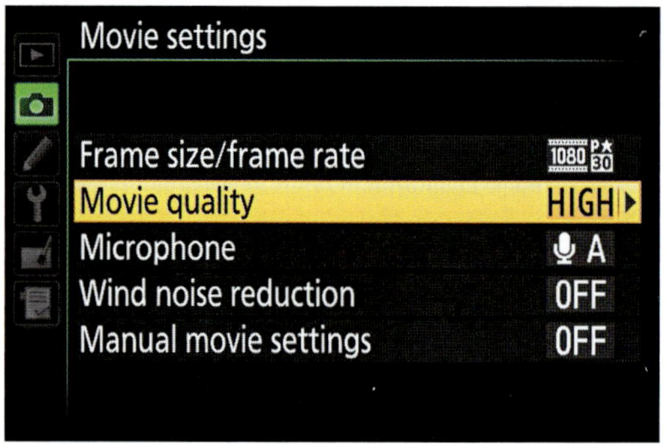

Manual Callout

Refer to page 174 of the Reference Manual PDF for a complete rundown on the movie recording settings.

Sound

The D5500 can record audio to go along with your video, but keep a couple of things in mind when using it. The first is to make sure you don't block the microphone located in front of the hot shoe on top of the camera. This should not be a problem if you are holding the camera as discussed in Chapter 1.

The next thing you need to know about the sound is that while the built-in microphone records in stereo, it is not the greatest quality and it will pick up the sound of the AF motor if you use autofocus while recording. The D5500 does have an external microphone jack on the side panel (**Figure 10.3**), so you might want to consider investing in an external microphone. A nice step up from the built-in microphone is the Nikon ME-1 external microphone, which also records in stereo but picks up less noise from the AF motor due to being mounted atop the hot shoe. You can watch and listen to a thorough review of the ME-1, along with some comparisons to other external microphone choices, at http://bit.ly/d5100Mic (the ME-1 is used on a D5100 in the review, but the microphone is the same).

You also have the option of turning off the audio altogether. This can be useful if the sound might be distracting or you plan on using your own soundtrack, to be added to the video at a later time.

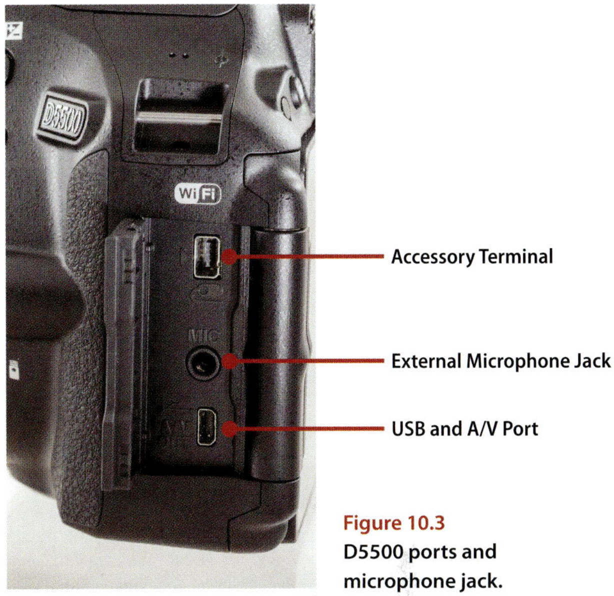

Figure 10.3 D5500 ports and microphone jack.

Turning off the sound

1. Following the directions for setting the movie quality above, locate the Movie Settings menu, and press the OK button.
2. Highlight the Microphone option, and press OK again (**A**).
3. Select the Microphone Off option, and press OK to lock in the change (**B**). Press the Menu button twice to return to shooting mode.

A

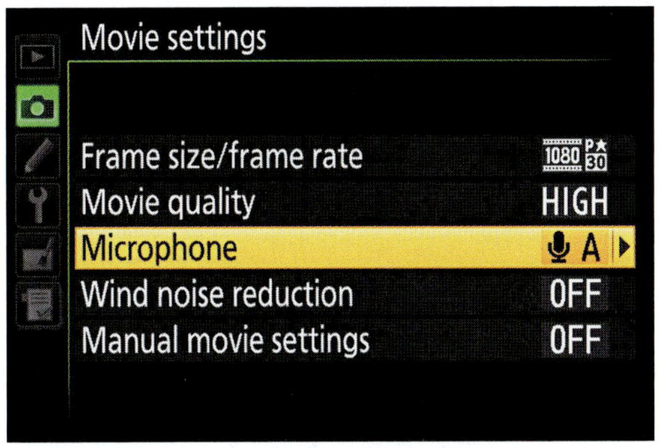

B

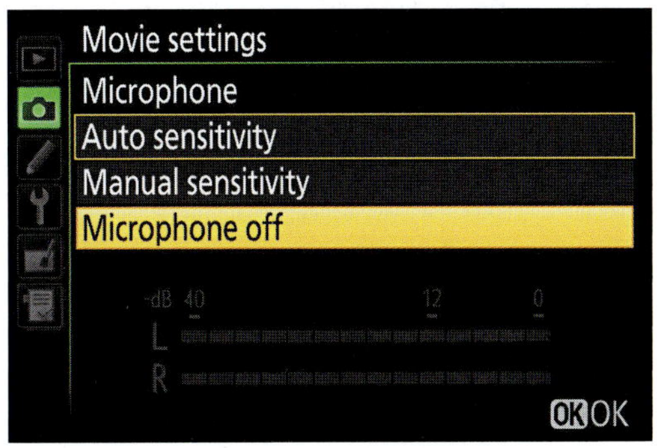

Focusing the camera

Once the video is recording, you have a couple of focusing options to choose from. To manually focus, simply slide the focus switch on the lens to the M position and then rotate the focus ring while recording. If your subject moves closer or farther from the camera position, you'll need to turn the focus ring on the lens in order to maintain sharp focus.

As I mentioned previously, you can also use the camera's autofocus during recording to keep your subjects in focus, but I don't recommend it. The option is a good idea on paper, but it has a long way to go in real life. You can certainly give it a try, but I think you'll find autofocus a bit too jarring (and noisy) as it hunts back and forth trying to keep even a slow-moving subject in focus.

Another option is to leave the focus mode in AF-S and then simply press the shutter release button to focus on your subject. Note that if you are recording sound with your video, autofocus and vibration reduction will be audible in your video, and they sound terrible. I usually let autofocus lock in focus first, and then slide the focus switch to M and take over from there.

It's All About the Lenses

Video cameras have been around for a long time, so why is it such a big deal that you can now use your dSLR camera to record video? The answer is simple: It's all about the lenses. If you have any experience using a video camcorder, you know that it always seems like everything is in focus. While this isn't necessarily a bad thing, it can also be pretty boring. Using dSLR video allows you to use faster lenses (larger apertures), which can give you shallower depth of field in your videos. This shallow depth of field can add a sense of dimension and depth that is lacking in most standard video cameras. The truth is that many videographers are turning their attention from video cameras costing many thousands of dollars to the much more affordable dSLR video cameras to produce similar high-definition results.

The D5500 not only allows you to capture video with a more shallow depth of field, but it also gives you the flexibility to use different lenses for different effects. While you may own only one lens right now, you can buy specialty lenses to enhance your video as well as your still capture. Any lens that you can use for still photography on your D5500 can also be used for video, including ultrawide lenses such as the AF DX Fisheye-Nikkor 10.5mm f/2.8G ED, the AF-S VR Zoom Nikkor 70–300mm f/4.5–5.6G IF-ED, the AF Micro Nikkor 60mm f/2.8D for getting extreme close-up videos, or even a Lensbaby (www.lensbaby.com) for creating movies with only small selective areas of the image in focus. The Lensbaby has to be used in Manual mode and is all manual focus, but the results are really different from what you get with a normal lens (and kinda fun).

Before you start buying new lenses, which can require quite an outlay of cash, I highly recommend that you check out a lens rental service like Borrow Lenses (www.borrowlenses.com) or Lens Pro to Go (www.lensprotogo.com). That way you can try out a really nice, expensive lens for a few days or a few weeks and see if it is something that's worth adding to your gear bag. I've done this several times and find the process and the cost to be very reasonable.

Accessories for Video

The next chapter is dedicated to accessories that will expand your photographic options, and many of those same accessories can be used for motion capture, too, but I want to mention a few video-specific accessories here.

Tripods

A tripod is not used in quite the same way for video as for still-image applications. When you are shooting video, you want to present a nice, smooth scene that is fairly free of camera shake. One example is the pan shot. When you are following a subject from side to side, you will want the viewer's attention to be focused on the subject, not the shaky look of the video. To help in this effort, your weapon of choice should be a tripod with a fluid head.

A fluid head looks a little different than a standard tripod head, in that it usually has one long handle for controlled panning. To really make things smooth, the head uses a system of small fluid cartridges within the panning mechanism so that your panning movements are as smooth as possible. For around $130, you can get a nice fluid pan head that will mount on your existing tripod legs (if your tripod has a removable head). Another option to consider is a dedicated video monopod, such as the Manfrotto Fluid Video Monopod (you can even get it with a panning head), which gives you the stability of a tripod but with a much smaller footprint.

Camera stabilizers

Aside from using a boom arm, there's really only one way to get jitter-free video on your camera while moving around: Use a steady device. You have probably heard of Steadicam rigs, but they can be cumbersome and expensive; frankly, they're overkill for the normal video situation. But some smaller, handheld rigs provide the same benefit without the cost and bulk, like the ModoSteady from Manfrotto. One of the big advantages of this rig is that it has three different setups to choose from. The steady mode hangs a counterbalance under the camera to allow you to capture fluid-looking video movement. You can also move the balance arm to a different position and use it as a shoulder rig, much like the stock of a rifle. Finally, you can open the handle and turn it into a small tabletop tripod. That's a lot of functionality for under $100.

Easier LCD vision

I have one problem with shooting video on the D5500, or any dSLR camera: I can't use the viewfinder as I record. Instead, I'm forced to use the rear LCD, and while it is very large and sharp, I tend to have to hold the camera fairly far away from my body to see the screen. But there is another way, and it is perfect for vision like mine.

To really get a good look at what is happening in your LCD, you should use a loupe like the Hoodman Cinema Kit Pro (www.hoodmanusa.com), which attaches to the camera for hands-free operation. Not only is it great for getting a better look at the LCD while recording, it also helps avoid glare on the screen while working outdoors (more on this in Chapter 11).

Get yourself a Mini-HDMI cable

When you are ready to play back your video, you can run the video directly from your camera (**Figure 10.4**) to your TV. You'll need to use a TV capable of displaying high-definition video, which also means that you will want to use an HDMI cable to connect the camera to the TV. HDMI (High Definition Multimedia Interface) cables will carry your uncompressed video to your HDTV in all its glory. The only problem is that your camera didn't have an HDMI cable included in the box when you bought it. This means you will have to purchase one to take advantage of the HD playback. If you are thinking that you already own an HDMI cable for connecting your other media components to your TV, you might want to take another look. Your camera uses a mini-HDMI connection, so most standard cables designed for video components won't work.

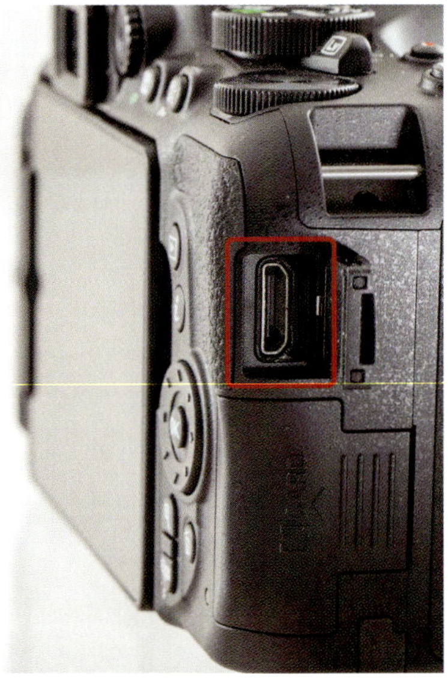

Figure 10.4 The D5500 HDMI port is located above the memory card slot.

If you do decide to purchase one, make sure you get a Mini-HDMI-to-HDMI cable. You can find them at most electronics stores where HD cameras and TVs are sold. (Here's a little hint for purchasing a Mini-HDMI cable: Search the Internet for the best prices. Most electronics stores have huge markups on cables, and you can usually find a suitable one online for about a third of the price of what you'd pay in your local store.)

Getting Shallow Depth of Field

As I said earlier, getting the look of a production cinema camera means working with shallow depth of field. When trying to get a large aperture in your video, you might find that the camera wants to use an auto-exposure mode to establish the correct camera settings for recording video. To get the benefit of a large aperture, you are going to need to start in Manual or Aperture Priority mode and set your aperture before switching to Live View. To illustrate what I am talking about, I captured two frames from two video clips for comparison. One clip was shot with the aperture set to f/2.8 (**Figure 10.5**), and in the other, I just changed the aperture to f/22 (**Figure 10.6**).

Can you see the difference in the depth of field in the two clips? Deciding what is in focus is a very powerful cinematic technique, and controlling the depth of field is a great way to hone in on the most important part of the scene.

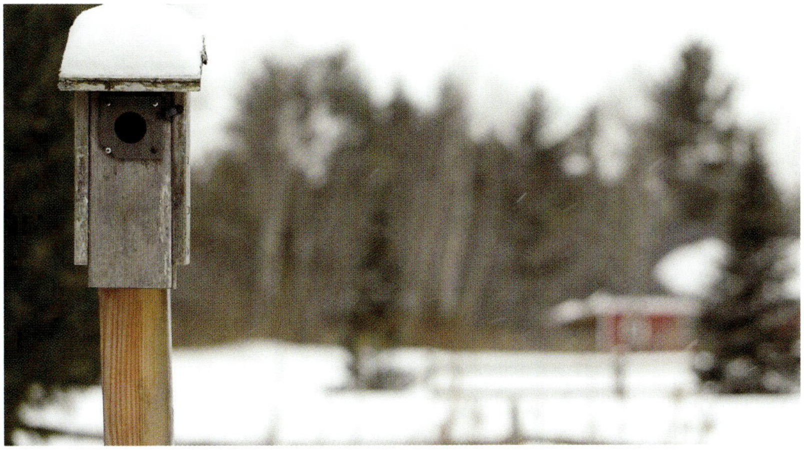

Figure 10.5
Frame of video shot at f/2.8, showing narrow depth of field.

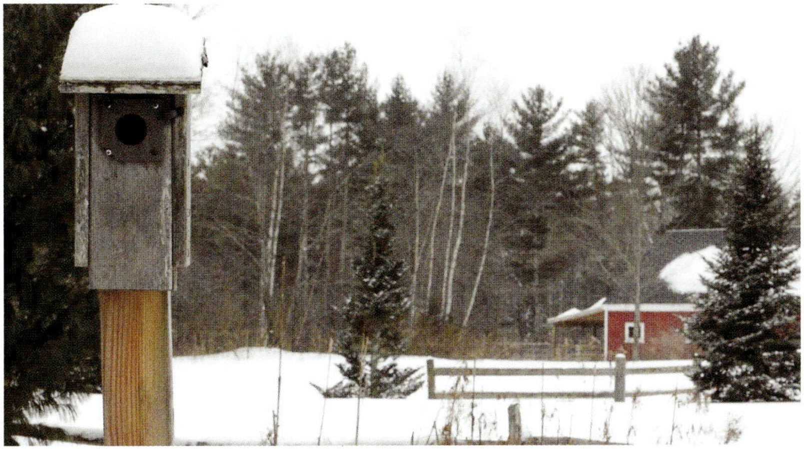

Figure 10.6
Frame of video shot at f/22, showing wider depth of field.

Giving a Different Look to Your Videos

Using picture controls

Something a lot of people don't realize: You can use the picture controls to give your video a completely different look. Sure, you can use the Standard control for everyday video, but why not add some punch by using the Vivid setting? Nothing says "HD" like bright, vivid colors. Or maybe you want to shoot a landscape scene. Go ahead and set the picture control to the Landscape setting to improve the look of skies and vegetation. If you really want to get creative, try using the Monochrome setting and shoot in black and white. The great thing about using the picture controls is that you will see the effect right on your LCD as you record, so you will know exactly what your video is going to look like. Want to take things up a notch? Try customizing the picture controls and do things like shoot sepia-colored video. Check out the "Classic Black and White Portraits" section of Chapter 6 to see how to customize the look of your Monochrome picture control.

Using effects modes

As discussed in Chapter 3, you can also use the effects modes when capturing video. You'll be hard-pressed to find an easier way to make your videos look different than shooting with the Miniature Effect mode, which not only makes things appear smaller but also speeds up the timeline when recording video. The Photo Illustration effect not only affects the color of the video but also gives it a sort of stop-motion animation effect. Try shooting some video using each effect to see the different results.

White balance

Another great way to change the look and feel of your video is to select a white balance that doesn't match your scene. You can completely change the mood of the video by selecting a white balance setting that is different from the actual light source you are working in. Don't be afraid to be creative and try out various looks for your video.

Tips for Better Video

Shoot short clips

Most professional video shot today is actually made up of very short video sequences that are edited together. If you don't believe me, watch any TV show and see how long you see an actual continuous sequence. I am guessing that you won't see any clip longer than about 10 seconds. Shooting small clips also gives the camera a chance to cool down. The camera really heats up inside when recording video, so keep an eye on the LCD to see if you get a temperature warning. You can thank music videos for shortening our attention span, but the reality is that your video will look much more professional if you shoot in shorter clips and then edit them together, which brings me to the next tip.

Stage your shots

If you are trying to produce a good-looking video, take some time before you begin shooting to determine what you want to shoot and where you want to shoot it from. You can mark the floor with tape to give your "actors" a mark to hit. You can also use staging to figure out where your lens needs to be set for correct focus on these different scenes.

Use Manual focus

This will be difficult at first, especially if you have never had to manually focus in the past, but with a little practice you can become fairly adept at the process. One benefit of focusing manually is that, depending on the lens you are using, you will avoid the noise of the autofocus motor, which can be picked up by the microphone if you are recording audio. More importantly, it puts you in the driver's seat for controlling what is in focus, which leads the viewer's eye to what you want to show. While in Live View, you can enable AF-F (not all of the effects modes support AF-F), which will try to keep the subject in focus continually even when recording video, but it may be too slow for your needs, or it may try to focus on something other than what you have in mind. Brushing up on your manual skills is only going to serve you well down the road. Set the camera lens to Manual focus, and then use the focus ring on the front of the lens.

Put your camera in a different place

It's possible that the one feature that really compelled you to buy the D5500 was the articulating LCD. Being able to see the screen from just about any angle gives you a lot of flexibility in where you put your camera while recording. You can place the camera on the ground or hold it way over your head and still see all of the action taking place. Use this to your advantage to capture video from angles that are different from the standard shooting position most people use when shooting video.

Avoid the quick pan

While recording video, your camera uses something called a rolling shutter, which, as the name implies, rolls from the top to the bottom of the frame. If you are panning quickly from one side to another, you will see your video start to jiggle as if it were being shot through Jell-O. This is something that can't be overcome except by using a slower panning motion. If you are going to be shooting a fast subject, consider using the Shutter Priority mode with a fast shutter speed. It won't eliminate the problem completely, but it should improve things a little.

Use a fast memory card

Your video will be recording at up to 60 frames per second, and as it is recording, it is placing the video into a buffer (temporary holding spot) while the camera writes the frames to your memory card. If you are using a slower card, it might not be able to keep up with the flow of video—the result being dropped frames. The camera will actually not record some frames because the buffer will fill up before the images have time to be written. This will appear as small skips in the video when you watch it later. You can prevent dropped frames by using an SD card that has a speed rating of Class 6 or higher (**Figure 10.7**). These cards have faster writing speeds and will keep the video moving smoothly from the camera to the card.

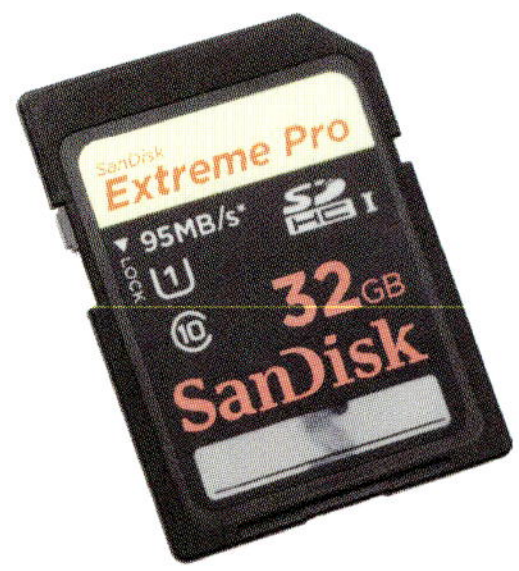

Figure 10.7
A fast card, such as this SanDisk SDHC Class 10, will help capture more of your video frames.

Turn off the sound

If a microphone upgrade is not in your near future, you might consider going silent. Earlier, I told you how to turn off the audio option while recording your video. The truth is that the built-in microphone does not produce audio that is up to the quality of the video. To make your videos stand out, try turning the microphone off and adding a music soundtrack. You will be amazed at how the right music can really enhance a video. Of course, you will need to do this on your computer, which will require special video-editing software (see the section on editing your video, later).

Watching and Editing Your Video

Watching video

There are a few different ways for you to watch your videos: in your camera, on your TV, and on your computer. To watch your video clips on your camera, simply press the Playback button, and press the OK button to activate the Play command. Pretty simple. The Multi-selector acts as the video controller and allows you to rewind and fast-forward as well as stop the video altogether.

If you would like to get a larger look at things, you will need to either watch the video on your TV or move the video files to your computer. To watch on your TV, you can use the A/V cable that came with your camera (the one with the red, yellow, and white jacks); it plugs into the small port on the side of the camera body. This will let you watch low-resolution video on your TV. To get the full effect from your HD videos, you will need to purchase an HDMI cable (as discussed previously), and your TV needs to support at least 720p and have an HDMI port. Once you have the cable hooked up to your TV (tune your TV to the channel used for HDMI input), simply use the same camera controls that you used for watching the video on the LCD.

If you would like to watch your video on your computer, you will first need to either download the files or access them using an SD card reader. Apple owners can use Apple's QuickTime Player to watch the video. If the video is too large for your screen, try pressing Command-0 (zero) to make it half-size, or Command-3 to fit the video to your screen. Microsoft Windows users can open videos using the Windows Media Player. This should be the default player for video files on your computer, so you should be able to just double-click a video file to open it in the Media Player. Resize the video by pressing Alt-1 for a 50 percent view. You can also download and install the free QuickTime Player on Windows (www.apple.com/quicktime).

Editing video on your camera

The D5500 has a very simple editing feature built into the camera's software that can be used for trimming the beginning or ending of a clip or saving out individual frames as JPEG stills, but it is a bit slow to use and drains your battery faster. To really edit your clips, I suggest copying them to your computer and using dedicated video-editing software, which will give you greater control and a much more user-friendly workspace.

Editing video on your computer

If you are a Mac owner, you can edit your HD video using the iMovie application. The latest version is chock-full of new video-editing features, including the ability to work with audio.

If you are using Windows, try the Windows Live Movie Maker for a nice, basic video-editing application. Many different applications for Windows editing exist, such as Adobe's Premiere Elements. You can find more information and download a trial version at www.adobe.com/products/premiereel. If you have Photoshop CS6 (or higher), you should definitely take advantage of the improved video-editing features that are now included.

Expanding your knowledge

I have given you a couple of quick tips and suggestions in this chapter to get you started with your movie-making, but if you really want to get serious, you need to know a lot more. Videography can be a complex endeavor, and there is much to learn and experiment with if you want to move beyond the simple filming of the kids in the backyard or the trip to the amusement park. If you really want to explore all your camera has to offer in the way of video movie-making, I suggest you check out *Creating DSLR Video: From Snapshots to Great Shots*. It is packed with everything you need to know about taking your dSLR video skills to the next level and beyond.

Chapter 10 Assignments

Even if you don't think you will be shooting much video, it pays to know how to do it because you just never know when it will come in handy. I have to admit that I used to turn up my nose at the video functions in dSLR cameras, but over time, I have come to really appreciate the ability to create multimedia projects that offer a greater range of expression. Who knows, you just might be the next big indie director.

Changing your focus

Several focus modes are available for the movie Live View mode, and you should give all of them a try before deciding which method works best for you. Try setting AF-S mode and focusing prior to shooting, and then shoot a sequence with AF-F mode to see if you prefer to have the camera autofocus continuously while you shoot.

Abandoning AF

Once you are comfortable with the autofocus methods, go ahead and turn autofocus off and go manual. The hardest part is getting used to which way the focus ring needs to turn for closer and farther focus points. Try this: Put a piece of tape on the lens barrel and write N and F (for near and far) on it so you know which way to go. Now try to capture a moving subject while adjusting focus.

Going shallow

Remember that one of the biggest advantages in using your D5500 for video is the shallow depth of field you can achieve. If you don't have a lens with a particularly large aperture, try using it wide open and getting close to your subject. The closer you are, the narrower the depth of field will look.

Share your results with the book's Flickr group!
Join the group here: flickr.com/groups/nikond5500_fromsnapshotstogreatshots

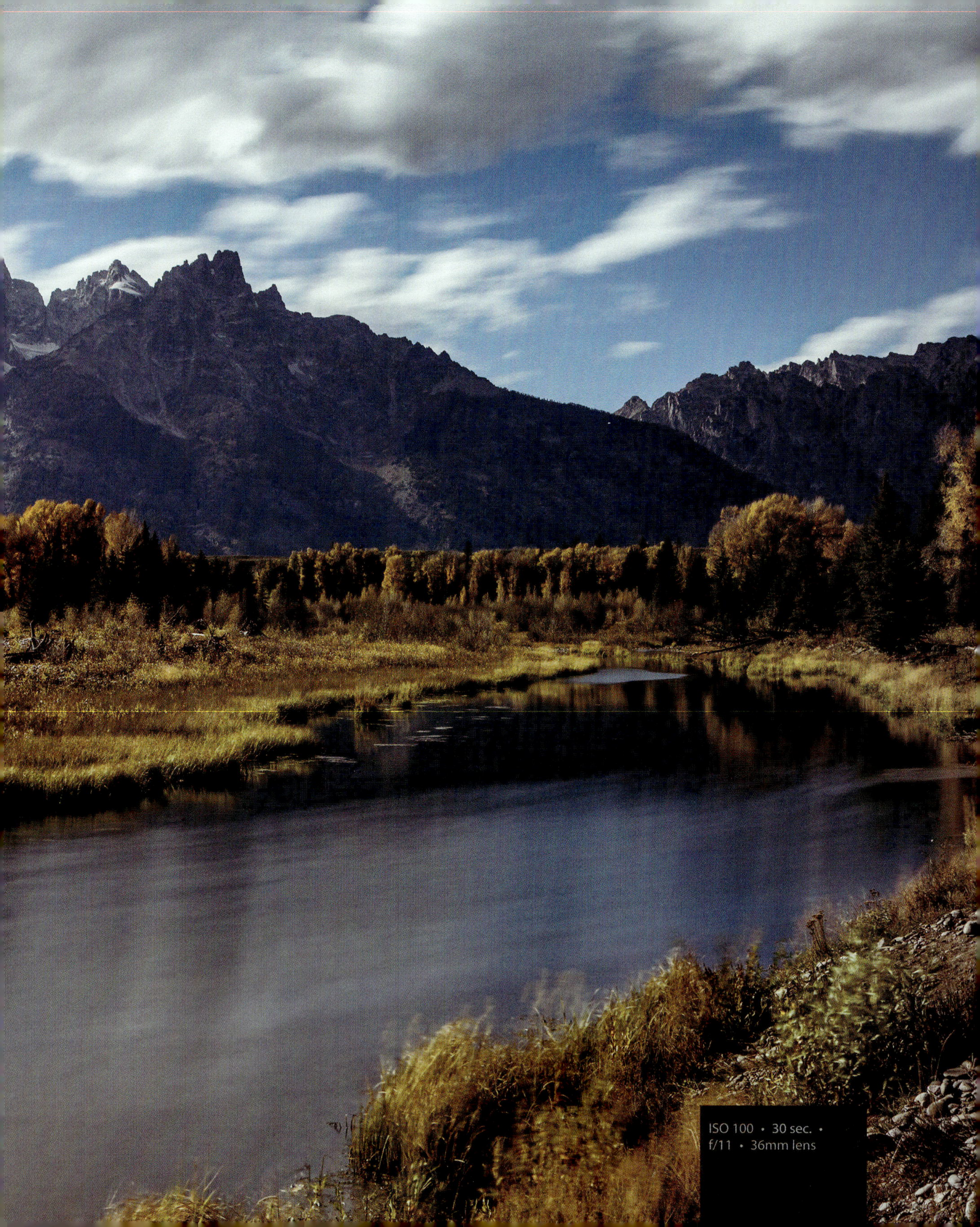
ISO 100 • 30 sec. • f/11 • 36mm lens

11

Accessorize

Upgrades and Accessories to Expand Your Camera's Creative Potential

If you bought your camera with a lens, you basically have everything you need to begin shooting with your D5500. I took great care to ensure that almost all of the techniques in this book can be used with your basic camera setup. That being said, some accessories are essential for certain types of photography. Others aren't necessarily essential, but they will improve the look of your images.

Let's take a look at some items that I believe are must-have accessories for your photography.

Filters

You should have several filters in your camera bag. Each one serves a unique purpose. Some say that digital imaging programs such as Adobe Photoshop can duplicate the effects that filters offer. This may be true for some effects, but some filters affect exposure time (like a neutral density filter for a silky waterfall look) and are nearly impossible to recreate in Photoshop.

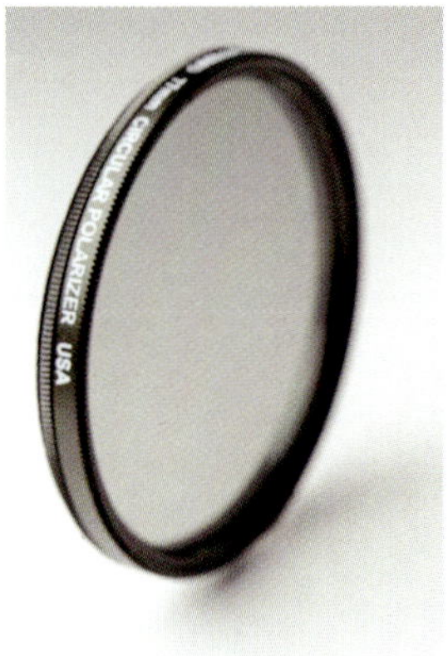

Figure 11.1 **A Tiffen circular polarizing filter.**

Polarizing

This filter ranks right up there at the top of the list of must-own photography accessories. You won't find a self-respecting landscape photographer who doesn't have at least one polarizer in her camera bag (**Figure 11.1**).

Light travels in straight lines, but the problem is that all those lines are moving in different directions. When they enter the camera lens, they are scattering about, creating color casts and other effects. The polarizer controls how light waves are allowed to enter the camera, letting only certain ones pass through. So what does that mean for you? Polarizing filters will make blue skies darker, vegetation color more accurate, and colors more saturated. Haze will be reduced, and images can look sharper (**Figures 11.2** and **11.3**). Not bad for a little piece of glass.

Most polarizers are circular and allow you to rotate the polarizing element to control the amount of polarization you want. As the filter is rotated, different light waves will be allowed to pass through, such as a reflection on a body of water (**Figure 11.4**). Turn the filter a little and the light waves from the reflection are blocked, making the reflection disappear (**Figure 11.5**). Another benefit of the filter is that it is fairly dark, so when used in bright lighting conditions, it can act as a neutral density filter (see the next section), allowing you to use larger apertures or slower shutter speeds. The average polarizing filter requires an increase in exposure of about one-and-a-half stops. This won't be an issue for you because you will be using the camera meter, which is already looking through the filter to calculate exposure settings. You should consider this effect on exposure settings if your intention is to shoot with a fast shutter speed or use a small aperture for increased depth of field.

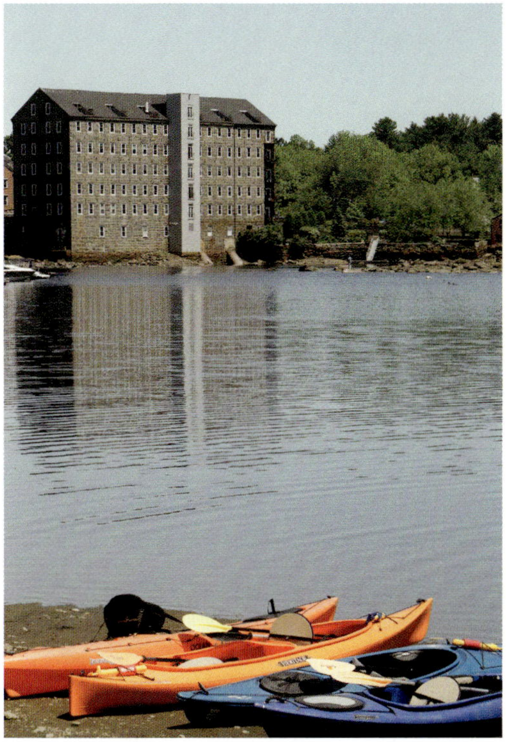

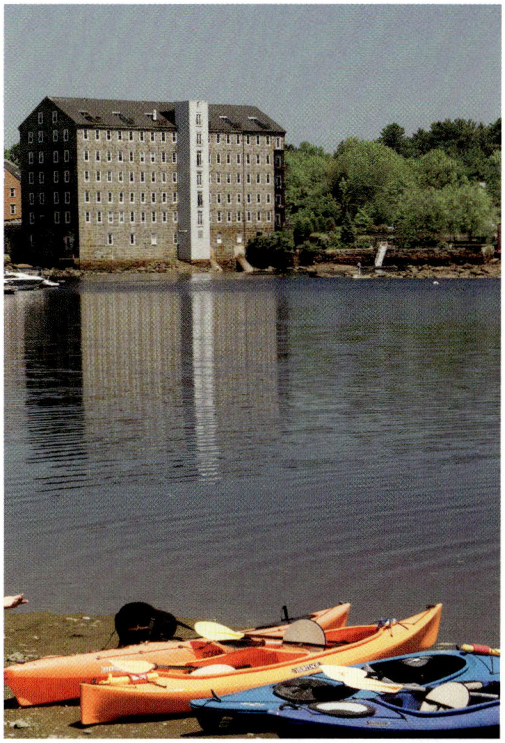

Figure 11.2 (left) Without a polarizing filter, the scene looks a little low on contrast and has a blue color cast from the sky.

ISO 200 • 1/200 sec. • f/9 • 70mm lens

Figure 11.3 (right) After I added a polarizer, the colors are much more accurate, the blue sky is darker, and the color cast is now gone.

ISO 200 • 1/125 sec. • f/9 • 70mm lens

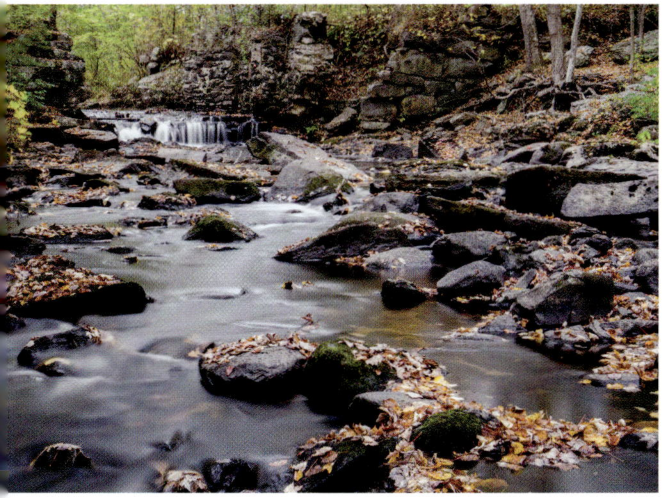

Figure 11.4 Before a polarizer is added, the sky is reflected in the water.

ISO 200 • 30 sec. • f/29 • 48mm lens

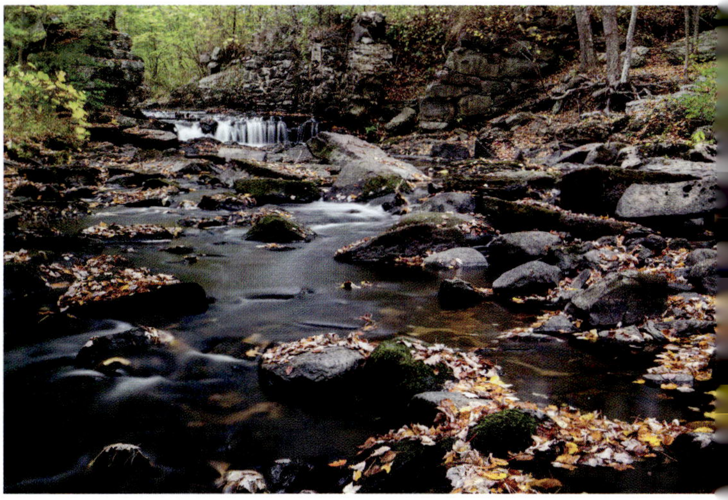

Figure 11.5 With a polarizer added, you can see through the surface of the water.

ISO 200 • 30 sec. • f/16 • 48mm lens

Neutral density (ND)

Sometimes there is just too much light falling on your scene to use the camera settings you want. Most often this is the case when you want to use a slow shutter speed but your lens is already stopped down to its smallest aperture, leaving you with a shutter speed that's faster than you want.

A classic example of this is shooting a waterfall in bright sunlight. To get a silky look to the water, the shutter speed needs to be about 1/15 of a second or slower. The problem is that a proper exposure for bright sunlight is f/16 at 1/100 of a second with the camera set to ISO 100 (this comes from the Sunny 16 rule). If my lens has a minimum aperture of f/22, the slowest shutter speed I will be able to use is 1/50 of a second.

The way around this problem is to use a neutral density (ND) filter to make the outside world appear a little darker. Think of it as sunglasses for your camera. ND filters come in different strengths, which are labeled as 0.3, 0.6, and 0.9 (though there are stronger filters available, such as the 10-stop ND filter from Lee). They represent a one-stop difference in exposure for each 0.3 increment. If you need to turn daylight into dark, the 0.9 ND filter will give you an extra three stops of exposure (**Figure 11.6**). This means that, in my earlier example, I could get an exposure of f/16 at about 1/10 of a second. This would be an ideal exposure for capturing a shot of silky-smooth water (**Figure 11.7**).

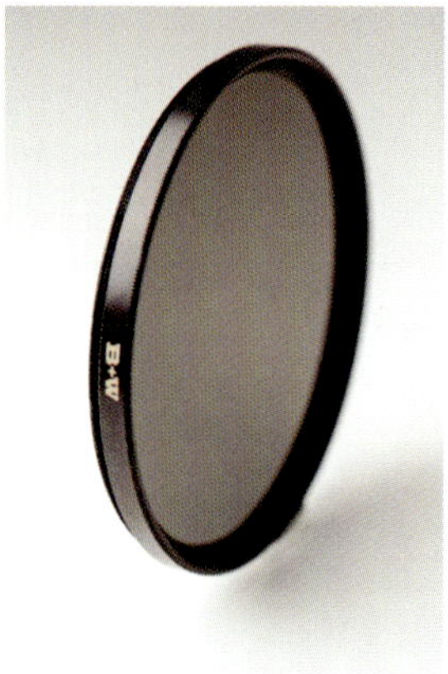

Figure 11.6 **A B+W 77mm 0.9 ND filter.**

To see more B+W filters, check out www.schneideroptics.com.

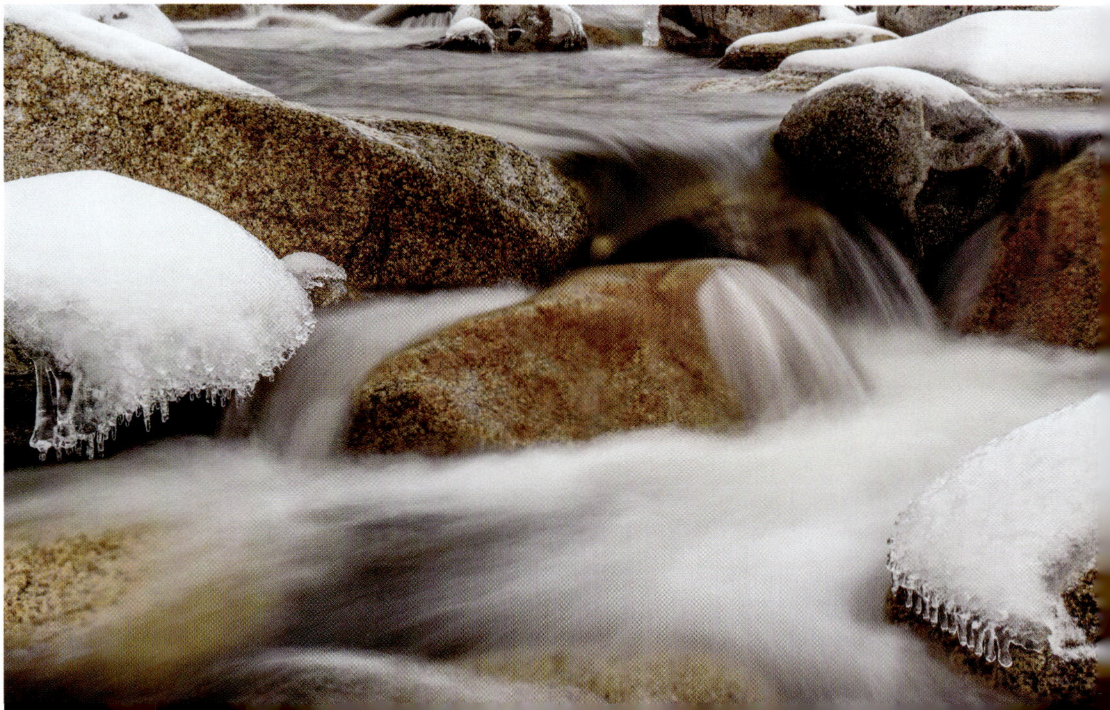

Figure 11.7
With a 0.9 ND filter, I was able to use a long shutter speed in daylight and transform the rushing water into mist.

ISO 100 • 1.3 sec. • f/16 • 18mm lens

Graduated ND

Another favorite of the landscape photographer, the graduated ND filter has the benefits of the standard ND filter but graduates to a clear portion (**Figure 11.8**). This allows you to darken just the upper or lower part of your scene while leaving the other part unaffected. This filter is most commonly used to darken skies that are too bright (**Figure 11.9**) without affecting the ground area (**Figure 11.10**). If a regular ND is used, the entire area will get darker, and there will be no visible change in the brightness ratio between the sky and the ground.

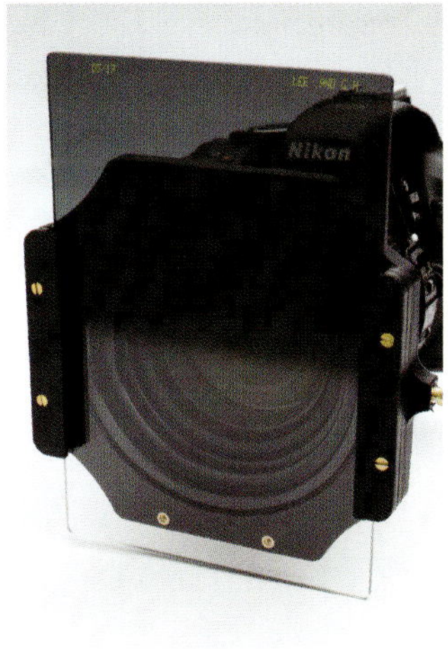

Figure 11.8
Graduated filters come in different strengths and transitions, from soft to hard, and allow you to expose for the darker areas (ground) without blowing out the brighter regions (sky).

You can purchase the graduated ND as a screw-on filter, but most photographers prefer to use the larger 4x6 version, which allows them to control exactly where the filter transitions from dark to transparent. Many options are available in graduated ND filters, such as the density factor (number of stops) and how gradual the transition is from dark to clear.

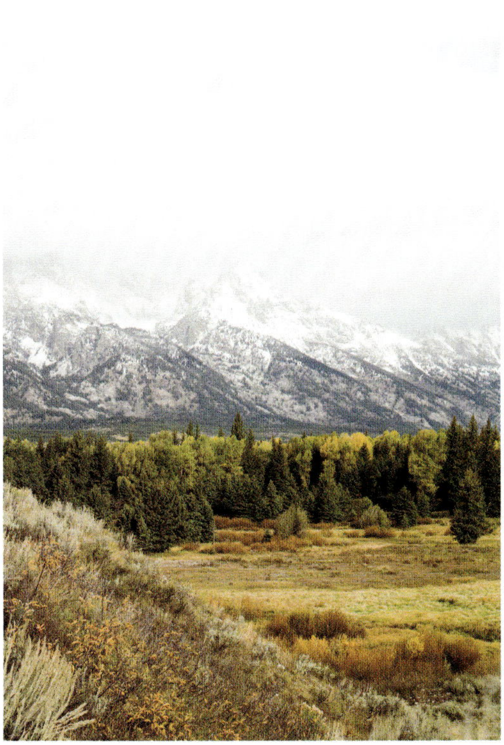

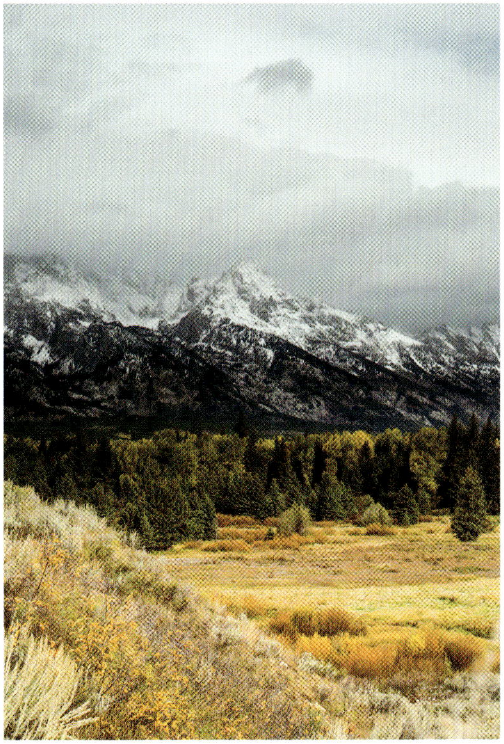

Figure 11.9 (left)
Even though the sky is filled with clouds, it is much brighter than the ground, and that makes for a tricky exposure situation.

ISO 100 • 1/40 sec. • f/11 • 60mm lens

Figure 11.10 (right)
With a 0.9 graduated ND filter placed over the sky, I was able to expose for the foreground and retain detail in the brighter mountains and sky.

ISO 100 • 1/40 sec. • f/11 • 60mm lens

Tripods

If you buy only one accessory for your photography, do yourself a favor and make it a tripod. In general, any tripod is going to be better than no tripod at all. A tripod makes your photos sharper and lets you shoot in any lighting condition. There are more choices in tripods than there are in dSLRs, so how do you go about choosing the right one for you? The main considerations are weight, height, and head.

The weight of your tripod will probably determine whether or not you will actually carry it along with you farther than the parking lot. Many different types of materials are used in tripods today. The lightest is carbon fiber, which is probably the most expensive as well. More than likely, you should consider an aluminum tripod that is sturdy and has a weight rating that is suitable for your camera as well as your lenses.

Make sure the tripod extends to a height that is tall enough to allow you to shoot from a comfortable standing position. Nothing ruins a good shoot like a sore back. Taller tripods need to be sturdier to maintain a rigid base for your camera. You will also want to consider how low the tripod can go. If you want to do macro work of low-level subjects such as flowers, you will need to lower the tripod fairly close to the ground. Many new tripods have leg supports that allow you to spread the legs very wide and get the camera low to the ground.

The other determining factor when purchasing a tripod is the type of head that it employs to secure the camera to the legs. There are two basic types of tripod heads: ball and pan. Ball heads use a simple ball joint that allows you to freely position the camera in any upright position and then clamp it down securely. This type of head is flexible and quick to use, but it can make it difficult for you to switch between portrait and landscape orientations. Ball heads tend to be slightly more expensive as well.

Pan heads employ a swivel and usually two hinged joints that allow the camera to pan left and right, move up and down, and adjust the position along the horizontal axis. Handles are typically employed to allow movement of the camera and lock down the position. The pan head is by and large the most popular tripod head style on the market. If you plan on shooting a lot of video with your D5500, you might want to consider the pan head since it will deliver more functionality for your videography, specifically in panning from side to side.

If you really want to make your tripod shooting move faster, consider buying a tripod that uses a quick-release head. Many styles of quick-release brackets are available; most use a small plate that screws into the bottom of the camera and then quickly locks into and releases from the tripod head.

The other thing to consider when purchasing a tripod is the leg-locking system. Whether it is a lever lock, locking rings, or some other system, make sure that you test it thoroughly to see how easy it is to lock and unlock the leg positions. Also check to see how smoothly the legs retract and extend. Avoid legs that stick because they will probably only get stickier over time.

There are many different brands of tripod to choose from, but I suggest sticking to Gitzo (www.gitzo.com), Giotto's (www.giottos.com), Manfrotto (www.manfrotto.com), and Really Right Stuff (www.reallyrightstuff.com) for rock-solid tripods and tripod accessories.

Remote or Cable Release

When shooting long exposures, you can use the self-timer to activate the camera, or you can get yourself a wireless remote or a cable release. My favorite option is the wireless ML-L3 (**Figure 11.11**), which uses an infrared beam (just like your TV remote) to fire the shutter from a distance of up to around 16 feet. Another option is the MC-DC2 remote release cord, which is an electronic release that attaches to the camera via the remote port and lets you trip the shutter. A remote release is the preferred tool when shooting with the camera set to Bulb (see Chapter 9).

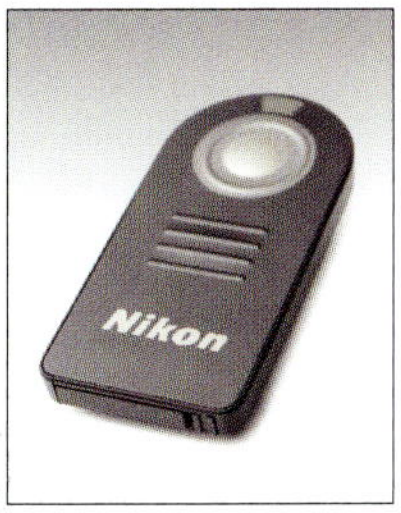

Figure 11.11
The Nikon ML-L3 wireless remote lets you activate the shutter without touching the camera.

The idea of the release is that it allows shutter activation without having to place your hands on the camera. This is the best way to ensure that your images will not be affected by camera shake. The ML-L3 sells for around $20, and the MC-DC2 for around $35. Both work not only with the D5500 but also with several other Nikon dSLR models. A remote also comes in handy for shooting macro work, where the tiniest vibration can affect the sharpness of your image.

To take advantage of the D5500's built-in Wi-Fi functionality, you'll need to download and install the free Wireless Mobile Utility (WMU) application (for Android or iOS) in your mobile device. Then you can enable the Wi-Fi feature in the D5500 Setup menu and connect the camera to your device via Wi-Fi. Once it's connected, you can remotely focus and trigger the camera shutter (**Figure 11.12**) from your mobile device and download the photos right to your device for easy sharing.

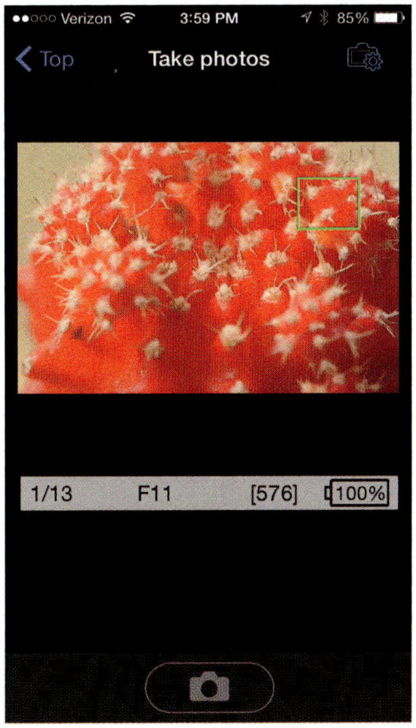

Figure 11.12
The Nikon WMU app provides a live view through the camera's lens right to your mobile device.

Manual Callout

To learn more about using the Wi-Fi feature on the D5500, check out page 224 in the Reference Manual PDF.

Macro Photography Accessories

Extension tubes

Extension tubes are like spacers between your lens and your camera. The tubes are typically hollow, and their sole purpose is to move the rear of the lens farther away from the camera body.

A lens can get only so close to a subject and still be able to achieve a sharp focus. This is because as the subject gets closer, the focal point for the lens moves back to a point where it is behind the image sensor. Using an extension tube lets you move that focal point forward by placing the rear of the lens a little farther away from the camera sensor, thus letting you get the lens closer to the subject and enlarging the subject in your picture.

The tubes come in varying sizes, which are typically measured in millimeters. The more common sizes are 12mm, 20mm, and 36mm. The longer the tube, the greater the magnification factor (up to 1:1). The tubes are best used with lenses that are 35mm in focal length and longer. A wide-angle lens will have such a short focusing distance that you will be right on top of your subject. Nikon manufactures several extension tubes, or you can buy them from third-party manufacturers. Prices vary, but you will pay more for tubes that utilize optics in their design. You can also purchase sets of tubes with varying lengths that can be used individually or stacked together for greater magnification.

Close-up filters

Another great way to jump into macro work is by purchasing a close-up filter (**Figures 11.13** and **11.14**). Close-up filters come in varying magnifications but tend to be a little more expensive than extension tubes. This is because they are usually made of high-quality glass that works in concert with the lens. The filters and lenses can have some advantages over tubes, too. Because they screw onto the front of your lens, close-up filters don't interfere with any of the communication functions between the lens and the camera body. They also result in less loss of light, so exposures can be slightly shorter than when you're using extension tubes. They do, however, work similarly to tubes in that they allow you to shorten the minimum focus distance of your lens so you can move closer to your subject, thereby increasing the size of the subject on your sensor. Close-up lenses usually

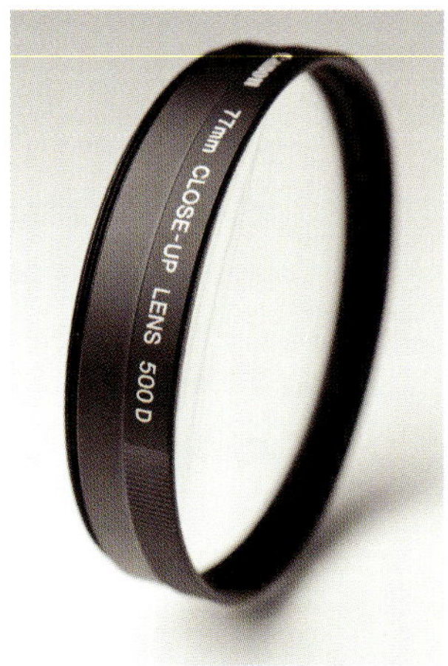

Figure 11.13 **The Canon 500 D close-up filter. Don't let the brand name fool you; the filter works with any lens.**

come in magnification factors like +1, +2, +3, +4, and +5. They can also be stacked, strongest to weakest, to increase the magnification factor.

The other difference is that close-up filters are usually screw-threaded onto your lens, which means you have to purchase a specific thread diameter. So if your favorite lens has a 68mm filter thread, that is the size you would use for the close-up filter. The big downside is that if you want to use different lenses that have different thread sizes, you will have to buy multiple filters. Just as with most glass filters, the larger the diameter, the higher the price. One solution is to work with a zoom lens so you can have a range of focal lengths to use with just one filter. Another solution to this problem is to use a step-up ring, which allows you to thread a large filter to a smaller lens. I purchase all my filters at 77mm and then use step-up rings to attach them to smaller-diameter lenses.

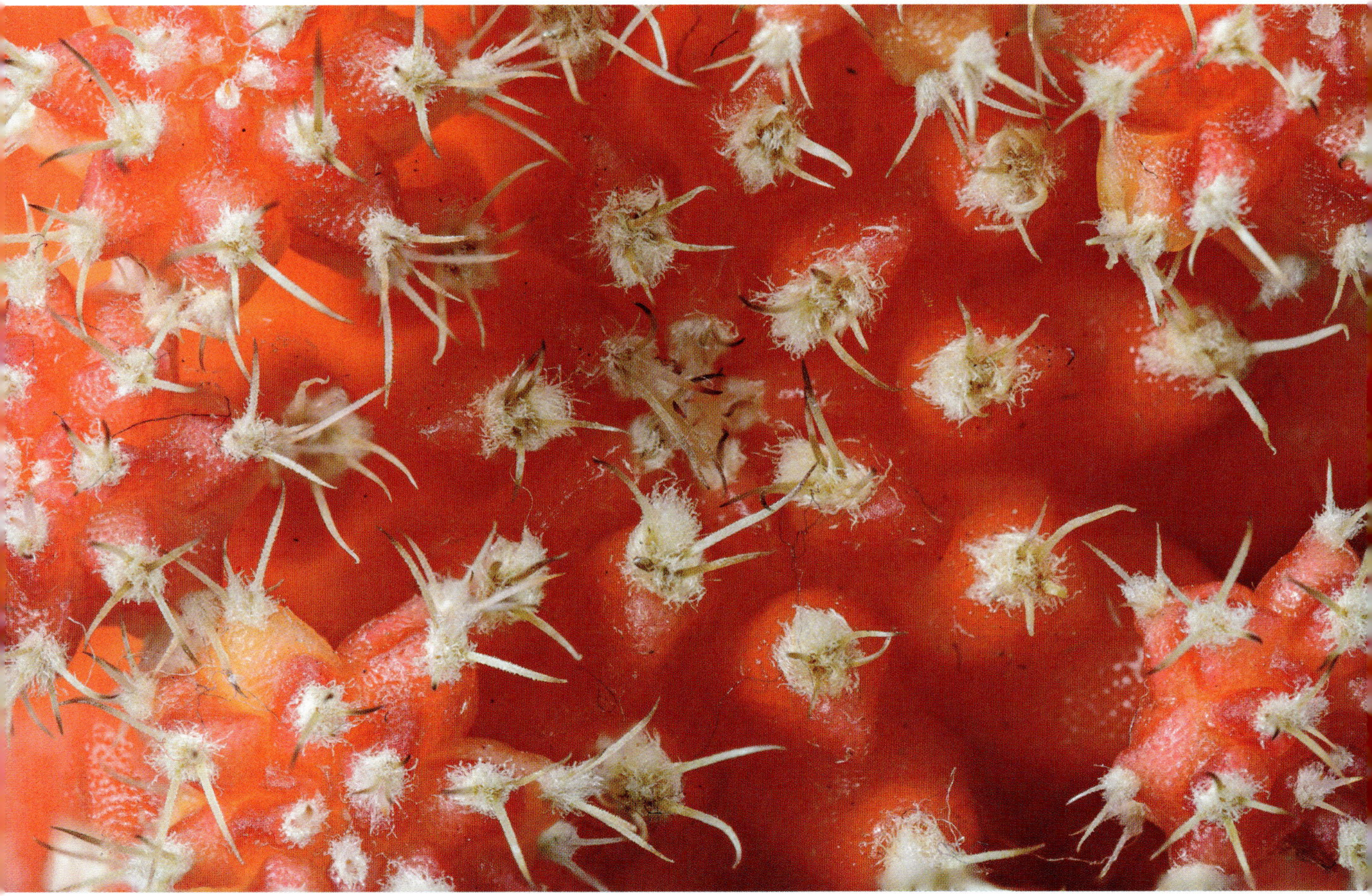

Figure 11.14 **I captured this cactus by using a Canon 500 D close-up filter on a 105mm lens and triggering the shutter via Wi-Fi.**

ISO 100 • 1/4 sec. • f/22 • 105mm lens

Hot-Shoe Flashes

Earlier in the book I covered the built-in flash and what you can accomplish with it. Now let me say that you really, really need to get yourself a hot-shoe mounted flash if you want to take better flash images (**Figure 11.15**). For one thing, the external flash is going to be much more powerful than the pop-up version. Also, there is much more flexibility in the Speedlight system of flashes than you could ever hope to get from the built-in version.

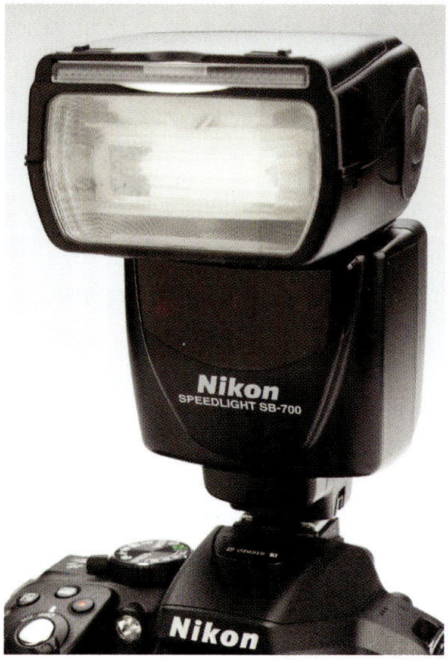

Figure 11.15 **The Nikon SB-700 is a nice companion to the D5500.**

Nikon currently has several Speedlight flashes for sale, but my recommendation is that you purchase the SB-700 or, better still, the SB-910 Speedlight. They will run somewhere in the neighborhood of $325 for the SB-700 and $545 for the SB-910, which can be a hard pill to swallow at first. The pill will go down much easier once you have used one of these powerful and flexible flashes. Not only will your on-camera flash photography be much better, but you also gain the option of moving to a wireless, off-camera flash system down the road.

Diffusers

While we're considering flashes, let's discuss a tool that lets you improve the light you are using in your portrait photography. A diffusion panel is a piece of semitransparent material, usually white, that you place between your light source and your subject. The fabric does as the name implies: It diffuses the light, spreading it out into a soft, low-contrast light source that makes any subject look better. You could make your own or buy one of the many commercially available versions. I like the Lastolite TriGrip diffuser (www.lastolite.com) because it folds up small and fits in my Think Tank bag. Another option to check out is the 5-in-1 reflector kit made by Westcott (www.fjwestcott.com). It not only has a very nice diffusion panel, but it also has reflective covers that slip over the diffusion panel so you can bounce some fill light into your scene. Best of all, the entire system is collapsible, so it fits into a small package for traveling.

Camera Bags

This topic is tricky because there is no one-size-fits-all answer. How much gear you want to carry, how big you are, and your own style will all influence your bag purchasing decision.

I like to travel with my photo gear. Typically, my travel involves flying. This means that all of my camera equipment travels in the cabin with me, not in the luggage compartment. I can't emphasize this enough: *Do not pack your camera in your checked luggage!* Thousands of cameras, lenses, and accessories are lost and stolen from checked luggage every year. The best way to ensure that doesn't happen to you is to bring your equipment on board and place it in the overhead storage. I like to bring my laptop as well, so I have found a couple of backpack camera storage systems that allow me to fit a camera body, several lenses, some accessories, my laptop, and even some snacks into one backpack-style bag that fits under the seat in front of me or in the overhead bin. I also prefer a backpack because I like the freedom of slinging the bag over my shoulder, leaving my hands free for other luggage. I am currently using a Think Tank Photo Airport Acceleration bag (www.thinktankphoto.com) for all my travel needs.

The other bag you should look into is something for everyday use. There are bags that are made to handle all sorts of camera bodies, lenses, and accessories, and they're usually completely configurable with moveable padded partitions so you can customize the bag. I spend most of my photographic life outdoors, so my current bag of choice is a rotation180° Professional (www.mindshiftgear.com), which is built for this kind of use. This backpack-style bag easily holds multiple camera bodies and lenses, extra batteries, memory cards, and plenty more. I'm a bit of a pack mule, so you might want something smaller to start with. I'd suggest checking out Mindshift's other backpack options.

These two bags are the ones I am using currently, but finding the perfect camera bag is truly the Holy Grail for photographers. The fact is you can go through a lot of them searching for one that perfectly fits your every need and never find it. I have several bags presently taking up residence in my closet.

Bits and Pieces

Speaking of camera bags, let me share with you a few items that always travel in mine.

The battle against dust is a losing one, but that doesn't mean you can't have your small victories. To help in the war against the dust speck, I carry three weapons of cleanliness.

The lens cloth

A good microfiber lens-cleaning cloth always comes in handy for getting rid of those little smudges and dust bunnies that seem to gravitate toward the front of my lens. There are lots of different brands, and any one will work. I use one called a Spudz, which folds into its own pouch and has the added benefit of being gray. This means that I can use it as a gray card to get meter readings in Spot metering mode, or as a way to correct the white balance in my images down the road when I bring them into my imaging software. Have a few of these on hand.

More information on Spudz cleaning cloths can be found at www.alpineproducts.com.

The LensPen

For really stubborn smudges on a lens, I pull out my trusty LensPen (**Figure 11.16**). This nifty little device has a soft, retractable dust-removal brush on one end and an amazing cleaning element on the other that uses carbon to clean and polish the lens element.

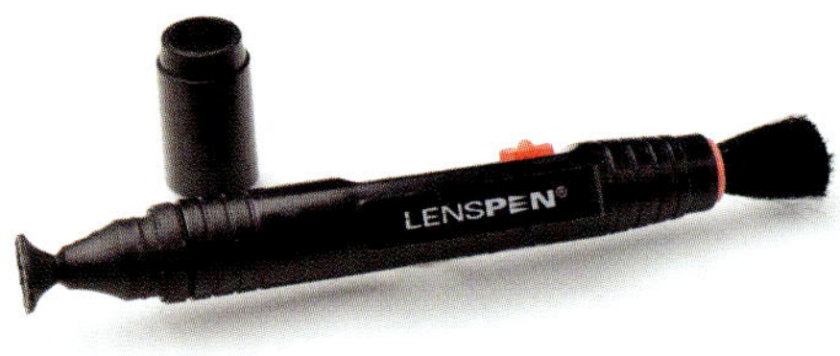

Figure 11.16 The LensPen lens-cleaning tool.

More information on LensPen products can be found at www.lenspen.com.

Air blowers

Some folks prefer to use canned compressed air to blow away dust, but the cans can sometimes release fluid when they are tilted. For this reason, I always use my Rocket-Air blower from Giotto's (**Figure 11.17**). This funny-looking device is great for getting rid of tough dust, and it uses a clean air path so the dust you are blowing away doesn't get sucked back into the ball and redeposited on your equipment the next time you use it.

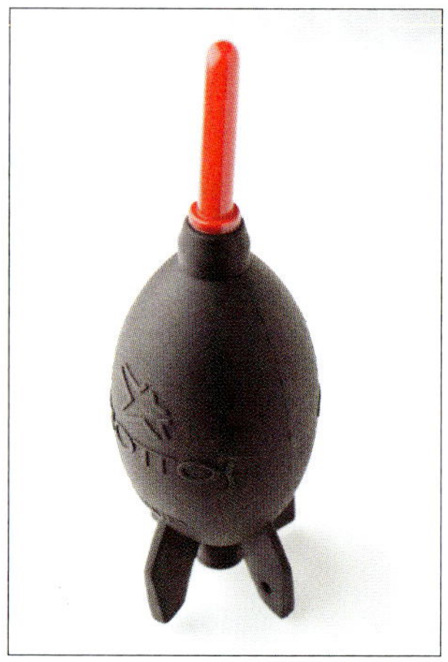

Figure 11.17 Giotto's Rocket-Air dust blower.

A loupe for your LCD

Having a large LCD is an amazing thing. The only problem is that it can be very hard to see in bright daylight conditions. I overcome this by using a Hoodman HoodLoupe. The loupe doesn't magnify your screen; it just provides a light-tight little tent that lets you get a better look at your rear LCD. It has a handy lanyard so you can hang it around your neck and keep it within easy reach for checking out those great shots you just took. If you are going to work in the bright sun, you will definitely want to get yourself one of these for your camera bag.

To check out all of the Hoodman accessories, head to www.hoodmanusa.com.

Conclusion

You can spend a lot of time worrying about having the right gadget, filter, or accessory to make your photography better. It can become an obsession to search for the latest thing out there. But here's the deal. You already have almost everything you need to take great pictures: an awesome camera and the knowledge necessary to use it. Everything else is just icing on the cake. So, while I have introduced a few items in this chapter that I believe will make your photographic life easier and even improve your images, don't get caught up in the technology and gadgetry.

Use your knowledge of basic photography to explore everything your camera has to offer. Test the limits of your camera. Don't be afraid to take bad pictures. Don't be too quick to delete them off your memory card, either. Take some time to really look at them and see where things went wrong. Look at your camera settings and see if perhaps there was a change you could have made to improve things.

Be your toughest critic and learn from your mistakes. With practice and reflection, you will soon find your photography getting better and better. Not only that, but your instincts will improve to the point that you will come upon a scene and know exactly how you want to shoot it before your camera even comes out of the bag. If you'd ever like to get some hands-on practice in the field, I'd love to have you join me in a workshop. Head over to www.thedigitalphotoworkshops.com, and use the code SNAPSHOTS to save $100 on the registration fee.

Index

B

C

D

E

F

L

M

N

O

P

Q

R

S

T